Internationalizing Media Studies

The explosion of transnational information flows, made possible by new technologies and institutional changes (economic, political and legal), has profoundly affected the study of global media. At the same time, the globalization of media, combined with the globalization of higher education mean that the research and teaching of the subject face immediate and profound challenges, not only as the subject of enquiry but also as the means by which researchers and students undertake their studies.

Edited by a leading scholar of global communication, this collection of essays by internationally acclaimed scholars from around the world aims to stimulate a debate about the imperatives for internationalizing media studies by broadening its remit, including innovative research methodologies, taking account of regional and national specificities and pedagogic necessities warranted by the changing profile of students and researchers and the unprecedented growth of media in the non-Western world.

Transnational in its perspectives, *Internationalizing Media Studies* is a much-needed guide to the internationalization of media and its study in a global context. The book is divided into four thematic sections:

- Internationalizing media research
- Broadening the field of media studies
- Regional perspectives on internationalization
- Pedagogic parameters: internationalizing media syllabi.

Contributors: Indrajit Banerjee, Oliver Boyd-Barrett, Sandra Braman, Naren Chitty, Nick Couldry, John D.H. Downing, Jan Ekecrantz, Gerard Goggin, Cees J. Hamelink, Andreas Hepp, David O. Lavin, Mark McLelland, Winston Mano, Tristan Mattelart, Vincent Mosco, Kaarle Nordenstreng, Monroe E. Price, Clemencia Rodríguez, Tarik Sabry, Daya Kishan Thussu, Elena Vartanova, Jair Vega, Stefaan Verhulst and Yuezhi Zhao.

Daya Kishan Thussu is Professor of International Communication at the University of Westminster in London. The founder and Managing Editor of the journal *Global Media and Communication*, his key publications include *News as Entertainment*, *Media on the Move*, *International Communication* and *Electronic Empires*.

Internationalizing Media Studies
Series Editor: Daya Kishan Thussu
University of Westminster

Internationalizing Media Studies
Edited by Daya Kishan Thussu

Internationalizing Media Studies

Edited by
Daya Kishan Thussu

Routledge
Taylor & Francis Group
LONDON AND NEW YORK

First published 2009
by Routledge
2 Park Square, Milton Park, Abingdon, Oxon, OX14 4RN

Simultaneously published in the USA and Canada
by Routledge
270 Madison Ave, New York, NY 10016

Routledge is an imprint of the Taylor & Francis Group, an informa business

Typeset in Bembo by
Taylor & Francis Books
Printed and bound in Great Britain by
CPI Antony Rowe, Chippenham, Wiltshire

British Library Cataloguing in Publication Data
A catalogue record for this book is available from the British Library

Library of Congress Cataloging in Publication Data
Internationalizing media studies / edited by Daya Kishan Thussu.
p. cm.
1. Mass media–Study and teaching. 2. Communication, International–Study and teaching. I. Thussu, Daya Kishan.
P91.3.I55 2009
302.23071–dc22

2008054206

ISBN10: 0-415-45529-4 (hbk)
ISBN10: 0-415-45530-8 (pbk)
ISBN10: 0-203-87738-1 (ebk)

ISBN13: 978-0-415-45529-9 (hbk)
ISBN13: 978-0-415-45530-5 (pbk)
ISBN13: 978-0-203-87738-8 (ebk)

Contents

Notes on contributors

Indrajit Banerjee has been the Secretary-General of the Asian Media and Information and Communication Centre (AMIC) since 2004 and is Associate Professor at the Wee Kim Wee School of Communication and Information at the Nanyang Technological University, Singapore. A PhD from the Sorbonne University, he was the Research Coordinator of the first UNDP Regional Human Development Report on ICTs and Human Development 2005. He was appointed to the Steering Committee of the World Congress on Communication and Development and was the coordinator of the first World Journalism Education Congress, 2007. Among his publications are *Asian Communication Handbook 2008*, *Internet and Governance in Asia: A Critical Reader* and *Rhetoric and Reality: The Internet Challenge for Democracy in Asia.*

Oliver Boyd-Barrett is Professor of Journalism at Bowling Green State University, Ohio. He has published 14 books as well as scores of articles and book chapters. Among his publications are: *Globalization of News* (Sage, 1998) and, most recently, *Globalization, Communications Media and Empire* (John Libbey, 2006). His current research projects relate mainly to media representations of the 'war on terror'.

Sandra Braman is Professor of Communication at the University of Wisconsin, Milwaukee, having just completed service as the Freedom of Expression Professor at the University of Bergen, Norway. Recent works include *Change of State: Information, Policy, and Power* (MIT Press, 2007) and the edited volumes *The Emergent International Information Policy Regime* (Palgrave Macmillan, 2004), *Biotechnology and Communication: The Meta-Technologies of Information* (Lawrence Erlbaum, 2004) and *Communication Researchers and Policy-Making* (MIT Press, 2003). Braman is currently doing research on relationships between communication and policy-making at the comparative, international and global levels, and on evidence of ways in which decision-makers working on the design of the internet engage with legal and policy issues in the published decision-making discourse.

Naren Chitty is Foundation Chair in International Communication at Macquarie University in Australia. He has authored and co-edited several books and journals. Professor Chitty is a former Secretary General of the International Association for Media and Communication Research and the editor-in-chief of the *Journal of International Communication*. His website is accessible at http://naren.chitty.googlepages.com/home.

Nick Couldry is Professor of Media and Communications at Goldsmiths College, University of London, where he is Director of the Centre for the Study of Global Media and Democracy. He is the author or editor of seven books, including most recently *Listening beyond the Echoes: Media, Ethics and Agency in an Uncertain World* (Paradigm Books, 2006) and (with Sonia Livingstone and Tim Markham) *Media Consumption and Public Engagement: Beyond the Presumption of Attention* (Palgrave Macmillan, 2007).

John D.H. Downing is Director of the Global Media Research Center in the College of Mass Communication and Media Arts, Southern Illinois University at Carbondale. His publications include *Internationalizing Media Theory* (Sage, 1996) and (with Charles Husband) *Representing 'Race': Racisms, Ethnicities and Media* (Sage, 2005). He is editor of the International Communication segment of the Blackwell *Encyclopedia of Communication* and general editor of the forthcoming *Encyclopedia of Alternative Media* (Sage).

Jan Ekecrantz was, until his timely death in 2007, Professor in Media and Communication Studies at the Department of Journalism at Stockholm University. He published extensively in English, French, Portuguese, Spanish, Finnish and Russian journals. His later work dealt with media cultures in Brazil, China and post-Soviet countries, to appear in book form as *Discourses of Change: Media and Transformations in East and West.*

Gerard Goggin is Professor of Digital Communication in the Centre for Social Research in Journalism and Communication, University of New South Wales, Sydney, Australia. His books include *Mobile Phone Cultures* (2007), *Cell Phone Culture* (2006), *Virtual Nation:The Internet in Australia* (2004) and *Digital Disability* (2003, with Christopher Newell). With Mark McLelland he is editor of *Internationalizing Internet Studies* (2008). Goggin is editor of the journal *Media International Australia.*

Cees J. Hamelink is Emeritus Professor of International Communication at the University of Amsterdam. He is currently Professor for Management of Information and Knowledge at the University of Aruba, Professor of Human Rights and Public Health at the Vrije Universiteit of Amsterdam, and Honorary Professor of the University of Queensland, Brisbane, Australia. He is also the editor-in-chief of the *International Communication*

Gazette and Honorary President of the International Association for Media and Communication Research. He is author of 17 monographs on communication, culture and human rights, among them *Cultural Autonomy in Global Communications* (1983), *The Politics of World Communication* (1994) and *The Ethics of Cyberspace* (2000).

Andreas Hepp is Professor of Communications and Head of the Institute for Media, Communication and Information at the Faculty of Cultural Studies, University of Bremen, Germany. He is author of four, co-author of two and co-editor of nine books and has written more than 90 articles and chapters in different academic journals and books. His main interests are in media, communication and cultural theory, media sociology, inter- and transcultural communication, cultural studies, media change, methods of qualitative media research and audience studies.

David O. Lavin is completing his PhD in the Department of Sociology at York University in Toronto. His major research interests are labour studies, political economy and communication/media studies.

Mark McLelland lectures in sociology in the School of Social Sciences, Media and Communication at the University of Wollongong and was the 2007/8 Toyota Visiting Professor of Japanese at the University of Michigan. He is co-editor of the collection *Japanese Cybercultures* (2003) and has published widely on the internet in Japan, most recently in *New Media and Society*. He is co-editor of *Internationalizing Internet Studies* (2008) with Gerard Goggin.

Winston Mano is Senior Lecturer in Media and Communication Studies at the University of Westminster in London. His research mainly focuses on radio, music, audiences, globalization, media democracy and development. He is a founding editor of the *Journal of African Media Studies* published by Intellect.

Tristan Mattelart is Senior Lecturer in International Communication at the French Institute of the Press (Institut français de presse), University of Paris 2. His publications include *Le cheval de Troie audiovisuel: Le rideau de fer à l'épreuve des radios et télévisions transfrontières* (1995); *La mondialisation des médias contre la censure: Tiers monde et audiovisuel sans frontières* (2002), and *Médias, migrations et cultures transnationales* (2007).

Vincent Mosco is Canada Research Chair in Communication and Society, Queen's University, Canada. Mosco graduated from Georgetown University in 1970 and received his PhD in Sociology from Harvard University in 1975. He is the author of numerous books on the media, telecommunications, computers and information technology. His most recent include *The Laboring of Communication* (Lexington, 2008); *Knowledge Workers in the Information Society* (edited with Catherine McKercher and published by Lexington, 2007) and *The Digital Sublime: Myth, Power, and Cyberspace* (MIT Press, 2004), which won the 2005 Olson Award for outstanding book in the field of rhetoric and cultural studies. He is also completing a revised edition of his 1996 book *The Political Economy of Communication*, which is to be published by Sage in 2009.

Kaarle Nordenstreng is Professor of Journalism and Mass Communication at the University of Tampere in Finland. He was head of research at the Finnish Broadcasting Company in the late 1960s, after which he moved to his present position. He has also served as a consultant to UNESCO (1969–75) and as vice-president of the International Association for Mass Communication Research (1972–8) as well as president of the International Organization of Journalists (1976–90). He has been visiting professor at the universities of California (UCSD), Maryland, Minnesota and Texas at Austin and has written or edited more than 30 books, including *Television Traffic – A One-way Street?* (1974), *Beyond National Sovereignty* (1993) and *Russian Media Challenge* (2001), as well as 400 scholarly articles and reports.

Monroe E. Price is Director of the Center for Global Communication Studies at the University of Pennsylvania's Annenberg School of Law and a professor at Cardozo School of Law in New York City. He is the author of *Media and Sovereignty: The Global Information Revolution and Its Challenge to State Power* (MIT Press, 2002).

Clemencia Rodríguez is Associate Professor at the University of Oklahoma. She has conducted research since 1984 on citizens' media in different international contexts, including Nicaragua, Colombia, Spain, Chile and among Latino communities in the United States. Her publications include *Fissures in the Mediascape: An International Study of Citizens' Media* (2001).

Tarik Sabry is Senior Lecturer in Media and Communication Theory at the University of Westminster, where he is a member of the Communication and Media Research Institute. He is the co-editor of two new scholarly journals: *Middle East Journal of Culture and Communication* and *Interactions: Studies in Communication and Culture*. His research interests include Arab cultural studies, Arab contemporary thought, media and migration, globalization and post-colonialism.

Daya Kishan Thussu is Professor of International Communication at the University of Westminster in London. A former associate editor of Gemini

News Service, a London-based international news agency, he has a PhD in International Relations from Jawaharlal Nehru University, New Delhi. Among his key publications are *News as Entertainment: The Rise of Global Infotainment* (Sage, 2007), *Media on the Move: Global Flow and Contra-Flow* (Routledge, 2007), *International Communication – Continuity and Change*, second edition (Hodder Arnold, 2006), *War and the Media: Reporting Conflict* (Sage, 2003) and *Electronic Empires – Global Media and Local Resistance* (Arnold, 1998). He is the founder and managing editor of the Sage journal *Global Media and Communication*.

Elena Vartanova is Professor, Deputy Dean for Research and head of Chair in Media Theory and Media Economics at the Faculty of Journalism, Moscow State University. She has published several monographs (in Russian) on the Nordic media model, European information society and media economics. She co-edited *Russian Media Challenge* (Kikimora, 2002, second edition) and has written a number of articles on Russian media in international journals.

Jair Vega is Professor at the Department of Communication at Universidad del Norte in Barranquilla in Colombia. His publications have appeared in *Investigación y Desarrollo*, *Forum Académico* and *Signo y Pensamiento*. Vega is international consultant for the Communication for Social Change Consortium (http://www.communicationforsocialchange.org/), the Communication Initiative (http://comminit.com/), GTZ, and the Pan American Health Organization.

Stefaan Verhulst is Chief of Research at the Markle Foundation in New York and Senior Research Fellow at the Center of Global Communications Studies, Annenberg School for Communications, University of Pennsylvania. He was the co-founder and director of the Programme in Comparative Media Law and Policy at Oxford University. Verhulst has served as consultant to various international and national organizations, including the Council of Europe, the European Commission, UNESCO, UNDP, USAID, the World Bank and DFID. His publications include *In Search of the Self: Conceptual Approaches to Internet Self Regulation* (Routledge, 2001), *Convergence in European Communications Regulation* (Blackstone, 1999), *EC Media Law and Policy* (AWL, 1998), *Legal Responses to the Changing Media* (Oxford University Press, 1998) and *Broadcasting Reform in India* (Oxford University Press, 1998).

Yuezhi Zhao is Professor and Canada Research Chair in the Political Economy of Global Communication at the School of Communication, Simon Fraser University, Canada. She is the author of *Media, Market, and Democracy in China* (1998), co-author of *Sustaining Democracy? Journalism and the*

Politics of Objectivity (1998) and co-editor of *Democratizing Global Media: One World, Many Struggles* (2005), *The Political Economy of Communication: A Reader* (2007) and *Global Communications: Toward a Transcultural Political Economy* (2008). Her latest book, *Communication in China: Political Economy, Power, and Conflict* (2008), explores China's rapidly evolving polity, economy and society through the prism of its communication system.

Introduction

Daya Kishan Thussu

Despite its extraordinary expansion as a field within higher education, media studies still remains a largely nationally bound and inward-looking area of academic enquiry. For an outsider to the field – in more ways than one – with a PhD in International Relations and experience of journalism and teaching and researching international aspects of media for nearly two decades, I would argue that such parochialism untenable in the age of globally mediated connectivity.

Emerging at the fringes of university life and therefore sometimes denied the status it deserved, media studies has often struggled to be taken seriously, partly because of this parochialism. Whatever the status of media studies within academe, though, there is little debate about the primacy of media in contemporary societies. Mass media, therefore, are an important arena for research in our media-saturated lives: they might influence in varied ways – cognitively, behaviourally, emotionally – the way we think about the world, socialize, vote in an election or go to war. *Why Study the Media?*, Roger Silverstone asked in his well-known book, and answered that it was 'because the media are central to our everyday lives that we must study them. Study them as social and cultural as well as economic and political dimensions of the modern world. Study them in their ubiquity and complexity. Study them as contributors to our variable capacity to make sense of the world, to make and share its meanings' (Silverstone, 1999: 2).

This formidable media power has been globalized in the era of multimedia conglomerates, deregulated and privatized communication systems (hard and software) and massive technological advances (Thussu, 2006; Thussu, 2007a; Arsenault and Castells, 2008). With the globalization of media and communication, media technologies and industries have created a culture in which people all over the world can watch and share experiences of media events, from sports and entertainment to war and humanitarian disasters, and, through advertisements, become consumers of free-market capitalism.

This book aims to contribute to the continuing debate in international communication studies on the imperative to broaden the discourse on the globalization of media and communication, going beyond what historian Niall Ferguson has called 'Angloblization'. The contributors to the book suggest that there is a pressing need for innovative research methodologies that fully take account of regional and national specificities, as well as the pedagogic necessities warranted by the growing internationalization of students and researchers and the unprecedented growth of media in the non-Western world, notably in such large Asian countries as China and India.

Rather than 'globalizing media studies', the book is called 'internationalizing media studies', indicating the continuing importance of the nation state in the contemporary media world. Despite exaggerated and premature obituaries of the nation state, it is fair to say that it is alive and well and more active today than it has ever been – whether it is invading Iraq or passing new international treaties or conventions or bailing out the corporate excesses of crony or casino capitalism, as evidenced in 2008. The nation states continue to be crucial in the study of media, though transnational networks are emerging that challenge and, in some cases, even subvert the nation state, particularly the weaker ones.

From its inception in Anglo-American academia nearly half a century ago, media studies has grown and matured as an academic field. The study of media has long been central to courses in communication studies in the US, with its various variants – from health, development, intercultural, political, international, global and participatory – to the more 'culturalist' approaches, associated with the European tradition of research. In much of the rest of the world, the dominant paradigm, emanating from the elite US media and communication studies departments, has been adopted or at least adapted. However, as media studies has expanded, it has included first feminist and, later, multicultural perspectives in its research agendas.

Feminism: the first intervention

The first major change in the field, which was founded largely by male academics mostly of a left-liberal ideological orientation, was the intervention of feminist critiques of media and popular culture. The gender imbalance was striking. In 1976, as James Curran has reminded us in the case of Britain, out of over thirty full-time permanent academic staff employed in pioneer media and cultural studies centres in Birmingham, Leeds, Leicester and the Polytechnic of Central London only three were women (Curran, 2006). The situation was not that dissimilar in other countries. Today, happily, the balance has been redressed to some extent. On the other hand, some might argue that the 'feminization' of media studies has contributed to a trend in 'softer' topics being researched and written about.

Race and ethnicity: the second intervention

The second prominent intervention in the study of media was the gradual importance being given to race and ethnicity, helped in no small measure by the contribution of scholars such as Stuart Hall in Britain and the general discourse of multiculturalism and post-colonialism, as well as a turn towards identity politics. Though this tradition broadened the scope of media and cultural studies, the remit was largely national – with the inherent danger that, for example, the diasporic and the distant communities were conflated, with a London suburb such as Southall being extrapolated to represent a culturally complex and multifaceted sub-continent like South Asia.

One outcome of these interventions was that gender and ethnic groups gained a greater focus of attention while class became less pronounced, reflecting the academic fashion of the 1980s and 1990s. The victory of capitalism in the Cold War disoriented the left in the West, including those in the academic community. Meanwhile the debate between political economy and cultural studies approaches to the study of media had become increasingly self-referential and unproductive.

Internationalization: the third intervention

The internationalization of the field can be seen as the third key intervention in the evolution of media studies. It might also help provide the academic respectability to which the field aspires to. The globalization of media together with the globalization of higher education provide excellent opportunities for researchers to broaden their intellectual horizons. Media and their study are in the process of transformation, necessitated by new global infrastructures, such as 'network' technologies, which have made redundant many traditional ways of teaching and researching the media. The notions of place, space and time have been challenged, making it imperative to invest in new research angles, approaches and methodologies. Already calls for the 'de-Westernization' of media studies have been made (Curran and Park, 2000).

Imperatives for internationalization

Globalization of the media means that research demands it

That media and communication have become a fast-growing area of academic enquiry internationally is a reflection of the huge impact of globalization on the media in recent years. The explosion of transnational information flows, made possible by new technologies and institutional changes – economic, political and legal – have profoundly affected global media production, distribution and consumption. Consequently, the emphasis is moving away from considering the role of media in the vertical integration of national societies, to examining transnational horizontal integration of media and communication processes, institutions and audiences.

Technological transformations have contributed to this shift, opening up huge possibilities of new subjects and materials for research in media, communication and culture. With the availability of digital television and online delivery mechanisms, there is a plethora of material now available to researchers. The digital revolution in communication and information technologies has triggered interactive and innovative ways in which media messages are produced and distributed in real time in a digitally linked globe. The Cold War concept of the 'free flow of information' has been given a new lease of life by the digital revolution and the internet. The Web 2.0 and the blogosphere, with its 'citizen journalists' and activists, are challenging the notion of editorial gatekeeping and bringing hitherto neglected or under-reported issues into the public discourse. The convergence of mobile technologies and broadband can now provide internet access at high speeds to a range of media – music, games, gambling, news, videos and personalized services. Particularly effective are the video-sharing sites such as YouTube, Facebook and MySpace; arguably the CNN effect of the 1990s has been supplanted by a 'YouTube effect'. With the Internet Corporation for Assigned Names and Numbers (ICANN) approving, in 2008, internationalized domain names, cyberspace is likely to have greater traffic and accessibility for content in such scripts as Arabic, Cyrillic and Devanagri as well as ideographic writing systems like Mandarin, Japanese and Korean. Easy to navigate, increasingly multi-lingual and sophisticated search engines have already ensured the globalization of 'social computing', with a myriad net-activists and bloggers producing and distributing information and entertainment within a 'global infotainment sphere' (Thussu, 2007b). This communicational connectivity is creating new horizontal media links among global, regional and national media, at a commercial corporate level through viral advertising networks (Thussu, 2007a; Arsenault and Castells, 2008), as well as alternative networks among indigenous (Wilson and Stewart, 2008) and political groups across the world, reflected, for instance, in the growth of Islamo-jihadist websites.[1]

International news networks, too, are challenging the established media order with a proliferation of diverse voices and views on global television and computer screens: Aljazeera English claims to be 'setting the news agenda', ostensibly privileging news from the global South; Telesur – the first pan-Latin American public broadcaster – complements such a news agenda. France 24 provides more coverage of Africa and the Arab world, while Russia Today, CCTV-9, Iran's Press TV and India's NDTV 24/7 offer distinctive perspectives on global issues. Adding to this multi-dimensional traffic is the growing phenomenon of the contra-flow of media products from the global South to the North and within the South; examples include Bollywood, Korean cinema, Japanese animation, Arabic news and Brazilian soap operas (Thussu, 2007a).

Globalization of higher education means that students demand it

Media studies is popular with students across the world. With the liberalization and expansion of the global economy, higher education has now become a transnational arena (Knight, 2003; Ninnes and Hellsten, 2005; Güriiz, 2008).

Students are becoming increasingly mobile, seeking higher education outside their own national systems and cultures. According to data from UNESCO and OECD, in 2007 some 2.73 million students were studying at a foreign university – most going to such countries as the US, Britain and Australia. This global market has seen the aspiration of other countries to set up hubs of international higher education in such places as Dubai, Singapore, Shanghai and Bangalore. Initiatives such as the European Union's Erasmus Mundus are promoting joint masters programmes with sponsorship for international students. Universities are more and more dependent on international students for their financial viability; in 2008 more than one third of all postgraduate students in Britain came from overseas.

However, as consumers of a highly priced and prized commodity, these students also have demands and expectations of their studies and bring different experiences of and perspectives on the world to their learning. There has been much work done in developing policy and practice in internationalizing the curriculum, particularly in Australia and North America, but in the UK the importance of this is only now being recognized.

An internationalized teaching and research agenda would encourage researchers to foster academic and professional links to develop joint projects to investigate transnational media and cultural phenomena. Already there is greater and more open communication among professional organizations in the field and increasing internationalization; the International Communication Association (ICA) has recently voted to 'become more international', while the International Association for Media and Communication Research (IAMCR) has a long and distinguished history of nurturing internationalization. Other regional professional organizations too are recognizing the benefits accruing from internationalization.

The 2008 crisis of US-led neo-liberal capitalism may also indirectly contribute to internationalization of media studies, as scepticism grows about the applicability of the US-dominated media and communication systems in other socio-economic and cultural contexts. This may indicate a broader geopolitical and economic shift, too, in evidence in the economic recovery in Russia and the resultant assertiveness of the Kremlin; China's double-digit economic growth and the extension of its influence in parts of the developing world; the rise of India as a software power, and the trend towards social democracy in Latin America.

The cracks and crises that have emerged in the neo-liberal model of globalization, threatening global economic stability, might provide an opportunity to rethink the limitations of neo-liberal ideology – an ideology which, in the words of one eminent commentator, has 'entered the bloodstream of media and cultural studies, almost without us noticing it' (Curran, 2006: 144). For an alternative, community-based capitalism to evolve, media and communication studies will have to be deployed effectively to truly reflect the landscape of a globalized and interconnected planet.

The book in outline

The book is divided into four parts. Contributors to the first part focus on how media and communication research can and should be internationalized. The second part of the book deals with broadening the field of media studies, taking on board new political, economic, legal and regulatory challenges unleashed by the globalization of media and communication industries and institutions. Chapters in the third part encompass regional perspectives on media studies, with examples from Latin America, Asia, the Arab world, as well as such major countries as China and Russia. The final part of the book engages with the teaching of media studies, with perspectives drawn from teaching of media in the US, the Nordic countries and Africa, in addition to discussions of media ethics and the internationalization of internet studies.

Internationalizing media research

In a context-setting chapter on internationalization, I discuss the changes in media and their study at a juncture when notions of place, space and time have been reconfigured. After providing a brief historical context to the evolution of media studies as an academic field, I critique the epistemological limitations of the study of the media, necessitated in part by the rise of 'Chindia' in global communication and media discourses. I also suggest how academics could contribute to the internationalization of media studies.

In their chapter, Andreas Hepp and Nick Couldry ask a very pertinent question – what should be the unit of comparison for comparative media research? Suggesting a transcultural approach for comparative research which goes beyond a nation-bound and territorialized view of 'media cultures', Hepp and Couldry criticize the 'container thinking' implicit in much contemporary comparative media research, and see cultural formations linked to race, gender and ethnicity, and deterritorialized popular cultures as 'cultural thickenings' or 'amalgamations'. Cultural perspectives also figure prominently in Tristan Mattelart's historical appraisal of theories of globalization and media internationalization. He critiques the tendency among the theorists of cultural globalization not to adequately take on board the contribution of critical political economy towards the internationalization of media and communication studies. Often, he notes, the version presented in sociological, anthropological or cultural studies paradigms is reductive, caricaturing political economists as doomsayers of global cultural homogenization.

That the World Wide Web – with its 'mingling of media' or 'multi-mediacy' – is central to the internationalization of media is emphasized by Naren Chitty in his contribution. Chitty frames this discussion of the web as the venue for the internationalization of media and exemplifies it with a study of various locally based websites of a transnational operation, the United Nations Development Programme. In his chapter, the late Jan Ekecrantz, in one of his last pieces, argues that, though media and communication studies have been international, their study needs to be more inclusive in the era of globalization, taking account of regional modernities and non-Western media thought and supporting this approach with comparative, cross-disciplinary case studies.

Broadening the field of media studies

One characteristic of this volume is that many of its contributors take a broad view of media studies as a field of academic enquiry. In her essay, Sandra Braman exhorts the academic community to take more seriously the legal aspects of media and their study in a global context, indicating the paucity of material on global legal media studies. She argues that globalization of law through the processes of government, governance and governmentality is of importance to media studies theoretically, as a research subject, and pedagogically. The necessity to develop comparative media law and policy research is also emphasized by Stefaan Verhulst and Monroe Price in their essay, arguing that such a change would enrich media studies. It is, they argue, essential for media and communication researchers to be aware of the bigger picture and how this might contribute to a better understanding of the field itself.

Oliver Boyd-Barrett urges media researchers to move away from the narrow confines of studying just 'the media', posing the question: can we talk about media solely from within the discipline of media studies? Instead, he makes a plea to extend the conversation of communication scholars with researchers studying such issues as global corporate power and corruption, the excesses of a market-driven democracy, environmental decay and wars over natural resources at a time when these are depleting rapidly. Another neglected area of media and communication studies is the role of the communication labour that provides the equipment that makes the globalization of media possible and which itself is increasingly becoming globalized. In their contribution, Vincent Mosco and David Lavin examine labour relations in international communication, showing how organizations that represent media and information workers are developing global strategies and using the media to participate in international activities. Their focus is on the Union Network International, a Swiss-based global labour federation that specializes in media, communication, information, and service workers.

Regional perspectives on internationalization

The five essays in this part explore regional and national perspectives on the internationalization of media and its study. In his reflections on the state of media studies in Asia, Indrajit Banerjee points to continuing contestation of the validity and legitimacy of an 'Asian' media studies discourse, despite the proliferation of media and communication schools across Asia and the steady improvement in the quality of research and scholarship. Banerjee, who has been active in internationalizing Asian media, not least by energizing the Singapore-based Asian Media Information and Communication Centre (AMIC), argues that the focus should be on developing local perspectives and models based on extensive and grounded research.

The most significant transformation in media in Asia has occurred in the continent's largest and fastest-growing country, a phenomenon deftly mapped by Yuezhi Zhao. Rather than focusing on transnational flows of media capital, forms, contents and influences, internationalizing media studies in the Chinese context, Zhao contends, requires articulation of the relationship between state and society within the Chinese media and communication system, as well as the ways in which social inequalities and injustices in China are structurally linked to transnational capitalism. Examining the media and cultural studies discourses in the Arab world, Tarik Sabry privileges a 'dialogical approach' (between Arab and Western scholars) as a better alternative to asymmetrical discourses of de-Westernization. De-Sovietization not de-Westernization is at the heart of Elena Vartanova's contribution. She examines the attempts to 'de-Sovietize' media studies in Russia, sometimes by adapting Western approaches and models by researchers accustomed to conceptual frameworks that took shape at a time of state-controlled or managed media. Vartanova suggests that de-Sovietization has entailed not only accepting Western concepts uncritically but also integrating Western media theories with indigenous communication traditions to create new concepts. The primacy of the local and the indigenous is also central to the chapter by Jair Vega and Clemencia Rodríguez, who report the findings of a case study of community radio in Colombia. This example shows the importance of political communication in Latin America, a region with a distinguished history of alternative media and one which media studies outside the continent could take more fully into account.

Pedagogic parameters: internationalizing media syllabi

How should media studies encompass the teaching of the internationalization of our field? The contributions in the final part of the book take up this challenge. In a short reflective piece, esteemed communication scholar Cees Hamelink makes a case for a reflexive approach to the glocalization of media ethics studies by fusing local moralities with engagement in the global challenge of discursive reflexivity. Kaarle Nordenstreng, another veteran commentator on international media, demands a more rigorous approach to media studies to compensate for the lack of scientific depth in the field. After examining the teaching of media in Scandinavia, he recommends the continuing study of the history of ideas in the field, as well as of the nature of the field. John Downing reports on the teaching of international media studies within the elite private and public universities in the United States, looking at the extent to which global media issues are taught and how far they are engaged with in textbooks. Downing notes that the trend is strongly in the direction of insularity rather than internationalism. In striking contrast to the US, the teaching of media is much more internationalized in Africa, as Winston Mano suggests in his chapter based on interviews with media scholars in Uganda, Nigeria, South Africa and Zimbabwe. The dependency on Western textbooks and other teaching materials has internationalized the study of media, though Mano argues for curricula that are informed by African epistemology and responsive to the needs of the continent. One major contributor to the internationalization of media studies is the growing use of the internet as a tool for education. Gerard Goggin and Mark McLelland underline the need to internationalize internet studies in order to go beyond Anglophone perspectives on the internet, as English-language users are being overtaken by other language communities, with pedagogical implications for media studies.

Across the chapters a few salient themes emerge. Despite their differences of perspective and diverse approaches, the contributors to this volume recognize the imperative to internationalize media studies. The continued dominance of a US–UK-centric epistemology for the study of mass media is another feature that cuts across geographical and cultural boundaries – with examples drawn from Africa to Russia to Asia. There is a general sense of disquiet with the nature of contemporary media studies and a need to reinvigorate it by extending its remit by entering into an intellectual and interdisciplinary dialogue with other social sciences, as well as non-Western theories and approaches.

Some of the chapters included in this volume were first presented at an international conference that I conceived and organized with the help of colleagues at the University of Westminster supported by the journal *Global Media and Communication*.[2] More than 250 scholars from around the world attended the event in London in September 2006. I want to take this opportunity to thank all my colleagues, especially Colin Sparks, Peter Goodwin, Winston Mano, Annette Hill and Sally Feldman, for their excellent support, as well as acknowledge the invaluable help provided by our three research students: Yael Friedman, Gabriel Moreno and Anastasios Maragiannis.

Edited books involve a great deal of work and organization and I feel privileged to have been able to benefit from the intellectual energy, range of perspectives and enthusiasm for academic enquiry of a group of high-calibre contributors from around the world. I remain very grateful for their involvement in this project. This volume is part of a new book series called *Internationalizing Media Studies* which I edit, and my hope is that the contributions in this collection will stimulate a wider debate about the pressing imperatives for internationalizing our rapidly growing and globalizing field.

Notes

1 The growing value and visibility of such alternative media discourses are noted by leading media journals, which have devoted special issues to alternative media research, for example *Media History* (2001), *Media International Australia* (2002), *Journalism: Theory, Practice and Criticism* (2003) and *Media, Culture and Society* (2003).

2 See the 2007 special issue of *Global Media and Communication*, vol. 3, no. 3, on the theme of Internationalizing Media Studies.

References

Arsenault, Amelia and Castells, Manuel (2008) The Structure and Dynamics of Global Multi-Media Business Networks, *International Journal of Communication*, 2: 707–48.

Curran, James (2006) Media and Cultural Theory in the Age of Market Liberalism, in James Curran and David Morley (eds) *Media and Cultural Theory*. London: Routledge, pp. 129–48.

Curran, James and Park, Myung-Jin (2000) Beyond Globalization Theory, in James Curran and Myung-Jin Park (eds) *De-Westernizing Media Studies*. London: Routledge, pp. 3–18.

Gürüz, Kemal (2008) *Higher Education and International Student Mobility in the Global Knowledge Economy*. Albany, NY: SUNY Press.

Knight, Jane (2003) *Internationalization of Higher Education Practices and Priorities*, International Association of Universities Survey Report. Paris: UNESCO.

Ninnes, Peter and Hellsten, Meeri (eds) (2005) *Internationalizing Higher Education: Critical Explorations of Pedagogy and Policy*. Dordrecht (Netherlands): Springer.

Silverstone, Roger (1999) *Why Study the Media?*. London: Sage.

Thussu, Daya Kishan (2006) *International Communication: Continuity and Change*. London: Hodder Arnold, second edition.

—— (2007a) Mapping Global Media Flow and Contra-flow, in Daya Kishan Thussu (ed.) *Media on the Move: Global Flow and Contra-flow*. London: Routledge, pp. 11–32.

—— (2007b) *News as Entertainment: The Rise of Global Infotainment*. London: Sage.

Wilson, Pamela and Stewart, Michelle (eds) (2008) *Global Indigenous Media: Cultures, Poetics, and Politics*. Durham, NC: Duke University Press.

Part I

Internationalizing media research

Part I

Internationalizing media research

Chapter 1

Why internationalize media studies and how?

Daya Kishan Thussu

International media and their study are in the process of transformation, spurred on by increasingly mobile and globally networked communication infrastructures. The multi-vocal, multi-directional and multi-layered media flows have also made redundant many traditional ways of thinking about the media (Thussu, 2007; Arsenault and Castells, 2008). The globalization of media industries and audiences, combined with the internationalization of higher education, mean that the research and teaching of the media face pressing challenges.[1] In particular, the transformation of media and communication in Asia – the world's most populous region with some of its fastest growing economies – has profound implications for what constitutes the 'global' in media and their study. As a relatively new field that is by its nature inter- and trans-disciplinary, media studies is well placed to draw in and deploy a range of paradigms and approaches, from the social sciences as well as arts and humanities, to look across borders and boundaries, between nations, cultures and academic disciplines (Downing, 1996; Curran and Park, 2000; Appadurai, 2001; Murphy and Kraidy, 2003; Abbas and Erni, 2005; Miike, 2006; Shome, 2006; Thussu, 2007; Connell, 2007; Sreberny, 2008; Tomaselli, 2008).

This chapter aims to delineate the changes in media and their study at a juncture when notions of place, space and time have been reconfigured, making it imperative to suggest new research angles and approaches, as well as methodologies, going beyond explicit or implicit assumptions for studying international social reality. After providing a brief historical context to the evolution of media studies as an academic field, the chapter critiques the epistemological limitations of the study of the media, necessitated in part by the increasing importance of China and India in global communication and media discourses. Finally, the chapter suggests some markers which could contribute to the internationalization of media studies.

Historical limitations and legacies

Like other new fields, the study of media emerged on the fringes of academic activities, initially in the United States, where communication became the subject of university research after the end of the First World War, when interest in the psychological potential of the media to shape people's views became apparent, reflected in such works as Walter Lippmann on public opinion (published in 1922) and Harold Lasswell on propaganda (published in 1927). The growing institutionalization of media and communication studies within the disciplines of sociology, politics and psychology led to the establishment of 'mass communication' as a new area of academic inquiry. Early work in the field demonstrated a positivist and empiricist orientation, with an emphasis on behavioural 'effects' research, and more applied aspects of communication, often influenced by political and economic interests. Such studies tended to have a national focus and largely ignored the transnational and historical contexts of communication and media.

In Europe, media and communication as a field of academic study took time to develop, though in Finland a college of journalism was established in 1925, in Czechoslovakia in 1928, and the Institut Français de Presse in Paris in 1937. After the Second World War, Europe's first international journal for media, *Gazette*, was founded in 1955 – four years after the launch of the US-based *Journal of Communication*. Academic study of media began in Italy in 1958 and in Spain in 1960, while such French scholars as Jacques Ellul, with his seminal work on propaganda, and Fernand Terrou, who founded the science of the press at the Sorbonne University, made notable contributions to the field (Vroons, 2005).

In Britain's class-dominated academe, where higher education was until the 1980s the preserve of a relatively small elite, media studies developed at the margins of traditional academic activities. Initially media studies was taught in the former polytechnics and was characterized as having a Marxist orientation – reclaiming and validating the experience of the working classes, with intellectual inspiration from such figures as Richard Hoggart, founder of the Birmingham Centre for Contemporary Cultural Studies, and Welsh scholar Raymond Williams at Cambridge University. The dominant 'culturalist' paradigm took a qualitative and critical approach and evolved in the 1970s to delineate the ideological role of the mass media (Scannell, 2007). Thus, in Britain, the study of media, culture and communication had a different trajectory from that of the US model of communication studies with its health, development, interpersonal and organizational variants. Despite its popularity among students, the media were not considered a 'proper' subject for academic study, and that rather condescending attitude towards the subject still persists in some quarters.

In parts of the world where the British educational model had a defining influence, such as in India, a similar attitude to studying the media can be detected. Generally in the global South, where the European colonial imprint was deeply ingrained in intellectual institutions, media and communication research was profoundly influenced by the Western or, more specifically, the American tradition of mass communication research, given its prominence during the Cold War. This was reflected also in a dependency relationship in the field of research, evident in the import of textbooks, journals, citations, employment of experts, and the funding, planning and execution of research. This situation was characterized, as Halloran has noted, 'by a one-way flow of values, ideas, models, methods and resources from North to South. It may even be more specifically a flow from the Anglo-Saxon language fraternity to the rest of the world' (Halloran, 1997: 39).

It is not surprising then that US approaches were enthusiastically adopted in media and communication courses around the developing world. The so-called modernization paradigm shaped the theoretical framework in relation to media and communication studies in much of the global South (Sparks, 2007). A dependency syndrome developed that privileged a type of data-driven research on the behaviour, attitudes and values of the people in the developing countries but largely failed to analyse the political, social and cultural contexts of communication. Continuities can be detected in a revised version of modernization theory which demonstrates an almost blind faith in the potential of the new information and communication technologies as agencies for development. This 'neo-developmentalist' view, under the banner of the globalization of the information society, legitimized an advanced telecommunication and computer infrastructure, through 'efficient' private corporations (Mosco, 1996). A valuable antidote to the modernization thesis, represented by critical research, analysed patterns of ownership and production in the media and communication industries, and located these within the context of national and transnational power relations. However, this tradition often took a deterministic line in which much of the South was seen as an undifferentiated 'other'.

To be sure, such limitations of scholarship were not specific to the study of media and communication but afflicted the social sciences more generally, being deeply rooted within European academic traditions. As Said has argued, in the European intellectual imagination the 'other' was created as part of an ideological Orientalist discourse, promoting and privileging European imperialist epistemology (Said, 1978). Such specialized journals as the *Journal asiatique* (established in 1823), the *Journal of the Royal Asiatic Society* (1834), and the *Zeitschrift der deutschen morgenländischen Gesellschaft* (1845), as well as 'learned societies', helped legitimize an intellectual discourse which was based principally on racialized and imperialistic categorizations of the non-European. As a recent study of higher education in colonial India argues, European epistemology was projected not just as one of many ways of knowing but as knowledge itself, undermining indigenous knowledge systems and traditions (Seth, 2007).

As British colonialism became entrenched in most of the globe during the nineteenth century, the hegemony of the English language was established, supplemented in the twentieth century by the growing relationship between American-led global capitalism – with its formidable media, cultural, corporate, military and communication networks – and the English language (Phillipson,1992). This severely disadvantaged scholars writing in other languages (even European ones). Translations, where they existed, were more often than not from English into other languages rather than the other way around (Ahmad, 1992).

As historian Dipesh Chakrabarty has argued in his provocative book *Provincializing Europe*, this led to what he termed 'asymmetric ignorance', indicating that the Western academy did not need to read specialists of non-Western histories. Long 'dead and gone' European intellectuals are routinely invoked as 'though they were our own contemporaries', Chakrabarty notes. Illustrating his point with an example from his native India, Chakrabarty wryly observes: 'Faced with the task of analyzing developments or social practices in modern India, few if any Indian social scientists or social scientists of India would argue seriously with, say, the thirteenth-century logician Gangesa or with the grammarian and linguistic philosopher Bartrihari (fifth to sixth centuries), or with the tenth- or eleventh-century aesthetician Abhinavagupta. Sad though it is, one result of European colonial rule in South Asia is that the intellectual traditions once unbroken and alive in Sanskrit or Persian or Arabic are now only matters of historical research for most – perhaps all – modern social scientists in the region' (Chakrabarty, 2007: 5–6).

That there exists in Western historical writing a pervasive Eurocentric or Occidental bias, as well as 'theft' by the West of the achievements of other cultures in such notable inventions as capitalism, democracy and individualism, is well documented by social scientist Jack Goody. He notes that although 'most historians aim to avoid ethnocentricity (like teleology), they rarely succeed in doing so because of their limited knowledge of the other (including their own beginnings). That limitation often leads them to make unsustainable claims, implicitly or explicitly, about the uniqueness of the West' (Goody, 2006: 4).

Escaping epistemological essentialism

Media studies, like other fields broadly within the arena of the social sciences and humanities, is affected by what might be called epistemological essentialism, rooted as it is within an Anglo-American intellectual tradition. There is increasing awareness of this rather limited epistemological engagement with other cultures and knowledge systems, especially in the context of global communication research. Even scholars working within international relations paradigms have begun to recognize this lacuna.[2] As the editors of a special issue on the theme of 'International Relations and the Challenges of Global Communication' of the British journal *Review of International Studies* noted: 'The conventional approach within IR has been, until recently, an attitude that "we" know all that there is – or is needed – to know about global communication, and therefore that there is no need to situate IR within the emerging dynamics of communication elsewhere' (Constantinou *et al.*, 2008:

7). They contended that 'theories of globalization that are credited for producing new imaginings of the global can be seen to have failed to globalize imagination, that is to retrieve and disseminate theories of the global from non-Western and non-metropolitan centres' (ibid.: 11).

The 'US–UK duopoly' in global media is also paralleled in the study of it, largely because of the dominance of English as the language of global communication, combined with the fact that the study of media emerged in the United States as an academic field, which is therefore home to the majority of textbook and journal publishing in the area, closely followed by Britain (Lauf, 2005). Siebert and his colleagues' book *Four Theories of the Press* (Siebert *et al.*, 1956), for example, was for decades a compulsory text for media courses around the world, though, as one critic noted, the book 'does not offer four theories: it offers one theory with four examples' (Nerone, 1995: 18). The authoritarian versus liberal media theory unsurprisingly remained the dominant paradigm in the study of media during the Cold War. Southern demands for a fairer and more balanced flow of information, leading to the 1970s debates within UNESCO about the creation of a New World Information and Communication Order, brought the global South, albeit briefly, into the global communication discourse (Thussu, 2006). The end of the Cold War and the disintegration of the Soviet Union prompted scholars to offer reflections on the transitional state of the media in the former communist countries of the Eastern bloc. Examining the change in 'mediatic processes' in Russia, Poland and Hungary between 1980 and 1995, Downing argued for 'the necessity for communication theorizing to develop itself comparatively, acknowledging in particular that to extrapolate theoretically from such relatively unrepresentative nations as Britain and the United States, is both conceptually impoverishing and a peculiarly restricted version of even Eurocentracism' (Downing, 1996: xi).

By the end of the 1990s, there was talk of 'de-Westernizing' media studies, part of 'a growing reaction against the self-absorption and parochialism of much Western media theory' (Curran and Park, 2000: 3). Despite the fact that research funding increasingly privileges comparative research, as Livingstone notes, 'comparative methodology is rather little discussed, with the consequence that too often research teams find themselves "reinventing the wheel" or, worse, repeating the mistakes of others' (Livingstone, 2003: 478). Meaningful endeavours at providing comparative models of media systems have ignored analysis beyond the Euro-American ambit, despite the extraordinary expansion of the media, especially in Asia (Hallin and Mancini, 2004). Similarly, comparative studies of global journalists (Weaver, 1998) and journalism research (Löffelholz and Weaver, 2008) operated within a Euro-Atlantic model (it is interesting to note that in neither book is there a discussion of journalism in India – home to one of the world's most diverse and dynamic mediascapes). Transnational and comparative research projects in areas such as political communication (Esser and Pfetsch, 2004) or news values (Shoemaker and Cohen, 2005) theorize broadly within the dominant Anglo-

American research orbit and rarely go beyond tokenism as far as the non-Western world is concerned. French scholarship in communication and media is generally self-contained and therefore intellectually smug, while in much of Asia, despite the massive expansion of media, its study remains largely derivative and lacking in indigenous theoretical underpinnings, though attempts have been made in recent years to 'decolonize' Asian media and cultural studies (Erni and Chua, 2005).

The 'Chindia' challenge

The most significant recent change in relation to the globalization of media is the rise of Asia, especially its two largest countries.[3] Any meaningful discussion of the internationalization of media studies, therefore, must take into account the rapid growth of China and India – the two ancient civilizations with huge potential to influence the emerging global 'knowledge society' – which are increasingly making their presence felt on the global scene (Goldman Sachs, 2007). Jairam Ramesh, political analyst and former economic advisor to the prime minister of India, is credited with the notion of 'Chindia' (Ramesh, 2005). The 'Chindia' phenomenon represents what has been termed the 'rise of the rest' in a 'post-American world' (Zakaria, 2008) and is likely to profoundly influence globalized media. The 'peaceful rising' of China and the economic growth of India (though deeply skewed in favour of a rich minority in both countries), coinciding with cracks within the neo-liberal model of US-led Western capitalism, are set to challenge conventional frameworks for the study of international media and communication. Their combined economic and cultural impact, aided by extensive global diasporas, is likely to create globalization with an Asian accent. With 56 round-the-clock news channels, India has the distinction of having the world's most linguistically diverse media landscape, while China has emerged as the planet's biggest mobile telephone market, having the highest blogger population as well as being the largest exporter of IT products. According to the World Association of Newspapers, in 2008 74 of the world's 100 largest-selling dailies were published in Asia, with China (107 million copies sold daily) and India (99 million) leading the pack. Moreover, outside the Anglo-American media ambit new configurations are developing: Indian entertainment corporations are looking east for markets beyond the diaspora. The success of the 2005 Chinese film *Perhaps Love* – the first musical since the 1950s and made with expertise from Bollywood – is indicative of the potential of a 'Chindia' cultural collaboration. Trade between the two Asian giants – negligible at the beginning of the 1990s – had grown to $40 billion by 2008, making India's eastern neighbour its largest single trading partner, overtaking the US.

The world's business elite have been quick to recognize this change. A 2003 cover story in *BusinessWeek* (December 8) on 'The Rise of India' focused on the 'low-cost, high IQ, English-speaking brain power' of India, while the story 'China Now' in the 31 December 2007 issue of *Newsweek* concluded that 'the much-heralded advent of China as a global power is no longer a forecast but a reality'. In 2007 the BBC, in association with PBS in the US, broadcast a six-part series called *The Story of India*, looking at the country not as an exotic place but as one of enterprise and innovation, a cradle of culture and science. The Canadian Broadcasting Corporation, in conjunction with New York Times TV and Germany's ZDF, produced a series called *China Rises* and its sequel *India Reborn*, a four-part documentary. A plethora of publications has appeared on both sides of the Atlantic about the globe's two 'mega-markets', ranging from journalistic accounts such as Smith, 2007 (*Sunday Times*); Emmott, 2008 (*The Economist*); Meredith, 2007 (*Forbes*); Engardio, 2007 ('the best minds' at *BusinessWeek*) and Zakaria, 2008 (*Newsweek*), to reports from the World Bank (Winters and Yusuf, 2006).

According to industry estimates, within a generation China and India will become the largest and the third largest world economies, respectively, in terms of purchasing power parity – together they will account for nearly 40 per cent of world trade (Goldman Sachs, 2007). This, notes Harvard professor Tarun Khanna, will be achieved as a result of Chinese and Indian managerial talent and distinctive approaches to business and entrepreneurship. 'The world's future', he writes, 'is irrefutably tied to that of China and India' and yet the United States 'is woefully uninformed about the past and present of both countries', noting that for most of the past 150 years less than 2 per cent of the major stories in any given year in the *New York Times* have been on China and India (Khanna, 2007: 2).

The US media may have been lacking in this area but the twinning of China and India as future major powers is noticed by the White House. If current economic trends continue, predicted a US government report, 'Rising Asia will continue to reshape globalization, giving it less of a "Made in the USA" character and more of an Asian look and feel. At the same time, Asia will alter the rules of the globalizing process. By having the fastest-growing consumer markets, more firms becoming world-class multinationals, and greater S&T stature, Asia looks set to displace Western countries as the focus for international economic dynamism.' The report, *Mapping the Global Future*, by the National Intelligence Council, added: 'The likely emergence of China and India, as well as others, as new major global players – similar to the advent of a united Germany in the 19th century and a powerful United States in the early 20th century – will transform the geopolitical landscape, with impacts potentially as dramatic as those in the previous two centuries. In the same way that commentators refer to the 1900s as the "American Century," the 21st century may be seen as the time when Asia, led by China and India, comes into its own' (US Government, 2004).

The rise, or, as Kishore Mahbubani has argued, 'the return' of Asia may signal a corresponding decline in the Western domination of world history of the last two centuries (Mahbubani, 2008). However, if one takes a long view of history, as British economic historian Angus Maddison has shown, until the eighteenth century China and India were the largest economies in the world, accounting for more than 60 per cent of global GDP: out of a world total of \$694.4 billion in 1820, at the international dollar rate of 1990, Asia's contribution to global GDP was \$410 billion, as against the West's \$175 billion (Maddison, 2001: 28).

India: software as soft power

As the Indian media and communication sector further integrates with the US-dominated transnational media conglomerates, benefiting from an English-fluent creative workforce as well as media outsourcing industries, in such areas as animation and post-production services for Hollywood and other industries, Indian cultural products are likely to have a transnational reach, attracting consumers beyond their traditional South Asian diasporic constituency. The availability of new delivery and distribution mechanisms coupled with the growing corporatization of its film factories and television industry have ensured that Indian content has entered the global media sphere, with the potential of pushing it in new directions. In 2008 the *Times of India* group acquired Britain's Virgin Radio, relabelling it as Absolute Radio, in the first such overseas acquisition by an Indian media corporation. Indian companies are investing in Hollywood production in what are emerging as significant synergies between Hollywood and Bollywood – the world's richest and its biggest film industries (Kavoori and Punathambekar, 2008). Already, Indian films are increasingly being watched by an international audience as well as a 24-million-strong Indian diaspora. Hindi films are shown in more than 70 countries: by 2004 exports accounted for nearly 30 per cent of the industry earnings while annual export earnings were in the range of \$220 million (UNESCO, 2005; UNCTAD, 2008).

Industry estimates show that the Indian entertainment and media industry will be worth nearly \$29 billion by 2012, with a compounded annual growth rate of 18 per cent between 2008 and 2012 (FICCI, 2008). The convergence between creative industries and information technology services is particularly strong in a country that has emerged as a global IT powerhouse. The information technology and IT-enabled services industries are central to India's integration into the global electronic economy: IT exports from India will reach \$148 billion by 2012. Underpinning this software is the hardware of India's indigenous space technology: in 2008 the Indian Space Research Organization made history by launching 10 satellites in one flight.

The 'peaceful rise' of China

China's economic development over the past quarter of a century has been unprecedented – since 2006 China has been the world's largest holder of foreign-currency reserves, estimated to be about \$2 trillion. In 2008, according to *Fortune 500*, three of the top ten global corporations were based in China, with PetroChina ranking second; China Mobile stood at number five, and Industrial and Commercial Bank of China at number six. China's creative economy – television, animation, design, publishing and digital games (Curtin, 2007; Keane, 2007) – is reshaping the traditional understanding of culture, as evident during the spectacular showcasing of China's sophisticated creative energy at the Olympics opening ceremony on 08.08.08. As one commentator noted: 'The rise of China has reached the stage of a transition from a simple "Made in China" brand to a dynamic "create/initiate in China" concept' (Wang, 2008: 270).

In communication hardware, too, China has demonstrated extraordinary growth – the China Great Wall Industry Corporation has launched more than 30 satellites in the past two decades, and in 2008 China became the third country in the world after the US and Russia to launch a manned space mission. China's 'growing soft power', notes one observer, 'has emerged as the most potent weapon in Beijing's foreign policy arsenal' (Kurlantzick, 2007: 5). To promote its cultural diplomacy, Confucius institutes, comparable to France's Alliance Française and Germany's Goethe Institute, have been set up around the world. The first was established in Seoul in 2004, and by 2007 210 institutes in 64 countries and regions were in operation (Wang, 2008).

Despite these achievements, it is fair to suggest that the 'Chindia' challenge is not going to undermine in the short run the multifaceted US domination of the world's media through what I have elsewhere described as 'the glocal Americana', ranging from children's programming (Disney) to youth (MTV) and sport (ESPN), to feature films (Hollywood), news and current affairs (CNN, Discovery) and the internet (Google) (Thussu, 2007). Yet as one commentator notes: 'As the world's largest country emerges not from within but outside the established post-World War II international order, it is a drama that will end with the grand ascendance of China and the onset of an Asian-centred world order' (Ikenberry, 2008).

The Chinese version of media marketization – where the state has played a central role in taming Anglo-globalization – and India's example of a multi-ethnic, multilingual and multicultural media system may offer interesting sites for future media and communication research. The 'Chindia' challenge may also have a long-term effect on how capitalism evolves and international relations are managed. Though both societies have formidable differences and their capitalistic paths have taken distinct trajectories, they also share compelling common elements, including a culture of thrift – of repair and recycling – in sharp contrast to the profligate consumerist, and ultimately unsustainable, culture of the dominant West.

Markers for internationalizing media studies

How will the 'Chindia' factor affect the internationalization of media studies? The study of media and communication is rapidly growing in both countries –

more than 700 communication and media programmes were being run in Chinese universities, paralleled by the publication of many Chinese-language journals in the field. The opening up of the media and communication sector has led to a mushrooming of, mostly market-driven, vocational and media research institutes in India. Both countries are also the source of a considerable number of postgraduate and research students studying media and communication in Western universities.

Globally, as media studies has grown and gradually gained acceptance as a legitimate area of academic inquiry, its research concerns and agendas have broadened (Downing, 1996; Curran and Park, 2000; Rantanen, 2005; Thussu, 2007). There is a need to develop original methodological approaches that encompass new phenomena and identify differences and similarities through comparative and collaborative research. To achieve this a broader theoretical framework is needed that draws from the best practices of both the critical as well as liberal traditions of media and communication scholarship. However, it is important to think beyond the idea of the West versus the Rest and the de-Westernizing discourse (given its negative connotations), and to 'decolonize' the way research in and about the majority world is conceived and conducted.

Historicizing media and culture

The first step is to rethink the manner in which the syllabi are planned, making them more inclusive and international. A truly internationalized curriculum means the integration of an international dimension into teaching and research. It is important to remind ourselves that modernity was not necessarily a manifestation of European ideas – there were other paths of progress.[4] A global history of institutionalized education would take into account non-European trajectories of knowledge-creation and dissemination. It would note, for example, that centres of higher education in Taxsila (in present-day Pakistan) and Nalanda, in India, existed for a millennium before universities were established in Europe; that Egypt's al-Azhar university, established in the tenth century, was set up more than a hundred years before the first university in Europe (Bologna University, founded in 1119).

In political science courses around the world, Niccolò Machiavelli's *The Prince* (published in 1513) is an essential text on Realpolitik – though the world's first treatise on statecraft, entitled *Arlhăshastra* (the treatise on economics), was compiled in the fourth century BC by Chanakya (also known as Kautalya), who taught at Taxsila. This work provided the framework for public administration in South Asia for centuries; even in contemporary India, Chanakya *niti* (policy) is part of the political lexicon (Rangarajan, 1992).

A global history of communication would include communication between non-European countries and cultures. It would note that the interest in Buddhist thought and texts in China led to Chinese scholars visiting Nalanda to exchange ideas on law, philosophy and politics (Sen, 2005). Such cultural interaction led to the translation into Chinese of the Sanskrit *Vajracchedikā-prajñāpāramitā-sūtra* (*Diamond Sutra*), the world's first printed book on paper, published in the ninth century (Chanda, 2007).

Many more people know (outside the Arab/Islamic regions) of Venetian traveller Marco Polo (1254–1324), who 'discovered' China, than have heard of the Moroccan explorer Ibn Battutah, who between 1325 and 1354 travelled around the Arab world all the way to China, via India, and whose written accounts based on his astute observations, *Rihlah*, remain an invaluable source for historians. There is a rich tradition of communication emanating from travel outside the Euro-Atlantic sphere, which looks beyond the tendency among Western travellers to 'discover' or 'categorize' the natives in often racialized systems of classification (Khair *et al.*, 2006).

The Islamic contribution to the social sciences, too, is profound. The roots of sociology, from which media studies has evolved, can be sought in the fourteenth-century Arab historian and philosopher Ibn Khaldun, in whose *Muqaddimah* ('Introduction to history') there are suggestions of the creation of a new social science, *ilm al-umran* (science of social organization).

An internationalized media history would take on board non-European trajectories. It would note that printing was invented in China not in Europe; that the first printing press in the Ottoman Empire was established in 1511, and in the Americas in Mexico in 1535. The history of journalism would include the name, for example, of Turkish journalist Ibrahim Şinasi (1826–70), considered the father of modern Turkish journalism, who established the journal *Tasvir-i-efkâr* ('Interpreter of ideas'). There is a strong tradition of anti-colonial journalism in Asia, represented by such leaders as Sun Yat Sen in his *Chung-kuo Jih-pao* (Chinese Daily Newspaper), founded in 1899, and Mahatma Gandhi, who edited for most of his political life the weekly newspaper *Young India* (later renamed *Harijan*). Such narratives of journalism do not make it into standard histories of political journalism (Muhlmann, 2008 [2004]). An internationalized media studies would give these broader versions of history the kind of prominence they deserve. There are very few comparative media history texts, an indication that historians don't do 'media', while, with a few honourable exceptions, most media scholars are not concerned with history, as media education is largely about contemporary social reality.

Taking religion seriously

For historical reasons, media studies has traditionally ignored the role of religion in social and political life. With a few notable exceptions (Mowlana, 1996; Gunaratne, 2005; Hoover, 2006), most research in the field tends to gloss over the study of religion – particularly within critical scholarship. In many parts of the world, religion defines people's culture and there is an increasing assertion of religious identity – discernible, for example, in the growth of Hindu nationalism in India, fundamentalist Christianity in the US and militant Islamism in many Muslim countries. Communicating religion through media has a long history – from Church propaganda to liberation theology in Latin America, from circulation of Hindu iconography to digital distribution of radical Islamist imagery. As Hoover has noted: 'Religion depends in some fundamental ways on ideas about the world, about difference, about solidarity, and about the condition of meaning and truth rooted in understandings of place. Scholarship in the world of religion has recognized the effects of globalization for some time but a more sustained focus on the role and implications of media in these issues awaits doing' (Hoover, 2006: 11).

In the post-9/11 world of an open-ended and global 'war on terror', representation of Islam in the world's media has become a pressing though controversial subject for research. The 'Chindia' connection is relevant here: both India and China represent cultures and civilizations whose roots are not in the Abrahamic religions. Their perception of Islam, therefore, is less likely to be influenced by discourses that refer to the crusades and the 'clash of civilizations'. Had British imperialism not divided India at independence in 1947, it would have been the world's largest Muslim country in terms of population. Today it has the world's third largest Islamic population. The media discourse in India on Islam – whether in news and current affairs or in the Bollywood representation of Muslims – is more nuanced than in the US-dominated Western media. To appreciate the complexity of Islam and its rich cultural heritage and various contemporary sub-cultures, media and communication scholars need to take its study seriously.

Decolonizing thoughts and theory

One key intellectual requirement for a truly internationalized media studies is what might be called the 'decolonization of thoughts and theory' to break free from the hegemony of Western or, more precisely, Anglo-American theorization on media. As Gramsci observed, 'every relationship of hegemony is necessarily an educational relationship and occurs not only within a nation, between the various forces of which the nation is composed, but in the international and worldwide field, between complexes of national and continental civilizations' (Gramsci, 1971: 350).

There exists, it has been suggested, 'an empire of knowledge, perhaps far more considerable than the empires we associate with Euro-American imperialism or with the large corporate undertakings that have divided much of the world among themselves, and it has shaped the categories through which we view the world; and since many of these categories are largely invisible, or bathed in the language of kindness, good intentions, and progress, they are more insidious in their operations than the forces and agents through which naked domination is exercised' (Lal, 2002: 4).

For colonized countries, the West was not just a geographical or political entity but a psychological category, and in countries such as India one way of surviving neo-colonialism was by 'domesticating the West' (Nandy, 1983: 108). Even in countries not directly colonized, such as Iran, Western intellectual influence and infatuation was profound – *Gharbzadegi* (loosely translated as Westoxication) was how Iranian author Jalal Al-e-Ahmad described the phenomenon in a book by the same title published in 1964 under the Shah's repressive regime. It was, notes an observer, 'one of the first attempts to dissect the cultural dimension of neo-colonialism' (Connell, 2007:119).

The empire of knowledge remains so deeply entrenched that it is not seen as inappropriate that two of London University's elite institutions are still called, in 2008 and without a trace of irony, 'Imperial College' and 'School of Oriental and African Studies'. As Western theories are tested in non-Western locales and found inadequate, a new kind of thinking is required which values ideas and perspectives emanating from non-metropolitan hubs of global knowledge centres. No research is neutral – it carries with it value systems, models and methods. In this context, arguments have been made for repositioning media and communication studies in Asia (Miike, 2006), the Middle East (Ayish, 2003; Sreberny, 2008) and Africa (Tomaselli, 2008). Internationalization has an influence on what is taught, how it is taught, and how it is assessed. Through this process, international perspectives become an integral part of the teaching methodology, content, structure and organization of courses, and the thinking of both staff and students. As a new and emerging field in its global context, media studies offers possibilities of breaking free from the constraints of Western discourses and thus decolonizing the research imagination.

Research imaginings and innovations

Internationalization of research and teaching means validating and valuing the experiences and perspectives of students and researchers from different cultures and traditions. To internationalize the teaching and research of media, a new research imagination is required which would entail what Appaduari has called 'deparochialization of the research ethic – the idea of research itself' (Appadurai, 2001: 15). In the era of 'grassroots globalization', he notes, the relationship between 'the knowledge of globalization and the globalization of knowledge' needs to be reappraised (Appadurai, 2001: 14).

The 'Chindia' challenge offers new incentives to 'Re-Orient' the research paradigm, in the words of development economist Andre-Gunder Frank (Frank, 1998). Such work as political scientist John Hobson's *The Eastern Origins of Western Civilization* provides a historical context in which to re-evaluate the role countries such as China have played in an earlier version of globalization (Hobson, 2004). Would a Chinese media perspective on events in Africa be less affected by the colonial mindset and therefore more representative of African realities? Would development discourse be different if it was shaped in New Delhi and Beijing rather than in New York, London or Paris? How would we be researching community media as well as communication through folk songs and popular theatre if we borrowed from other traditions? Should researchers not consider consulting, for example, the work of medieval mystic Kabir (1398–1448), whose poems of penetrating wit and profound wisdom travelled across South Asia, making him one of the most quoted poets in the region (Dharwadker, 2003)? Media researchers are so steeped in Western disciplinary canons that they do not perceive the need for what Shome has called 'transnational interdisciplinarity', which would encourage researchers to 'engage in, and try to connect to, knowledge formations and vocabularies that reside in other modernities and other temporalities that are either refused recognition, or are not adequately translated, in machines of knowledge production' (Shome, 2006: 3).

Beyond tokenism and derivative discourses

Despite the exponential expansion of media in the non-Western world, its study in metropolitan centres remains largely insignificant, not to say tokenistic. A majority of academics working in the field are writing and researching primarily for a Western research community – the dominant culture of higher education research funding as well as the political economy of academic publishing also promote this orientation (Ahmad, 1992). The academic 'other' is often added as an afterthought or a token – sometimes a pragmatic imperative for research funding, at other times an exotic 'cosmopolitan' presence. The globalization of higher education is gradually changing this, as researchers and academics from diverse cultural and intellectual backgrounds become involved in transnational research projects, and though many internalize and thus work within the dominant paradigm, some are succeeding in broadening the terms of discourse. There is a need, as Slater has recognized, to develop a perspective which emphasizes the importance of 'learning critically' from post-colonial writers and theorists 'who have represented and continue to propel forward intellectual life beyond and with the West' (Slater, 2004: 232).

In much of the former communist bloc, as well as the global South, the study of and research into media are in their early stages and often the academic discourse is derivative, drawing on work done mainly in the US and in Europe, though in some regions – dependency theorists in Latin America and post-colonial literature from India are notable exceptions – innovative and experimental research is beginning to take shape. The pressing need for 'a commitment to empirical research' as well as 'real interdisciplinarity' has been rightly emphasized (Murphy and Kraidy, 2003: 306).

Imperatives for internationalization

The globalization of media studies is increasingly challenging traditional complacency, prompted also by the changing profile of the student body as well as the growing ethnic and cultural diversity of faculty within metropolitan academia, and global and regional mobility within the scholarly community. An internationalized media studies would further erode tokenism in research in the metropolitan centres and energize academics in the South and those who write about the South to go beyond derivative discourses. The availability of new digital technologies and open source materials can further the cause of greater media literacy. For this to happen, there is a need to foster institutional and individual intellectual links across various disciplines and undertake grounded research that questions old paradigms and provides material for new theorization. However, internationalization is not without its many impediments. What are the most appropriate research methods and methodologies to analyse meaningfully diverse media cultures? How does one construct comparative international research while maintaining professional integrity and a set of quality standards? What criteria should universities adopt in developing a core curriculum for the study of global media? What human and material resources would be needed to reorient faculty to enable them to teach and research other media and cultures?

These impediments apart, there is a moral imperative to internationalize. In an era of globalization, the media could contribute to the creation of a 'second superpower' – world public opinion. However, with the rapid privatization of the means of communication and media and the promotion of a global consumerist culture, predicated on the supremacy of the market, the public aspects of the media are under constant threat. An antidote is urgently needed to an unsustainable commercial model of media – a global public media benefiting from a global 'creative commons', where free access to knowledge is guaranteed (Lessig, 2004).

Such a moral imperative will propel academics to develop an innovative, integrated and imaginative research agenda that would promote media deployment for global public good: for conflict resolution; for intercultural and international tolerance; and for tackling such daunting problems as poverty, disease, political, economic or social oppression, environmental sustainability and the militarization of space.

Notes

1 The *Journal of Communication* ran two special issues: 'The State of the Art in Communication Theory and Research', Part I December 2004 – Vol. 54, Issue 4, and Part II September 2005 – Vol. 55, Issue 3. Also see the 2004 special issue of *Javnost – The Public*, Vol. 10, No. 3, on the theme of 'New Perspectives on Critical Communication Studies'. A change of attitude towards embracing internationalism is discernible in such journals as *Theory, Culture & Society*, whose 2006 special issue, Vol. 23, Nos. 7–8, carried reflections on the globalization of cultural studies, with contributions from Japan, India and South Africa. Another indication of the internationalization theme is that the journal *Gazette* was renamed in 2006 as the *International Communication Gazette*, 'in order to better reflect our editorial aims and scope', as its Editor-in-Chief noted. Also see 2007 special issue of the journal *Global Media and Communication*, Vol. 3, No. 3, as well as articles in the 2007 special issue of *Nordicom Review*. For an Asian perspective on

communication – 'Towards an Asian Theory of Communication' – see the 2000 special issue of *Asian Journal of Communication*, Vol. 10, No. 2.

2 One recent example of interdisciplinary research is the 2007 issue of the Australian journal *Millennium: Journal of International Studies*, Vol. 36, No. 1, which ran a special forum on how Edward Said's work could be deployed in international relations. Also see the March 2008 special issue of the *ANNALS of the American Academy of Political and Social Science* on the theme of 'Public Diplomacy in a Changing World'.

3 Though demonstrating exceptional economic growth in recent years, both countries have a very low per capita income in comparison to the Western world, and inequality within their societies is getting more pronounced. Both countries aspire to leadership in the global South – the China–Africa summit of 2006 and India–Africa summit of 2008 are a case in point. The strategic and economic links between India and the US, reflected in the 2008 nuclear agreement, can also be considered as contributing to rivalry between the two Asian giants with old histories and new geopolitical ambitions.

4 See, for example, essays in the 2007 special issue on 'An Intellectual History for India' of the journal *Modern Intellectual History*, Vol. 4, No. 1, with contributions on how ideas travelled to, from and within nineteenth- and twentieth-century India. For the neglect of history in the study of political communication see the 2001 special issue of the journal *Political Communication*, Vol. 18.

References

Abbas, Ackbar and Erni, Nguyet John (eds) (2005) *Internationalizing Cultural Studies: An Anthology*. Malden, MA: Blackwell.

Ahmad, Aijaz (1992) *In Theory: Classes, Nations, Literatures*. London: Verso.

Appadurai, Arjun (2001) Grassroots Globalization and Research Imagination, in Arjun Appadurai (ed.) *Globalization*. Durham, NC: Duke University Press.

Arsenault, Amelia and Castells, Manuel (2008) The Structure and Dynamics of Global Multi-media Business Networks, *International Journal of Communication*, 2: 707–48.

Ayish, Mohammad (2003) Beyond Western-Oriented Communication Theories: A Normative Arab–Islamic Perspective, *Javnost* (The Public),10(2): 79–92.

Chakrabarty, Dipesh (2007) *Provincializing Europe: Postcolonial Thought and Historical Difference*. Princeton, NJ: Princeton University Press, second edition.

Chanda, Nayan (2007) *Bound Together – How Traders, Preachers, Adventurers and Warriors Shaped Globalization*. London: Yale University Press.

Connell, Raewyn (2007) *Southern Theory: The Global Dynamics of Knowledge in Social Sciences*. Cambridge: Polity.

Constantinou, Costas, Richmond, Oliver and Watson, Alison (2008) Editors' Introduction: International Relations and the Challenges of Global Communication, *Review of International Studies*, 34: 5–19.

Curran, James and Park, Myung-Jin (2000) Beyond Globalization Theory, in James Curran and Myung-Jin Park (eds) *De-Westernizing Media Studies*. London: Routledge, pp. 3–18.

Curtin, Michael (2007) *Playing to the World's Biggest Audience: The Globalization of Chinese Film and TV*, Berkeley: University of California Press.

Dharwadker, Vinay (2003) *Kabir: The Weaver's Songs*, New Delhi: Penguin.

Downing, John (1996) *Internationalizing Media Theory: Transition, Power, Culture*. London: Sage.

Emmott, Bill (2008) *Rivals: How the Power Struggle between China, India and Japan Will Shape Our Next Decade*. London: Allen Lane.

Engardio, Peter (ed.) (2007) *Chindia: How China and India are Revolutionizing Global Business*. New York: McGraw-Hill Professional.

Erni, John Nguyet and Chua, Siew Keng (eds) (2005) *Asian Media Studies: Politics of Subjectivities*. Cambridge: Blackwell.

Esser, Frank and Pfetsch, Barbara (eds) (2004) *Comparing Political Communication: Theories, Cases and Challenges*. Cambridge: Cambridge University Press.

FICCI (2008) *The Indian Entertainment and Media Industry – A Growth Story Unfolds*. London: PriceWaterhouseCoopers in association with the Federation of Indian Chambers of Commerce and Industry.

Frank, Andre-Gunder (1998) *ReOrient: Global Economy in the Asian Age*. Berkeley: University of California Press.

Goldman Sachs (2007) *BRICs and Beyond*. New York: Goldman Sachs Global Economics Department.

Goody, Jack (2006) *The Theft of History*. Cambridge: Cambridge University Press.

Gramsci, Antonio (1971) *Selections from the Prison Notebooks*, edited and translated by Quintin Hoare and Geoffrey Nowell Smith. London: Lawrence and Wishart.

Gunaratne, Shelton (2005) *The Dao of the Press – A Humanocentric Theory*. Cresskill, NJ: Hampton Press.

Hallin, Daniel and Mancini, Paolo (2004) *Comparing Media Systems: Three Models of Media and Politics*. Cambridge: Cambridge University Press.

Halloran, James (1997) International Communication Research: Opportunities and Obstacles, in Ali Mohammadi (ed.) *International Communication and Globalization*. London: Sage.

Hobson, John (2004) *The Eastern Origins of Western Civilization*. Cambridge: Cambridge University Press.

Hoover, Stewart (2006) *Religion in the Media Age*. London: Routledge.

Ikenberry, John (2008) The Rise of China and the Future of the West: Can the Liberal System Survive?, *Foreign Affairs*, January/February.

Kavoori, Anandam and Punathambekar, Aswin (eds) (2008) *Global Bollywood*. New York: New York University Press.

Keane, Michael (2007) *Created in China: The Great New Leap Forward*. London: Routledge.

Khair, Tabish, Edwards, Justin, Leer, Martin and Ziadeh, Hanna (eds) (2006) *Other Routes: 1500 Years of African and Asian Travel Writing*. Oxford: Signal Books.

Khanna, Tarun (2007) *Billions of Entrepreneurs: How China and India are Reshaping Their Futures – and Yours*. Cambridge, MA: Harvard Business School Press.

Kurlantzick, Joshua (2007) *Charm Offensive: How China's Soft Power is Transforming the World*. London: Yale University Press.

Lal, Vinay (2002) *Empire of Knowledge: Culture and Plurality in the Global Economy*. London: Pluto.

Lasswell, Harold (1927) *Propaganda Techniques in the World War*. New York: Alfred Knopf.

Lauf, E. (2005) National Diversity of Major International Journals in the Field of Communication, *Journal of Communication*, 55(1): 139–51.

Lessig, Lawrence (2004) *Free Culture: How Big Media Uses Technology and the Law to Lock Down Culture and Control Creativity*. London: Penguin.

Lippmann, Walter (1922) *Public Opinion*. New York: Free Press.

Livingstone, Sonia (2003) On the Challenges of Cross-National Comparative Media Research, *European Journal of Communication*, 18(4): 477–500.

Löffelholz, Martin and Weaver, David (eds) (2008) *Global Journalism Research: Theories, Methods, Findings, Future*. Oxford: Blackwell.

Maddison, Angus (2001) *The World Economy: A Millennial Perspective*. Paris: OECD.

Mahbubani, Kishore (2008) *The New Asian Hemisphere: The Irresistible Shift of Global Power to the East.* New York: Public Affairs.
Meredith, Robyn (2007) *The Elephant and the Dragon – The Rise of India and China and What it Means for all of Us.* New York: W. W. Norton.
Miike, Yoshitaka (2006) Non-Western Theory in Western Research? An Asiacentric Agenda for Asian Communication Studies, *Review of Communication*, 6(1–2): 4–31.
Mosco, Vincent (1996) *The Political Economy of Communication: Rethinking and Renewal.* London: Sage.
Mowlana, Hamid (1996) *Global Communication in Transition: The End of Diversity?* Thousand Oaks, CA: Sage.
Muhlmann, Geraldine (2008) *A Political History of Journalism*, Cambridge: Polity. First published in 2004 as *Une histoire politique du journalisme*, Paris: Presses Universitaires de France.
Murphy, Patrick and Kraidy, Marwan (eds) (2003) *Global Media Studies: Ethnographic Perspectives.* New York: Routledge.
Nandy, Ashis (1983) *The Intimate Enemy: Loss and Recovery of Self under Colonialism.* New Delhi: Oxford University Press.
Nerone, John (ed.) (1995) *Last Rights: Revisiting Four Theories of the Press.* Urbana: University of Illinois Press.
Phillipson, Robert (1992) *Linguistic Imperialism.* Oxford: Oxford University Press, fourth edition.
Ramesh, Jairam (2005) *Making Sense of Chindia: Reflections on China and India.* New Delhi: India Research Press.
Rangarajan, L.N. (1992) *The Arlhãshastra.* New Delhi: Penguin.
Rantanen, Terhi (2005) *The Media and Globalization.* London: Sage.
Said, Edward (1978) *Orientalism.* New York: Penguin.
Scannell, Paddy (2007) *Media and Communication.* London: Sage.
Sen, Amartya (2005) *The Argumentative Indian.* London: Penguin.
Seth, Sanjay (2007) *Subject Lessons: The Western Education of Colonial India.* Durham, NC: Duke University Press.
Shoemaker, Pamela and Cohen, Akiba (2005) *News around the World: Content, Practitioners, and the Public.* London: Routledge.
Shome, Raka (2006) Interdisciplinary Research and Globalization, *Communication Review*, 9: 1–36.
Siebert, Fred, Peterson, Theodore and Schramm, Wilbur (1956) *Four Theories of the Press: The Authoritarian, Libertarian, Social Responsibility and Soviet Communist Concepts of What the Press Should Be and Do.* Urbana: University of Illinois Press.
Slater, David (2004) *Geopolitics and the Post-colonial: Rethinking North–South Relations.* Cambridge: Blackwell.
Smith, David (2007) *The Dragon and the Elephant: China, India and the New World Order.* London: Profile Books.
Sparks, Colin (2007) *Globalization, Development and the Mass Media.* London: Sage.
Sreberny, Annabelle (2008) The Analytic Challenges of Studying the Middle East and Its Evolving Media Environment, *Middle East Journal of Culture and Communication*, 1(1): 8–23.
Thussu, Daya Kishan (2006) *International Communication – Continuity and Change.* London: Hodder Arnold, second edition.
—— (ed.) (2007) *Media on the Move: Global Flow and Contra-flow.* London: Routledge.
Tomaselli, Keyan (2008) Repositioning African Media Studies, *Journal of African Media Studies*,1(1): 9–22.

UNCTAD (2008) *Creative Economy Report 2008*. New York: United Nations Conference on Trade and Development.

UNESCO (2005) *International Flows of Selected Cultural Goods and Services 1994–2003*. UNESCO Institute for Statistics, Paris: United Nations Educational, Scientific and Cultural Organization.

US Government (2004) *Mapping the Global Future: Report of the National Intelligence Council's 2020 Project*. Washington, DC: National Intelligence Council.

Vroons, Erik (2005) Communication Studies in Europe: A Sketch of the Situation around 1955, *Gazette: The International Journal for Communication Studies*, 67(6): 495–522.

Wang, Yiwei (2008) Public Diplomacy and the Rise of Chinese Soft Power, *The ANNALS of the American Academy of Political and Social Science*, (616): 257–73.

Weaver, David (ed.) (1998) *The Global Journalist: News People around the World*. Cresskill, NJ: Hampton Press.

Winters, Alan and Yusuf, Shahid (eds) (2006) *Dancing with Giants: China, India and the Global Economy*. Washington: World Bank Publications.

Zakaria, Fareed (2008) *The Post-American World*. London: Allen Lane.

Chapter 2

What should comparative media research be comparing?

Towards a transcultural approach to 'media cultures'

Andreas Hepp and Nick Couldry

The methodological base of international media research is comparative: but what should be the unit of comparison? So far the criteria of difference have been mostly 'national-territorial': the nation state is taken as the unquestioned starting point in comparing media production, representation, reception and appropriation in different countries. While this makes sense in specific fields of media research (media systems, political economy), which, like most media politics, remain territorially bound in many respects, it ignores other phenomena which may need to be formulated outside the frame of the 'national-territorial': cultural formation linked to race, gender and ethnicity, and deterritorialized popular cultures. In addition, it obscures our view of what 'media cultures' might be in an era of media flows that consistently overlap national borders.

Based on these considerations we want to argue in this chapter for a 'transcultural approach' to comparative media research. This transcultural approach does not start with the 'state' and its territoriality as the essential centre of comparison but outlines a more complex horizon for carrying out media research by comparing different media cultures understood as specific, if often blurred, cultural 'thickenings'. To make such an approach understandable we first criticize the 'container thinking' implicit in much of the present comparative media research. Then we outline our understanding of media cultures as 'cultural thickenings' or 'amalgamations'. Based on this we finally explain a 'transcultural approach' as a specific way of comparing media cultures. Overall we hope to develop arguments that provoke us to think about comparative media research in a new way.

It is important to emphasize at the outset that we see our argument as just one perspective on a very complex theoretical problem. If we look from the perspective of national cultural discourse, we must agree with Ulf Hannerz that (national) cultures can no longer be seen as based simply on what is shared by their members since 'contemporary complex societies systematically build nonsharing into their cultures' (Hannerz, 1992: 44). Seen from outside that national perspective, we can still think of media cultures or diaspora cultures, for example, as based principally on shared meanings but only on condition that we give up the assumption that such sharing takes place necessarily, or even importantly, within the container of national territories. It is the latter perspective whose implications we develop here, since it is the prospects for comparing 'media cultures' – as part of a wider internationalizing of media and cultural research – with which we are more broadly concerned.[1]

'Container thinking' in comparative media research

The problem diagnosed

Within sociology in general, and sociology of globalization in particular, we find an increasing critique of the 'container thinking' found in traditional sociology. A number of major sociologists have developed this critique.

For example, Ulrich Beck (1997: 49) has criticized the fact that 'sociology as intellectual order-keeping power' brought forward a 'container theory of society'. This container theory is manifested by the circumstances that, in most (functional) sociology, societies are by definition subordinated to states: 'societies are state societies, social orders are state orders' (Beck, 1997: 49).[2] In this sense we are speaking of an American, German or British society, which is then thought of as bordered by a 'state container' as a 'territorial entity'. The argument Ulrich Beck develops here is that while such a way of thinking might be appropriate for theorizing modern states at their beginning, it is not sufficient for social forms in times of globalization which transgress national borders and build up transnational social spaces.

Ulrich Beck is not alone in making these arguments. Anthony Giddens had already mentioned in *Consequences of Modernity* the disembedding forces of modernity which for him consequently result in the processes of globalization. For sure, his critique of the concept of the nation state and national society is not as far reaching as Ulrich Beck's, but nevertheless Giddens reminds us that with globalization all 'societies are also interwoven with ties and interconnections which crosscut the socio-political system of the state and the cultural order of the "nation"' (Giddens, 1990: 14).

John Urry and Manuel Castells are two academics who have taken this discussion further (cf. the discussion in Moores, 2008). For instance, John Urry (1999) argued in his book *Sociology Beyond Societies* for a discipline of sociology that researches and theorizes social processes beyond the unquestioned concept of a (national and territorially bound) society. How this can be undertaken is outlined in his book *Global Complexity*, in which Urry (2003) tries to theorize transnational social forms using the concepts of 'network' and 'fluid'. In a comparable focus we can understand Manuel Castells' (1996) concept of the 'network society'. Despite the criticisms that can be made of this concept, its power can be seen in the attempt to describe social structures and their transformation beyond a national-territorial frame. Network structures and spaces of flows are articulated across territorial borders and nation states (Hepp, 2006; Hepp, 2009).

We can sum up such a critique of 'container thinking' within social theory in three points (Hepp, 2004: 13). First, it is a critique of the container concept of the state, a rejection of thinking of the (nation) state as something like the 'reservoir of society'. Second, it is a critique of thinking that the nation state is territorialized, i.e. that 'national cultures' are unquestionably related to a defined territory of living. Third, it is a critique of theorizing these national and territorially bound 'container societies' as functionally integrated, which ignores all the disembedding, transgressing and dysfunctional processes of contemporary social life. In this sense a critique of 'container thinking' within social theory has to be contextualized within critiques of continued functionalist thinking in social research, and particularly media research (Couldry, 2003, 2005a, 2005b): that anti-functionalist argument should therefore be assumed to run implicitly in parallel to our explicit argument here.

The problem persists

If we contrast these arguments with current discussions in media and communication studies, one arrives at the striking result that within international media research such 'container thinking' has yet to be superseded. Of course there are a number of works arguing exactly in such a direction, of which John Tomlinson's (1999) book *Globalization and Culture* is an important example. Nevertheless in our view this is not the dominant trajectory. Again, we would like to take some well-known examples to substantiate this.

The first example is the book *De-Westernizing Media Studies*, edited by James Curran and Myung-Jin Park (2000a). This book has the very important role of reminding us of the implicit 'Western-centrism' in much of the present international media research. So the book is welcome in arguing for a more open-minded research perspective beyond the dubious centring of research on Western models.

In the introduction James Curran and Myung-Jin Park (2000b) frame the whole book by arguing for a perspective beyond 'the self-absorption and parochialism of much Western media theory' (Curran and Park, 2000b: 3). Beginning with Siebert *et al.*'s (1956) *Four Theories of the Press*, they criticize Western models for their blind acceptance of evaluating media communication in different regions of the world. In a specific sense we can locate the modernization and media imperialism perspectives on international communication in this pattern, as they start with Western models of cultural change. The important point for our argument is that Curran and Park locate theories of globalization also within their critique. While globalization theory is right in criticizing a Western centrism, they argue, it is not able to theorize the power relations of global capitalism, as political economy in media and communication did, because it has abandoned a focus on the nation state as the relevant unit of comparison:

> Indeed, cultural globalization is viewed as positive precisely because it is thought to weaken the nation. By contrast the political economy literature offers a less schooled approach, with one strand attacking the corrupting legacy of nationalism as the worm inside the apple of social democracy, and disputing liberal notions of state as illusory. But this tradition, in all its diversity, still tends to see the state as potentially the instrument of popular countervailing power and progressive redistribution, and views the nation as the place where democracy is mainly organised.
>
> (Curran and Park, 2000b: 11)

Curran and Park argue that the nation state continues to be relevant in comparative media research. Their main argument is that 'communications systems are still in significant aspects national' and that the 'nation is still a very important marker of difference' (Curran and Park, 2000b: 11f.). Because of that, they not only organized the book *De-Westernizing Media Studies* around the (itself Western) concept of national media systems; they also developed a state-centred model to compare these media systems, using the dichotomies 'neo-liberal' vs. 'regulated' and 'democratic' vs. 'authoritarian'. In this sense, their 'de-Westernized' model of doing comparative media research starts with the state as the unit of comparison, but claims that at least in part the related media systems have to be described with more context-sensitive categories than previously. This generates the structure of the book as a whole. Divided into sections ('transitional and mixed societies', 'authoritarian neo-liberal societies', 'authoritarian regulated societies', 'democratic neo-liberal societies' and 'democratic regulated societies'), certain aspects of national media systems are discussed in the context of an increasing media globalization, while the implicit state reference point for comparison remains intact.

This trajectory also marks other publications on comparative media research. A further example is the book *Comparing Media Systems* by Daniel Hallin and Paolo Mancini. The arguments of the book have a comparable starting point, pointing out that 'most of the literature on the media is highly ethnocentric, in the sense that it refers only to the experience of a single country' (Hallin and Mancini, 2004: 2). While this understanding of ethnocentrism is, for sure, itself quite restricted, it is nevertheless their point of departure to develop an exploratory system for doing comparative media research. In so doing, Hallin and Mancini (2004: 66–86) develop three models of media systems, the 'polarized pluralist model' (typical of France, Greece, Italy, Portugal and Spain), the 'democratic corporatist model' (typical of Austria, Belgium, Denmark, Finland, Germany, the Netherlands, Norway, Sweden, Switzerland) and the 'liberal model' (typical of Britain, the United States, Canada, Ireland).

It is beyond the scope of this chapter to discuss these different 'models' in detail. More important, in any case, is how the 'models' are constructed as reference points of comparative media research. Based on the state as reference point, and media systems as political frameworks, of (mass) media communication, Hallin and Mancini's 'models' are typified by referring to certain kinds of states. While such a procedure might be understandable for political aspects of media communication which, as we noted at the outset, remain at least to some extent state-related (since political legitimization is based on decisions by people living in specific states),[3] and while the tremendous advance of the model is its more open, pluralistic normative perspective (cf. Couldry, 2005a and 2005b; McQuail, 2005; Hardy, 2006), the remarkable point is that Hallin and Mancini also make cultural conclusions based on their models, claiming that a state's relation to a model not only says something about its political media system, but also about its society and (media) culture. It is not that we rule out such cultural consequences of Hallin and Mancini's model; our argument, however, is that such consequences need to be argued for on a stronger basis than the assumption that each nation has a distinctive and territorially bounded culture, including a distinctive media culture.

In these two frameworks for comparative media analyses, we find once more, and perhaps unwittingly, the 'container thinking' so criticized in present social and cultural theory. Much current media research has an implicit 'territorial essentialism', even as it tries to move towards rigorous international comparison. The state remains the principal reference point of comparative research, on the basis of which media systems, media markets and media cultures are theorized. One can call this an 'international (and intercultural) approach' to comparative media research which might be visualized as shown in Figure 2.1 (Hepp, 2006: 78–80).

Our contention about this 'international approach' is not to deny that there are aspects of media communication related to the state that must be discussed in a (territorialized) state frame (see above), but rather to note the tendency in comparative media research to date to essentialize the relation between state,

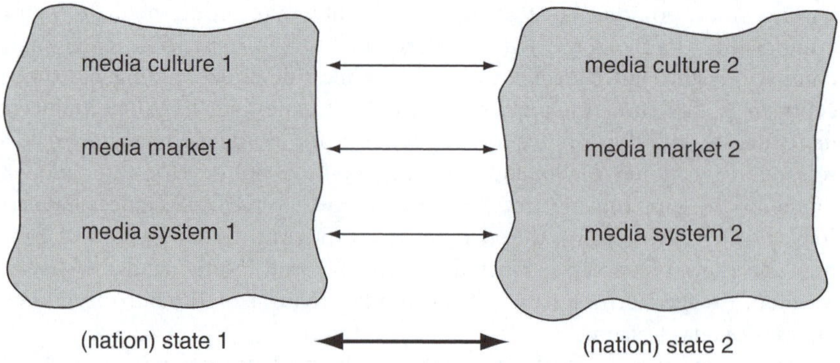

Figure 2.1 International and intercultural approach to comparative media research

(political) media system, media market and media culture into a model of binary comparison or what we might call a binary comparative semantic.[4] But if we focus on questions of media culture, in particular, this 'territorial essentialism' is highly problematic, since contemporary media cultures are not per se bound in such national containers, and so are not necessarily available to be compared in this way.

Media cultures as territorialized and deterritorialized thickenings

If we focus more on questions of media cultures than media markets or media systems, different types of argument are necessary. Note that this does not mean that our argument in what follows has no consequences for questions of (media) politics: indeed, the current crisis of traditional politics in many countries (including the UK) remains closely tied to the histories of particular states as the continuing, if no longer fully legitimate, focus of political culture (cf. Couldry *et al.*, 2007).

When speaking about 'media cultures' specifically, we include all cultures whose primary resources of meaning are accessible through technology-based media. From this point of view, all media cultures have to be theorized as translocal phenomena, inasmuch as media make translocal communicative connections possible (Hepp, 2004: 163–94). They are not 'placed' at a defined locality but are articulated through 'disembedded' communicative processes, while still being related to a greater or lesser number of localities within or beyond particular national or regional boundaries.[5] This said, we can understand media cultures as based on a connectivity of communication processes that might be focused around a relatively centralized power structure (as with traditional mass media) or marked by a more multi-centred power structure (as many hope for the internet).[6] They may be larger or smaller in terms of the contents and interests which focus together. We need to allow also for 'media cultures' which are highly generalized, for example different ways in which the celebrity/audience relationship is worked out in different media/political territories – a point to which we return later.

Describing media cultures in this sense as translocal phenomena, we also refer to a specific understanding of culture. Some time ago Jan Nederveen Pieterse (1995) divided principal understandings of culture into two, a territorial one and a translocal one. The essence of his arguments is that territorial concepts of culture are inward-looking, endogenous, focused on organicity, authenticity and identity, whereas translocal concepts of culture are outward-looking, exogenous, focused on hybridity, translation and identification. Based on our arguments, it seems helpful to us to understand cultures in general in a translocal frame: all present cultures are more or less hybrid, have to translate, change their identities and so on. In contrast to this, what is problematic for a general territorial conceptualization of culture is that it refers to the already criticized container thinking of nation states. With this concept, cultures are from the beginning interpreted as national cultures of territorial states; no other template or model is considered. More helpful than such territorial bordering is to suggest that cultures – as the sum of the classificatory systems and discursive formations on which the production of meaning draws (see Hall, 1997: 222) – transgress the local without being necessarily focused on territoriality as a reference point of their meaning articulation. In this sense, cultures are a kind of 'thickening' (Löfgren, 2001) of translocal processes of the articulation of meaning. Such a theorization opens the possibility of understanding territorialization, and deterritorialization, as contested practices through which specific cultures are articulated in their particularity – by the media and beyond (García Canclini, 1995, 2001).

By focusing on this framework, it will be possible to describe the development of European media cultures during the last hundred years in a different way (cf. Hepp, 2008). One can take, for instance, the works of Benedict Anderson, Orvar Löfgren or David Morley as examples of this. The rise of national cultures is related to the diffusion of the so-called mass media. When different locales are very intensively connected by media, different people can be involved in a communicative process, and the construction of a common 'imagined community' (Anderson, 1983), 'home territory' (Morley, 2000) or 'cultural thickening' (Löfgren, 2001). Such reflections refer to the level on which questions of territory pertain to translocality. One can take television history as an example. First, television was marketed in the 1950s as global, when it was called a 'window to the world'. Second, television had to be appropriated locally, that is to say it had to find its place in local life. And third, the horizon of its first representations had the tendency of being nationally territorial, because the first important television events were national celebrations, national football games or national serial productions, but also the borders of TV networks broadcasting were the borders of nations. Like the print media and the radio before it, television helped to construct the territorialized 'cultural thickening' of a nation.

David Morley's metaphor of the 'home territory' is, at this point, important in a dual sense. On the one hand, it shows the specificity of these national media cultures. It is possible to describe national media cultures whose translocal communicative thickening has been territorialized in such a way that national frontiers are the main borders of many communicative networks and flows. The process of thickening of the national imagined community was territorially bound. On the other hand, Morley's metaphor of the home territory shows us quite clearly that this territoriality of the media-influenced home no longer exists in a pure form. In the time of globalization, communicative connectivity is becoming more and more deterritorialized. With the distribution of media products across different national borders and the emergence of the internet, global communicative connectivity grows, which makes the thickenings of national media cultures relative and overlapping. One must contextualize them as part of different networks of the media.

This means that the borders of the 'cultural thickenings' to which we belong do not necessarily correspond with territorial borders, even though territories continue to have a high relevance as a reference point for constructing national community. Rather, deterritorial thickenings gain relevance with increasing global media connectivity. If we take the case of media cultures today, we can say that we have both moments at the same time: on the one hand, territorially focused thickenings of communicative connections (hence it still makes sense to talk about mediated regional or national translocal communities as reference points of identities)[7] but, on the other hand, communicative thickenings across territorial borders, thickenings which offer the space for deterritorialized translocal communities with corresponding identities. Analytically, we can make here a four-level distinction between ethnic, commercial, political and religious aspects. On the level of ethnicity we have an increasing number of communicative thickenings of minority groups and diasporas.[8] On the commercial level a high number of deterritorial popular cultural communities, like youth cultures, sports communities and fan networks, are discussed in much present research.[9] On the political level over the last decades deterritorial social movements like the critical globalization movement have gained relevance.[10] And on the religious level we see different belief communities like religious or spiritual groups, which define themselves in particular as not territorially bound.[11] One can argue that all of these examples are based on translocal media connectivity and specific cultural thickenings which operate across territorial boundaries; each offers an important resource point for current identities.

But how can we do comparative media research in such a frame? This question will be discussed in the last section of our chapter.

A transcultural approach – or how can we compare?

The arguments we have developed concerning questions of media cultures have the aim of showing that media cultures have something to do, on the one hand, with 'territorialization' – here understood as a specific process of meaning articulation – and, on the other hand, with 'deterritorialization' in the sense that many present cultural forms cannot be related to specific territories. All this shows how problematic an essentialist territorialized 'container thinking' is for doing comparative research on media cultures. But where to start if we still want to do comparative research? The answer we want to outline in the following involves developing a new comparative semantic that we will call a 'transcultural approach' (see Figure 2.2).

By using the term 'transcultural', we do not intend to indicate that we should only focus on forms which are standardized 'beyond' or 'across' cultures. Rather, we borrow the term from Wolfgang Welsch (1999), who used

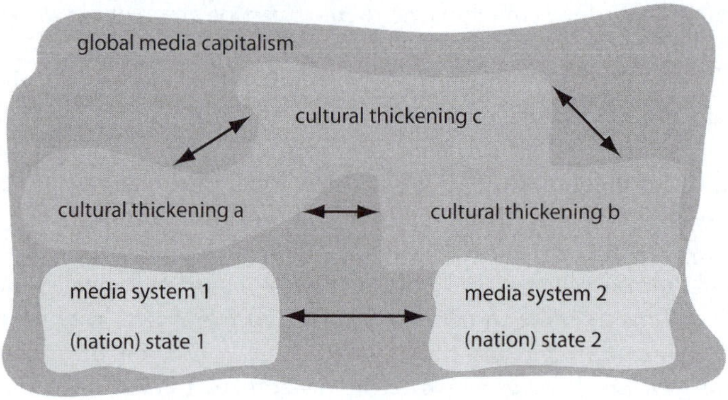

Figure 2.2 Transcultural approach to comparative media research

it to indicate that in present times important cultural phenomena cannot be broken down into dimensions of traditional cultures based in specific territories. Instead, contemporary cultural forms are increasingly generated and communicated across various territories.

The transcultural comparative semantic we want to suggest takes the existence of global media capitalism as a starting point. Across different states global media capitalism becomes a structuring force in the sense that in different regions of the world media communication is more and more considered as an 'exchange of economic good' and not only as a communication process with the aim of better reciprocal understanding (cf. Herman and McChesney, 1997; Hesmondhalgh, 2002). Nevertheless, we have to bear in mind that this global media capitalism does not standardize the articulation of meaning because of its 'over-determination' of meaning (Ang, 1996). Quite often global media capitalism rather seems to be a source of ongoing cultural fragmentation, contestation and misunderstanding – not only between national cultures but also across them.

Within global media capitalism, political media systems are the most territorially related entities, because the legitimacy of political decision-making is still, to a high degree, state related. Nevertheless, as soon as questions of media culture come to the fore, based on our previous arguments it becomes obvious that either cultural thickenings can be broadly territorialized (as with national cultures, articulated with reference to a state and its territory) or they can transgress states and their territories. Examples we have mentioned of this are diasporas, popular cultures, social movements or religious belief communities. The articulation of these communities refers to deterritorialized transmedial communicative spaces.

Concerning the question 'How to compare?', a 'transcultural approach' overcomes the binary of an 'international approach' without excluding the state as a possible reference point of comparison. In detail this means that a 'transcultural approach' does not operate with a concept of media cultures enclosed by territorial states but with an understanding of the thickening of these phenomena in the frame of an increasingly global communicative connectivity. Such a 'comparative semantic' tries to consider the specificity of such thickenings and the complex interrelations between them.

Discussion by way of examples

Based on our arguments above, we want to take two examples from our present research to show how useful a 'transcultural comparative semantic' is.

Our first example is a research project on the Catholic World Youth Day as a media event.[12] At first glance this research project seems to be 'comparative' in a traditional sense, as it investigates the media event within Germany and Italy. Nevertheless, there are at least three arguments why research on media events like the World Youth Day must be conducted 'transculturally'.

First, the research project shows that this media event has in particular a central role within the deterritorial belief community of Catholicism. These findings can be carried out for both the German and Italian media coverage, as in both cases this belief community was the main meaning horizon of the media event. Second, the fact that the local happenings of the World Youth Day in Cologne were mediatized meant, in the media coverage of both states, that their plurality was reduced to the single story of the papal visit to Cologne as the core of the media event. Both in Italy and in Germany this focusing of the media coverage resulted in comparable patterns and forms of staging the sacred figure of the Pope as a 'celebrity', who, within the deterritorialized staging of Catholicism and its Catholic youth culture, seems to work as a kind of general 'brand'. Third, we can also see differences between the discussion of the event in the German and Italian media. For example, within the German media relations were discussed between a possible re-emergence of religion (of which the World Youth Day was considered an example) and a new conservatism in the context of German elections. Also the official position of the Pope on sexual morality played a significant role in the media coverage in Germany but not in Italy.

It is not possible to discuss the results of this empirical study in detail here.[13] Nevertheless, these points demonstrate the need for a 'transcultural approach' in this research: on the one hand, such a mode of comparison offers the chance to typify forms and patterns across territorial and national cultural frames, with Catholicism in focus as a mediated cultural thickening of its own. This makes sense as the increase in a new form of Catholic youth spirituality is important across Germany and Italy, and as the shaping forces of the mediatization of religion are the same in both contexts. So there are core aspects of the media event that can be ascertained across different territorial frames. At the same time, the media event of the Catholic World Youth Day is marked by various aspects of national contextualization. The media event has a 'thematic core' shared by different states, territories and 'their' national cultures, which relates to the mediatization of a deterritorialized culture of Catholicism around its 'brand' the Pope, but is thickened in a specific way in the context of different national (and regional) media.

Only a transcultural perspective allows for such complexities within contemporary mediated communication. A traditional international or intercultural approach forces this event into the 'container' of a national culture, and so distorts it. There is no national cultural unit 'at the heart' of this media event, which was always from the beginning translocal in its production and reference points.

Our second example is deliberately more diffuse, since we want to use it to broach the difficult question of where we set the limits to the term 'media culture', and whether it is possible that, notwithstanding the global flows of celebrity signs, there might, paradoxically, be national celebrity cultures that would come within our definition of 'media cultures'. If so, this would return us to Hallin and Mancini's problematic, but on terms based more securely in a translocal approach.

It is beyond doubt that the celebrity's role in global media capitalism generates cultural 'thickenings' across national borders around particular major celebrities, particularly in those domains less dependent for transmission on language: music, sport, film, fashion. When Japanese and UK fans of The Beatles meet on Liverpool's Beatles Trail, they act out a shared but translocal fan culture even though they may lack the common language to articulate what it is they share. The necessary translocality of such media cultures was brought home to one of the authors when he was on holiday in China and walked into the garden of a hotel in Xi'an, only to find, in front of a traditional pagoda and lake setting, a bronze sculpture of David Beckham's torso, arms uplifted to salute the crowd's adulation after a goal, and displaying one of his more recent haircuts. A member of the same (UK) tour group asked in puzzlement, 'But why?', on the basis that Beckham is an English footballer, not realizing that Beckham the brand is much 'bigger' in Asia than in Britain. Whatever the national origins of Beckham's celebrity, Beckham the brand must be understood as from the outset transnational in nature. In this way, celebrity generates examples of media cultures that cannot be understood as other than translocal and transnational.

But that is not the end of the story, because it is equally obvious, if difficult to articulate precisely, that the way the relationship between 'celebrity' and its opposite (call it 'ordinary life') is lived out differs in, say, the USA from in the UK or France, let alone China or Iran. Can we therefore imagine nationally distinct celebrity cultures with distinct 'values' and ritual forms in these territories, even though many of the reference points of those cultures would be globally shared (we have in mind much more than national variations in how a particular celebrity icon is interpreted)? This is an interesting but completely unexplored territory which reveals what is at stake in the move beyond the 'national container' notion of culture. Here, because of the pervasive globalization in the celebrity industry, it is the national dimension of celebrity culture (in the broad sense, obviously there are local celebrities only known on a small scale) that has to be argued for, not the global or translocal dimension.

The argument needs to be made, as discussed earlier, by identifying the factors which in particular locations and to different degrees lead to distinct 'cultural thickenings' around the basic forms of celebrity and fandom. One factor that is likely to be distinctive is religion's role in supplying models for, or reasons for forbidding or suppressing, the adulation of exceptional figures. While religion, interestingly, is ignored in Hallin and Mancini's model for comparing media systems, elements included in that model could also be relevant here: for example, the relative dominance for a long period of market-based media (USA), the closeness or distance of media outlets from civil society (US versus Sweden), and the changing economics (and resource distribution for traditional news-gathering) within particular countries' media industries, especially their newspapers. This is an area still to be explored, but it suggests how territorially based factors could inflect media cultures, many of whose reference points are from the outset transnational. This illustrates, therefore, how we might approach those media cultures which are nationally distinct from within an overall approach to culture which is 'transnational', not 'international'.

Conclusion

We hope that these two examples have shown how a transcultural perspective can help us to do comparative media and communication research in times of media globalization. If we no longer take the state territory as an unquestioned and essentialized starting point, we can be much more open to contemporary media cultures' complex interrelations. Media cultures are by no means limited to 'nation state cultures'. Many aspects of media cultures have to be thought beyond such a narrow frame.

This is especially the case for highly controversial, power-related and contested aspects of contemporary culture: Catholicism and the deterritorial Catholic belief community are one example, while Islam, including its more politicized dimensions, is another. When, following the 7 July 2005 bombings in London and in the wake of the foiled bomb plot against planes leaving London in August 2006, neighbours of those involved or arrested expressed to journalists their shock at how people who enjoyed routine aspects of local culture (fish and chips from the local takeaway, talk about the local football team) could also be involved in such events,[14] they expressed the tension between a traditional place-bound notion of culture and a different notion of culture which is from the start mediated and translocal. The tension, however, appears as such mainly from an external perspective, since it is both possible and increasingly likely to combine both types of culture (and more) in one life.

It is only through a fully transcultural frame of analysis that we can properly grasp such tensions and in that way move, we hope, one stage closer to a genuinely comparative and internationalized account of media's role in our everyday lives.

Notes

1 This chapter is a more developed version of our joint paper presented to the Internationalizing Media Studies conference at the University of Westminster, September 2006. Thanks to the conference's organizers and to our audience there.
2 Translated from the German edition.
3 Nevertheless, we have to have in mind that especially in the context of media globalization different forms of 'deterritorialized media politics' gain relevance, as the discussion about global media governance shows (see O'Siochru *et al.*, 2002; Guerrieri *et al.*, 2004; Raboy, 2004).
4 Also if more than two media cultures, markets and systems are compared in this way, that basic argumentative structure remains binary in the sense of comparing closed dualities.
5 It is important, however, not to confuse two questions: the degree to which a locality is translocally connected through communication and the degree to which people living in that locality live their life within the physical space of that locality. The latter can never be reduced to zero since as physical beings we must all reside somewhere.
6 While we don't discuss questions of power on the following pages (because we want to focus on outlining founding ideas for doing comparative media research), these arguments show how far our thinking is related to questions of power. See for this, concerning digital media, Couldry and Curran (2003).
7 One example would be the identity of different German federal states like Bavaria or Bremen, another example the different national identities within Europe. In addition, the construction of Europe itself is a space of communicative connectivity, and the originating European identity is historically a territorially bound process (cf. Kleinsteuber and Rossmann, 1994; Morley and Robins, 1995).
8 See, besides others, Tölölyan (1996); Cohen (1997); Dayan (1999); Naficy (2001); Georgiou (2004); Silverstone and Georgiou (2005).
9 Some important examples of research on this are Amit-Talai and Wulff (1995); During (1997); Hills (2002); Pilkington *et al.* (2002); Storey (2003).
10 Again just a few examples of research on this are Porta *et al.* (1999); Cohen and Rai (2000); Touraine (2002); Klein (2000); Hepp and Vogelgesang (2005).
11 Cf. Knoblauch (1989); Hoover and Lundby (1997); Habermas (2005); Beyer (2006); Sumiala-Seppänen *et al.* (2006).
12 The research project 'Situational Community-Building by Religious Hybrid Events: The 20th World Youth Day 2005 in Cologne – The Mediatization Perspective' was founded by the German Research Foundation (DFG) and is part of a wider research consortium.
13 For some of the results of the research project see Hepp and Krönert (2009).
14 See, for example, published under the subheading 'community reaction', the recollection by Kamran Siddique, 'My Friend: the Football Fan Who Dreamed of Being a Doctor', *Guardian*, 15 August 2006, page 5.

References

Amit-Talai, Vered and Wulff, Helena (eds) (1995) *Youth Cultures: A Cross-Cultural Perspective*. London: Routledge.

Anderson, Benedict (1983) *Imagined Communities: Reflections on the Origins and Spread of Nationalism*. New York: Verso.
Ang, Ien (1996) *Living Room Wars: Rethinking Media Audiences for a Postmodern World*. London: Routledge.
Beck, Ulrich (1997) *Was ist Globalisierung? Irrtümer des Globalismus – Antworten auf Globalisierung*. Frankfurt a.M.: Suhrkamp.
Beyer, Peter (2006) *Religions in Global Society*. London: Routledge.
Castells, Manuel (1996) *The Rise of the Network Society: The Information Age. Economy, Society and Culture*. Vol. 1. Oxford: Blackwell.
Cohen, Robin (1997) *Global Diasporas: An Introduction*. Seattle: University of Washington Press.
Cohen, Robin and Rai, Shirin (2000) Global Social Movements: Towards a Cosmopolitan Politics, in R. Cohen and S.M. Rai (eds) *Global Social Movements*. London: Athlone, pp. 1–17.
Couldry, Nick (2003) *Media Rituals: A Critical Approach*. London: Routledge.
—— (2005a) Comparing Media Systems: Three Models of Media and Politics, *Political Studies Review*, 3: 304–6.
—— (2005b) Media Rituals: Beyond Functionalism, in E. Rothenbuhler and M. Coman (eds) *Media Anthropology*. Thousand Oaks, CA: Sage, pp. 59–69.
Couldry, Nick and Curran, James (eds) (2003) *Contesting Media Power: Alternative Media in a Networked World*. London: Rowman and Littlefield.
Couldry, Nick, Livingstone, Sonia and Markham, Tim (2007) *Media Consumption and Public Engagement: Beyond the Presumption of Attention*. Basingstoke: Palgrave Macmillan.
Curran, James and Park, Myung-Jin (eds) (2000a) *De-Westernizing Media Studies*. London: Routledge.
Curran, James and Park, Myung-Jin (2000b) Beyond Globalization Theory, in J. Curran and M.-J. Park (eds) *De-Westernizing Media Studies*. London: Routledge, pp. 3–18.
Dayan, Dayan (1999) Media and Diasporas, in J. Gripsrud (ed.) *Television and Common Knowledge*. London: Routledge, pp. 18–33.
During, Simon (1997) Popular Culture on a Global Scale: A Challenge for Cultural Studies?, *Critical Inquiry*, 23: 808–21.
García Canclini, Nestor (1995) *Hybrid Cultures: Strategies for Entering and Leaving Modernity*. Minneapolis, MN: Minnesota University Press.
—— (2001) *Consumers and Citizens: Globalization and Multicultural Conflicts*. Minneapolis, MN: Minnesota University Press.
Georgiou, Myria (2004) Mapping Diasporic Media across the EU: Addressing Cultural Exclusion, EMTEL Research Paper. http://www.emtel2.org/.
Giddens, Anthony (1990) *The Consequences of Modernity*. Cambridge: Polity.
Guerrieri, Paolo, Lapadre, P. Lelio and Koopmann, Georg (2004) *Cultural Diversity and International Economic Integration: The Global Governance of the Audio-visual Sector*. Cheltenham: Edward Elgar.
Habermas, Jürgen (2005) Religion in the Public Sphere, http://www.holbergprize.no/ [3.8.2006].
Hall, Stuart (1997) The Centrality of Culture: Notes on the Cultural Revolutions of Our Time, in K. Thompson (ed.) *Media and Cultural Regulation*. London: Sage, pp. 207–38.
Hallin, Daniel and Mancini, Paolo (2004) *Comparing Media Systems: Three Models of Media and Politics*. Cambridge: Cambridge University Press.
Hannerz, Ulf (1992) *Cultural Complexity*. New York: Columbia University Press.

Hardy, Jonathan (2006) Reassessing Hallin and Mancini's Media Models. Paper presented at the conference 'Internationalizing Media Studies: Imperatives and Impediments', University of Westminster, London, 15–16 September 2006.

Hepp, Andreas (2004) *Netzwerke der Medien: Medienkulturen und Globalisierung*. Wiesbaden: VS.

—— (2006) *Transkulturelle Kommunikation*. Konstanz: UVK (UTB).

—— (2008) Translocal Media Cultures: Networks of the Media and Globalisation, in A. Hepp, F. Krotz, Friedrich, S. Moores and C. Winter (eds) *Connectivity, Networks and Flows: Conceptualizing Contemporary Communications*. Cresskill, NJ: Hampton Press, pp. 33–58.

—— (2009) Transculturality as a Perspective: Researching Media Cultures Comparatively, in *Forum: Qualitative Social Research*, 10(1), Art. 26.

Hepp, Andreas and Krönert, Veronika (2009) Religious Media Events: The Catholic "World Youth Day" as an Example for the Mediatisation and Individualisation of Religion, in N. Couldry, A. Hepp and F. Krotz (eds) *Media Events in a Global Age*. London: Routledge, forthcoming.

Hepp, Andreas and Vogelgesang, Waldemar (2005) Medienkritik der Globalisierung: Die kommunikative Vernetzung der globalisierungskritischen Bewegung, in A. Hepp, F. Krotz and C. Winter (eds) *Globalisierung der Medien*, Wiesbaden: VS, pp. 229–60.

Herman, Edward and McChesney, Robert (1997) *The Global Media: The New Missionaries of Corporate Capitalism*. London: Cassell.

Hesmondhalgh, David (2002) *The Cultural Industries*. London: Sage.

Hills, Matthew (2002) *Fan Cultures*. London: Routledge.

Hoover, Stuart and Lundby, Knut (eds) (1997) *Rethinking Media, Religion and Culture*. New Delhi: Sage.

Klein, Naomi (2000) *No Logo: Taking Aim at the Brand Bullets*. London: Flamingo.

Kleinsteuber, Hans-Jürgen and Rossmann, Thorsten, with Kulbatzki, Arnold C. und Thomaß, Barbara (1994) *Europa als Kommunikationsraum: Akteure, Strukturen und Konfliktpotenziale in der europäischen Medienpolitik*. Opladen: Leske + Budrich.

Knoblauch, Hubert (1989) Das unsichtbare neue Zeitalter: New Age, privatisierte Religion und kultische Milieus, *Kölner Zeitschrift für Soziologie und Sozialpsychologie*, 41: 504–25.

Löfgren, Orvar (2001) The Nation as Home or Motel? Metaphors of Media and Belonging, *Sosiologisk Årbok*: 1–34.

McQuail, Dennis (2005) Book Review: Comparing Media Systems: Three Models of Media and Politics, *European Journal of Communication*, 20: 266–8.

Moores, Shaun (2008) Conceptualizing Place in a World of Flows, in A. Hepp, F. Krotz, Friedrich, S. Moores and C. Winter (eds) *Connectivity, Networks and Flows: Conceptualizing Contemporary Communications*. Cresskill, NJ: Hampton Press, pp. 183–200.

Morley, David (2000) *Home Territories: Media, Mobility and Identity*. London: Routledge.

Morley, David and Robins, Kevin (1995) *Spaces of Identity: Global Media, Electronic Landscapes, and Cultural Boundaries*. London: Routledge.

Naficy, Hamid (2001) *An Accented Cinema: Exilic and Diasporic Filmmaking*. Princeton, NJ: Princeton University Press.

Nederveen Pieterse, Jan (1995) Globalization as Hybridization, in M. Featherstone, S. Lash and R. Robertson (eds) *Global Modernities*. London: Sage, pp. 45–68.

O'Siochru, Sean, Girard, W. Bruce and Mahan, Amy (2002) *Global Media Governance: A Beginner's Guide*. Lanham, MD: Rowman and Littlefield.

Pilkington, Hilary, Omel'chenko, Elena, Flynn, Moya, Starkova, Elena and Bliudina, Ul'iana (2002) *Looking West? Cultural Globalization and Russian Youth Cultures*. Philadelphia: Pennsylvania State University Press.

Porta, Donatella della, Kriesi, Hanspeter and Rucht, Dieter (eds) (1999) *Social Movements in a Globalizing World*. London: Macmillan.
Raboy, Marc (2004) The WSIS and Its Legacy for Global Governance, *Gazette*, 66: 225–32.
Siebert, Fred, Peterson, Theodore and Schramm, Wilbur (1956) *Four Theories of the Press*. New York: Illinois University Press.
Silverstone, Roger and Georgiou, Myria (2005) Editorial Introduction: Media and Minorities in Multicultural Europe, *Journal of Ethnic and Migration Studies*, 31: 433–41.
Storey, John (2003) *Inventing Popular Culture: From Folklore to Globalization*. Oxford: Blackwell.
Sumiala-Seppänen, Johanna, Lundby, Knut and Salokangas, Raimo (eds) (2006) *Implications of the Sacred in (Post)Modern Media*. Göteborg: Nordicom.
Tölölyan, Khachig (1996) Rethinking Diaspora(s): Stateless Power in the Transnational Moment, *Diaspora*, 5: 3–36.
Tomlinson, John (1999) *Globalization and Culture*. Cambridge: Polity.
Touraine, Alain (2002) The Importance of Social Movements, *Social Movement Studies*, 1: 89–95.
Urry, John (1999) *Sociology Beyond Societies: Mobilities for the Next Century*. London: Routledge.
—— (2003) *Global Complexity*. Cambridge: Polity.
Welsch, Wolfgang (1999) Transculturality – The Changing Forms of Cultures Today, in Bundesminister für Wissenschaft und Verkehr and Internationales Forschungszentrum für Kulturwissenschaften (eds) *The Contemporary Study of Culture*. Vienna: Turia & Kant, pp. 217–44.

Chapter 3

Globalization theories and media internationalization

A critical appraisal

Tristan Mattelart

Since the end of the 1980s the development of theories of cultural globalization, in the Anglo-Saxon academic field, has resulted in a deep transformation in the ways of thinking media internationalization. The critical political economy of communication, which since the 1960s has played a key role in analysing media internationalization, has been supplanted by disciplines that until the late1980s had rarely addressed the international dimensions of media.

Theories of cultural globalization, as we will try to show here, are the product of a convergence in theory among cultural studies, anthropology and sociology, which regardless of their disciplinary differences tend to think of the cultural consequences of globalization along the same lines. As such, they propose a new dominant paradigm to apprehend the consequences of media internationalization – a paradigm which has deconstructed the perspectives of political economy and replaced them with a radically different vision.

The aim of this chapter is to show, through some of the key texts, how these theories of cultural globalization have emerged and to underline some of the major ruptures that they have entailed in the ways of thinking media internationalization.

The 'flexibility' of the global economy

Theories of cultural globalization have brought about new ways of perceiving the world capitalist system and, therefore, the transnational media system. The world capitalist system was represented in the works of critical political economy in the 1970s and in the early 1980s as producing cultural standardization. Since the late 1980s, it is increasingly described as generating cultural diversity, even if placed under the sign of commodification.

The key work behind this theoretical change was published in 1989 by the British geographer David Harvey, *The Condition of Postmodernity*. In many respects, this book laid the foundations for the emergence of globalization theories. Harvey's main hypothesis is that the changes that the world capitalist system has been experiencing since the beginning of the 1970s have important effects on contemporary culture. The multinational, 'Fordist' regime of accumulation that dominated between 1945 and 1973, characterized by a system of mass production and mass consumption, was succeeded, argues Harvey, by a more global and more 'flexible' regime of accumulation, one that is marked by an increased 'geographical mobility', by 'greatly intensified rates of commercial, technological, and organizational innovation', by its ability to answer to rapid shifts in consumption practices, and by its ability to explore 'highly specialized and small-scale market niches' (Harvey, 1989: 124, 147, 156).

Now, with each one of these regimes of accumulation is associated a specific mode of social and political regulation that is also a specific cultural order. Thus, Fordism has to be conceived 'less as a mere system of mass production and more as a total way of life' in which media, advertising, and their standardized contents played a central part. They participated in articulating, on an international scale, mass production with mass consumption: 'Mass production meant standardization of product as well as mass consumption; and that meant a whole new aesthetic and a commodification of culture' (Harvey, 1989: 135).

The flexible regime of accumulation has led to the development of a new, highly commodified cultural order in which the media more than ever play an essential role in sustaining high levels of consumption. Accelerated rates of consumption, fast-changing fashions, and expanding small-scale market niches increasingly require, explains Harvey, 'the mobilization of all the artifices of need inducement and cultural transformation that this implies'. Nevertheless, the new cultural order is not seen as producing cultural 'standardization' but as generating, on the contrary, that world of cultural fragmentation that characterizes the postmodern condition. 'The relatively stable aesthetic of Fordist modernism has given way to all the ferment, instability, and fleeting qualities of a postmodernist aesthetic that celebrates difference, ephemerality, spectacle, fashion and the commodification of cultural forms' (Harvey, 1989: 156).

For thinking the link he establishes between 'the dynamics of political economy' and those of 'cultural change', Harvey proposes the very influential concept of 'time-space compression'. The development of a new regime of flexible accumulation, he suggests, has resulted in the rise of 'an overwhelming sense of compression of our spatial and temporal worlds' that is one of the major features of the 'postmodern condition'. By that concept of 'time-space compression', the geographer aims at describing 'processes that so revolutionize the objective qualities of space and time that we are forced to alter, sometimes in quite radical ways, how we represent the world to ourselves' (Harvey, 1989: 211, 240).

Harvey thus articulates the accelerated turnover time in production, the increased pace of consumption, the faster spread of commodities on a global scale, the increased cultural confrontations it produces, with the development of a postmodern culture that stresses the 'fragmentation, discontinuity', 'ephemerality, collage', or 'instability' of identities (Harvey, 1989: 44, 302).

The rise of postmodernist cultural forms has not led, however, notes Harvey, 'to any diminution of corporate power'; quite the opposite. The new regime of flexible accumulation has indeed been accompanied by deregulation processes that have been conducive to increased logics of 'monopolization' and to 'massive mergers' on a global scale (Harvey, 1989: 157–8). Represented in the context of Fordism as being a force of cultural 'standardization', the media are henceforth seen as propagating a fragmented mass culture, placed under the sign of cultural 'difference', even if mediated by an ubiquitous corporate power.

Between homogenization and heterogenization

The link that Harvey established between the emergence of new forms of economic organization and the development of a new cultural order influenced the writings of Stuart Hall, a key figure of British cultural studies, and led him to re-examine the role of mass culture in global times. Considering the flexible character of the new regime of accumulation described by Harvey as consubstantial with the 'process which is called globalization' and with the 'opening up of new global markets', Hall shows how these phenomena force us to reconsider the nature of the world capitalist system and, consequently, that of the mass culture which irrigates it (Hall, 1997a [1991]: 30).

With the globalization processes of the late 1980s and early 1990s, he argues, 'new regimes of accumulation [arose], much more flexible regimes, founded not simply on the logics of mass production and mass consumption but on new flexible accumulation strategies, on segmented markets, on post-Fordist styles of organization, on lifestyle and identity-specific forms of marketing, driven by the market, driven by just-in-time production, driven by the ability to address not the mass audience, or the mass consumer, but penetrating to the very specific smaller groups, to individuals, in its appeal' (Hall, 1997a [1991]: 30).

The advent of these new regimes of accumulation is the main factor leading Hall to question the idea that with the global spread of capitalism 'all particularity would disappear'. Globalization, he argues, has been thought 'in too unitary a way', represented as absorbing all the differences. It is necessary to move away from this 'notion of [a] singular, unitary logic of capital which does not mind where it operates' in order to fully understand the issues of globalization (Hall, 1997a [1991]: 23, 29, 30).

Not that he underestimates capital's ability 'to commodify everything, which is certainly one part of its logic'. But at the same time, alongside this tendency to commodify everything, there is 'another critical part of its logic which works in and through specificity'. 'At a certain point', writes Hall, 'globalization cannot proceed without learning how to live and working through difference' (Hall, 1997a [1991]: 29, 31).

Thus, globalization has to be seen, according to Hall, as a 'contradictory' process, where tendencies to homogenization and tendencies to heterogenization coexist. And the study of 'global mass culture' is a laboratory to understand this double movement between homogenization and heterogenization. Global mass culture is undoubtedly carrying a 'homogenizing form of cultural representation', dominated as it is by Western technologies, capitals, companies and imaginaries. 'But the homogenization is never absolutely complete', writes Hall, since this 'over-corporate, over-integrated … form of economic power … lives culturally through difference', or even through 'the proliferation of difference' (Hall, 1997a [1991]: 8, 31).

Thus the critical political economy analysis that the transnational media system carries the threat of cultural homogenization has been supplanted by the analyses of it as contributing, to a certain extent, to cultural diversity.

Deconstructing national identity

If the logic of 'time-space compression' demands an examination of the nature of the world capitalist system, it also raises the question of the nature of national culture and national identity. How, in a time when the seeming death of distance facilitates transnational encounters of identities and cultures, can one continue to think these with the same categories as previously? 'Cultural identities', writes Hall, 'everywhere are being relativized by the impact of time-space compression' (Hall, 1992: 306).

Analysis of the cultural dimensions of globalization took shape in an intellectual environment in which notions of national identity and national culture – largely mobilized by the political economy during the 1970s and the early 1980s – were being increasingly criticized and condemned for their essentialism. Instead, conceptions of identity and culture that take into account the central role of transnational cultural flows were being preferred.

Concepts of national identity and national culture, argues Hall in several texts published in the early 1990s, should not be regarded as given, but as ideological productions aiming at 'absorbing all the differences' – whether of class, of gender, ethnic or regional – that constitute the nation, in order to represent it as 'a homogeneous entity' (Hall, 1997a [1991]: 2).

Logics of globalization nevertheless put these ideological constructions 'under considerable pressure'. The interdependence of 'the global economy' results in 'the erosion of the nation-state and identities which are associated with it'. Increased flows of migration break ethnically homogeneous representations of national identity. The advent of a 'new form of global mass culture' challenges the continuity of so-called national cultures (Hall, 1997a [1991]: 25–7).

Globalization processes offer then, according to Hall, a favourable context to break with 'the old logics of identity'. At odds with these 'old logics', he presses us to think identities 'as never completed, never finished; … they are always … in process', being in constant 'formation' under the influence, in particular, of external cultural contacts (Hall, 1997b [1991]: 42–3, 47).

Hall stresses indeed the key role that transnational cultural flows play in the constitution of cultural identities. For that reason, he places the concept of diaspora at the heart of his theorization of identity. This concept is used 'metaphorically, not literally', to describe a conception of identity 'defined, not by essence or purity, but by the recognition of a necessary heterogeneity and diversity …; by hybridity' (Hall, 1990: 235).

Cultural mélanges activated by transnational flows become, with these writings, one of the major characteristics of the contemporary cultural condition. Globalization, explains Hall in another text, published in 1995, 'obliges us to conceptualize culture in new ways'. 'Culture is not settled, enclosed or internally coherent. In the modern world, culture, like place, is a meeting point, where different influences, traditions and forces intersect' (Hall, 1995: 178, 187).

This transformation in the ways of conceptualizing identities and cultures has had profound effects on the ways of thinking the cultural consequences of globalization. As long as cultures were conceived as homogeneous entities, with a high degree of coherence, globalization could only be perceived as having a deeply unsettling influence on them. 'With its accelerated flows of goods, peoples, ideas, and images, … its time and space convergences, its migratory movements of people and cultures, globalization is calculated to disturb culture's settled contours', notes Hall (Hall, 1995: 176).

With the adoption of a more syncretic conception of culture, global flows are not seen any more as disturbing 'culture's settled contours' but, on the contrary, as participating in the redefinition of these increasingly moving contours. To describe the way in which cultures are, in the contemporary world, 'forced to interact – often in profoundly asymmetrical ways in terms of their relative power' – Hall has recourse to the concept of 'transculturation', which he borrows from Mary Louise Pratt. It describes the processes by which a dominated culture 'appropriates' the codes of the dominant culture, to create new 'hybrid' or 'creole' cultural forms (Hall, 1995: 193, 196).

In this perspective, the 'invasion of foreign influences and images from the new global cultural industries' is not regarded – as it could be in the writings of the critical political economy of the 1970s or the early 1980s – as dislocating 'established traditions and customary ways of life', but as contributing to give birth to cultures which are 'the result of some never-completed, complex process of combining elements from various cultural repertories … , "new" cultures which are related but which are not exactly like any of the originals' (Hall, 1995: 176, 193).

The creolization of world cultures

Transnational cultural flows, rather than threatening local cultures, are able to contribute to their renewal; this argument has also become dominant in certain anthropological works. While Hall develops his thesis on new forms of transnational contacts in times of globalization without making reference to theories of political economy, Swedish anthropologist Ulf Hannerz bases his argument largely on a critique of them. So, in an article published in 1989 in *Public Culture*, he challenges 'the alarmist view of the threat of global cultural homogenization' propagated, in his opinion, by political economy writings – he quotes Cees Hamelink (1983). The anthropologist sets against these writings a resolutely more optimistic perspective, a perspective more confident in the local cultures' ability to adopt foreign influences, even if the pessimistic views of Hamelink cannot, explains Hannerz, because of the 'asymmetry' of cultural exchanges, 'be dismissed out of hand' (Hannerz, 1997a [1989]: 13–15).

Scenarios of world cultural homogenization are based, notes Hannerz, on 'established assumptions' about the 'cultural purity and authenticity' of local cultures that would be 'threatened with extinction through the importation of "cheap foreign junk"'. In this perspective, the relationship between local and transnational culture 'can only be one of competition'. Turning away from this conception of culture, the anthropologist puts forward an alternative that enables him to understand the 'creative interaction between the transnational and the indigenous' (Hannerz, 1997a [1989]: 15–16).

Hannerz proposes, then, the concept of 'creolization' to suggest 'that cultures, like languages, can be intrinsically of mixed origins, rather than historically pure and homogeneous'. As an example of the ways in which particular cultures incorporate 'global cultural flows' to give birth to creolized cultures, Hannerz evokes the sitcoms produced in Nigeria – a country where he has conducted much of his anthropological fieldwork. Born of the encounter between their overseas models and a local culture, Nigerian sitcoms mobilize their local viewers in greater numbers than the many 'old American serials' that are broadcast. 'Local cultural entrepreneurs', writes Hannerz, 'have gradually mastered the alien cultural forms' and, in 'taking them apart, tampering and tinkering with them', succeeded in creating new cultural forms in tune with local realities (Hannerz, 1997b [1991]: 124, 127).

The dynamics of the creolization of cultures described by Hannerz rest on a conception of the market as generating cultural diversity which is not far removed from that developed by Hall. The anthropologist underlines, indeed, the ability of 'the cultural entrepreneurs of the periphery [to] carve out their own niche, find their own market segment, by developing a product more attuned to the characteristics of their local consumers'. If the market can be a 'force of global homogenization', he concludes, it is also, thanks to the logics of segmentation, a crucible 'of cultural innovation through creolization' (Hannerz, 1996: 74).

This firm belief that transnational cultural flows can generate cultural diversity is also found in other anthropological works. To the term 'creolization' employed by Hannerz, the Indian anthropologist Arjun Appadurai, who lives in the United States, prefers that of 'indigenization', used to describe how societies and cultures appropriate transnational flows.

'The central problem of today's global interactions is the tension between cultural homogenization and cultural heterogenization', writes Appadurai in a famous article published in 1990 in *Public Culture*. He does not underestimate the expansionist logics of the 'instruments of homogenization'. But in opposition to the arguments of 'cultural homogenization' – fuelled according to him by the writings of Cees Hamelink (1983), Herbert Schiller (1976) and Armand Mattelart (1983) – he stresses the increasing logic of the 'cultural heterogenization' of the world. What the theses of 'Americanization' or 'commoditization' fail to consider, he argues, is in particular 'that at least as rapidly as forces from various metropolises are brought into new societies they tend to become indigenized in one or other way' (Appadurai, 1990: 295; see also Appadurai, 1996: 32).

A new way of thinking the issues raised by transnational media flows thus took shape at the end of the 1980s and at the beginning of the 1990s, more or less explicitly in rupture with the writings of critical political economy of the 1970s and the early 1980s. These writings privileged the study of the transnational media system, examining closely the strategies of its main actors, documenting the realities of the unequal exchange, underlining logics of domination, and worrying about the threat that these could constitute to the national identity of Third World countries. To these writings, theories of cultural globalization answer by emphasizing, for their part, the logics of appropriation that particular cultures deploy towards global cultural flows.

'Cultural pluralism' in times of globalization

For Roland Robertson, to whom is sometimes attributed the paternity of globalization theories in the field of the social sciences, the cultural effects of globalization have also to be thought as a dialectical process between homogenization and heterogeneization. However, in accordance with the cultural studies and anthropological writings looked at previously, the sociologist tends, in his analysis of this dialectical process, to put the stress above all on the logics of cultural heterogenization.

In the same vein as David Harvey, Robertson defines globalization as a concept referring both 'to the compression of the world and the intensification of consciousness of the world as a whole'. The sociologist borrows from Harvey and the cultural studies the idea that globalization – 'as a form of "compression" of the contemporary world' – 'relativizes' or, better, 'challenges' the 'stability' of cultural representations. One of the 'major features of globalization [being] the compression of the world, one of its main consequences is an exacerbation of collisions' among cultures or among societies, putting under pressure the categories used to perceive these (Robertson, 1992: 8, 29, 141).

Like Hall, Robertson thus questions the concepts of national culture and local culture and presses us to think about the way in which these national or local cultures are also fed by global flows. 'The cultures of particular societies are, to different degrees,' he writes, 'the result of their interactions with other societies in the global system' (Robertson, 1992: 113).

Robertson also raises, in the same way, the question of the nature of 'global culture', too often represented as carrying cultural standardization in his eyes. 'It would not be too much to say that the idea of global culture is just as meaningful as the idea of national-societal, or local, culture.' The 'consumerist global capitalism' has indeed learnt how to exploit local differences to make profits: 'the contemporary capitalist creation of consumers frequently involves the tailoring of products to increasingly specialized ... markets – so-called "micro-marketing"'. To those who condemn the role played by global capitalism in 'the commodification and homogenization of culture', Robertson thus answers that, on the contrary, 'the production and consolidation of difference and variety is an essential ingredient of contemporary capitalism' (Robertson, 1992: 100, 114, 173).

Robertson describes then globalization as a dialectical movement in which the global is enriched by local specificities – to which it gives a universal reach – and in which the local is, for its part, enriched by the influences stemming from the global system. The sociologist synthesizes this in a famous formula, in which he defines globalization as a 'two-fold process involving the universalization of particularism and the particularization of universalism' (Robertson, 1992: 102).

With Robertson, 'cultural pluralism' becomes in this way one of the 'constitutive feature[s]' of globalization. 'The insistence on heterogeneity and variety in an increasingly globalized world is', he stresses, 'integral to [his] globalization theory' (Robertson, 1992: 61, 131).

Globalization and self-identity

In harmony with these writings analysing the way in which global flows reconfigure local cultures, the British sociologist Anthony Giddens is concerned with how global flows reconfigure individual identities.

'Modernity is inherently globalizing', explains Giddens in his book *The Consequences of Modernity*, published in 1990. One of modernity's great characteristics is indeed the 'disembedding of social systems', notion by which the sociologist describes, in particular, the way in which social relations develop outside physical settings of interaction. Modernity, he writes, increasingly fosters 'relations between "absent" others, locationally distant from any given situation of face-to-face interaction. In conditions of modernity, place becomes increasingly phantasmagoric: that is to say, locales are thoroughly penetrated by and shaped in terms of social influences quite distant from them.' By this process, modernity connects the local with the global, affecting 'the lives of many millions of people' (Giddens, 1990: 17–20).

Globalization is nevertheless, in Giddens's work as in Robertson's, 'a dialectical process'. According to the sociologist, 'local transformation is as much a part of globalization as the lateral extension of social connections across time and space'. That is why he complements 'the notion of disembedding with one of reembedding' (Giddens, 1990: 64, 79). And to describe this last notion, Anthony Giddens studies in particular how disembedding logics of globalization transform individuals' ordinary experience.

The 'dialectic of the local and the global' is at the heart of the book he published in 1991, *Modernity and Self-Identity*, where he analyses the consequences of globalization for individual lives. In this book, he studies 'the two poles of the dialectic of the local and the global in conditions of high modernity', namely 'transformations in self-identity and globalization'. The key idea of the book is that, under the effect of the 'disembedding, globalizing tendencies of modernity', the individual becomes, more and more, a reflexive individual – an individual who is increasingly able to compose his own identity thanks to the widened mediated experience to which he henceforth has access. 'In a post-traditional social universe, ... in which the reordering of time and space realigns the local with the global, the self undergoes massive change. ... On the level of the self, a fundamental component of the day-to-day activity is simply that of choice.' If, 'by definition, tradition or established habit orders life within relatively set channels', globalizing logics of modernity, for their part, by the access they offer to the outside world, confront 'the individual with a complex diversity of choice' (Giddens, 1991: 21, 26, 32, 80).

Media play a key role in this 'plurality of choices': 'With the increasing globalization of media, a multifarious number of milieux are, in principle, rendered visible to anyone who cares to glean the relevant information.' And this mundane mediated experience is, according to Anthony Giddens, positively incorporated in the day-to-day conduct of individuals, enriching what he calls the 'reflexive project of the self'. The media are in this way major sources from which individuals negotiate their identities. 'Although every one lives a local life, phenomenal worlds for the most part are truly global' (Giddens, 1991: 32, 84, 187).

The widened horizon of experience that enriches individuals' lives is largely the product of the increased circulation of consumer goods and commercial media within the framework of the global capitalist system. Giddens recognizes this: the 'plurality of choices' he highlights 'is in some substantial part the very outcome of commodified processes' (Giddens, 1991: 199).

Commodification can of course be 'inimical' for 'the reflexive project of the self', notes the sociologist. But, rather than being seen as carrying threats of cultural 'standardization', commodification processes are, in his work, in many respects, mainly regarded as feeding a variety of self-identities. 'Market-governed freedom of individual choice becomes an enveloping framework of individual self-expression' (Giddens, 1991: 197, 199).

From the greater cultural diversity generated by the flexible regime of accumulation of the world capitalist system to the larger variety of cultural choices that the individual (and the consumer!) experiences, thanks to the media, the increasing cultural heterogenization of the world is, as we can see, one of the main arguments common to writings on cultural globalization.

A scientific dispossession

Cultural studies, anthropology and sociology took a long time to discover the central role that media ubiquity plays in the reconfiguration of identities and cultures. Why wait until the end of the 1980s to become aware of a reality that the critical political economy emphasized, from a radically different point of view, as far back as the end of the 1960s? The interpretative frameworks proposed by the new approaches have nonetheless become dominant. To study the emergence of the theories of cultural globalization is then also to study the history of a scientific dispossession. With their development, the critical political economy of communication, after having played a pioneering role in the analysis of the issues raised by media internationalization, has indeed been largely marginalized.

Newcomers to the analysis of the cultural consequences of media ubiquity ignore, at best, the literature produced before them on the question. There is not the slightest trace, in the writings of David Harvey, Roland Robertson or Anthony Giddens, of the works of the political economy of communication. Elsewhere, when they are quoted, it is summarily, without ever entering into the complexity of their arguments, which are quickly schematized as the so-called theses of 'cultural imperialism'.

Ignored, these works have also been caricatured and denigrated to establish the new paradigm of globalization. One book has played an important role in this context, published by the British sociologist John Tomlinson in 1991 under the title *Cultural Imperialism*. Adopting a deliberately 'nomadic discourse', the author sets out to tear to pieces the theses of Herbert Schiller, based primarily on two articles, published in 1979 and 1985, and on the first chapter of *Communication and Cultural Domination* (Schiller, 1976). The criticism of the writings of Armand Mattelart is based on two works of the 1970s – *How to Read Donald Duck* and *Multinational Corporations and the Control of Culture*, translated into English respectively in 1975 and 1979 (Dorfman and Mattelart, 1975 [1971]; Mattelart, 1979 [1974]) – and chooses to overlook the important revisions made to his thought as far back as the beginning of the 1980s (Tomlinson, 1991: 35–45).

Working only with references in English, Tomlinson reduces the 'cultural imperialism' theses to an abstract intellectual construction, not contextualized, frozen in the early 1980s, produced primarily by American or European researchers speaking, without of course having the legitimacy to do so, in the name of the masses of the Third World. The epigraph that introduces the book sums up well his intention. It quotes these words of Gilles Deleuze to Michel Foucault: 'You were the first to teach us something absolutely fundamental: the indignity of speaking for others' (Tomlinson, 1991).

Alternately ignored, caricatured, mummified or vilified, the critical political economy of communication has been in this way resolutely disqualified as a legitimate approach to understanding the processes of increasing cultural transnationalization, to the benefit of the new perspectives proposed by cultural studies, anthropology and sociology. Theories of cultural globalization have indeed partially been built against a caricatured perception of those of political economy, whose contribution has been reduced to warnings against the threat of global cultural homogenization. Its contribution having been reduced to this alarmist scenario, it has been easy then to set against it another, more positive, view that puts forward the increasing cultural heterogenization of the world. Tomlinson's book illustrates this: after having demolished the theses of 'cultural imperialism', he indeed praises, in his conclusion, the fruitfulness of the research perspectives opened up by the topic of 'globalization' (Tomlinson, 1991: 175).

Another book written by Tomlinson – *Globalization and Culture*, published in 1999 – is representative of the paradigm shift that occurred in the 1990s with the advent of the theories of cultural globalization. Taking explicitly the opposite view to Herbert Schiller's analyses on the 'global capitalist monoculture', Tomlinson, following Giddens, examines in this book the way in which 'cultural commodities' contribute 'to the general experience of "cultural disembedding" … typical of modern societies' (Tomlinson, 1999: 81, 105).

Rather than considering these cultural commodities 'as simply images of a depressing global standardization or homogenization', Tomlinson explores the ways in which they contribute to the rise of a 'cultural awareness which is, in various senses, "global"', making a reference to Robertson. 'It does imply that "the global" increasingly exists as a cultural horizon within which we (to varying degrees) frame our existence' (Tomlinson, 1999: 30, 105).

Thanks to the media and to new communication technologies, individuals thus have, according to Tomlinson, a 'growing awareness of the significance of "remote forces" well beyond the limits of the local or national contexts where they live'. And this mundane mediated experience furnishes individuals with a 'cultural resource' which enables them to broaden their cultural horizons (Tomlinson, 1999: 30, 114).

Conclusion

With the theories of cultural globalization, cultural studies, anthropology and sociology have become in the Anglo-Saxon academic world, within the space of ten years, major disciplines within which the effects of media internationalization are analysed. In the meantime, critical political economy has lost much of the influence it had exerted on the ways of thinking these realities.

The contribution of the new approaches needs to be emphasized. They encourage a view of the heterogeneity of media production within the transnational system; they alert us to the ambiguity of such concepts as national identity or national culture, employed, sometimes imprudently, by critical political economy; they demand a more precise analysis of the complex ways by which transnational flows are appropriated by individuals or cultures.

However, these new approaches leave also a number of important questions unresolved. The realities of cultural globalization tend in particular in these perspectives to be studied mainly in specific relation to the complex processes of appropriation. The comprehensive framework where these appropriations take place is, for its part, systematically ignored. Writings on cultural globalization are indeed characterized by their complete lack of interest in a careful analysis of the transnational media system, its architecture, its actors, their interactions, the realities of world communication flows, the values they spread globally.

Moreover, whereas the media are key constituents of their theoretical apparatuses, none of the anthropological or sociological works quoted earlier study in detail their nature, their insertion in a commercial mode of production and consumption, and the relations of domination that structure them. The media constitute in these writings, in many respects, magic objects endowed with extensive powers: cultural resources, thanks to which national cultures and individual identities are redefined, major players of the global cultural mélange. As magic objects, the media remain in these works, largely, black boxes; theories of cultural globalization are not on the whole articulated with media theory.

A paradox deserves to be underlined here: theories of cultural globalization think the effects of media internationalization without thinking the processes of media internationalization! What is then the heuristic character, to understand the issues raised by these processes of internationalization, of analyses studying the complexity of the modes of indigenization of transnational flows, without studying either the nature or the origin of these same flows?

These new approaches apprehend moreover the cultural consequences of globalization in largely speculative terms. The sophistication of their theoretical analyses contrasts strongly with the poverty of their empirical analyses. While these works celebrate the advent of creole, hybrid, transcultural or cosmopolitan identities and cultures in times of globalization, they do not describe meticulously the ways in which individuals or cultures are actually confronted with transnational media flows.

By ignoring world communication realities, by neglecting the need to study with precision the concrete interactions that take place at the local level, theories of cultural globalization tend to magnify the logics of appropriation of global flows, without considering either their limits or their contradictions. As such, these new perspectives run the risk of being considered sophisticated theoretical constructions legitimizing, probably unintentionally, the free flow of the major players of the global system.

References

Appadurai, Arjun (1990) Disjuncture and Difference in the Global Cultural Economy, *Public Culture*, 2(2): 1–24.

—— (1996) *Modernity at Large: Cultural Dimensions of Globalization*, Minneapolis: University of Minnesota Press.

Giddens, Anthony (1990) *The Consequences of Modernity*. Cambridge: Polity.

—— (1991) *Modernity and Self-Identity: Self and Society in the Late Modern Age*, Stanford, CA: Stanford University Press.

Hall, Stuart (1990) Cultural Identity and Diaspora, in Jonathan Rutherford (ed.) *Community, Culture, Difference*. London: Lawrence and Wishart, pp. 222–37.

—— (1991; 1997a) The Local and the Global: Globalization and Ethnicity, in Anthony King (ed.) *Culture, Globalization and the World-System*. Minneapolis: University of Minnesota Press, pp. 19–39.

—— (1991; 1997b) Old and New Identities, Old and New Ethnicities, in Anthony King (ed.) *Culture, Globalization and the World-System*. Minneapolis: University of Minnesota Press, pp. 41–68.

—— (1992) The Question of Cultural Identity, in Stuart Hall, David Held and Tony McGrew (eds) *Modernity and Its Futures*. Cambridge: Polity, pp. 273–316.

—— (1995) New Cultures for Old, in Doreen Massey and Pat Jess (eds) *A Place in the World? Places, Cultures and Globalization*. Oxford: Oxford University Press, pp. 175–211.

Hamelink, Cees (1983) *Cultural Autonomy in Global Communications*. New York: Longman.

Hannerz, Ulf (1989; 1997a) Notes on the Global Ecumene, *Public Culture*, 1(2): 66–75; reprinted in Annabelle Sreberny-Mohammadi, Dwayne Winseck, Jim McKenna and Oliver Boyd-Barrett (eds) *Media in Global Context: A Reader*. London: Arnold, pp. 11–18.

—— (1991; 1997b) 'Scenarios for Peripheral Cultures', in Anthony D. King (ed.) *Culture, Globalization and the World-System: Contemporary Conditions for the Representation of Identity*. Minneapolis: University of Minnesota Press, pp. 107–28.

—— (1996) *Transnational Connections: Culture, People, Places*. London: Routledge.

Harvey, David (1989) *The Condition of Postmodernity: An Enquiry into the Origins of Cultural Change*. London: Basil Blackwell.

Mattelart, Armand (1979 [1974]) *Multinational Corporations and the Control of Culture: The Ideological Apparatuses of Imperialism*. Sussex: The Harvester Press.

—— (1983) *Transnationals in the Third World: The Struggle for Culture*. Sussex: Bergin and Garvey.

Mattelart, Armand and Dorfman, Ariel (1975 [1971]) *How to Read Donald Duck: Imperialist Ideology in the Disney Comic*. New York: International General.

Robertson, Roland (1992) *Globalization: Social Theory and Global Culture*. London: Sage.

Schiller, Herbert (1976) *Communication and Cultural Domination*. White Plains, NY: International Arts and Sciences Press.

Tomlinson, John (1991) *Cultural Imperialism*. London: Pinter.

—— (1999) *Globalization and Culture*. Cambridge: Polity.

Chapter 4

Frames for internationalizing media research

Naren Chitty

Nothing exemplifies contemporary challenges to media research more than does the web, creating as it does a new virtual geographical landscape, one that has connecting spaces that are not too far removed in effect from the wardrobe leading to Narnia (Lewis, 1950). The web, with its 'mingling of media' or 'multi-mediacy', and its immediacy – instantly linking between media and cultural, economic, political and social domains – provides an expedient frame for internationalizing media. Web media forms and content are shaped by multi-mediacy and immediacy. And web users must surely, under a constructivist logic, interact with web media to shape this character. The web is a plexus of venues. It is important to understand the web venues as 'storied places', with architectural hierarchies (Sundén, 2006: 287). The first part of this chapter provides a discussion of the nature of the web as venue. Seven propositions are made in this regard, the seventh unfolding into a matrix of immediacy. Websites of an organization that operates across the immediacy matrix, the United Nations Development Programme (UNDP), are subjected to a sociographical and iconographical analysis in the second part. The aim is to find out how the UNDP-constructed storied venues promote organizational identity while providing avenues for 'grassrooting' or interaction with local places (Castells, 2005: 627–36).

Web as venue

The web is the new medium for the presentation and projection of organizational and individual self in the networked world. Self sets an individual apart from others and expresses personhood through thoughts and deeds. The corporate self seeks projection through various media that record deeds, selectively perhaps, and convey thought. Observers construct images of organizations or individuals by decoding their thoughts and deeds or the descriptions of such by third parties. Depending on the goal orientation of an organization, it will seek to achieve results in one or more areas such as image projection, trade and information transfer/exchange. Web 'spaces' are essentially particular kinds of social 'spaces' in which organizations and individuals are able to interact in ways such as the above.

I am not enthusiastic about the use of the term web 'space'. An ontological discussion of space may reveal the roots of my disquiet about the use of the term in relation to the web. Einsteinian physics informs us of the inseparability of space and time. When we speak of physical space today, we refer in fact to space-time. Non-physical space-time is mind, individual and collective, bounded only by memory, perception, cognition, affection and creativity – influenced by the experience of space-time. Constructs in non-physical space-time are mental and in our experience may be conveyed to others through physical media of communication, whether script, music, sculpture, oral history. Lefebvre's conception of time as the categories of change and stability in relation to motion in space reinforces Einstein in the social world, that 'there can be no time without space and vice versa' (Bolin, 2006: 71). Lefebvre constructed social space as an intermediary category between mental and physical space (Lefebvre, 1991). 'This social space or the space of social life contains … three elements: conceived, perceived and lived in space. In their turn these elements are connected to three spatial components in the production of space, representations of space, representational spaces or spaces of representation and spatial practice'(Ek, 2006: 47).

If space and time are mutually inextricable, the phrase 'social space' becomes shorthand for social space-time. Social space-time has geo-social (e.g. states, provinces), architectural (e.g. buildings, rooms), socio-natural (e.g. beaches), and mediated (e.g. newspapers, broadcasts, web pages) settings. It consists of extensions of mind – constructs or constructions. Extensions are tools for operating in social space-time. With constant use they begin to be reified through a process Hall calls 'extension transference' (Hall, 1977: 31). Our world of social constructions and constructs is very real to us.

Social space-time settings have a variety of functions, deriving originally perhaps from generic human needs. These functions may be described and social loci characterized as transactional. Social transactions take place in such loci. Transaction, as social interaction, is the essence of the social. Transaction may take place at serendipitous gatherings of individuals. Gatherings may also be convened at designated venues. Websites are designated venues for particular transactions, exchanges of various kinds of values. One can actually stumble serendipitously on a designated venue. The importance of the term 'venue' is that it draws in satisfactorily the notions of time and location into social space. The space-time continuum is as true in the social as it is in the physical domain: social space does not exist outside of time, as recognized by Massey (Massey, 2005: 130).

Do social space-time, or 'venue', and individual mind influence each other? 'Venue' is mostly collective mind. It shapes and is also shaped by individual minds. One might go further, from a constructivist viewpoint, to argue that ontography changes the nature of space-time, even generates space-time. And ontography is informed by phenography. The construction of space through words and mathematical symbols takes place incessantly in the realm of quantum physics. Much of this is space of belief in the messages of science. Ontographical processes related to Newtonian and social realities are vastly separated but there are some similarities that are noteworthy. The positivist finds a wealth of material that is physical, observable and measurable in both domains. However, positivism is less advantaged when the fundamental nature of space-time is investigated at the level of quantum physics. Mathematics and language are often the only scientific tools at this level. Where observation and measurement of 'things' themselves is not possible, researchers observe effects and theorize thereafter.

Under a symbolic interactionist perspective, one that arises from George Herbert Mead's insights (Mead, 1934), the quantum physicist's description of quantum space may be viewed as being linked by the languages of analysis and description (such as mathematics and English) to 'transactional venues', notably those for scientific and wider communities. The use of metaphor from everyday life, terms such as 'string theory', ties the moment of theorization at the quantum level to the everyday social context. A positivist approach may also be employed in developing social ontographies. The organizational structures of several nations and international organizations may be examined and commonalities determined. The institution of levels of organization as political acts leads to the construction of such levels and the shaping of social reality. At the same time theorization, for instance theorization on whether structure inhibits agency and how agency inhabits structure, can shape the construction of new ontographies.

There are seven propositions I wish to make about transactional venues. The first proposition is that features in transactional venues resonate with features from physical space-time. A fundamental characteristic of space-time is its hybridity. The anabolism and katabolism of space-time are associated with an inseparably hybrid and incessantly hybridizing nature. Matter and energy engage in all manner of comings together and goings apart. Proposition five elaborates on proposition one. The second proposition is that transactional venues are striated to varying degrees. Deleuze and Guattari speak of politically striated (state controlled) and smooth (nomad's) space (Deleuze and Guattari, 2004: 361–2). Transactional venues are held together by lexical rules arising from legal, political, economic, religious, cultural institutions and readings and practices arising from people. There is a constant tension between rules and people's ways.

The third proposition is that transactional venues are socially constructed and socially experienced. Words and other symbols are pieces of mind that are used to construct venues. Words and other symbols are spaces in themselves, being packed with meanings and histories that the mind can unpack, if equipped to do so. Iconography may be employed to tag culture, history and ideology onto venues.

A fourth proposition is that hybridity is a process. Whereas historical examples of hybridity may be described in terms of particular symbolic plateaus (Lasswell, 1965a, 1965b), current examples of hybridity are constantly evolving. Hybridization is a process that connects all of humanity and hybrid forms are interconnected and constantly changing.

A fifth proposition is that a major transaction in a venue is the production of hybridity, the generation of transduction. The hybridization that takes place in a venue is an active process, one of continuous transformation through transduction – or the moving of concepts between knowledge domains (Simondon, 1989, 1995). In the selection of concepts for the presentation of group self or individual self, there is individuation at the organizational and individual levels respectively. 'Simondon's concept of individuation does not introduce a division between a molecular domain (intensity) and a molar one (extensity) so much as it mediates between such domains' (Hansen, 2001).

At one end of the spectrum, institutions seek to build communities of identity. At the other end are individuals, inhabitants of nation states and territories across the world, who engage in personal individuation, including the individualizing of venues that they visit, in which they undertake transactions or which they inhabit. Kraidy makes a useful distinction, in terms of the political use of venues, between dominance (under cultural imperialism), resistance/adaptation (under cultural pluralism) and hybridity (under critical transculturalism) (Kraidy, 2005: 150). Lie makes a distinction, for analytical purposes, between 'different states of liminality' that he identifies as 'the state of cultural coexistence, the state of intercultural negotiation, and, the state of intercultural transformation towards hybridized transculturality' where 'different cultural elements have come to be known, accepted, shared and lived by different cultural groups. The entanglement has formed a new culture' (Lie, 2002: 19–20). I would argue that culture is like a river, similar but never the same in two places. There are multiple sources from and myriads of environments and materials through which a culture flows. We can freeze cultural moments, we can construct periods with the use of labels, but culture is fluid, multilayered, multi-sourced and has multiple influences on 'itself' and others.

A sixth proposition is that the construction of web architecture follows readings of constructions of social organization. There is the common-sense geographical ontography that cascades from global through regional to national to sub-national region to local area. There are various scholarly ontographies of social organization ranging from the political dichotomies of global and local or centre and periphery to more elaborate constructs. Global is usually represented through the use of key symbols of the international political economy. Local is usually represented through the use of key symbols of local culture, dress, buildings, religious festivals.

The seventh proposition is that ontographical constructs are useful heuristics for the analysis of the web architecture of an organization. Heuristics are extensions and we must ever be careful of creeping extension transference. The seven propositions draw attention to the need to develop ontographies of mediated social contexts that incorporate local and global dimensions. This is undertaken below.

Constructing an heuristic framework

Transactional venues, virtual or otherwise, are linked in a transactional plexus related to production, reproduction, exchange, individuation and transduction. Venues could be broad or narrow, ranging from the world market, through the Chinese diasporic community in the United States, to a telephone conversation between two teenage girls in Sydney. Gottmann's 'transactional metropolis is connected to, and interwoven with, other transnational centers, forming metropolitan networks within national territories and across international boundaries', in relation to 'terms of employment, hosting environment, interweaving of quaternary activities, evolution of urban centrality' (Corey, 1983: xvii). Is the global–local binary an adequate planetary ontography of all that is global, local and in between? Planetary ontographies need to go beyond simple geographies of our planetary society. Should sociographies be drawn empirically from the organization concerned, whether the organization is the formal international system that has been constructed around international organizations and regimes, a business corporation, a religious organization or a community centre?

Thrift argues that '[s]pace is no longer seen as a nested hierarchy moving from "global" to "local". This absurd scale dependent notion is replaced by the notion that what counts is connectivity' (Thrift, 2004: 59). The alternative notion of folded space, manifold space offers opportunities for unfolding (Doel, 2000: 127–8). The word 'develop' arose from an old French word meaning 'to unfold'. We can imagine the histories that are folded in space, histories of developments that we need to 'develop', as we used to do with old-fashioned photographic film, before we can form a picture of a venue. Indeed time (history and past foldings and the present, future, actual and possible unfoldings and foldings respectively) is contained in 'venue'. But false histories may also be folded into venues. Myths of national origin are glaring examples.

While there has been an academic migration from modern centralism to postmodern decentralism, large organizations continue to construct themselves and their web identities on the basis of nested hierarchies. For this reason one needs to reflect on sociography in analysing web pages of international or transnational agencies. One can do so while continuing to privilege connectivity and agency as values. Nesting may be conceived of sans an ideology of hierarchy. Folders or folds may be viewed as nesting in social space without any absolute hierarchy. Hierarchy or the lack thereof would be in the eyes of the beholder – or in the mind's eye of the projecting agent.

At least six conceptualizations of the global and local have been made in the last decade as a matrix (Chitty, 1994a, 1994b, 2000, 2002, 2004; Pettman, 2000; Lipschutz, 2001; Kraidy, 2003; Jansson, 2006; Perlas and Strawe, undated). Lipschutz, arriving at his position via Foucault and feminism, uses matrix in relation to the global political economy in an article that is broadly compatible with the incorporation of structure and agency in my own matrix framework

(Lipschutz, 2001: 323). Describing a political economy centred around agents, rather than people in structures, he associates the economic order with a matrix. 'While we have been instructed to watch disorder and fear for our future, we have become ever more tightly entangled in that new Order – that Matrix – from which there is no escape' (Lipschutz, 2001: 325). Pettman uses the term matrix as a frame for a world politics which he conceives of as Babushka dolls representing states, firms and individuals (Pettman, 2000: 215–24). In a third independent development, Kraidy addresses a slightly different 'theoretical matrix [that he proposes for international communication and that] … begins with the global level, going through the regional, national, provincial and ending with the local … overlapping and mutually influencing contexts of action' (Kraidy, 2003: 38). Both Kraidy's proposed framework and my framework draw on Robertson's glocalization insights (Robertson, 1994: 33–52). I have, in my framework, inter-nestled matrices. These matrices host actors that have political, economic and cultural goals, as well as material and non-material 'products' and 'imports'. Instead of the administrative matrix of my heuristic, one that escapes diplomatic minefields associated with the concept of state, Kraidy has a 'national' level because 'the nation state persists as an influential player in globalization'. He has a provincial level that my matrix heuristic does not have, but does not include the equivalent of an individual matrix. Another difference is that Kraidy does not view his levels as part of a larger system (Kraidy, 2003: 38).

Jansson's epistemology of texture employs a matrix with three values of scale (regional, institutional and global) and three values of space (mediatization of space, mediation of space and a mediatized sense of space). He argues that a 'third dimension, time, might as well be included in the picture, pointing to the process of texturation – the tension field between durability and change' (Jansson, 2006: 101).

Perlas and Strawe discussed social threefolding (state, market and civil society) in the age of the empire matrix, in 2003. The empire matrix (United States of America) is the economics-driven globalizing polarity (imperial individuation), in contrast to the polarity of individual individuation, of emancipation of the individual from group conditioning, that contributes to social change. It is the argument of Perlas and Strawe that the polarities need to be harmonized so that individualism serves the global community (Perlas and Strawe, undated).

My own heuristic describes five matrices, one embedded in the other, linking the global political economy and regional, administrative and ethno-historical matrices to individuals. This matrix is an arena of transactional venues, networks of individuals, ethno-histories, administrations, regions and political economies. These may also be considered to be interlocking sub-systems of a confederal planetary social organization within the international system. However, sociographical categories are constantly evolving, being replaced by new ones – by fiat – and being perceived variously by actors. My heuristic should be viewed as adjustable, one that may be modified based on the perceived sociographic reality, as one changes the focus of a pair of binoculars. I do not intend that it be reified or subjected to extension transference. But, certainly, in examining the web architecture of international organizations, it would be useful to first calibrate, with a sociographic construct, the organization's structure as revealed in the storied web venues with a sociographic construct.

Encompassing all, in the matrix heuristic, is the physical environment or N-matrix (see Table 4.1). Engaging with the N-matrix, in both value-extractive (economic) and value-nurturant (ecological) modes, is the global political economy or P-matrix. Like all other matrices other than the N-matrix, the P-matrix is fundamentally a comprehensive human collectivity, resource environment and arena of venues. The P-matrix consists of people, their material and non-material products (including institutions) and relationships with each other and with products. In other words, it refers to people and culture, where culture consists of social constructs. Individual matrices are also particular in that they are human singularities.

Within the socially all-encompassing P-matrix are sub-arenas. The way in which these sub-arenas are perceived and constructed varies by region, state, organization. I identify regional matrices, administrative matrices and ethno-historical matrices as matrices that may be found between the P and I-matrices. An E-matrix may be an arena or plexus of venues for people of Chinese

Table 4.1 Matrix framework

Matrix	*Description*
I:I-matrix	1. Individual (actor) 2. Individual's non-material 'products' and 'imports': values, attitudes, beliefs and behaviour; 3. Individual's material products and acquisitions.
II: E-matrix	1. Ethno-historical actors; 2. Ethno-historical actors' non-material 'products' and 'imports': values, attitudes, beliefs and behaviour; 3. Ethno-historical actors' material products and acquisitions
III: A-matrix	1. Administrative collectivities' actors; 2. Administrative actors' non-material 'products' and 'imports': values, attitudes, beliefs and behaviour; 3. Administrative actors' material products and acquisitions.
IV: R-matrix	1. Regional actors; 2. Regional actors' non-material 'products' and 'imports': values, attitudes, beliefs and behaviour; 3. Regional collectivities' material products and acquisitions
V: P-matrix	1. Global actors; 2. Global actors' non-material 'products' and 'imports': values, attitudes, beliefs and behaviour; 3. Global actors' material products and acquisitions.
VI: N-matrix	Material conditions for human transactions.

origin, within an A-matrix or administrative matrix that coincides with a nation state or that crosses national borders. An E-matrix could include a diasporic community. Today an A-matrix often hosts a plexus of interacting diasporic communities. Interfacing E-matrices play a particularly dynamic role in the construction of new hybridities. The problem of conceptualizing the political relationships between China, Hong Kong and Taiwan wanes in importance when China, because of its size, is treated as an R-matrix or regional matrix, with its provinces, special administrative regions and Taiwan being treated as A-matrices.

Matrices are embedded successively in each other from individual to political economic and may be reduced to symbols in an individual matrix. It is not a great insight to say that the world may be reduced to words. Words may also be used to change the world. Each matrix is an arena or plexus of transactional venues that contains actors, non-material products and imports (values, attitudes, beliefs and behaviour) and material products and acquisitions. These values, quantitative or qualitative as they may be, bridging seamlessly from global to individual venues and products, include messages or narratives that may be imported or exported by actors within each matrix (Chitty, 2004).

The UNDP website

The UNDP is a P-matrix organization, with headquarter's staff, drawn from various A and E-matrices, who operate within a P-matrix organizational culture. It also has regional and national offices. UNDP activities are spread across the developing world. The UNDP is a venue for global policy production, programme development, funding and service delivery in the area of development. It engages in processes of global social change through transduction. It has the challenge of bridging between multiple venues of international, national and sub-national transduction. New informational technology provides a limited opportunity to achieve this end, by at least netting those who have access to the internet, in one way or the other. The UNDP shares with other organizations the need for individuation at the organizational level. 'As a governance structure, consisting of networks of states and non-state actors, rather than a government exercising sovereignty on behalf of a people, the UN system must relentlessly seek to decrease the natural distance between ordinary folk throughout the world and the steel and glass organs and Weberian processes of the UN … access needs also to be built into structures of governance, and the creative use of telecommunication technology can allow for participation between actors at different levels and within different cultures' (Chitty, 2005: 11).

This chapter does not seek to discuss the UN's effectiveness in building participatory governance structures. Rather, it examines a few key features in the UNDP's web-delivered individuation. In particular it discusses meanings attached to design elements chosen by the UNDP for individuation across various matrices in which it chooses to present itself.

People tend to individualize venues that they inhabit or in which they undertake transactions. One might say that places are spaces that have been individualized by experience or by the artificial provision of references that create ambience and therefore invite revisiting and 'place-ization'. 'Since the 1980s cultural studies has shown a growing interest in questions of space and place influenced in particular by Foucault and his intersections of discourse, space and power. In this context, a place is understood to be a site or location in space constituted and made meaningful by social relations of power and marked by identifications or emotional investments. As such, a place can be understood to be a bounded manifestation of production of meaning in space' (Barker, 2004: 144).

On the other hand, institutions may use venues to homogenize and universalize certain aspects of behaviour. In international structures like that of the UNDP, there is a tension between the universalizing of policy, including policy on communication, presentation of messages, and the overall architecture that connects numerous venues located in various matrices.

> In order to analyze the landscapes of representation, we need to consider the signifying practices that are fundamentally constituent of culture and society. On the one hand, these are the signifying practices strategically developed in order to actively attain effects, for example marketing, public relations, branding and other campaigning, and commercial and political communication. On the other hand, there are also more subtle and not always conscious practices around media use, which lead to cultural patterns (taste communities, for example).
>
> (Bolin, 2006: 80)

We can expect physical venues at UNDP headquarters in New York to reflect signifying practices associated with the ostensibly global P-matrix rather than with any ostensible A-matrix (e.g. Australian) or E-matrix (e.g. Chinese Australian) venues. There are two principal strategic reasons why elements of local place may be incorporated in a global venue. One is the need for a globally individuating organization to interface with third sector 'grassrooting' impulses (Castells, 2005: 627–36). A second is because of the individuation needs of individuals associated with an organization, employees or customers and partners. A physical venue at UNDP headquarters may be peopled by individuals who carry with them histories and cultures from one or more folds in space-time. An Indian national at UNDP headquarters in New York could have references on display, or for purposes of personal individuational support, to his ethnic origins, family in Bombay, schooling in Britain, university in Boston, postings in Beijing, Berlin and Beirut, and marriage to a Barbadian. Personal individuation is not necessarily a form of resistance to organizational individuation. The two forces of individuation can be resolved in a benign balance by the individual.

The same is true for websites, except that unlike the UNDP's physical headquarters in New York, the virtual home page flows into workstations (at home, at work and at play) across the globe. Broader localization strategies seek to represent the varied nature of membership with E-matrix references, thereby making venues more familiar and friendly.

The transactions offered in the different UNDP web venues were found to be representational (public relations), educational, informational, individuational and transductional. Transduction was discernible in relation to knowledge, values and signs from other transaction venues. The study was limited to an examination of how UNDP websites project their individuation imperatives. The web architecture was examined in order to reveal how the UNDP deals with individuation in various matrices. In July 2006 the UNDP web architecture was in partial congruence with the matrix heuristic, with recognition of P, R and A-matrices. E and I-matrices did not figure in the UNDP web architecture, but there was ethnographic iconography on the home page and one A-matrix exception referred to below.

Individuation was sought on the UNDP home page through classical Graeco-Roman iconography, of an Apollonian character, associated with the public architecture of Western empires. Empires are mega venues that generate hybridity while resisting its polluting influence in important expressions of public life (for as long as possible), as in Roman and post-Roman European imperial architecture. Gina Chitty takes the view 'that the Anglo-Saxon project of empire worked through a projection of an imperial Apollonianism' (G. Chitty, 2005: 106). Nietzsche describes the origin of Ancient Greek dramatic tragedy in terms of a contest of principles, summarized by Raymond Geuss and Ronald Speirs thus:

> Nietzsche names each of these principles after an ancient Greek deity (Apollo, Dionysius) who can be thought of as imaginatively representing the drive in question in an especially intense and pure way. 'Apollo' embodies the drive towards distinction, discreteness and individuality, towards the drawing and respecting of boundaries and limits; he teaches an ethic of moderation and self-control. The Dionysiac is the drive towards the transgression of limits, the dissolution of boundaries, the destruction of individuality, and excess.
>
> (Nietzsche, 1999)

Apollonian iconography is easily recognizable all over the world, and it is not surprising that it is used by the United Nations Organization (UNO) for individuation. Other organizations, such as corporations, may utilize different visual references such as logos, images, symbols, fonts and layouts. The dominant Apollonian symbols on the UNO's portal page were the globe, centred on the north pole, an appropriate P-matrix symbol. The globe was framed by Augustan laurel leaves (Apollo's bay or *Laurus nobilis*) signifying peace, set against the sky blue of the UNO. The laurel leaves also evoked classical Apollonian order. The page was available in English, Arabic, Chinese, French, Russian and Spanish. The banner at the top of the English page depicted eight faces, of both genders, all ages and representing a wide spectrum of ethno-cultural backgrounds. It provided a counterpoise to the classic P-matrix symbolism of the UN emblem. The UNDP headquarters website also showed signs of being a P-matrix venue. Available in English, French and Spanish, it drew on Apollonian iconography, the masthead banner consisting of an inflated segment of the UN emblem in blue on a darker blue background. The font used on this page was 'Arial', a classic unembellished type. Transduction was evident in reports being drawn from different parts of the world, from A-matrices, but having been filtered through the UNDP headquarter's newsroom. There were five news stories listed at the top and a section entitled 'UNDP around the world' at the bottom. The five news stories were about a West Africa conference on the diamond trade (30 June), Nepal's trade potential (29 June), the agenda for trade in the Asia-Pacific (29 June), emissions-free fuel-cell buses in Beijing (20 June), and CNN's Femi Oke returns to Liberia, inspired by the UNDP's work (16 June).

The section entitled 'UNDP around the world' had stories from Afghanistan ('Helping legislators engage with their local communities') and Cambodia ('Learning to live with HIV'). Four of the five news stories came from the UNDP newsroom, presenting R and A-matrix news to an educated readership who may be presumed to be journalists, the UN community, government officials, NGO workers, researchers and students. Only the Chinese story was not from the UNDP newsroom, but from the UNDP in China.

The UNDP in China website was available in English and Chinese. Both versions had standard modern images with the regulation UNDP masthead banner consisting of an inflated segment of the UN emblem. The English version had a directory that was divided into 'most recent speeches and "most recent media advisories"'. The links to MDGs (Millennium Development Goals) in various provinces led to pages that depicted individuation at the level of the A-matrix institution, with little transduction being demonstrated. There were links to UNDP headquarters and the UNDP in other countries. Interestingly, from the point of view of being 'storied', there were no direct links from the UNDP headquarters site to its regional offices for Asia, such as that in Thailand at the UNDP Regional Centre in Bangkok. The Regional Centre in Bangkok (July 2006) site explained that the Asia-Pacific region had two regional centres (Colombo and Bangkok) and one sub-regional centre (Suva). Rather, there were direct links to A-matrix offices grouped under 'regions'. This may reflect a desire of the UNDP to project itself as being composed of A-matrix members. The UNDP Regional Centre in Bangkok (July 2006) site also had the Apollonian blue laurel logo banner, offering no regional images. It had links to other regional and sub-regional centres. The UNDP Regional Centre in Colombo (July 2006) site had local scenes on the masthead banner. The updated UNDP Regional Centre in Colombo (13 September 2007) site had a map of the region.

The UNDP (July 2006) Thailand page was replete with Thai iconography in celebration of the King's 60-year reign. There were links to the P-matrix and R-matrix UNDP sites. The UNDP in Sri Lanka (July 2006) site incorporated a considerable number of local scenic and cultural visuals under the standard Apollonian UNDP masthead. The site had links with stories about the UNDP in other countries. The Kingdom of Cambodia (July 2006) UNDP website was stamped with signifiers of Western modernity on its front page but drew in I-matrix views in 'A view from the inside' that were contrasted with 'A view from the outside'. The insiders' views included photographs of individuals, with names, ages, occupations, where from, where living now, best day, worst day, hopes and dreams and message to the world. While these views and facts are presented in 100 words or less, there is at least an attempt at creating a transduction footpath (rather than avenue) between ordinary people and the UNDP web network.

The UNDP appeared to be following the conventional wisdom of consolidating corporate image and values through an integrated architecture for its websites. This is very much a function of individuation of the UN at the larger or P-matrix level and the facilitating of a P-matrix character, presence and presentation of regional information. The putative target audience consists of members of urban society across the world, journalists, the UN community, policy-makers, NGO workers, researchers and students. There is little concession, and then only at national level (e.g. in Cambodia), to the use of the internet for a more participatory form of governance, which may supplement rather than replace the present public informational style. One possibility for generating participation is to develop moderated weblog or discussion groups on various policy areas that ordinary people may use to express their views. An example of this may be seen on the website of the *Nation* newspaper in Bangkok. Another strategy would be to humanize the United Nations by allowing UN officials to have their own webpages, now easily constructed and hosted on various web venues such as Google and MySpace, to be linked to their names within the organizational setting. The UNDP would be better able to benefit from the multi-mediacy and its immediacy, in balancing the forces of individuation and increasing stakeholder participation, if it considered options such as these.

This chapter has emphasized the universality of hybridity, and favoured the use of the notion of transactional venues rather than space in describing the web. It has drawn on sociographies and iconographies to discuss web architecture in terms of individuation and transduction. The use of UNDP websites as an example has shown how different iconographies are used to address the individuation needs of the organization and individual, and that the use of the lens of sociography reveals the degree of 'grassrootedness' of an organization's web architecture.

References

Barker, C. (2004) *The Sage Dictionary of Cultural Studies*. London: Sage.

Bolin, G. (2006) Electronic Geographies, in J. Falkheimer and A. Jansson (eds) *Geographies of Communication: The Spatial Turn in Media Studies*. Göteborg: Nordicom, pp. 67–86.

Castells, M. (2005) Grassrooting the Space of Flows, in A. Abbas and J. Erni (eds) *Internationalizing Cultural Studies: An Anthology*. Malden: Blackwell, pp. 627–36.

Chitty, G. (2005) Public Postures, Private Positions: Baila and Sydney Sri Lankans. Unpublished thesis. Macquarie University, Australia.

Chitty, N. (1994a) Communicating World Order, *Journal of International Communication*, 1 (2): 100–19.

—— (1994b) *Framing South Asian Cooperation: An Examination of Regional Views on South Asian Cooperation*. New Delhi: South Asian Publishers.

—— (2000) A Matrix Model for Framing Newsmedia Reality, in A. Malek and A. Kavoori (eds) *The Global Dynamics of News*. Stanford, CA: Ablex, pp. 13–30.

—— (2002) Mapping Know-ware Land, in N. Chitty (ed.) *Mapping Globalization: International Media and a Crisis of Identity*. Penang: Southbound, pp. 1–13.

—— (2004) Configuring the Future: Framing International Communication within World Politics in the 21st Century, *Journal of International Communication*, 10(2): 42–66.

—— (2005) Introduction, *Journal of International Communication*, 11(2): 9–13.

Corey, K. (1983) An Introduction to the Transactional City, in J. Gottmann (ed.) *The Coming of the Transactional City*. College Park: University of Maryland Institute of Urban Studies, pp. xi–xvii.

Deleuze, G. and Guattari, F. (2004) *A Thousand Plateaus*. London: Continuum.

Doel, M. (2000) Unglunking Geography: Spatial Science after Dr. Seuss and Gilles de Leuze, in M. Krang and N. Thrift (eds) *Thinking Space*. London: Routledge.

Ek, R. (2006) Media Studies, Geographical Imaginations and Relational Space, in J. Falkheimer and A. Jansson (eds) *Geographies of Communication: The Spatial Turn in Media Studies*. Göteborg: Nordicom, pp. 45–66.

Hall, E. (1977) *Beyond Culture*. New Jersey: Anchor Books.

Hansen, M. (2001) Internal Resonance, or Three Steps toward a Non-viral Becoming, *Culture Machine*, 3. Available online at http://culturemachine.tees.ac.uk/Cmach/Backissues/j003/Articles/hansen.htm (accessed 8 May 2007).

Jansson, A. (2006) Textural Analysis: Materializing Media Space, in J. Falkheimer and A. Jansson (eds) *Geographies of Communication: The Spatial Turn in Media Studies*. Göteborg: Nordicom, pp. 87–106.

Kraidy, M. (2003) Glocalization as an International Communication Framework, *Journal of International Communication*, 9(2): 29–49.

—— (2005) *Hybridity or the Cultural Logic of Globalization*. Philadelphia, PA: Temple University Press.

Lasswell, H. (1965a) *World Politics and Personal Insecurity*. New York: Free Press.

—— (1965b) *World Revolutionary Elites*. Cambridge, MA: MIT Press.

Lefebvre, H. (1991) *The Production of Space*. Oxford: Blackwell.

Lewis, C.S. (1950) *The Lion, the Witch and the Wardrobe*. London: Geoffrey Bles.

Lie, R. (2002) Spaces of International Communication. Barcelona: IAMCR annual conference, pp. 1–44.

Lipschutz, R. (2001) Because People Matter: Studying Global Political Economy, *International Studies Perspectives*, 2(4): 321–39.

Massey, D. (2005) *For Space*. Cambridge: Polity.

Mead, G. (1934) *Mind, Self and Society*. Chicago, IL: University of Chicago Press.

The Nation. The Nation weblog. Available: www.nationmultimedia.com/webblog/ (accessed 14 July 2006).

Nietzsche, F. (1999) *The Birth of Tragedy and Other Writings*, ed. R. Geuss and R. Speirs, trans. R. Speirs. Cambridge: Cambridge University Press.

Perlas, N. and Strawe, C. (n.d.) Importance of Social-Threefolding in the Age of the Empire Matrix. GlobeNet3. Available: http://www.globenet3.org/Features/Feature_Empire_Matrix.shtml (accessed 7 July 2006).

Pettman, R. (2000) *Commonsense Constructivism or the Making of World Affairs*. New York: M.E. Sharpe.

Robertson, R. (1994) Globalization or Glocalization?, *Journal of International Communication*, 1(1): 33–52.

Simondon, G. (1989) *Du Mode d'existence des Objets Techniques*. Paris: Aubier.

—— (1995) *L'individu et sa Genèse Physico-biologique*. Grenoble: Jerome Millon.

Sundén, Jenny (2006) Digital Geographies: From Storyspace to Storied Places, in J. Falkheimer and A. Jansson (eds) *Geographies of Communication: The Spatial Turn in Media Studies*. Göteborg: Nordicom, pp. 279–96.

Thrift, N. (2004) Intensity of Feeling: Towards a Spatial Politics of Affect, *Human Geography*, 86(1): 57–78.

UN (United Nations). Available: www.un.org (accessed 7 July 2006).

UNCG (2002) Report of the United Nations Communications Group at Its First Annual Session, Rome, 27–8 June 2002. Available: ceb.unsystem.org/hlcp/documents/UNCG-reports-misc/UNCG-final-report-2002.pdf (accessed 31 January 2006).

UNDP (United Nations Development Programme). Available: www.undp.org (accessed 7 July 2006).

UNDP, Kingdom of Cambodia. Available: www.un.org.kh/undp (accessed 7 July 2006).

UNDP, Newsroom. Available: http://content.undp.org/go/newsroom (accessed 7 July 2006).

UNDP, UNDP in China. Available: www.undp.org.cn/ (accessed 7 July 2006).

UNDP, UNDP Regional Centre in Bangkok. Available: http://regionalcentrebangkok.undp.or.th/ (accessed 7 July 2006).

UNDP, UNDP in Sri Lanka. Available: www.undp.lk/ (accessed 7 July 2006).

UNDP. Who Are We and What Do We Do? A World of Development Experience. Available: www.undp.org/about/ (accessed 13 July 2006).

Chapter 5

Media and communication studies going global[1,2]

Jan Ekecrantz

How is media research to be conducted in a globalized world? Are new paradigms and methodologies needed when the nation state is no longer an unproblematic measure of everything, or a presupposed conceptual frame, in a world where global interdependencies and transborder exchanges are supposedly more significant than structures and processes contained within national borders? The geopolitical and geo-cultural consequences of the collapse of the Soviet Union in conjunction with the ICT revolution have changed the terms of everything 'international' and raised academic concerns about 'space' in general. Not only media systems, but also political and economic systems generally, are in flux in the new millennium.

There is an often-noted new instability in the world after the fall of the Berlin Wall, the crackdown in Beijing in 1989 and, not least, after 9/11 in 2001. Media studies shares with sociology and political science difficulties in coming to grips with the realities of a transnationalized and transforming world. One explanation is a certain, lingering 'methodological nationalism' (Beck, 2002), implying that the nation state still provides the presupposed and mostly implicit conceptual frame, even when the focus is on phenomena beyond the nation state. Considerable thinking is called for and much is also going on, not least in the field of globalization studies, with its notorious problematization of all kinds of borders, including disciplinary ones. For many decades, media and communication studies have contributed substantially to our general knowledge of international conditions and processes. There may be a problem with the older disciplines, from which communication research originated, in that they have not incorporated this body of knowledge into their own thinking, modern media and modern media studies now often being a white spot (in sociology, political science, literary theory, etc.). This may also explain what seems to be a diminishing inflow into media studies from its 'founding' disciplines. It should be remembered that a series of original, path-breaking thinkers in our field came from outside media and communication studies: Max Horkheimer, Theodor Adorno, Jürgen Habermas, Raymond Williams and many others. On the other side of the North Atlantic, we find many other scholars coming from the 'outside' and producing modern classics in our field – from Robert Park and Paul Lazarsfeld to Herbert Schiller.[3]

It seems to be the case that media and communication studies, now a discipline in its own right, has lost touch with these other disciplines, which, in turn, have now largely eliminated media from their research agendas and curricula. As a consequence, they often regard media as epiphenomena, or neglect them altogether.[4]

This is the classical problem of an increasing division of intellectual labour at a time when integrated and truly interdisciplinary approaches and transnational theorizing are needed more than ever, owing to the increasing complexity of and interdependencies in a globalized world. Media studies (and its forerunners) originated as a cross- or interdisciplinary undertaking. Now it is, in most places, a discipline in its own right with regard to academic institutionalization. With this come academic prestige, professorships and research funding. But there are also problems and costs associated with being a specialized discipline.

In the field of media and communications, an increased division of intellectual labour runs counter to developments in the late-modern world, where the 'system of the media is losing its specificity and becoming an integral part of the economic, cultural and political system' (Martín-Barbero, 1993: 215). This is just one dimension of globalization that impacts on national systems. Globalization means increased complexity (change and heterogeneity) and this is the new raison d'être for cross-disciplinarity. Media studies has always been international, long before 'globalization' was coined in the early 1990s by Roland Robertson (1992), sociologist of religion. There have been a number of approaches in internationally oriented media and communication studies, from international news and propaganda to *Four Theories of the Press* (Siebert *et al.*, 1956), and media and development (Lerner, 1958; Lerner and Schramm, 1967; Pye, 1963). Later came the cultural imperialism critique (Schiller, 1969, 1976) and the NWICO process (see Carlsson, 2005), then media globalization and new media studies. Much of this is covered by international communication (Thussu, 2006), a field that has bordered on and sometimes been interfolded with international politics, international sociology, translocal anthropology and other fields. Media studies has also taken on board, in innovative ways, theory complexes such as world system theory (McPhail, 2006), modernity theory (Thompson, 1995), media and migration (Appadurai, 1996), the network society (Castells, 1996), diaspora studies (e.g. Tsagarousianou, 2004), and research on the new (informatized) wars (Kaldor, 1999). Most recently, studies of new global social movements and media have proved to be fertile ground for cross-breeding between several fields, as in research on civil society media (e.g. Atton, 2002; Couldry and Curran, 2003).

I will continue on this track and argue for: (1) more dialogue with 'non-Western' theory and research perspectives, (2) more basic cross-disciplinarity, and (3) a stronger focus on global inequalities and social transformation. These research concerns are interrelated and mutually reinforcing. Globalization forces us not only to focus more on *transnational* phenomena in general, but also to highlight *social change and difference*, which are almost unprecedented in pace and scope and directly and indirectly caused by globalization processes. Stability and equality do not characterize contemporary societies. Further, as increasingly central institutions around the world, the media are deeply ingrained in most societal processes. This calls for broad and integrated approaches in media studies, for cross-disciplinarity in a very basic sense: as theorizing and empirical research *across both disciplinary and socio-cultural borders*. Such *transnational theory-building* would seem necessary to take care of some of the new complexities in the contemporary world and its *media-driven modernities*. What they have in common are the facts of change and difference, and the centrality of the media as institutions. Theorizing media and social change in a globalized world implies questioning some received categories and distinctions based on assumptions that no longer hold.

These arguments will be developed in the following. Far from proposing a new theory of media and globalization, I will try to show how media studies can and needs to be opened up to experiences and realities outside the centre of the world system. I will first wind back half a century, when media and social development were frequently on the agenda of development research, then reflect on the contemporary scene, which is largely characterized by global divides and their concomitant media phenomena. Following this will be a brief section on the meanings of 'de-Westernization' and the decreased relevance of some firmly rooted disciplinary distinctions. This theme will then be concretized using Russian, Brazilian and Chinese examples.

Media and the development of underdevelopment

A brief history of internationally oriented studies of media and social change could start with the Schramm, Lerner and Pye era in mass communication research. In the 1950s and 1960s there was a strong reliance on the purportedly universal correlation between growth in media consumption and political democratization and social development in general.[5] It was assumed, by Daniel Lerner and others, that the media created a psychic mobility among people living in the countryside in traditional (i.e. pre-modern) societies, in turn resulting in geographic and then social mobility, owing to people's longing for a modern life and salaried employment in the cities. The media served as 'mobility multipliers', thus contributing to the 'passing of traditional society', to refer to the title of Lerner's famous book.[6] This was before the decolonization of several countries in Africa and the democratization of Latin American countries, processes that had nothing to do with the rise of public media, at least not in the former colonies. This was also before the cultural imperialism thesis, associated above all with Herbert Schiller, who stated that the content of media worldwide was strongly dominated by imperial, that is US military, economic, political and ideological, interests (Schiller, 1969, 1976). And the world had not yet seen the 'barrios', 'favelas' and 'banlieus' surrounding the megacities of Asia, Africa and South America, which housed millions of unemployed and destitute. This is where Lerner's mobile hordes ended up, once they got moving – for reasons other than media consumption.

At the time, the given fact was that the statistical correlation between the number of radio and TV receivers per capita, on the one hand, and participation in elections and a number of welfare indicators, on the other, tended to be quite strong (around +0.40 across all countries). It should also be underlined that an important component of the theoretical setup was developmentalism, a belief in unilinear development.[7] Socio-economic differences between countries were translated into a time scale – there were underdeveloped, developing and developed countries – assuming a considerable time lag separating the former from the latter.[8] Difference related to dominance and exploitation in the contemporary world was not yet on the media research agenda, but was to be focused on by dependency theory in the 1970s.

The correlation was mostly a spurious one. If one bothered to look at partial correlations, one could easily see that it did not hold for most of the countries in the world – not for the 'underdeveloped' or the most 'developed'. In the poorest and richest countries, respectively, more media meant more market, but not more democracy – media development being above all a consequence and indicator of economic growth.

For the ten richest countries, there was even a strong negative correlation between the number of TV sets and political participation. There were also some significant clusters. One group of countries stood out as relatively media-saturated, but this had no relationship whatsoever to socio-economic or political development. More media did not mean that these countries were better off in other respects. To this group belonged most of the Latin American countries, many of them then with authoritarian military regimes and a heavy influx of commercial US television, the developmental potential of which was questioned early on by Latin American intellectuals.[9]

The manifold lessons from these statistical exercises are still valid, and yet these studies largely overlooked:

1 socio-economic differences within countries (Sklair, 1995/7);
2 global power relationships – centre–periphery relations;
3 the relation between the two – Norths and Souths reproducing themselves on national and local levels, thus producing a globalization of poverty (Nederveen Pieterse, 2004a, 2004b);
4 the fact that authoritarianism is perfectly compatible with free market commercialism. This creates problems for attempts at homogenizing categorizations of national media systems (cf. post-Soviet Russia and China, below);
5 the fact that media functions cannot be universally ascertained. In particular, socio-economic level and position in the world system determine uses and political effects of the media system on social, cultural and political life and processes.

A generation later, the difficulties in finding easily applicable classificatory principles for the purposes of comparative media research are reflected in attempts to sort countries in terms of their media systems, one reason being that these systems are reflections of complex and differentiated socio-economic orders. Curran and Park, in their groundbreaking *De-Westernizing Media Studies* (2000), introduced the following two major dimensions as a way of sorting the media systems in today's world: *democratic* vs. *authoritarian* and *neo-liberal* vs. *regulated*. However, these authors had to include an extra, fifth category for '*transitional or mixed societies*', including China, Eastern Europe, Russia, South America and the Middle East. This 'rest', particularly interesting from the point of view of theorizing media and social change, comprises the most dynamic regions, the new media modernities. It is obvious that we need to introduce other dimensions as well. It is even reasonable to ask whether there exist any *non*-transitional or *non*-mixed societies. At least it seems as if most countries are moving along both these dimensions – and others.

I will return to this comparative model, but here we can use it to speculate about the directions in which these countries might be moving – given the axes of the model. In which of the four possible directions are China, Russia and the rest of the 'transitional and mixed' nations moving? And how far have they advanced in the six, seven years since the publication of this book? One thing we know for sure is that the direction of change, given the alternatives defined by this model, depends greatly on interdependent economic and political developments globally *and* nationally. We also know that things move fast in the globalized world and that that in itself creates social and political tensions that have to be taken into consideration when theorizing media and social change.

Postmodern poverty

Fifty years after the 'media and development' paradigm (and the Bandung conference) and 25 years after the cultural imperialism critique, the geopolitical structure of the First, Second and Third Worlds and one of the two super states has evaporated with the Cold War. Some 50 new countries have seen the light of day and television and the internet have turned into dominant media worldwide. Internet access is restricted, but nevertheless a significant factor, in Third World countries. Television, however, has a strong presence even in poor countries (I will reflect on this fact below). During the same period, socio-economic cleavages within as well as between countries have increased. This also runs parallel to the introduction of parliamentary democracy in Africa, Latin America and most recently in the post-Soviet world. This 'misfit' between economy and politics needs to be taken into account in any analysis of national or local media systems and cultures.[10]

The World Bank's development reports show how the Gini index[11] has developed in a select number of countries over the past 50 years. These are within-country measures, and there is a general long-term increase in economic inequality. Three groups of countries emerge from these statistics:

1 *extreme inequality*: many Latin American countries (the situation in the sub-Saharan region is even worse according to other data); Gini exceeds 0.50;
2 *strong and steadily increasing inequality*: USA, UK, China, Russia, India; Gini within the 0.35–0.40 range;
3 *moderate inequality* (as everything is relative): continental and northern Europe; Gini below 0.35.

This is about differences *between* countries with respect to differences *within* countries. How does this 'correlate' with media systems and media cultures? The *first* group, with extreme inequality, is with few exceptions composed of democratic, capitalistic countries with colonial and authoritarian pasts (including apartheid) under military regimes. The media systems are advanced and strictly commercial, especially when it comes to broadcast media (e.g. the Globo and Televisa media empires).

The *second* group is a mixed bag of old and new capitalistic economies, including some old empires, some of the largest parliamentary democracies, but also China.[12] The media systems vary considerably, but things in common include strong central (federal) governments and big, more or less globalized, media corporations with large nationwide audiences.

The *third* group includes a number of European countries (EU members or not), many of them, especially in the north, (post-)welfare societies with public service media as one component of the media structure. Were we to use the above categories, these European systems would be deemed 'democratic and regulated' (Curran and Park, 2000).[13]

Inequalities based on economic factors, gender, ethnicity, etc., and class cleavages are the causes of many other conditions, such as crime, violence, corruption, trafficking and HIV/AIDS (Marmot, 2005; Wilkinson, 2006). If equality is taken to be an aspect of democracy (for instance as equality of life chances), one has to conclude that economic growth and marketization have little, if anything, to do with democratization. This goes against the grain of liberal political science, but, nevertheless, the empirical foundations for this conclusion are overwhelming.

In a study of 14 countries, picked to represent the three groups above, I plotted economic equality (global ranking based on Gini values) against press freedom (global ranking based on interviews and official data) and then dichotomized these variables (high and low positions in the world ranking). The overall correlation is almost non-existent, meaning that the degree of equality is not linked to the level of press freedom. For instance, in Egypt there are restrictions on press freedom, but the country has relatively high equality. In South Africa, as in Brazil, the situation is the opposite: enormous cleavages and booming, non-censored commercial media. This is the static picture. In order to capture the dynamics of media and economic growth, I plotted economic growth between 1990 and 2004 (change in global ranking) against press freedom.

The important finding here is that the most expansive new capitalist economies have the poorest record when it comes to press freedoms, parliamentary democracies or not, but with old or neo-authoritarian traits. We are beginning to discern a pattern in which a number of fast-moving capitalist economies (Russia and China being two of them) are also moving in the direction of neo-liberalism *and* neo-authoritarianism. This is happening not with the help of old-fashioned, state-driven propaganda machineries, but in media environments seemingly based more on the pleasure principle, which is supportive of both nationalism and patriotism, than on the reality principle, to put it in Freudian terms (Stallybrass, 1996). This is not to say that reception is predictable, just that hundreds of millions of people are continuously exposed to the production of consensus from above.

More sophisticated indicators and statistical analyses could probably take us a little further along this path of enquiry, but in order to better understand media in a globalized world we have to think through some concepts in media and communication studies, developed mostly within the European/Anglo-American orbit. What does it mean, for a start, to move beyond the national confines?

De-Westernizing as de-disciplining

With the globalization rhetoric that came to the fore in the 1990s, a number of concepts have become problematic and there are many suggestions as to how to get 'beyond' or 'deconstruct' this and that. What follows is my own contribution to this particular genre. First, the urge for 'internationalization', within academia and elsewhere, leads us to a number of related, but more far-reaching, concepts:

Internationalizing (for instance, media studies), in a strict sense, refers to relations between or comparisons across nations or nation states. In international politics, a political science sub-discipline, this is often unproblematic. It is about interstate relations and activities, or nation-based comparisons, period. To the extent that the nation as such is problematized, however, 'international' dissolves into something 'foreign' or, for that matter, 'global'.[14] In a much broader sense, as pointed out in the introduction, it may include both comparative approaches and global and transnational processes (Thussu, 2006).

Transnationalizing reflects, on the one hand, the conceptual change from 'multinational' (no centre) to 'transnational' corporations (operating from core centres in the world economy). On the other, it is an expression of an ambition to move beyond methodological nationalism and 'transnationalize' theory, which I interpret as a way out of locally produced universalizations (wherever they are produced). A third meaning would be a focus on cross-border or translocal processes, mostly reflecting the 'de-territorialization' of communication practices.

De-Westernizing (to pick up on Curran and Park's book title) resounds with an ambition to make room in media studies for perspectives in the East and South. It also implies that we, at the end of the day, give up our Western canons in favour of African, Asian and Latin American ones. Before that, it would be a great step forward to have these different canons productively confront each other in truly globalized media studies. This agenda of caveats (or 'de-'catchwords) for the global age is far from exhaustive. I have already pinpointed methodological nationalism, which would entail a *denationalizing* of media studies, a giving up of concepts firmly rooted in the figure of thought (or mental container) of the nation state and its inherited institutions and national myths. A *de-colonizing* of media and communication studies, originating in core imperial and colonial nation states, takes a great deal of imagination, a 'planetary' perspective (Dussel, 1998) or 'thinking from the border', from outside European and north American modernities (Mignolo, 2000).

All this adds up to a *de-disciplining* of media and communication studies. I started out with a call for more dialogue with 'non-Western' theory and research perspectives, more cross-disciplinarity, and a return to historical, disciplinary roots, reinserting media in the social and the cultural. From this follows, among other things, a questioning of basic categories and a deconstruction of disciplinary dichotomies such as *Politics/Culture*,[15] *Symbolic/Material, Public/Private, Real/Unreal, Fact/Fiction, Time/Space*,[16] *Production/Consumption, Word/Image, Text/Reader, Self/Other, We/Them*.[17]

This is not the place to discuss these further, beyond the selective footnote explications. Instead, we shall see how the criticism applies to the situation in some concrete societies. Even cursory studies of some 'non-Western' worlds confirm that globalized media studies would benefit considerably from a further dissolution of these binary opposites or, as the case may be, from further inquiries into the inherent dialectics that come into play in actually existing societies. The deconstruction of some such dichotomies does not constitute philosophical word play, but something that is already affected by the media in their *mediation*, in its broadest sense, not least between institutions.

Difference and change in media modernities

In recent years I have studied media developments and media cultures in 'post-authoritarian', 'neo-authoritarian' systems, 'new democracies', and whatever other labels have been used (the 'rest' category). These societies, for instance Brazil, China and Russia, have served as laboratories for natural experiments in media and social change (Ekecrantz *et al.*, 2003). They have many things in common, distinguishing them from most other countries: size, rapid immersion into the world capitalist system (ratified by WTO or Nafta membership),[18] economic growth, democratic deficits by the exclusion of large groups in terms of class, gender and ethnicity from public spheres, economic and social cleavages, and political, cultural and regional divisions, thus problematizing the notion of the nation as a homogeneous and meaningful unit. Cleavages exist not only between countries in the North and South, respectively, but very much within nation states, the poor and the rich often within arm's length.[19]

What they also have in common is that they are *media modernities*, short for media-driven modernities. How do media mediate between the social classes and between other groupings, producing a mediated visibility with repercussions for social relations and struggles? National, urban bourgeoisies are certainly visible in news, entertainment and advertising, and this applies to Brazil, Russia and China (cf. Lerner's model).[20]

The media modernities of these huge polities are thus based on differentiations that are political, social, regional and temporal, but also ideological and cultural. All of these are heightened by the rapid transformations. The different Chinas, for example (Zhao, 2003), are bound to produce diverging discourses, impossible to harmonize in a unified hegemonic order, even when history is sometimes effectively suppressed – or when foreign news and the internet are censored (Lagerkvist, 2006).[21]

In post-Soviet Russia, the relationship between politics and economy, with media as mediator, defies most known models. The first years of the 1990s were characterized by independent media that operated as a 'fourth power' (1991–5). Then entered a highly politicized media system that operated in a society turned into a spectacle (1996–2000). This fragmented 'media-political system'[22] operates in a fully fledged commercial environment. However, the fluidity of the 'Russian' media system[23] has its spatial counterparts. In 87 out of 89 regions in Russia, one finds seven different 'media models'.[24] This raises doubts as to whether there exists a 'Russian' or, for that matter, a 'Brazilian' or 'Chinese' media system.

Before Putin's presidency (2000–8), Brian McNair saw the implications of the Russian system in terms of a new and unique form of capitalism that seriously threatened the democratic transition: 'In this respect Russia, for all its robber-baron primitivism, may turn out to be a pioneer of the media-driven capitalism of the twenty-first century, in which the controllers of information in all its commodity forms – journalism, entertainment, computer software, data services – are established as the key sub-sector of the capitalist owning class as a whole' (McNair, 2000: 89). What could now best be described as media-driven state capitalism, a system yielding both financial and political profits, defies most known media models. Outside academia, however, it has been subjected to both intellectual criticism and literary satire.[25] This appeals not least to the younger generations, who are turning away from television. These Russian generations today seem totally alienated from official politics, as enacted on national TV channels, today directly or indirectly controlled by the Kremlin.[26] They tend to 'adapt to any conditions and turn to private lives as spheres of self-realization while almost completely ignoring the virtual community of the nation state' (Zassoursky, 2004). To the extent that this is a valid description of today's Russian youth, it has gone a long way since the attempted coup in August 1991, when various groups of young people were active on the barricades, embodying a politics of pleasure which challenged the dominant meaning of politics (Pilkington, 1994: 303ff.), or since young protesters spread red paint on the White House in Moscow as a demonstration against the first war in Chechnya.

One may not agree with all of these analyses, but they have served here to concretize my thesis that some prevailing disciplinary dichotomies (politics/economy/culture) – and Western institutional models – do not hold. A lack of institutional stability and national homogeneity undermines methodological nationalism. Political communication forms in northern and southern mainland China, closer to Westernized Hong Kong, are almost as varied as popular cultural forms in different parts of Brazil, from Afro-Brazilian capoeira in the north-east to favela hip hop in Rio, to gaucho cowboy culture in the south.

The spatial structures of modernity have a temporal side. The timing and speed of entry into the world capitalist system and the rate at which a society has been transformed in the recent past ('keeping pace with time' in today's official Chinese rhetoric) seem to be significant factors for at least two reasons. First, there exists a collective experience of change in society and in everyday life for a large portion of the population. Zhen describes how this is related to 'a larger cultural anxiety about temporality … the rapid transition from socialism to a market economy … different temporalities – old and new, socialist and capitalist, global and local – have collided … the perils of speed have made anxiety a central feature of public discourse' (Zhen, 2001: 132). This quote certainly apostrophizes the collapse of some received dichotomies as far as rapidly transforming societies are concerned.

Conclusion

The emerging global system of social classes and power structures is the most significant trait pertaining to 'globality', which means that there are winners and losers and all kinds of widening gaps and divisions. The rise to power of global elites is mirrored at the other end of the socio-economic scale in the masses of forced national and international migrants and hundreds of millions of unemployed owing to economic globalization – read capitalist expansion – in new world regions led by globalized elites with their feet in transnational corporations and neo-liberal governments.[27] Comparative cross-disciplinary case studies can take us a long way if we are interested in getting to know what all this means in actually existing media modernities. Let me conclude by returning to the introductory arguments for basic cross-disciplinarity in media studies and pointing to some such efforts under way.

A new *macro-sociology of media* would focus on the intersection of global and national class systems and the ways in which they shape the media, media cultures and mediated conflicts. Other cross-disciplinary encounters have already made an imprint in global media studies. *Anthropology*, for instance, is a relative newcomer in media studies, but it could contribute substantially to our understanding of translocality and 'transmodernity', based on a de-territorialized notion of culture that privileges *routes* instead of *roots* (Clifford, 1997). *Comparative literature* could show us experiences of media modernities outside the North Atlantic orbit. Latin America and Asia, for instance, provide us with a wealth of literary reflections on what it means to live in media-saturated urban environments (if read in that way) far away from the core areas of the moderrn world system – as did many of the classical modernist authors in Europe.[28]

Comparative media history is needed to unravel the deep historical structures of today's global communications, such as the circuits of commerce that produced Western and other modernities in the first place ('globalization' being the cause, not the consequence, of modernity – in this perspective). I have already mentioned the field of *new global social movements*.

Globalizing media and communication studies thus implies more than an aggrandizement of the research object and more than adding countries to the bag of comparisons. For one thing, it is about the inclusion of other kinds of media users, cultural producers and political animals than those typified or implicated in much research – those who happen to live in rich countries, who are targeted as consumers or even citizens with entertainment or information, while sitting comfortably in their homes after work. This was the type codified within the paradigm of affluence out of which mass communication research sprang in the post-war period.[29] As we all know, however, there are masses of non-rich people 'out there' (also in the rich parts of the world) and they are not consumers, do not think of themselves as citizens of a polity and do not come home after work, because they have no work and hence no leisure time and no place to spend it anyway. But they also have in common that they inhabit, and are dependent on what goes on in, heavily media-saturated societies. This is a historically new equation or paradox, calling for new alliances in media studies, both between and beyond disciplines and their national habitats.

Notes

1 Originally published in Ulla Carlsson and Knut Helland (eds) *Media Structures and Practices: As Time Goes by . . . Jubilee Issue of Nordicom Review 2007*. Nordicom, Göteborg University, pp. 169–81.

2 Draws on three papers presented, respectively, at the IAMCR conference in Cairo, 24–8 July 2006, the conference 'Internationalizing Media Studies: Imperatives and Impediments', University of Westminster, London, 15–16 September 2006, and the Russia in Flux Research Programme Seminar, Academy of Finland, Helsinki, 27 October 2006.

3 Zelizer (2004) has reviewed a broad range of contributions to journalism studies from many different disciplines. A similar treatment of media studies, as a broader field, would require a book series.
4 See, for instance, Downing's (1996) criticism of political science for its neglect of media and communication aspects, also when it is concerned with political influence.
5 See, for example, Lerner (1958), Pye (1963) and Lerner and Schramm (1967).
6 See also Thompson's retrospective discussion and contextualization of Lerner's book 40 years after the publication of *The Passing* (Thompson, 1995: 188–97).
7 See McPhail (2006) for brief overviews of models at the time, including the economic growth model. Rostow's theory of stages is now, after 1989, being reintroduced in a new shape in much 'transition' research. Updates of the debate on developmentalism are found in Hemer and Tufte (2005).
8 This was a form of 'denial of coevalness': people in 'backward' parts of the world are not really our contemporaries (Fabian, 1983).
9 For data on the phenomenal, continued growth of media around the world, Latin America included, between the 1970s and the late 1990s, see Carlsson (2005: 209).
10 In the following, I have used secondary data and done some simple calculations myself. The IAMCR paper 'Cairo 2006' gives a more complete picture.
11 Roughly speaking, the Gini index measures the ratio between the income of the richest and that of the poorest. It ranges from 1 (maximum inequality: one person has all the income) to 0 (no one has more than any other).
12 According to other estimates, China belongs in the first group.
13 Or 'democratic corporatist/polarized pluralist', to use the typology suggested by Hallin and Mancini (2004).
14 In Swedish academia, an 'international publication' may be a text (1) in an 'international' journal (in one of the so-called world languages), or a text either (2) published in English, anywhere, for instance by Nordicom in Gothenburg, or (3) published abroad, in any language.
15 See Brooksbank Jones (2000) on 'the progressive "enculturing" of politics in response to deepening social divisions'; 'the political significance of cultural practices in extra-institutional politics', and 'the imbrication of culture and politics (as analytic categories and as practices)'. See also Sassen (2006) on how cultural events become political, e.g. street activities, and about the increasing importance of the non-formal forms and places of politics: real political processes that cannot be contained within the formal political system. I have tried to systematize this thematic in Ekecrantz (2006).
16 See Bakhtin (1934/5) on the study of chronotopes (timespaces) as determining, together, the capacities of fictional genres; Wallerstein (1997) shows how the temporal and the spatial are interlinked in sociological and historical forms of knowledge.
17 There is a risk that the ubiquitous criticism of this figure of thought just reproduces orientalism by producing a similarly universalist (meta)discourse. Sardar voices a concern over representations of the 'Other' in history, anthropology and politics: 'Postmodernism's obsession with representation of the Other in fiction is designed to project this representation back as reality and hence shape and reshape the Other according to its own desires' (Sardar, 1998: 176). We/them is an often taken-for-granted distinction, sometimes downplaying similarities and mystifying difference (not least when the 'East–West' dyad is called forth).
18 In Brazil and China, half of the gigantic populations are younger than 25–27, which means that in China this group amounts to some 650 million people.
19 The richest person in Brazil, the owner of the Globo empire, has his well-guarded mansion on a slope in Rio de Janeiro, with favelas uphill.
20 A Russian reality soap showing the everyday life of the immensely rich in a secluded block on the edge of the Moscow River attracted a huge audience.

21 Chin-Chuan Lee catches this well: 'In China the media have been battling a confluence of ideological currents and moulding a hybrid ideology ridden with conflicting identities, images, and subjectivities. In this sense, the media have been a site of ideological contestation and accommodation, derived from the ambiguities and contradictions between the revolutionary rhetoric of Communism and the practical discourses of marketization' (Lee, 2003: Introduction).
22 Termed the 'media-political complex' by Curran and Park (2000:14).
23 This is based on Zassoursky (2004), but there are other such short-term periodizations.
24 The market model; the transitional to market model; the conflict model; the modernized Soviet model; the paternalistic Soviet model; the authoritarian Soviet model; the depressed model (Koltsova, 2006:166).
25 As in the works of Viktor Pelevin, for instance *Generation P* and the not yet translated *Vampyre*. Among other critical analysts, Irina Petrovskaya and Alexij Pankin should be mentioned.
26 Through state channels or large holdings in companies such as Gazprom, in its turn owner of major media since the ousting of media moguls and oligarchs such as Berezovskij and Guzinski.
27 The transnational capitalist class as conceived of by Leslie Sklair is composed of four groups or fractions: (1) TNC executives and their local affiliates, (2) globalizing state bureaucrats, (3) globalizing politicians and professionals, and (4) consumerist elites (merchants, media) (Sklair, 1995: 299ff.).
28 Like Joseph Conrad and James Joyce, see Donovan (2001).
29 From Paddy Scannell's presentation at the Westminster conference (see note 2). Book forthcoming.

References

Appadurai, Arjun (1996) *Modernity at Large: Cultural Dimensions of Globalization*. Minneapolis: University of Minnesota Press.

Atton, Chris (2002) *Alternative Media*. London: Sage.

Bakhtin, Mikhail (1934–5[1981]) *The Dialogic Imagination*. Austin: University of Texas Press.

Beck, Ulrich (2002) The Cosmopolitan Society and Its Enemies, *Theory, Culture and Society*, special issue on: *Cosmopolis*, 19(1–2): 17–44.

Brooksbank Jones, Anny (2000) Cultural Politics in a Latin American Frame, in A. Brooksbank and Ronaldo Munch (eds) *Cultural Politics in Latin America*. Basingstoke: Macmillan.

Carlsson, Ulla (2005) From NWICO to Global Governance of the Information Society, in Oscar Hemer and Thomas Tufte (eds) *Media and Glocal Change: Rethinking Communication for Development*. Clacso/Nordicom: Buenos Aires/Gothenburg.

Castells, Manuel (1996) *The Information Age: The Rise of the Network Society*. Oxford: Blackwell.

Clifford, James (1997) *Routes: Travel and Translation in the Late Twentieth Century*. Boston, MA: Harvard University Press.

Couldry, Nick and Curran, James (eds) (2003) *Contesting Media Power: Alternative Media in a Networked World*. Lanham, MD: Rowman and Littlefield.

Curran, James and Park, Myung-Jin (eds) (2000) *De-Westernizing Media Studies*. London: Routledge.

Donovan, Stephen (2001) Literary Modernism and the Press, 1870–1922, dissertation, Department of English, Göteborg University.

Downing, John D.H. (1996) *Internationalizing Media Theory: Transition, Power, Culture.* London: Sage.

Dussel, Enrique (1998) Beyond Eurocentrism: The World-System and the Limits of Modernity, in Fredric Jameson and Masao Miyoshi (eds) *The Cultures of Globalization.* Durham, NC, and London: Duke University Press, pp. 3–31.

Ekecrantz, Jan (2006) Espetáculos midiazados e comunicações democráticas: entre a hegemonia global e a ação cívica, in Rousiley Maia and Maria Céres Castro (eds) *Mídia, Esfera Pública e Identidades Coletivas,* Belo Horizonte: Editora UFMG, pp. 93–116.

Ekecrantz, Jan, Maia, Rousiley and Castro, Maria Céres (2003) Media and Modernities: The Cases of Brazil and Russia, in *Stockholm Media Studies I,* Stockholm: JMK.

Fabian, Johannes (1983) *Time and the Other: How Anthropology Makes Its Object.* New York: Columbia University Press.

Hallin, Daniel and Mancini, Paolo (2004) *Comparing Media Systems: Three Models of Media and Politics.* Cambridge: Cambridge University Press.

Hemer, Oscar and Tufte, Thomas (eds) (2005) *Media and Glocal Change: Rethinking Communication for Development.* Clacso/Nordicom: Buenos Aires/Gothenburg.

Kaldor, Mary (1999) *New and Old Wars: Organized Violence in a Global Era,* Cambridge: Polity.

Koltsova, Olessia (2006) *News Media and Power in Russia.* London: Routledge.

Lagerkvist, Johan (2006) *The Internet in China: Unlocking and Containing the Public Sphere.* Lund: Department of East Asian Languages.

Lee, Chin-Chuan (ed.) (2003) *Chinese Media, Global Context.* New York: Routledge/Curzon.

Lerner, Daniel (1958) *The Passing of Traditional Society.* New York: Free Press.

Lerner, Daniel and Schramm, Wilbur (eds) (1967) *Communication and Change in the Developing Countries.* Honolulu: East-West Center.

McNair, Brian (2000) Power, Profit, Corruption, and Lies: The Russian Media in the 1990s, in James Curran and Myung-Jin Park (eds) *De-Westernizing Media Studies.* London: Routledge, pp. 79–94.

McPhail, Thomas (2006) *Global Communication: Theories, Stakeholders, and Trends.* Oxford: Blackwell.

Marmot, M. (2005) *Status Syndrome: How Your Social Standing Directly Affects Your Health.* London: Bloomsbury.

Martín-Barbero, Jésus (1993) *Communication, Culture, Hegemony.* London: Sage.

Mignolo, Walter D. (2000) *Local Histories/Global Designs: Coloniality, Subaltern Knowledges and Border Thinking.* Princeton, NJ: Princeton University Press.

Nederveen Pieterse, Jan (2004a) *Globalization and Culture: Global Mélange.* Oxford: Rowman and Littlefield.

—— (2004b) *Globalization or Empire?* New York: Routledge.

Pilkington, Hilary (1994) *Russia's Youth and Its Culture: A Nation's Constructors and Constructed.* New York: Routledge.

Pye, Lucian (ed.) (1963) *Communications and Political Development.* Princeton, NJ: Princeton University Press.

Robertson, Roland (1992) *Globalization: Social Theory and Global Culture.* London: Sage.

Sardar, Ziauddin (1998) *Postmodernism and the Other: The New Imperialism of Western Culture.* London: Pluto.

Sassen, Saskia (2006) *Territory, Authority, Rights: From Medieval to Global Assemblages.* Princeton, NJ: Princeton University Press.

Schiller, Herbert (1969) *Mass Communication and American Empire.* Boston, MA: Beacon Press.

—— (1976) *Communication and Cultural Domination*. New York: M.E. Sharpe.

Siebert, Fred, Peterson, Theodore and Schramm, Wilbur (1956) *Four Theories of the Press: The Authoritarian, Libertarian, Social Responsibility and Soviet Communist Concepts of what the Press Should Be and Do*. Urbana: University of Illinois Press.

Sklair, Leslie (1995) *Sociology and the Global System*. London: Prentice Hall.

—— (1995/7) Classifying the Global System, in Annabelle Sreberny-Mohammadi, Dwayne Winseck, Jim McKenna and Oliver Boyd-Barrett (eds) *Media in Global Context: A Reader*. London: Arnold, pp. 41–7.

Stallybrass, Julian (1996) *Gargantua: Manufactured Mass Culture*. London: Verso.

Thompson, John (1995) *The Media and Modernity: A Social Theory of the Media*. Cambridge: Polity.

Thussu, Daya Kishan (2006) *International Communication: Continuity and Change*. London: Hodder Education, second edition.

Tsagarousianou, Roza (2004) Rethinking the Concept of Diaspora: Mobility, Connectivity and Communication in a Globalized World, *Westminster Papers in Communication and Culture*, 1(1): 52–66.

Wallerstein, Immanuel (1997) Spacetime as the Basis of Knowledge, http://www.binghamton.edu/fbc/iwsptm.htm.

Wilkinson, R.G. (2006) *The Impact of Inequality: How to Make Sick Societies Healthier*. London: Routledge.

Zassoursky, Ivan (2004) *Media and Power in Post-Soviet Russia*. London: M.E. Sharpe.

Zelizer, Barbie (2004) *Taking Journalism Seriously: News and the Academy*. London: Sage.

Zhao, Yuezhi (2003) 'Enter the World': Neo-liberal Globalization, the Dream for a Strong Nation, and Chinese Press Discourses on the WTO, in C.C. Lee (ed.) *Chinese Media, Global Context*. New York: Routledge/Curzon, pp. 32–56.

Zhen, Zhang (2001) The 'Rice Bowl of Youth' in Fin de Siècle Urban China, in Arjun Appadurai (ed.) *Globalization*. Durham, NC: Duke University Press.

Part II

Broadening the field of media studies

Chapter 6

Globalizing media law and policy

Sandra Braman

Communication networks have long provoked the development of new forms of transnational governance, including both the first international organization (the ITU, to regulate the telegraph, in the 1860s) and the first global organization with regulatory-like powers (ICANN, to manage the internet, in the 1990s). The literature on international and comparative media law and policy is well developed,[1] but the difference between international and global organizations is significant: the first involves geopolitically recognized states, while the second also includes civil society entities such as non-governmental organizations (NGOs) and corporations in decision-making. The effective appearance of non-state actors in law making and implementation marks a dramatic turn in relations among states, societies and legal systems that highlights the need to globalize, as well as internationalize, media law and policy.

The impact of globalization is most visible in the formation of law-making institutions at the global level, but goes far beyond. The modes of policy transfer and coordination through which the legal dimension of globalization is accomplished are referred to as policy convergence (Jordan, 2005); harmonization is the outcome of such processes when they result in conformance of the laws of multiple states with each other. Legal globalization reaches the very foundations of jurisprudence, the principles and arguments upon which law making and interpretation are based (Twining, 2000). As a consequence, the opening of the twenty-first century is considered equivalent in historical importance to the period during which the international system of geopolitically recognized states first formed several hundred years ago (Kirby, 2006). Since differences in jurisprudence both manifest and justify differences in the ways that democracy is theorized and implemented (Edelman, 2005), these developments are of enormous political importance.

Harms argued as early as 1980 that communication policy should always be thought of in global terms, mainstream authors such as Mowlana (1996) called for a turn from international to global communication by the mid-1990s, and by the close of that decade doing so had become so common that it could be referred to as a cliché (Cunningham *et al.*, 1998). However, this insight has not yet widely infiltrated the study of media law and policy beyond the work of those doing research on ICANN (see, notably, Mueller, 1999). Credit must go, therefore, to the few existing exemplars, such as research on the use of public diplomacy to align media policies of transition societies with those of other nations (Price and Thompson, 2002), policy convergence efforts that appear in government commitments to the use of communication in health campaigns (Smith *et al.*, 2004; Taylor, 2004), antitrust law as applied to media and telecommunication oligopolies (Donovan, 2006), and treatment of consumer fraud (Rabkin, 2007).

The relative paucity of analysis is problematic because globalizing media law and policy is of constitutional significance, for all communication issues are of constitutional status (Tribe, 1985). Uncertainty regarding jurisdiction can leave crucial constitutional values to self-regulation (Dommering, 2006). Arguments for shifting the constitutional act to the international level support moving even further away from society-oriented principles (see, for example, Petersmann, 1991). The threat to freedom of expression and related civil liberties is thus of intense concern. Pool (1983) long ago warned that as diverse legal systems dealing with communication converge in response to technological change, it was likely that the most restrictive of available models would come to dominate. Competition, it turns out – rather than freedom of speech or the public interest – is the most important explanatory variable for legal globalization, whether that competition is economic (Howard, 2007; Swank, 2006) or political (Murillo and Martinez-Gallardo, 2007). If Sassen (2003) is correct that we are currently only in the 'incipient' phase of legal globalization, achieving a better understanding of how these processes unfold is critical.

This chapter introduces frameworks being used to analyse legal globalization across the law as they appear in *government* (formal institutions of the law), *governance* (decision-making with structural effect whether it takes place within the public or private sectors, and formally or informally), and *governmentality* (cultural predispositions and practices that enable and sustain governance and government) (Braman, 2006). This allows us to identify corresponding lacunae in the literature on the globalization of media law and policy and to explore the implications of both models and lacunae for theory, research and teaching. International law and policy is now a sub-set of global media law and policy, and comparative research is critical for understanding the processes by which globalization of the law takes place. Because research on international and global organizations, regional integration and multilateral treaties is relatively well represented in the media policy literature, the focus here is on other types of processes by which the law is becoming globalized. Many of these are relatively new, while others simply become more visible when the analytical lens is widened.[2]

The processes of policy convergence

Legal theory historically has been bound tightly to specific states (Street, 2003); as comparative legal scholar Ugo Mattei (1998) notes, most attorneys and legal thinkers operate as if they believe the country in which they live has a monopoly on the production of law. Thus it should not be surprising that most research on and theorization of globalization have taken place in fields other than the law (Berman, 2005b). The notion of an 'international plane' of law, however, first appeared in 1911 (Charnovitz, 2003), appreciation of the importance of transgovernmental relations through informal and non-governmental processes was evident by the mid-1970s (Keohane and Nye, 1977), and by the late 1980s the concept of internationalization had become a 'codeword' for modern legal development (Blume, 1989: 12). Today it is not possible to fully understand cross-border norm development and policy convergence solely within the bounds of international law. Legal scholars are interested in non-state actors, revisiting the concept of citizenship, and developing new theoretical and pragmatic approaches to state actions that take place beyond their geopolitical borders. It may or may not be coincidental that so much of this literature is dominated by thinkers from the US during a period in which a great deal of harmonization of the legal field also involves its 'Americanization' (Dezalay and Garth, 1996).

The linkage between jurisprudence and specific states is also a strength, because it means that new legal theories, practices and institutions always accompany changes in political form (Mattei, 1998). The very phrase 'international law' was coined by Jeremy Bentham in 1789 at a time when the 'law of nations' had to cope with the appearance of new states, and new types of states. The use of political theory to study globalization of the law significantly enriches analytical opportunities (Charnovitz, 2003). The extent to which current media laws and regulations should be deemed repressive, for example, can only be evaluated within the context of historical trends (Najjar, 1998). Taking an historical perspective also makes clear what is not unique about current circumstances. Previous waves of legal globalization included the spread of Roman law across Europe and the diffusion of European legal models during the colonial era (Kelemen and Sibbitt, 2004). Perceptions that current legal innovations have their origination in American practices are not always historically accurate (Schick, 2006). And the purportedly 'stable' system of sovereignty and territoriality that globalization is said to challenge may never have actually existed (Berman, 2005b).

Many key moments in the history of internationalization and globalization of the law involved the media. Experience with the telegraph convinced European governments that their regulatory interests differed from those of private parties (Pircher, 1987). Negotiations over the First World War peace treaty introduced a role for journalists in peace-making and transparency and the free flow of information as international policy principles (Blanchard, 1986). The Second World War brought new transatlantic partnerships in matters involving global communication (Headrick, 1990), and that war's atrocities catalysed development of international human rights laws that include protections for speech-related civil liberties (Dennis, 2006). Satellites required global coordination and, by introducing 'open skies' as another policy principle, significantly raised the relative salience of information policy issues (Oettinger, 1980).

Communication-based collaboration within the peace movement across state borders in the 1980s (Faber, 1982) launched the current round of growth of international non-governmental organizations (INGOs). The Helsinki Final Act for the Commission on Security and Cooperation in Europe (CSCE) placed human rights and civil liberties on a par with other principles of international law for the first time (Nordenstreng and Kleinwachter, 1991). The European Commission has stimulated harmonization processes in a wide range of issue areas that affect the media and/or generate a climate in which communication policy may be 'hauled' into harmonization, including finance (Warren, 1990), culture (Smith, 1990), research and technological innovation (Petrella, 1996), and policing (Occhipinti, 2003). Hauled harmonization occurs in one issue area when it is believed necessary in order to effect desired convergence in other issue areas (Margheritis and Maldonado, 2007).

The internet is of course a premier generator of both jurisdictional tensions and regulatory experiments (Bellia, Berman and Post, 2007; Berman, 2005a; Froomkin, 1997; Zittrain, 2005). The policy convergence effected by the need to cope with the internet is likely to transform national legal systems more deeply than has ever been accomplished by traditional international or transnational law (Hughes, 2003). Evidence of this convergence can be found in a number of areas. There is so much interplay among courts in diverse jurisdictions dealing with copyright (Cho, 2007; Proulx, 2005), for example, that some claim an international fair use doctrine is beginning to emerge (Okediji, 2000). Harmonization of laws dealing with libel (Yanchukova, 2003), e-commerce (Gaskin, 1999), and cybercrime (Downing, 2005) is increasing.

The characteristics of global communication policy problems Harms (1980) identified are worth revisiting. These are issues that require world-scale solutions (or separate local solutions in widely disparate countries); exist in at least three cultural regions; require more than one and usually several different disciplines in order to achieve a resolution; have been recognized by experts and government agencies in different regions; are the subject of scholarly research and policy deliberation at international meetings; have received attention over the last decade and will continue to receive such attention during the next decade; can be treated separately or autonomously (or, alternatively, as interdependent matters); and must be solved or they will aggravate and/or prevent the achievement of solutions to other problems.

Issue trends, technological change, the evolution of organizational and political forms, and content-based factors all contribute to legal globalization (Bennett, 1991b; Simmons, Dobbin and Garrett, 2006). Numerous typologies of types of policy convergence have been offered. Randeira (2007) offers a fourfold breakdown based on the locus of initiation: the simultaneous operation of multiple international or supranational norms operating only beyond the level of the state, changes in national laws, the impact of alternative 'people's policies' with a national or supranational character, and project law (rules, obligations and procedures generated by international organizations and donor agencies). Berman (2005b) distinguishes among categories according to the type of actors involved: transnationalization of the legal process itself, involvement of non-traditional legal actors in traditional legal processes, and the transnationalization of international norms by classical legal actors such as judges. Busch and Jorgens (2005) offer a typology based on mode of operation, principal motivations of policy-makers, and the degrees of freedom with which national-level policy-makers can influence the content and autonomously decide on the adoption of a policy: cooperative harmonization, coercive imposition, and interdependent but uncoordinated diffusion. Others include domination, elite networking, penetration, and institutional isomorphism in their analyses. Since convergence processes evolve, in most cases separate mechanisms will play roles at different times. Issue-oriented analyses of policy convergence processes unfortunately often confuse different types of regulation and modes of policy diffusion (Dommering, 2006).

Even when causal factors are present and there are deliberate efforts to promote harmonization, legal globalization does not always occur (Busch and Jorgens, 2005). Ideas travel more easily than do policy tools (Radaelli, 2005). Things may look alike on paper but not be so in practice. Types of bureaucracy, government capacity to handle conflict, the nature of policy processes, and actors' preferences can all have an influence. Dynamic relations among transnational corporations, non-market entities, and the actions of states can yield a range of possibilities for resolving particular global policy issues locally, as research has found both in the developing world (Jasanoff and Martello, 2004) and in the more developed societies of the North and West (Piven, 2001). Finally, efforts at global governance may simply fail (Van den Bossche and Alexovicova, 2005).

Globalization of the law through government

Globalization of media law and policy is a matter of *government* when it takes place through the practices, programmes, institutions, and decision-making procedures of geopolitically recognized entities. This occurs in the course of foreign policy, judicial thinking, and transformations of the form of the state itself.

Foreign policy

Hegemonic states extend their influence through diffusion (Kelemen and Sibbitt, 2004) or imposition (Bartholomew, 2006) of elements of their legal systems. Foreign policy-makers tend in this direction when they seek to avoid uncertainty (O'Heffernan, 1991) or internationalize markets (Dyson, 1986). Often governments make decisions and institute programmes that are *de facto* media law and policy in pursuit of other foreign policy goals (Blanchard, 1986; Winseck and Pike, 2007). Arms control treaties, for example, include numerous provisions of this type (Braman, 1991).

In the face of judicial, legislative or popular resistance to such activities, this may be accomplished by executive fiat (Biegel, 2001). Early twenty-first century struggles over expanding executive power within the United States include a growing literature analysing presidential options regarding extraterritorial applications of US law from this perspective (see, for example, Posner and Sunstein, 2007; Effron, 2003). Intergovernmental collaborations among law-makers can also accomplish this goal. Deliberate efforts of this type are multiplying; the International Network on Cultural Policy, for example, involves ministers of culture from around the world who discuss trade issues that have an impact on culture (Magder, 2006). These are not meetings at which international or global laws are made but, rather, venues in which policy concepts are developed collaboratively for subsequent implementation at the national level.

The judiciary

The constitutional status of communication policy makes the role of the judiciary as a globalizing force particularly important. Judicial treatment of problems involving foreign spaces and actions is not new. US court decisions have been used to justify extraterritorial extensions of the law since at least the close of the nineteenth century (Burnett, 2005). Legal foundations for doing so have been located even earlier (Schoen, Falchek and Hogan, 2005; Teitel, 2005), going as far back as foundational documents like constitutions (Sepper, 2006).

Logistical, communicative, evidentiary and theoretical developments are all means by which the judiciary contributes to legal globalization. Beginning with regular meetings of judges from European countries in the mid-1980s and expanding to worldwide conferences of judges in the mid-1990s, face-to-face meetings among those responsible for jurisprudence from different countries have helped develop an epistemic community in support of legal globalization (Berman, 2005a). Judges stimulate globalization of the law when they try to reduce tensions between the US and foreign sovereigns (Posner and Sunstein, 2007), interpret US statutes so that they apply extraterritorially (Keithley, 2005), and resolve conflicts between statutes and international treaties (Effron, 2003). Courts increasingly cite foreign court precedents (Baker, 2006; Benvenuto, 2006) and use evidence from foreign jurisdictions (Bennett, 1991a). National courts at times rely upon international customary law to support state-level decisions, and international courts treat national court decisions as evidence of state-level custom and practice (Moremen, 2006).

Theoretical work undertaken by the judiciary involves reconceptualizing the actors and processes that are the subject of litigation (Sachs, 2006) and development of new normative frameworks (Schmitt, 1999). One of the most interesting theoretical developments taking place takes advantage of an old US law, the Alien Torts Act of 1789. This statute has been used to analyse human rights cases in US courts to deal with activities involving repressive governments of other countries. Today it is also being used in disputes over transnational corporate activities that take place in countries other than those of the court involved (Schoen, Falchek and Hogan, 2005; Teitel, 2005).

State form

The assumption that all democratic states in the developed world are alike is invalid, for there are significant differences even among European countries that begin with how the state itself is understood (Alber, 2006; Michaels and Jansen, 2006). Superb comparative studies of states by Greenfeld (1992) and Silberman (1993) provide theoretically and empirically rich detail about ways in which states that are commonly treated as if they are similar in form differ in a number of ways of importance for information, communication and culture. That said, it is also true that the number of states is multiplying and the range of types of states is either growing (Hill, 1991) or, more plausibly, becoming recognized theoretically. The result, as with the multiplication of the number of international laws and law-making institutions (Seastrum and Getlan, 2001), is exacerbation of venue shopping choices and jurisdictional dilemmas. Existing states also find their legal systems challenged and ultimately transformed as a result of migration (Taki, 2005), expansion of the population in borderlands (Berman, 2005a), and/or diffusion of the borderland condition itself (Bauman, 2002).

New types of states produce legal innovations. 'Responsible port states', for example, are understood to have mandatory extraterritorial responsibilities (Molennar, 2007). The 'preventive state', based on a constitutional model that is paternalistically focused on non-political security threats, creates a detention regime with media dimensions (Sajo, 2006). Brooks (2005) argues that international organizations often do not succeed in efforts to restore 'failed states' to the status of 'successful' states because they are thinking exclusively in terms of Western models when there are other alternatives available.

The 'cunning' state, for example, deliberately manipulates responses to demands from the international community and models of approaches to the law in order to serve domestic goals. Strategies of the cunning state include flouting conditionalities associated with funding and treaty requirements, partial implementation of policy prescriptions, restriction of monitoring to selected domains of policy, and successfully preventing infringement of sovereignty in areas deemed to be particularly important. As cunning states communicate and collude with each other in the use of such strategies, patterns of legal globalization that may not align with those of hegemonic states and regions are appearing (Randeira, 2007).

Globalization of the law through governance

Globalization of media law and policy is a matter of *governance* when it takes place through the formal and informal practices, programmes, institutions and decision-making procedures of both public and private sector entities. This path towards legal globalization is of rising importance as a result of shifts in relations among states, the law, international organizations, and civil society. Research in this area focuses on the multiple formations of transnational civil society, private law and legal services, and the architecture of technologies and technological systems.

Transnational civil society

Whether driven by transnational political activity (Turner, 1992), the exigencies of the European Union (Cox, 1999), claims that the concept of citizenship has been incompletely theorized (Sunstein, 1996), or appreciation of the impact of international and global decision-making on individual citizens (Charnovitz, 2003), today the notion of citizenship is being reconsidered both theoretically and pragmatically. The familiar argument that states are 'imagined communities', of course, provides a rationale for taking seriously other relevant communities for political purposes (Berman, 2005b). Specialized communities, such as those of organized labour and diasporic movements, provide insight into the unpredictability and diversity of developments taking place in this area.

Though much of the literature treats the involvement of civil society in international and global law and policy as if it is a recent development, here, too, there is a history. During the nineteenth century non-state actors played important roles internationally in issues such as anti-slavery, the peace movement, and Red Cross activities (Berman, 2005b). Journalists and other civil society actors were actively involved in negotiations during the Paris 1919 peace talks (Blanchard, 1986). During the same period, Jane Addams – an early innovator in the development of civil society institutions – argued that citizens and community groups have an important role to play in international organization discussions because official delegates to meetings of such groups are not likely to know much about modern social thought and thus may otherwise have no means of understanding the importance of certain concerns. By the mid-1950s, Article 71 of the UN Charter was understood to justify the involvement of NGOs in international organizations (Charnovitz, 2003).

Among those who do research on or are involved as advocates in global media policy-making, the focus has been on civil society as represented by issue-oriented NGOs. Twenty-first-century meetings of the World Summit on the Information Society (WSIS) process provide examples of both practice and research of this type (see, for example, Calabrese, 2004; Raboy, 2004). However, the greatest success in terms of a strengthened legal presence for members of civil society at the global level has been in the very different arena of investors' rights (Van Harten, 2005). For those concerned about media policy, this may be an even more important dimension of civil society activity, given the global nature of media consolidation (McChesney, 1999).

Trade unions offer a particularly interesting example of global civil society efforts because of their birth in the belief that international processes of capital accumulation would force workers around the world to join together. International Framework Agreements now adapt and extend representation in a manner that parallels to some extent the strengthening of the global legal power of the investors whose capital is at stake (Fairbrother and Hammer, 2005). Migration also provides openings for legal globalization via governance. Cross-border communications and collaborations among those in diasporic communities contribute to what Karim (2006) describes as 'globalization-from-below'. Such groups contribute to policy convergence when they succeed in pressuring their home states to include absent citizens within a state for legal purposes (Fitzgerald, 2006) and conform to international human rights standards (Brainard and Brinkerhoff, 2006). Other areas of civil society activity that contribute to legal globalization via governance include the increasingly popular practices of privately providing law and order, adoption of managerial values and principles in state administration (reversing the post-Second World War directionality), and the spread of notions of corporate social responsibility (Rus, 2004).

Those who assume that strengthening civil society will improve the global situation for communicative rights and civil liberties confront at least two challenges. First, civil society groups represent all political positions from the most conservative to the most progressive, with the greatest current successes being achieved by those who are oriented around capital accumulation. Second, activity does not necessarily yield intended, or any, results. Transnational activists and advocates are often isolated from domestic social movements and find themselves unable to bridge the local and the global, undermining the ability of transnational coalitions to achieve their goals (Tarrow, 2005). Theatrical or carnivalesque protests may express political frustrations but do not often have traceable political impacts (Chvasta, 2006). The processes by which international and global decision-making take place so differ from those found at national and sub-national levels that NGOs can find it difficult to operate effectively (Steinhardt, 2005). Even when there is civil society participation in international or global meetings, it receives relatively little media coverage, in turn further limiting impact (Bennett *et al.*, 2004).

Private law and legal services

One of the most striking changes in relations among law, society and the state in recent decades has been the ever-increasing privatization of formerly public functions as the welfare state undergoes dismantling. (Deregulation, liberalization, forebearance from regulation, and privatization are all different regulatory and legal processes, but the common linkage of privatization with deregulation in the telecommunications and broadcasting industries from the 1980s on has caused many to inaccurately conflate these processes. All involve changes in regulation, but it is privatization that shifts policy processes from government to governance.) From the perspective of legal globalization, privatization increases the importance of the roles of private law relative to those of public law. The private provision of legal and cognate services is also a means by which legal globalization takes place through the processes of governance rather than government.

Privatization of public functions is occurring to such an extent that some believe private entities performing sovereign functions should be offered the same immunity to which states are entitled (Wen, 2003). Digitization of legal databases by private entities facilitates the use of cross-national arguments, precedents, and types of evidence (Katsh, 1989). Satellite communications provide an interesting terrain for examining the globalizing effects of privatization. These systems inherently have global functions even though they are put in place by and serve specific states (Gabrynowicz, 2005). Significant elements of both access to data collected by such satellites (Florini and Dehqanzada, 2001) and the system that manages satellite communications (Thussu, 2002) have been privatized. The first of these, in particular, has had a multiplier effect, for the ability to obtain data from around the world has also been of deep value to NGO groups engaged in transnational issue-oriented advocacy and activism.

Private law includes those areas of the law that are open to ordering by private parties rather than the state. Private law has been particularly important in recent decades for the media because, as a result of digitization, there have been so many legal issues for which there was previously no law at either the national or international levels. As a result, law firms such as Debevoisier and Plimpton have had a great deal of global influence because the development of contractual arrangements on behalf of their private clients has established legal principles that then serve precedential roles for public law – law made by geopolitically recognized governments (see, for example, Bruce, Cunard and Director, 1986). There are two different ways of thinking about the impact of globalization on relationships between private and public law, however. For those who claim that 'all law is public law' because private law operates within the public law context, changing the role of the state then changes the nature of the law. For those who claim that private law is already independent of the state, however, changes in the role of the state that result from globalization have no impact on the nature of the law (Michaels and Jansen, 2006).

Globalization of the delivery of legal services was under way before the formation of the World Trade Organization (WTO) (Dezalay, 1989, 1990), but the General Agreement on Trade in Services (GATS) administered by the WTO made it much easier for large firms based in one country to operate globally (Dezalay and Garth, 1996). Software is now being written specifically to support the globalization of legal services (see, for example, Contreras and

Poblet, 2005). The same developments are under way with cognate services such as accounting (Dilevko and Gottlieb, 2002). Use of the same accounting systems and techniques globally has an impact on the law by providing the information architectures through which media law and economic decision-making are implemented (Braman, 1993).

Technological systems

The structuration functions of computer code mean that the global architecture of the telecommunications network and of services offered through that network also serves law-like functions (see, for example, Biegel, 2001; Lessig, 1999; Shah and Kesan, 2003). Technical standard-setting, of course, has always been dominated by private sector decision-makers even when there is ultimately a public sign-off (Schmidt and Werle, 1998). Standardization processes are so important economically that they can introduce new legal issues (Hayashi, 1992).

Globalization of the law through governmentality

Globalization of media law and policy is a matter of *governmentality* when it is driven by cultural habits and predispositions that enable and sustain both governance and government. The term is Foucaultian, but other important work contributing to our understanding of culture and the law comes from the law and society movement (Sarat and Kearns, 1998) as well as the anthropology of law (Moore, 2001, 2005). Governmentality contributes to legal globalization in the areas of legal consciousness, cultural citizenship and popular culture.

Legal consciousness

Law is, in Clifford Geertz's phrase, a 'distinctive manner of imagining the real' (1983: 193). Legal consciousness is what people think of as natural and normal ways of doing things (Kennedy, 1980); law operates by influencing how we think and how we relate to each other (Berman, 2005b). Because we 'imbibe' legal culture, even non-enforceable conventions and law-like decisions of non-governmental actors can have a law-like effect (Merry, 2003). Individuals, then, are active participants in the process of constructing the law and legality. Research on legal consciousness includes attention to soft law and the diversity of sources of law creation and adjudication. In the area of media policy, cultural citizenship and popular culture are of particular importance.

While promoting legal consciousness is often an explicit goal of those agencies that seek to export democracy, the direction in which transformations of legal consciousness will go cannot always be predicted. It is commonly believed that intensification of the rule of law will lead to an expanding interest in rights, but the reverse may take place. Engel (2005), for example, found that in northern Thailand the introduction of new narratives about and conceptions of injury and compensation inclined the population towards an increased reliance on Buddhist concepts that justified *refraining* from engagement with the legal system in pursuit of compensation.

Some innovative work is being done on legal consciousness and the globalization of media law and policy. Yar (2005) looks at film piracy not as a crime wave but as a product of shifts in attitudes towards intellectual property rights, and Liang (2005) understands the circulation of 'non-legal' media as an aspect of the shifting nature of citizenship today. Unfortunately, many transnational issues of importance simply do not appear in legal consciousness, such as many of those raised by satellites and, for a long time, international trade (Gabrynowicz, 2005).

Cultural citizenship

Cultural citizenship involves the political implications of media-oriented dimensions of legal consciousness. While some activists and advocates are explicit, deliberate and self-aware in their declarations of cultural citizenship, the notion also refers to everyday activities of 'ordinary people'. Global cultural citizenship shares with cultural citizenship at the national level the rights to belong to a community, offer one's views, and express one's preferences; the responsibilities of cultural citizenship include respecting other people's tastes and how other people differ from oneself (Hermes, 2006). Cultural citizenship can also include the idea that rights inhere in groups as well as individuals (Delanty, 2006). Operationalization of cultural citizenship in the area of media policy includes extending laws that protect journalists' rights to citizen media (Deuze, 2006), the development of specific rights and responsibilities for the media (Stevenson, 1997), and encouragement to maximize shared media opportunities (Frith and Tsao, 1998).

Hermes (2006) argues that cultural citizenship includes making popular culture one's own. He identifies several contributions of popular culture to citizenship: it makes us feel welcome and offers a means of identifying with each other, it allows us to fantasize about our hopes and fears for the social future about which policy-making is taking place, and it links the domains of the public and the private. The difference between popular and elite discussions of globalization is notable (Waisbrod, 1998) – while elites have tended to be almost exclusively positive, it has never been off limits among popular audiences to suggest that in some dimensions globalization should be slowed, halted or reversed. Analysis of popular discourses by which people link the local and the global can be a source of new policy concepts (Clarke and Gaile, 1997). The act of consumption, too, is increasingly suffused with citizenship characteristics (Scammell, 2000).

Implications for media studies

Legal globalization through the processes of government, governance and governmentality is of importance to media studies theoretically, as a research subject, and pedagogically.

Theory

With the long history of intertwined media and political systems at the national level, the shift to a global environment necessarily introduces new theoretical issues. The Axford and Huggins (2001) collection identifies many of the elements of media policy that have been transformed as a result of globalization, including the nature of citizenship (Coleman, 2001), the political audience (Huggins, 2001), political leadership (Stromer-Galley and Jamieson, 2001) and governance itself (Newton, 2001).

Responses to these challenges are beginning to appear. Chakravartty and Sarikakis (2006) frame contemporary media policy issues as global, and Katz (2005) addresses ways in which globalization of markets and the modelling of new regulatory approaches has affected media policy across states. Bertrand (2003) has reconsidered the principles and practices of media ethics for a globalized world. We have looked at the use of state-level media policy as a tool of power in the international arena (Braman, 1995), and at press–state relations under conditions in which globalization has undermined the effectiveness of the state itself (Waisbrod, 2007).

Much, however, remains to be done. Relationships between media and political structures remain critically important but must be conceptualized in quite different ways to be adequate for understanding global rather than national processes, and to cope with governance and governmentality as well as government. While revisiting press–state relations in the twenty-first century is of value for thinking about media policy at the national level (Hallin and Mancini, 2004), the question of relationships between transnational media corporations and global civil society is a different matter. Dutton (2007) took a valuable first step in thinking about the role of the media vis-à-vis power in governance and governmentality as well as government with his suggestion that the internet serves as a 'fifth estate', ensuring the accountability of both public and private parties around the world. This is useful as a concept, and also as a model for innovative thinking about what is changing in our environment. Indeed, in this period it is particularly important to visit emerging and conflicting media policy-making processes theoretically (Braman, 2004a).

Research

If we put together a matrix of the legal globalization processes discussed here, most of the cells would be empty of media policy research. Thus the chapter can be read as a research agenda. Work on the globalization of media law and policy outside of ICANN has just begun, and lags behind what is being done in other areas of the law.

We do have materials such as textbooks on internet law that present the points of law in US court cases involving foreign content, content producers and/or internet users (see, for example, Bellia, Berman and Post, 2007; Radin and Rothschild, 2007). A few models of work that connects the globalization of media law and policy to the conversation taking place in other arenas of the law can be found, such as research on the role of the international community as media regulator in post-transition societies (Goldberg, 2002), the impact of regionalization on national media policies in Europe (Sarikakis, 2002), and the privatization of functions of international organizations with media policy-making responsibilities (Thussu, 2002).

We know next to nothing, however, about many critically important questions. How do legal developments favouring investors in transnational corporations affect the media in particular? How is harmonization of surveillance practices and censorship across states coming about? How does the necessity of relying upon private sector internet service providers (ISPs) radically change relations between the polity and the state when it comes to free speech issues? Many more such questions can be asked.

Pedagogy

Our responsibility is to contribute to the development of global citizens as well as global media policy researchers. The extent and sophistication with which we think about globalization of laws and policies that affect the media are of importance not only theoretically, but for practice as well. Thus there is reason to take note of the findings of a proprietary study undertaken for the Ford Foundation which found that the subject of global media law and policy is fractured across courses and disciplines in such a way that it is unlikely that any student would receive exposure to the whole (Braman, 2003). The study of global governance mechanisms, such as ICANN, is most common in courses on technology; international organizations such as the ITU and the World Intellectual Property Organization (WIPO) are introduced most frequently in information science syllabi for international information policy courses; bilateral and multilateral agreements such as those of the European Commission (EC) and the North American Free Trade Agreement (NAFTA) are almost exclusively dealt with in political science; comparative law is occasionally mentioned in international communication courses; mention of the global market for law is professor-specific and quite rare; anthropologists pay some attention to legal culture; and emerging legal trends and issues receive non-comprehensive and acontextual introductions in a few 'new media' or 'technology and society' courses. Those who teach complain that there are very few teaching materials available in the areas of international, global and comparative communication law. And the problem is cascading, for those who have not studied the subject in graduate school are also less likely to teach it, or to see the necessity of its inclusion in a curriculum.

Pedagogy can itself contribute to legal globalization processes; Latin American law schools, for example, work on strengthening the role of the judiciary to help diffuse the rule of law in their societies (Fuentes-Hernandez, 2002). The processes of legal globalization would be only one element of a syllabus or curriculum in global media policy, but introducing to students this significant change in the very way that policies are made could have a powerful perceptual effect.

Scholars from law schools and from communication or media studies departments differ in their analytical approaches (Pasadeos, Bunker and Kum, 2006), but what law schools are learning about the incorporation of legal globalization into their curricula provides some insight for those in media studies. The effort to train law students for citizenship in a global world can be wrenching in the context of an academic tradition entirely focused on one nation's legal traditions and modes of reasoning (Nussbaum, 2003). Thus New York University law school stresses building cultural humility into core courses as well as exposing students to a broader range of modes of legal reasoning as a means of cross-cultural exposure, rather than limiting the 'global' content to just a few examples of cases or regulations from other societies (Sexton, 2001). The job is difficult. More and more law schools now include rhetoric about legal globalization in their marketing materials, but this is rarely borne out by realities. Indeed, Mattei (2002) suggests that this language is often used as cover for further diffusing US approaches to the law.

Conclusions

Media policy creates the context within which other legal decision-making takes place. Even though those in media studies have been among the most aggressive thinkers and researchers regarding globalization, in the area of media law and policy attention largely remains riveted to the state level. The overtly political nature of national laws and regulations that affect the media, and the tight linkages between media conglomerates and those with political power, may be distracting both theorists and researchers from exploring legal globalization of media policy to the extent under way in other issue areas. Fully globalizing media studies, however, requires analysis of legal structures at the global level as they are beginning to appear in governance and governmentality as well as government. While state-level, international and comparative media law and policy analysis continue to be important – and do provide insight into globalizing processes – the global policy environment may ultimately encompass these developments. Thus the introduction offered here to the types of processes by which the law is becoming globalized may, it is hoped, provide a referential research agenda.

Notes

1 The notion of 'information law and policy' is an umbrella concept to refer to all law and policy dealing with any aspect of information, communication and culture (Braman, 2006). This chapter focuses on media law and policy as a sub-set of information law and policy. Increasingly, of course, the dividing lines are difficult to draw (Braman, 2004b).

2 Though some observers believe that the lack of an international organization focused on a particular area of the law means that there is no supra-state law, for example, other approaches may have been successful over long periods of time. We have seen this in the case of regulation of foreign direct investment (FDI), for example. Avi-Yonah (2003) argues that there is no supra-state law dealing with FDI because no international organization is responsible for it, but Elkins *et al.* (2006) point out that FDI has been the subject of policy through the different techniques of bilateral treaties for many years.

References

Alber, J. (2006) The European Social Model and the United States, *European Union Politics*, 7(3): 393–419.

Avi-Yonah, R.S. (2003) National Regulation of Multinational Enterprises: An Essay on Comity, Extraterritoriality, and Harmonization, *Columbia Journal of Transnational Law*, 42(1): 5–34.

Axford, B. and Huggins, R. (eds) (2001) *New Media and Politics*. London: Sage.

Baker, J.S., Jr. (2006) Citing Foreign and International Law to Interpret the Constitution: What's the Point? *Albany Law Review*, 69: 683–96.

Bartholomew, A. (2006) *Empire's Law: The American Imperial Project and the 'War to Remake the World'*. London: Pluto Press.

Bauman, Z. (2002) Reconnaissance Wars of the Planetary Frontier Land, *Theory, Culture and Society*, 19(4): 81–91.

Bellia, P.L., Berman, P.S. and Post, D.G. (2007) *Cyberlaw: Problems of Policy and Jurisprudence in the Information Age*, 3rd edn, St Paul, MN: Thomson/West.

Bennett, C.J. (1991a) How States Utilize Foreign Evidence, *Journal of Public Policy*, 11: 31–54.

—— (1991b) What Is Policy Convergence and What Causes It? *British Journal of Political Science*, 21(2): 215–33.

Bennett, W.L., Pickard, V.W., Iozzi, D.P., Schroeder, C.L., Lagos, T. and Caswell, C.E. (2004) Managing the Public Sphere: Journalistic Construction of the Great Globalization Debate, *Journal of Communication*, 54(3): 437–55.

Benvenuto, O.J. (2006) Reevaluating the Debate Surrounding the Supreme Court's Use of Foreign Precedent, *Fordham Law Review*, 74: 2695–2759.

Berman, P.S. (2005a) Choice of Law and Jurisdiction on the Internet, *University of Pennsylvania Law Review*, 153(6): 1819–82.

—— (2005b) From International Law to Law and Globalization, *Columbia Journal of Transnational Law*, 43(2): 485–556.

Bertrand, C. (2003) *An Arsenal for Democracy: Media Accountability Systems*. Cresskill, NJ: Hampton Press.

Biegel, S. (2001) *Beyond Our Control: Confronting the Limits of Our Legal System in the Age of Cyberspace*. Cambridge, MA: MIT Press.

Blanchard, M.A. (1986) *Exporting the First Amendment*. New York: Longman.

Blume, P. (1989) The Economics of Legal Information. Paper presented to the 8th European Conference of Critical Legal Studies, Budapest, Hungary, October.

Brainard, L.A. and Brinkerhoff, J.M. (2006) Sovereignty under Siege, or a Circuitous Path for Strengthening the State? Digital Diasporas and Human Rights, *International Journal of Public Administration*, 29(8): 595–618.

Braman, S. (1991) Contradictions in Brilliant Eyes, *Gazette*, 47(3): 177–94.

—— (1993) Harmonization of Systems: The Third Stage of the Information Society, *Journal of Communication*, 43(3): 133–40.

—— (1995) Horizons of the State: Information Policy and Power, *Journal of Communication*, 45(4): 4–24.

—— (2003) *Media Policy Education: The Gap between Curriculum and Need*. New York: Report to the Ford Foundation.

—— (ed.) (2004a) *The Emergent Global Information Policy Regime*. Houndmills: Palgrave Macmillan.

—— (2004b) Where Has Media Policy Gone? Defining the Field in the Twenty-First Century, *Communication Law and Policy*, 9(2): 153–82.

—— (2006) *Change of State: Information, Policy, and Power*. Cambridge, MA: MIT Press.

Brooks, R.E. (2005) Failed States, or the State as Failure? *University of Chicago Law Review*, 72(4): 1159–96.

Bruce, R.R., Cunard, J.P. and Director, M.D. (1986) *From Telecommunications to Electronic Services: A Global Spectrum of Definitions, Boundary Lines, and Structures*. London: Butterworths.

Burnett, C.D. (2005) Untied States: American Expansion and Territorial De-annexation, *University of Chicago Law Review*, 72(3): 797–879.

Busch, P. and Jorgens, H. (2005) The International Sources of Policy Convergence: Explaining the Spread of Environmental Policy Innovations, *Journal of European Public Policy*, 12(5): 860–84.

Calabrese, A. (2004) The Promise of Civil Society: A Global Movement for Communication Rights, *Continuum*, 18(3): 317–29.

Chakravarty, P. and Sarikakis, K. (2006) *Media Policy and Globalization*. Edinburgh: Edinburgh University Press.

Charnovitz, S. (2003) The Emergence of Democratic Participation in Global Governance (Paris, 1919), *Indiana Journal of Global Legal Studies*, 10: 45–77.

Cho, T.M. (2007) Hollywood vs. The People of the United States of America: Regulating High-Definition Content and Associated Anti-piracy Copyright Concerns, *Marshall Review of Intellectual Property Law*, 6: 525–49.

Chvasta, M. (2006) Anger, Irony, and Protest: Confronting the Issue of Efficacy, Again, *Text and Performance Quarterly*, 26(1): 4–16.

Clarke, S.E. and Gaile, G.L. (1997) Globalization and the Changing US City: Dimensions of Transformation – Local Politics in a Global Era: Thinking Locally, Acting Globally, *Annals of the American Academy of Political and Social Science*, 551: 28-43.

Coleman, S. (2001) The Transformation of Citizenship?, in B. Axford and R. Huggins (eds) *New Media and Politics*. London: Sage, pp. 109–26.

Contreras, J. and Poblet, M. (2005) NetCase: An Intelligent System to Assist Legal Services Providers in Transnational Legal Networks, *Law and the Semantic Web*, 3369: 218–32.

Cox, R.W. (1999) Civil Society at the Turn of the Millennium: Prospects for an Alternative World Order, *Review of International Studies*, 25(1): 3–28.

Cunningham, S., Jacka, E. and Sinclair, J. (1998) Global and Regional Dynamics of International Television Flows, in D.K. Thussu (ed.) *Electronic Empires: Global Media and Local Resistance*. London: Arnold, pp. 17–26.

Delanty, G. (2006) Cosmopolitan Citizenship, in J. Blau and K. Smith (eds) *Public Sociologies Reader*. Lanham MD: Rowman and Littlefield, pp. 37–50.

Dennis, M.J. (2006) Application of Human Rights Treaties Extraterritorially to Detention of Combatants and Security Internees: Fuzzy Thinking All Around?, *ILSA Journal of International and Comparative Law*, 12: 459–80.

Deuze, M. (2006) Ethnic Media, Community Media and Participatory Culture, *Journalism*, 7(3): 262–80.

Dezalay, Y. (1989) Putting Justice 'into Play' on the Global Market: Law, Lawyers, Accountants, and the Competition for Financial Services, *Tidskrift für rattssociologi*, 6(1–2): 9–67.

—— (1990) The *Big Bang* and the Law: The Internationalization and Restructuration of the Legal Field, *Theory, Culture and Society*, 7: 279–93.

Dezalay, Y. and Garth, B.G. (1996) *Dealing in Virtue: International Commercial Arbitration and the Construction of a Transnational Legal Order*. Chicago, IL: University of Chicago Press.

Dilevko, J. and Gottlieb, L. (2002) Subject Access to Government Documents in an Era of Globalization: Intellectual Bundling of Entities Affected by the Decisions of Supranational Organizations, *Government Information Quarterly*, 19(2): 123–45.

Dommering, E. (2006) Regulating Technology: Code Is Not Law, in E.J. Dommering and L.F. Asscher (eds) *Coding Regulation: Essays on the Normative Role of Information Technology*. The Hague: T.M.C. Asser Press, pp. 1–17.

Donovan, L.M. (2006) Importing Plaintiffs: The Extraterritorial Scope of the Sherman Act after Empagran, *Iowa Law Review*, 91(2): 719–49.

Downing, R.W. (2005) Shoring up the Weakest Link: What Lawmakers around the World Need to Consider in Developing Comprehensive Laws to Combat Cybercrime, *Columbia Journal of International Law*, 43: 705–62.

Dutton, W. (2007) *Through the Network (of Networks): The Fifth Estate*. Oxford: Oxford Internet Institute, Oxford University, Inaugural Lecture, 15 October.

Dyson, K. (1986) West European States and the Communication Revolution, in K. Dyson and P. Humphreys (eds) *The Politics of the Communications Revolution in Western Europe*. London: Frank Cass, pp. 10–55.

Edelman, M. (2005) Written Constitutions, Democracy, and Judicial Interpretation: The Hobgoblin of Judicial Activism, *Albany Law Review*, 68: 585–96.

Effron, R.J. (2003) Secrets and Spies: Extraterritorial Application of the Economic Espionage Act and the TRIPS Agreement, *New York University Law Review*, 78(4): 1475–1517.

Elkins, Z., Guzman, A.T. and Simmons, B.A. (2006) Competing for Capital: The Diffusion of Bilateral Investment Treaties, 1960–2000, *International Organization*, 60(4): 811–46.

Engel, D.M. (2005) Globalization and the Decline of Legal Consciousness: Torts, Ghosts, and Karma in Thailand, *Law and Social Inquiry*, 30(3): 469–514.

Faber, M.J. (1982) The Peace Movement in Europe, in P. Radhakrishna and M. Agrawal (eds) *Arms and Survival*. New Delhi: Satvahan, pp. 208–17.

Fairbrother, P. and Hammer, N. (2005) Global Unions: Past Efforts and Future Prospects, *Industrial Relations*, 60(3): 405–31.

Fitzgerald, D. (2006) Rethinking Emigrant Citizenship, *New York University Law Review*, 81 (1): 90–116.

Florini, A.M. and Dehqanzada, Y.A. (2001) The Global Politics of Commercial Observation Satellites, in J.C. Baker, K.M. O'Connell and R.A. Williamson (eds) *Commercial Observation Satellites: At the Leading Edge of Global Transparency*. Santa Monica, CA: RAND Corporation, pp. 443–8.

Frith, K.T. and Tsao, J. (1998) Advertising and Cultural China: Challenges and Opportunities in Asia, *Asian Journal of Communication*, 8(2): 1–17.

Froomkin, M. (1997) The Internet as a Source of Regulatory Arbitrage, in B. Kahin and C. Nesson (eds) *Borders in Cyberspace*. Cambridge, MA: MIT Press, pp. 129–63.

Fuentes-Hernandez, A. (2002) Globalization and Legal Education in Latin America: Issues for Law and Development in the 21st Century, *Penn State International Law Review*, 21: 39–59.

Gabrynowicz, J.I. (2005) The Perils of Landsat from Grassroots to Globalization: A Comprehensive Review of US Remote Sensing Law with a Few Thoughts for the Future, *Chicago Journal of International Law*, 6: 45–67.

Gaskin, J. (1999) Policing the Global Marketplace: Wielding a Knife in a Gunfight, *Columbia Journal of Transnational Law*, 38: 191–208.

Geertz, C. (1983) Local Knowledge: Law and Fact in Comparative Perspective, in *Local Knowledge: Further Essays in Interpretive Anthropology*. New York: Basic Books, pp. 167–234.

Goldberg, D. (2002) The International Community as Media Regulator in Post-Conflict Societies, in M. Raboy (ed.) *Global Media Policy in the New Millennium*. Luton: University of Luton Press, pp. 163–80.

Greenfeld, L. (1992) *Nationalism: Five Roads to Modernity*. Cambridge, MA: Harvard University Press.

Hallin, D.C. and Mancini, P. (2004) *Comparing Media Systems: Three Models of Media and Politics*. Cambridge: Cambridge University Press.

Harms, L.S. (1980) An Emergent Communication Policy Science: Context, Rights, Problems, and Methods, *Communication*, 5: 65–87.

Hayashi, K. (1992) From Network Externalities to Interconnection: The Changing Nature of Networks and Economy, in C. Antonelli (ed.) *The Economics of Information Networks*. Amsterdam: North-Holland, pp. 195–215.

Headrick, D.R. (1990) *The Invisible Weapon: Telecommunications and International Relations, 1851–1945*. New York: Oxford University Press.

Hermes, J. (2006) Hidden Debates: Rethinking the Relationship between Popular Culture and the Public Sphere, *Javnost/The Public*, 13(4): 27–44.

Hill, C. (1991) Diplomacy and the Modern State, in C. Navari (ed.) *The Condition of States*. Milton Keynes: Open University Press, pp. 85–101.

Howard, P.N. (2007) Testing the Leap-Frog Hypothesis: The Impact of Existing Infrastructure and Telecommunications Policy on the Global Digital Divide, *Information, Communication and Society*, 10(2): 133–57.

Huggins, R. (2001) The Transformation of the Political Audience, in B. Axford and R. Huggins (eds) *New Media and Politics*. London: Sage, pp. 127–50.

Hughes, J. (2003) The Internet and the Persistence of Law, *Boston College Law Review*, 44: 359–96.

Jasanoff, S. and Martello, M.L. (2004) *Earthly Politics: Local and Global in Environmental Governance*. Cambridge, MA: MIT Press.

Jordan, A. (2005) Policy Convergence: A Passing Fad or a New Integrating Focus in European Union Studies?, *Journal of European Public Policy*, 12(5): 944–53.

Karim, K.H. (2006) Nation and Diaspora: Rethinking Multiculturalism in a Transnational Context, *International Journal of Media and Cultural Politics*, 2(3): 267–82.

Katsh, E. (1989) *The Electronic Media and the Transformation of the Law*. New York: Oxford University Press.

Katz, Y. (2005) *Media Policy for the 21st Century in the United States and Western Europe*. Cresskill, NJ: Hampton Press.

Keithley, T. (2005) Does the National Labor Relations Act Extend to Americans Who Are Temporarily Abroad?, *Columbia Law Review*, 105(7): 2135–70.

Kelemen, R.D. and Sibbitt, E.C. (2004) The Globalization of American Law, *International Organization*, 58:103–36.

Kennedy, D. (1980) Toward an Historical Understanding of Legal Consciousness: The Case of Classical Legal Thought in America, 1850–1940, *Research in Law and Sociology*, 3: 3–24.

Keohane, R. and Nye, J. (1977) *Power and Interdependence*. Toronto: Little, Brown.

Kirby, M. (2006) International Law: The Impact on National Constitutions, *American University Law Review*, 21: 327–64.

Lessig, L. (1999) *Code and Other Laws of Cyberspace*. New York: Basic Books.

Liang, L. (2005) Cinematic Citizenship and the Illegal City, *Inter-Asia Cultural Studies*, 6(3): 366–85.

McChesney, R. (1999) *Rich Media, Poor Democracy: Communication Politics in Dubious Times*. Urbana, IL: University of Illinois Press.

Magder, T. (2006) International Agreements and the Principles of World Communication, in J. Curran and D. Morley (eds) *Media and Cultural Theory*. London: Routledge, pp. 164–76.

Margheritis, A. and Maldonado, M. (2007) Regional Integration and (Hauled) Integration Policy: What Does the European Experience Teach Us?, *Journal of European Public Policy*, 14(1): 152–66.

Mattei, U. (1998) *Comparative Law and Economics*. Ann Arbor: University of Michigan Press.

—— (2002) Some Realism about Comparativism: Comparative Law Teaching in the Hegemonic Jurisdiction, *American Journal of Comparative Law*, 50: 87–98.

Merry, S.E. (2003) Constructing a Global Law: Violence against Women and the Human Rights System, *Law and Social Inquiry*, 28(4): 941–77.

Michaels, R. and Jansen, N. (2006) Private Law beyond the State? Europeanization, Globalization, Privatization, *American Journal of Comparative Law*, 54: 843–89.

Molennar, E.J. (2007) Port State Jurisdiction: Toward Comprehensive, Mandatory and Global Coverage, *Ocean Development and International Law*, 38(1–2): 225–57.

Moore, S.F. (2001) *Law as Process: An Anthropological Approach*. Münster: Lit Verlag.

—— (ed.) (2005) *Law and Anthropology: A Reader*. Oxford: Blackwell.

Moremen, P.M. (2006) National Court Decisions as State Practice: A Transnational Judicial Dialogue?, *North Carolina Journal of International Law and Commercial Regulation*, 32: 259–309.

Mowlana, H. (1996) *Global Communication in Transition: The End of Diversity?* Thousand Oaks, CA: Sage.

Mueller, M. (1999) *Ruling the Root: Internet Governance and the Taming of Cyberspace*. Cambridge, MA: MIT Press.

Murillo, M.V. and Martinez-Gallardo, C. (2007) Political Competition and Policy Adoption: Market Reforms in Latin American Public Utilities, *American Journal of Political Science*, 51(1): 120–39.

Najjar, O.A. (1998) The Ebb and Flow of Press Freedom in Jordan, 1985–97, *Journalism and Mass Communication Quarterly*, 75(1): 127–42.

Newton, K. (2001) The Transformation of Governance?, in B. Axford and R. Huggins (eds) *New Media and Politics*. London: Sage, pp. 151–71.

Nordenstreng, K. and Kleinwachter, H. (eds) (1991) *Confidence-Building in the Non-military Field*. Tampere: University of Tampere.

Nussbaum, M.C. (2003) Cultivating Humanity in Legal Education, *University of Chicago Law Review*, 70: 265–79.

Occhipinti, J.D. (2003) *The Politics of EU Police Cooperation: Toward a European FBI?* Boulder, CO: Lynne Rienner.

Oettinger, A.G. (1980) Information Resources: Knowledge and Power in the 21st Century, *Science*, 209: 191–8.

O'Heffernan, P. (1991) *Mass Media and American Foreign Policy: Insider Perspectives on Global Journalism and the Foreign Policy Process.* Norwood, NJ: Ablex.

Okediji, R. (2000) Toward an International Fair Use Doctrine, *Columbia Journal of Transnational Law*, 39: 75–175.

Pasadeos, J., Bunker, M.D. and Kum, J.S. (2006) Influences on the Media Law Literature: A Divergence of Mass Communication Scholars and Legal Scholars?, *Communication Law and Policy*, 11(2): 179–207.

Petersmann, E. (1991) *Constitutional Functions and Constitutional Problems of International Economic Law.* Fribourg: University Press.

Petrella, R. (1996) Globalization and Internationalization: The Dynamics of the Emerging World-Order, in R. Boyer and D. Drache (eds) *States against Markets: The Limits of Globalization.* London: Routledge, pp. 62–83.

Pircher, W. (1987) Tours through the Back-Country of Imperfectly Informed Society, in J.D. Slack and F. Fejes (eds) *The Ideology of the Information Age.* Norwood, NJ: Ablex, pp. 63–77.

Piven, F.F. (2001) Globalization, American Politics, and Welfare Policy, *Annals of the American Academy of Political and Social Science*, 577: 26–35.

Pool, I.d.S. (1983) *Technologies of Freedom.* Cambridge, MA: Belknap Press.

Posner, E.A. and Sunstein, C.R. (2007) Chevronizing Foreign Relations Law, *Yale Law Journal*, 116(6): 1170–1228.

Price, M.E. and Thompson, M. (eds) (2002) *Forging Peace.* Bloomington: Indiana University Press.

Proulx, V. (2005) Borrowing from our Common Law Cousins: American and British Influences on the Merger of Canadian Trademark and Internet Domain Name Laws, *Arizona Journal of International and Comparative Law*, 22: 505–82.

Rabkin, M.A. (2007) When Consumer Fraud Crosses the International Line: The Basis for Extraterritorial Jurisdiction under the FTC Act, *Northwestern University Law Review*, 101 (1): 293–330.

Raboy, M. (2004) The World Summit on the Information Society and Its Legacy for Global Governance, *Gazette*, 66(3–4): 225–32.

Radaelli, C.M. (2005) Diffusion without Convergence: How Political Context Shapes the Adoption of Regulatory Impact Assessment, *Journal of European Public Policy*, 12(5): 924–43.

Radin, M. and Rothschild, J. (2007) *Internet Commerce: The Emerging Legal Framework*, 2nd edn, St Paul, MN: Foundation Press.

Randeira, S. (2007) The State of Globalization: Legal Plurality, Overlapping Sovereignties and Ambiguous Alliances between Civil Society and the Cunning State in India, *Theory, Culture and Society*, 24(1): 1–33.

Rus, E.P. (2004) The Lasting Marriage between Nation and State Despite Globalization, *International Political Science Review*, 25(3): 251–7.

Sachs, S.E. (2006) From St. Ives to Cyberspace: The Modern Distortion of the Medieval 'Law Merchant', *American University International Law Review*, 21: 685–812.

Sajo, A. (2006) Terrorism, Globalization and the Rule of Law: From Militant Democracy to the Preventive State?, *Cardozo Law Review*, 27: 2255–94.

Sarat, A. and Kearns, T.R. (1998) The Cultural Lives of Law, in A. Sarat and T.R. Kearns (eds) *Law in the Domains of Culture.* Ann Arbor: University of Michigan Press, pp. 1–20.

Sarikakis, K. (2002) Supranational Governance and the Shifting Paradigm in Communications Policy-Making: The Case of the European Parliament, in M. Raboy (ed.) *Global Media Policy in the New Millennium*. Luton: University of Luton Press, pp. 77–92.

Sassen, S. (2003) The Participation of States and Citizens in Global Governance, *Indiana Journal of Global Legal Studies*, 10(5): 5–31.

Scammell, M. (2000) The Internet and Civic Engagement: The Age of the Citizen-Consumer, *Political Communication*, 17(4): 351–5.

Schick, S.E. (2006) Globalization, Bankruptcy and the Myth of the Broken Bench, *American Bankruptcy Law Journal*, 80: 219–58.

Schmidt, S.K. and Werle, R. (1998) *Coordinating Technology: Studies in the International Standardization of Telecommunications*. Cambridge, MA: MIT Press.

Schmitt, M.N. (1999) Computer Network Attacks and the Use of Force in International Law: Thoughts on a Normative Framework, *Columbia Journal of Transnational Law*, 37: 885–937.

Schoen, E.J., Falchek, J.S. and Hogan, M.M. (2005) The Alien Tort Claims Act of 1789: Globalization of Business Requires Globalization of Law and Ethics, *Journal of Business Ethics*, 62(1): 41–56.

Seastrum, E.C. and Getlan, M.S. (2001) The Globalization of International Trade Litigation: AD/CVD Litigation – Which Forum and Which Law?, *Brooklyn Journal of International Law*, 26: 893–916.

Sepper, E. (2006) The Ties that Bind: How the Constitution Limits the CIA's Actions in the War on Terror, *New York University Law Review*, 81(5): 1805–43.

Sexton, J.E. (2001) Developing Cooperation in International Legal Education: Curricular Responses to Globalization, *Penn State International Law Review*, 20: 15–18.

Shah, R. and Kesan, J. (2003) Manipulating the Governance Characteristics of Code, *Info*, 5(4): 3–9.

Silberman, B.S. (1993) *Cages of Reason: The Rise of the Rational State in France, Japan, the United States, and Great Britain*. Chicago: University of Chicago Press.

Simmons, B.A., Dobbin, F. and Garrett, G. (2006) The International Diffusion of Liberalism, *International Organization*, 60(4): 781–810.

Smith, A. (1990) Towards a Global Culture?, *Theory, Culture and Society*, 7: 171–91.

Smith, R., Woodward, D., Acharya, A., Beaglehole, R. and Drager, N. (2004) Communicable Disease Control: A 'Global Public Good' Perspective, *Health Policy and Planning*, 19(5): 271–8.

Steinhardt, B. (2005) Three Cheers for International Cooperation, *Index on Censorship*, 34 (3): 44–9.

Stevenson, N. (1997) Globalization, National Cultures and Cultural Citizenship, *Sociological Quarterly*, 38(1): 41–67.

Street, P. (2003) Stabilizing Flows in the Legal Field: Illusions of Permanence, Intellectual Property Rights and the Transnationalization of Law, *Global Networks*, 3(1): 7–28.

Stromer-Galley, J. and Jamieson, K. (2001) The Transformation of Political Leadership?, in B. Axford and R. Huggins (eds) *New Media and Politics*. London: Sage, pp. 172–90.

Sunstein, C.R. (1996) *Legal Reasoning and Political Conflict*. Oxford: Oxford University Press.

Swank, D. (2006) Tax Policy in an Era of Internationalization: Explaining the Spread of Neo-liberalism, *International Organization*, 60(4): 847–82.

Taki, T. (2005) Labor Migration and the Language Barrier in Contemporary Japan: The Formation of a Domestic Language Regime of a Globalizing State, *International Journal of the Sociology of Language*, 175–6: 55–81.

Tarrow, S. (2005) The Dualities of Transnational Contention: 'Two Activist Solitudes' or a New World Altogether?, *Mobilization*, 10(1): 53–72.
Taylor, A.L. (2004) Governing the Globalization of Public Health, *Journal of Law, Medicine and Ethics*, 32(3): 500–8.
Teitel, R. (2005) The Alien Tort and the Global Rule of Law, *International Social Science Journal*, 57(3): 551–61.
Thussu, D.K. (2002) Privatizing Intelsat: Implications for the Global South, in M. Raboy (ed.) *Global Media Policy in the New Millennium*. Luton: University of Luton Press, pp. 39–53.
Tribe, L.H. (1985) Constitutional Calculus: Equal Justice or Economic Efficiency?, *Harvard Law Review*, 98: 592–621.
Turner, B. (1992) Outline of a Theory of Citizenship, in C. Mouffe (ed.) *Dimensions of Radical Democracy: Pluralism, Citizenship, Community*. London: Verso, pp. 33–62.
Twining, W. (2000) *Globalization and Legal Theory*. London: Butterworths.
Van den Bossche, P. and Alexovicova, I. (2005) Effective Global Governance by the World Trade Organization, *Journal of International Economic Law*, 8(3): 667–90.
Van Harten, G. (2005) Private Authority and Transnational Governance: The Contours of the International System of Investor Protection, *Review of International Political Economy*, 12(4): 600–23.
Waisbrod, S. (2007) Democratic Journalism and Statelessness, *Political Communication*, 24(2): 115–29.
Warren, M.G. (1990) Global Harmonization of Securities Laws: The Achievements of the European Communities, *Harvard International Law Journal*, 31: 185–232.
Wen, A.H. (2003) Suing the Sovereign's Servant: The Implications of Privatization for the Scope of Foreign Sovereign Immunities, *Columbia Law Review*, 103: 1538–87.
Winseck, D.R. and Pike, R.M. (2007) *Communication and Empire: Media, Markets, and Globalization, 1860–1930*. Durham, NC: Duke University Press.
Yanchukova, E. (2003) Criminal Defamation and Insult Laws: An Infringement on Freedom of Expression in European and Post-Communist Jurisdictions, *Columbia Journal of Transnational Law*, 41: 861–94.
Yar, M. (2005) The Global 'Epidemic' of Movie 'Piracy': Crime-Wave or Social Construction?, *Media, Culture and Society*, 27(9): 677–96.
Zittrain, J.L. (2005) *Jurisdiction*. New York: Foundation Press.

Chapter 7

Changing paradigms of media research and practice in contexts of globalization and terror

Oliver Boyd-Barrett

The '9–11' attacks of 2001 on the World Trade Towers in New York and on the Pentagon in Washington, and the ensuing 'war on terrorism', at least as construed by the United States, constituted a significant opportunity for media scholarship to reconsider certain pre-existing frames of thought or paradigms of its discipline. I shall consider five principal outcomes of this opportunity, namely the implications for (1) the 'propaganda model' as a tool for explaining the behaviour of news media in Western democracies; (2) 'objectivity as strategic ritual' and whether standard journalistic methodologies provide tolerably good service; (3) discourses of globalization, glocalization and hybridity for understanding the media in a global context, as opposed to earlier discourses of imperialism; (4) presumptions as to the benign intent of modern government; and (5) the prospects for media analysis as a lone discipline.

Validity of the 'propaganda model'

Herman and Chomsky (1988/2002) propose that media news is distorted by five filters in the production process. These are the business interests of corporations that own media; dependence on advertising for a substantial share of revenues; professional practices, including dependence on official sources; fear of 'flak' – the punishment that aggrieved news sources can exercise on journalists or their employers, and shared ideology between powerful sources, media owners and journalists.

This model of propaganda does not say much about propaganda as such, as represented, for example, in the works of Edward Bernays (1928) or Jacques Ellul (1965/73), or in disciplines that focus on propaganda such as rhetoric (from Aristotle through to Kenneth Burke, 1968) and the psychology of persuasion (e.g. Cialdini, 1998), not to mention the propaganda strategies articulated in army manuals (US Government, 1979) and, more recently, Entman's (2004) influential 'framing' analysis.

Herman and Chomsky's model is primarily structural. Features of content that it does address, such as media neglect of the victims of US foreign policy, emerge as consequences of structure. Yet if one examines some of the most egregious examples of propaganda in mainstream media – as often occurs in media collusion, generally at senior levels, with intelligence sources – one must address not so much the impersonal issues of structure, but the deeply personal issues of *agency* and responsibility (see Boyd-Barrett, 2003, 2004a, 2004b, 2007a, 2007b). All phenomena are related to structural preconditions, to be sure, but this is insufficient reason to attribute to structure the power of determination. Humans are born into a world that is not of their own making and, by virtue of being alive, they act upon the world and change it. Some will change it more than others. Acknowledgement of agency is essential for political practice and hope for change. This is the promise of such dissectors as FAIR, Media Reform and Media Lens that routinely castigate the media, challenge the practice of journalists and, at their most revealing, engage them in critical discussion (Media Lens, 2007).

The discipline of media studies was in great measure founded upon the study of 'effective' propaganda and persuasion. This would be a suitable time to return to that foundation, more critically, taking full measure of the extent to which we, the students, have been duped by our objects of study, taking into account but going beyond structural preconditions, taking into account and going beyond the construction and reception of representations, moving into the black box itself, exposing the deals and the dealers and their acolytes, witting and unwitting.

'Objectivity as strategic ritual'

Is Tuchman's (1978) summary of the journalistic routines that are said to guarantee balance among (usually 'authoritative', which is to say 'powerful') sources the best we should or could expect? If even the minimum standards of this approach were applied consistently, there might be hope. Experience repeatedly demonstrates that on the 'important' issues that command the support of elite interests, mainstream media succumb, with or without the benefit of 'strategic' ritual, to complicity with power. Consider, as examples: (1) coverage of the 1964 Gulf of Tonkin incidents (rarely acknowledged, even now, for the flimsy pretexts they served for official commitment of US forces to Vietnam); or (2) Judith Miller's front page *New York Times* stories in the 2003 lead-up to the US invasion of Iraq (Boyd-Barrett, 2004a), based on compromised and duplicitous 'anonymous' sources – war propaganda of which competent senior staff were surely aware, whatever protestations of incompetence they later served up in mock penitence, and (3) a mere three years later the byline of Miller's quondam coauthor, Michael Gordon, that graced another front page story of the *New York Times*, based mainly on unnamed US government sources, again in contravention of the newspaper's own rules of conduct, heralding a US propaganda campaign to blame the violence of Iraq on Iran (Mitchell, 2007).

With mainstream complicity, the US administration ratcheted up its accusations against Iran. The media obligingly ignored or marginalized evidence of local insurgent arms-production capability; covert US efforts to destabilize Iran, and evidence of Saudi military support of Sunnis. This last was foregrounded temporarily in July 2007, on the eve of US administration closure of a large arms deal with Saudi Arabia. In an editorial on 8 July, the *New York Times*, cognizant that over 70 per cent of Americans opposed continuation of the war, admonished the administration for its 'failure' in Iraq. It bewailed the irony of continuing 'sectarian' violence in the presence of over 100,000 US troops. It overlooked the possible role of US covert operations in such violence. The admonishment came four years too late. In choosing to pontificate on 'failure', the *New York Times* ignored an alternative criterion of success/failure, namely the effectiveness of administration pressure on its puppet regime to secure passage of an oil bill that would concede enormous profits to US oil corporations (Cogan, 2007).

The notion that mainstream media are motivated by the thirst to uncover scandal, and to that extent, therefore, will protect the public against the most egregious abuses of power, is wishful thinking. Well-documented critiques of the official 9–11 report, many by established scholars and journalists (Ahmed 2002, 2003, 2005; Chossudovsky, 2005; Griffin, 2004a, 2004b, 2007; Lance, 2003, 2006), show that the best that mainstream media can accomplish, in face of the darkest suspicions of foreknowledge and even complicity on the part of the 'secret government', if not of government officials (suspicions shared by more than a third of the US population, see Berger, 2006), is to ridicule those who ask pointed questions, while investing absolutely nothing in original investigative reporting of these gravest issues.

The propaganda model speaks to the limitations of the classic approach to journalism. Can we say of this Anglo-American practice that none the less it performs reasonably well for much of the time and represents the best we should hope for? Implicitly supporting this view, proponents of the Anglo-American tradition proclaim its universality. US reporting textbooks are staple training fodder as far afield as Argentina and the Ukraine.

The classic model of journalistic story-telling is to tell stories backwards, in a so-called pyramid structure that packs the main points of newsworthiness into a lead paragraph. The inherent consequence for most readers, I argue, is confusion, misinformation and loss of context. It takes readers too many years to learn how to navigate around the worst pitfalls of these narrative defects; many, especially the young, have abandoned the effort. Because it privileges the newest development, which generally has only a trivial place in the unfolding of the overall story over time, pyramid journalism suppresses fundamental context. Whatever context is included is simplistic and selective, with a view to minimizing controversy and fitting the space 'available'. Across a limited range of genres (e.g. political, foreign, sports, fashion), whose purpose is to rationalize the deployment and routine of correspondents, Western journalism presents the world as hopelessly fragmented, often pretending an equality between items that are not at all equal in their real-life consequences for society or, worse, giving high exposure to stories that have no real importance to anyone (e.g. celebrity coverage) and only modest priority to items that portend catastrophe (e.g. the rapid decline of species).

Genres are not neutral. The genre of war coverage plays into the hands of power. It focuses on covering the action of 'official' conflicts between standing armies, when it should be critically investigating the pretexts for war, and the role of intelligence and covert forces in providing the pretexts (Boyd-Barrett, 2004b). The rush to speed, 'balance' and 'impartiality' distracts from selectivity in choice of stories, one-sided framing of issues, and obsequious dependence on powerful, 'authoritative' sources. The production system of journalism is deeply autocratic: behind a smokescreen of occupational myths about derring-do and investigative reporting a small group of senior news editors and their managers (chosen or approved by proprietors and publishers whose interests are profit and/or political influence) highlight the stories that titillate, yet routinely deceive by failing to ask the right questions or to search for the right information to answer them. Younger reporters are instructed what to cover, while older reporters routinely cover the events and personalities of a given 'beat'. What any journalist writes is subject to the rewriting of sub-editors, whose judgements more mature reporters try to anticipate. Columnists have greater freedom; there are few of them, and their skills typically lie in acerbic wit or the weaving of canny argument on the basis of secondary evidence. They typically lack the resources or inclination for independent investigation.

While it fails to deliver on either impartiality or balance, journalism inappropriately promotes these concepts as fail-safe guarantors of 'truth', whereas at least as often it is disciplined argument and polemic at the command of passion and perseverance, and in combat with counter-polemics, that most dramatically achieve these outcomes. Exposure of the failures of mainstream US journalism in its coverage of the run-up to war in Iraq owes as much to the craft of documentary and sometimes partisan polemic of a Michael Moore (2004) (*Fahrenheit 9/11*), Danny Schechter (2005) (*Weapons of Mass Deception*), Robert Greenwald (2004 and 2006) (*Uncovered, Iraq for Sale*), or Loretta Alper and Jeremy Earp (2007) (*War Made Easy*) as to the skills of revered print reporters such as Seymour Hersh. There are many paths to truth and meaning, and the Anglo-American model has no monopoly on them. Universalization of the presumed excellence of impartiality and balance is ethically problematic. Do all sources and events deserve 'impartial' and 'balanced' coverage, even in the case, say, of regimes that are manifestly profoundly corrupt, criminal and immoral?

Mainstream journalism privileges the 'fact'. The problem of selectivity – the determination of which 'facts' to highlight and which to exclude – is dealt with by the term 'newsworthiness'. This fuzzy neo-magical term is a blend of marketing, cultural bias and propaganda. 'Episodic' journalism practice naively promotes the statements of powerful or 'authoritative' people as the equivalent of 'facts', and assumes that truth can be accessed by pitting such statements against each other. The only sense in which such statements have the status of 'fact' is that journalists can show that they were uttered. Not only do journalists frown upon theorizing ('speculation'), but their implicit theory as to the worth of authoritative sources is patently absurd, since clearly authorities can and do frequently lie. Journalists prize the 'authoritative' statement because they are reluctant to attribute motive to action. Motives cannot generally be seen, but statements can be heard. Determination of motive often requires intelligent speculation, the triangulation of different sources of evidence, and accurate prediction on the basis of such speculation (or theory). This comes close to social science and constitutes a worthy approach to truth-seeking. The practice and presumptions of journalism are embedded in all kinds of implicit theory, theories that would be more easily testable if made explicit. But making theories explicit is tantamount to confessing that theory has a place in journalism, which for many is a sacrilegious thought.

Imperialism and globalization

The principal message of the invasions and occupations of Afghanistan in 2001 and of Iraq in 2003, and the establishment of dependent puppet governments lacking the legitimacy even to control their capital cities, let alone their national territories, is that the fundamental character of transnational relationships between unequal powers of the nineteenth and twentieth centuries, and the means used to sustain power, have not changed much after decades of supposed de-colonization.

For a brief period in the 1960s it seemed a new era had dawned. Scarred by traces of neo-imperialism, Western powers seemed set on pluralistic sharing of power. Third World attempts at liberation from the shackles of neo-imperialism, through strategies of nationalization and import substitution, collapsed under the weight of covert Western destabilization, seduction by 'economic hit men' (Perkins, 2005) into overwhelming debt, elite cooption and corruption. The resulting domination of the global economy by Western-based multinationals in collaboration with local elites, serving the interests of transnational political, financial and industrial plutocrats and loosely regulated by Western-controlled global institutions, was thought by some to have ushered in a benign era – of globalization. Often reviled for its intensification of the distance between rich and poor, globalization has inspired relatively inconsequential debates about such matters as cultural standardization and hybridity, at the expense of matters of unparalleled importance in the history of the human race that pertain to the survival of the species and of the planet. The underlying character of globalization is similar to that of imperialism. Both are narratives of domination and exploitation, by powerful class and financial interests of the developed nations, over territory, people and resources, through the application of guile, magic (technology), persuasion and/or force, cooption of local elites, and the suffocation of oppositional thought by means of obfuscating imported Western ideologies of religion, politics and entertainment, and their associated bureaucracies of clergy, charlatan peddlers of (un)representative democracy, and commercial mass media.

With 50 years' perspective, we should conclude that the process of decolonization following the Second World War was far more painful and tragic than most Western media disclosed at the time. Its successor, neo-liberal modernization, is the only route permitted the 'developing world' by the West, and it has temporarily benefited the middle classes of many of these countries.

There is nothing modern about patterns of control over large expanses of territory through force, religion and trade. To confine our understanding of globalization to the division of the world into nation states is to make a fetish of the nation state (the enforced equivalence of political control, territory and, to varying degrees, tribal identity). Over time globalization inevitably undergoes changes of form, so that today the role of multinational institutions of finance, trade and investment, and the inclusiveness of the global economy and worldwide networks of communications and media, are more commanding features than they were one or two hundred years ago. This realization has been appropriated within a research dialectic whose focus is the significance that it should attribute to 'globalism' in contrast to less extensive territorial forms of human organization and culture (including the national, regional, ethnic), or even whether territory itself has been overemphasized at the expense of boundary-less networks of communication, human movement and trade. Terms such as transnational, translocal, transcultural, glocal and hybrid have been useful for a while, but such discourse can invite intellectual tourism and romanticizing of the local. There are few elements of the local that have not been impacted by the national, regional or global. What constitutes the local is defined by human perceptions, memory and power relations: the local is always a construction, no less so than the national or global. The local frequently articulates itself in terms of traditions that, by the standards of modern cosmopolitans, are reactionary, as in the case of male-dominated, patriarchal societies.

The locally invisible local: a case study

The limitation of terms such as 'global' and 'local' is suggested by the iconic power of a hero of the Cuban revolution, Che Guevara. Guevara was not Cuban, but Argentinian. His Cuban comrades considered him ambivalently as un-Caribbean, ascetic and disciplined. Guevara's iconicity rests principally on two photos, of which one, by Alberto Korda, was taken on an impulse as Guevara climbed the platform at a political rally in post-revolutionary Cuba (Castaneda, 1997). His bereted head looks upwards against a clear sky with apparent visionary pride and resolution. The second photo was taken immediately after Guevara's execution in Bolivia in 1967. His eyes are open, lips set in a benign smile. These photos acquired global significance not for what they were actually about (Guevara's foreign campaigns might be criticized as hopeless, Quixotic escapades) but because they were transplanted in May 1968 to the streets of Paris, and reabsorbed as components of a local struggle over education. A global icon, emerging from Guevara's death at the hands of Bolivian military, supported by CIA intelligence, loses the ambiguity of Guevara's local, if state-sponsored and transnationally orchestrated, campaigns, and is grafted on to a different local context, student riots in Paris, that then acquires its own global iconicity of rebellious youth, in conjunction with superficially similar but really quite different episodes manifest that year from Berkeley, California, to Budapest in Hungary, and Mexico City.

Guevara was born in the city of Rosario in Argentina. Rosario's identity as a city of Argentina acquired meaning only in the second half of the nineteenth century under the aggression of Generals Sarmiento and Roca on behalf of the centrist oligarchs of Buenos Aires. Guevara's birthplace in an apartment at 480 *Calle Entre Rios* had no plaque on the exterior, street level, at the time of writing. A plaque had been promised in the 1990s following lively civic debate, but a small bomb explosion outside the premises discouraged implementation. A new owner of the home had planned to convert it into a museum. At the time of this author's visit in 2007, locals living or working within metres of the house were unaware of where exactly Guevara had been born or even who he was. Thus the 'local' is not necessarily recognized in the local. A small commemoration some blocks away from the birthplace consists of a brick monument bearing a painted likeness, a far cry from the opulent and imposing statues that commemorate national founders and liberators in almost every city of South America. Guevara gets a passing mention, at best, in the tourist literature supplied by the city, whose main pride is a monument that celebrates the nation of Argentina, its flag and constitution.

The flag of Argentina represents a nation imposed in the nineteenth century on a vast hinterland of South America by the dominant Spanish clique of Buenos Aires, opponents of federalism, in battles against caudillos of various stripes, all of whom contributed to the despoliation of indigenous peoples. Guevara was a Bolivarian: he believed that the whole of South America should be a single entity. In this vision, the separate flags of South America represent a retrograde step, a collective vulnerability to the manipulations of the United States. In place of the potential iconicity of Rosario as symbol of international revolution against the artificial boundaries of bourgeois nation states, therefore, the city's governors determined that it should iconize the (local) nation and the flag.

A few kilometres from Rosario's city centre is the impoverished neighbourhood of Barrio Toba, harbouring a high concentration of the Toba, an indigenous people, one of twenty that populated this territory before the construction of the nation. In July 2007 the barrio hosted the first ever National Meeting of the Indigenous Nations and Peoples of Argentina. They protested the loss of their lands to multinational companies (first, the cattle companies, now agribusiness multinationals sweeping up what arable land remains after a century of environmental degradation) and the nation's disregard of their constitutional rights. Article 75.17 of the National Constitution recognizes the rights of the original inhabitants to land, the management of natural resources and bilingual education. The provision has been consistently and brutally violated. In Rosario, therefore, a city that more than any other in Argentina celebrates the national flag of a country that came into existence only in 1875, and whose original peoples were massacred at the hands of a 'national' hero, General Rocas, two 'locals' are ignored, the local birth of an international and anti-national revolutionary, and the local reality of indigenous suppression by multinational corporations in complicity with the ruling national and local elites. We can say that this is a city that denies its 'local' in explicit celebration of the national, and in implicit complicity with the multinational.

While we may make play of the ironies of local, ethnic, immigrant, regional, national, international and of the global forces that constantly and dialectically interact with this history, eventually the attempt and its rationale prove abstract, pointless and unworthy, against the much more important narrative, I suggest, of power struggles for social justice, human dignity and species survival that surely have strongest moral claim upon our attention.

Many recent writers on media and globalization (Curran and Park, 2000; Sparks, 1998; Boyd-Barrett, 1998; Kraidy, 2005; Straubhaar, 2007; Tunstall, 2007) have stressed the relative weakness of global (Western) media organizations and their media export activity in important regional markets, as assessed in terms of audience size, and their contrast with the intensifying vibrancy of national and local media and the development of export markets by hitherto 'Third World' countries such as Brazil in its sale of telenovelas worldwide, or India in the distribution of 'Bollywood' movies to an Indian diaspora. Such evidence is evoked to undermine theories of cultural imperialism and globalization. This limited perspective employs measures of significance that do not include actual influence on cognition, attitude or behaviour, and looks solely at manifest content to the exclusion of such considerations as the interlocking business and political interests of media owners, the role of multinational advertising as a sponsor for local media, and the local assimilation of Western commercial business models. It assumes, optimistically, that local media represent authentic local culture and disregards how celebration of the 'local' functions ideologically to obscure its incorporation within a globalized economic system.

Dispensing with the myth of benign government

Here I deal with the notion (common in the West, less so elsewhere) that government, far from being an essentially benign, if often incompetent, force upon which we should depend for security and welfare, is often a malign force, whose agents have in the past and still today routinely engage in the most nefarious of crimes in the pursuit of class, sectional and personal interest. While most if not all Western governments have been and still are culpable in this respect, it is likely that governments with the greatest level of power and resource are the most culpable. The case of Britain, for example, has been dealt with by Mark Curtis (2003). The worst of these crimes tend to be committed against people in other countries, as, for example, in Iraq since the invasion of 2003. The best available methodology for assessing the number of Iraqis who died as a result of the US invasion gives a figure of 600,000 by 2006. Blum (2003) catalogued over 50 episodes since the Second World War where the US deliberately and often covertly destabilized regimes that it did not consider sufficiently docile. Many of these were democracies. The consequences, as in Iran after US destabilization of its (democratic) regime in 1953, or as in Chile after destabilization of its (democratic) regime in 1973, included death and suffering on a massive scale. Worse even than covert destabilization has been the sequence of wars in which the US has engaged since the Second World War, many of them as a result of pretexts that the US itself created. The clearest example is the fabrication of the Gulf of Tonkin incidents in 1964, but nearly every US military engagement is rife with similar doubts and duplicities (see Boyd-Barrett, 2004b and 2007a).

The grand bogeyman of the post-war era, from 1944 to 1990, was Soviet communism, and fear of the bogeyman was stoked continuously, from the fabrications of Senator McCarthy in the early 1950s, to gross US government exaggerations of Soviet military power. By applying the label of communism to anyone it did not like (e.g. anti-imperial nationalists such as Ho Chi Minh of Vietnam, or Sukarno of Indonesia), the US sought to rid itself of even relatively minor sources of hindrance to its ambitions for global power, and to enrich the defence industries and other special interests in the process. Suspicions of administration involvement, whether indirect (allowing it to happen) or direct (actual complicity), in the events of 9/11, arise from a well-founded tradition of grave popular distrust of the US political system, and of the 'secret government' of intelligence agencies and covert forces that routinely directs or circumvents it, presumably at the behest of the military-industrial complex which depends on military engagement as the basis for its huge claims on government (taxpayer) money. Inasmuch as the US has real enemies, including Jihadist fundamentalists, these have often been nurtured by the US itself, as chronicled by Chalmers Johnson (2000, 2003). In *Blowback* he describes 9/11 Jihadism as a form of pay-back for US support for the Taliban during the Soviet occupation of Afghanistan in the 1980s. Western complicity in the nurture of its own enemies is manifested in frequent revelations concerning covert penetration, incitement and manipulation of terrorist groups in the pursuit of covert domestic and foreign policy goals (Boyd-Barrett, 2007a).

In the US, critical elements of a European-style post-war 'deal' between ruling elites and returning veterans were barely attempted. Over 60 years after the introduction of universal health care in Great Britain and its spread throughout most of the developed and even into the developing world, the US lacks such care, and some 50 million Americans are without health insurance. As Moore (2007) demonstrates in his popular documentary *Sicko*, even those who have health insurance, and pay heavily for it, are worse off than those who receive free care elsewhere. Other areas of domestic life reveal the state as deeply malign: they include the relentless drive by the Bush Junior administration to dismantle labor, disability, and environmental protections on behalf of corporate interests, with dire consequences for the quality of such basics of life as air and water. We may safely conclude that the Bush administration protects big business interests at the expense of large numbers of premature deaths and disease among Americans. Other examples include the reluctant, deceitful response to the massive threats of global warming and climate change; reckless dismantling of nuclear weapons proliferation treaties; the miserable administration response to the havoc wrought on New Orleans by Hurricane Katrina in 2006; the slow response to large-scale corporate theft from company pensions, and to other massive scams (such as that of Enron and the electricity power cuts that Enron engineered in southern California in 2000–1); protections afforded by the administration to US pharmaceutical companies (e.g. restrictions imposed on cheap drug imports from Canada); inadequate testing of genetically modified foods; approval of oil drilling in the wilderness of Alaska despite the modest yields anticipated; reduction of protections against tree felling in national parks; non-competitive bidding for huge defence contracts granted to companies that time and time again show themselves unable or unwilling to deliver quality, as in the case of Halliburton and its subsidiary KBR; a level of incarceration by an increasingly privatized prison system that is among the highest in the world; a law enforcement system that frequently entails the shooting of innocent people and abuse or torture of prisoners.

Government, through which the corporate and private plutocracy speaks by means of moneyed manipulation of the remaining shell of a system of 'representative' democracy (in which the masses are 'represented' by millionaires and billionaires with whom they have virtually nothing in common), seems increasingly to target its own people as the enemy. A media system that served the people would be more inclined to treat government as the enemy. Media scholarship has failed to appreciate that just as penetration of mainstream media by intelligence services and propaganda activity is not something incidental, but is intrinsic, to the operation of media in corporatized democracies, and therefore should have major implications for theorizing about the media, so should theory assimilate the realization that media do not merely service corporatized government, but they serve governments whose intentions, in profound respects, are malign, even towards their own people. Further, these governments act within a system of global power relations in which the US has for some decades acted and continues to act as an imperial power, and many of the corporatized democracies (and other systems of government) around the world are subalterns in this system. Up to 2003 the US had set up close to 1,000 military bases worldwide (Johnson, 2003), and there has been considerable further construction activity in Afghanistan, Iraq and Central Asia. Their purpose is global, regional and local control at the behest of a globally networked elite powered from its center in a US corporate plutocracy in alliance with the military-industrial complex. In 2007 the US was spending almost $229 billion on arms a year; this represented 46 per cent of the global total (Associated Press, 2007). The next largest was US ally Britain, which spent $59 billion, or 5 per cent of the total. In May 2007 the House of Representatives approved a $646 billion defence bill (Flaherty, 2007). These are the logistics of an imperial power whose strength most countries of the globe are simply unable to resist. That such imperial power can coexist with the appearance of 'local' media containing primarily 'local' content may speak either to the subtlety of soft power of imperial conquest or to the ease with which they distract the public from the reality of power relations.

US mainstream media rallied in support of President Bush during his 2003 build-up to invasion of Iraq, on false pretences, and similarly obliged his administration when it beat the drums for war against Iran from 2005 onwards, all in accordance with neo-conservative strategic thinking that had been available to the public from the 1990s. This unanimity of media support was tantamount to complicity, but was sometimes transparent, as confessed openly, for example, by the chief of news at CNN, Eason Jordan, when he told his viewing public that he had sought Pentagon vetting for the list of ex-military news commentators that he planned to use for coverage of the invasion (Alper and Earp, 2007). Following the US invasion of Afghanistan – a supposed reprisal for Afghan Taliban harbouring of Al Qaeda, the alleged culprits of 9/11 – Eason had instructed his news staff not to dwell too much on the casualties of US bombing without making it clear that the bombing was in retaliation for what CNN at that time claimed were the 5,000 casualties of 9/11 (that number was later reduced to 3,000). In the case of British Prime Minister Tony Blair, press complicity was exposed when the Cabinet Office finally released telephone records showing that Blair had had personal conversations with media mogul Rupert Murdoch on several occasions at critical points in Blair's premiership, including in the run-up to British involvement in the 2003 invasion of Iraq (Grice, 2007). These conversations were succeeded by dramatic headlines in support of British policy and against its opponents. In an earlier war, Kosovo, a 'handful of military personnel from the Third Psychological Operations Battalion, part of the airmobile Fourth Psychological Operations Group based at Fort Bragg, in North Carolina, had worked in CNN's headquarters in Atlanta' (Cockburn, 2000), working as regular employees of CNN. During this war, 'Christiane Amanpour, CNN's leading foreign correspondent, and a woman whose reports about the fate of Kosovan refugees did much to fan public appetite for NATO's war, [was] literally and figuratively in bed with spokesman for the US State Department, and a leading propagandist for NATO during that war, her husband James Rubin' (Cockburn, 2000). After the US invasion of Iraq, Amanpour complained that CNN 'was intimidated' by the Bush administration and Fox News, which 'put a climate of fear and self-censorship' (P. Johnson, 2003). The President of Fox News, Roger Ailes, had been hired by Fox owner Rupert Murdoch, who recognized that Ailes was one of the most important and effective PR strategists for the Republican Party. After 9/11, Ailes, 'as president of the "fair and balanced network," advised Bush on how to sell the Iraq war to the American people' (Stauber, quoted by Scheff, 2003).

Media studies as (in)sufficient unto itself

Can we talk about media solely from within the discipline of media studies? There is a limit to how many important insights we can learn about media simply from within the discipline of media studies itself. Where do the media stand in relation to the fundamental questions of the future and the well-being of the human condition? We have to ask, first of all, what are the factors that most affect the survival and health of humanity? And then we have to consider to what extent are news media exacerbating the problems, and to what extent are they contributing to solutions to these problems? Since the problems of the human condition increasingly have to do with such issues as corporate power and corruption, a global financial system that is beyond the control of regulators, the decay of corporate-driven democracy, global warming, pollution, wars over resources, the decline of gasoline supply, the future of coal and nuclear power, and so on, there is good reason to want to extend the conversation of communication scholars to directly involve the scholars of disciplines with whom they have had little previous dialogue.

Changing paradigms and the implications for media studies

What might we hope for from media systems in an age such as ours, were a 'public sphere' approach to media communication to prevail? We would expect diversity of ownership and great diversity of access. We would see the dilution of traditional models of journalism, which have functioned to close down critical thought, in favour of models that stimulate and engage with critical thought, and that function not so much to protect citizen-consumers but to show them how best to protect themselves, models that keep their distance from the major centres of power in society. Needless to say, when we look at the old media, we see no such features. These media are heavily concentrated; they are themselves major players in the multinational corporate universe; many of them have international presence but are mostly engaged in projects of cultural localization that misrepresent local cultures, minimize local cultural diversity and obfuscate the reality of the global economic and political order that increasingly shapes the local. These media are everywhere subservient to political power and engage proactively in propaganda functions of the state regardless of the formal properties of the political systems that host them. The internet is everything that the old media are not, except that it is (1) largely inaccessible to at least half of the world's population; (2) functionally inaccessible, by reason of low-grade distribution speeds and/or insufficient supply of computers and similar outlets, for approximately another quarter of that population; (3) subject to monopolistic controls of giant cable and telephone companies over the distribution of internet content; (4) subject to oligopolistic market control over the content that most competitively attracts audience attention, namely the web services of the traditional media conglomerates, and (5) affected by the continuing intellectual conditioning and dumbing-down of mainstream media culture and education which depresses the uses to which the internet is generally put.

References

Ahmed, N. (2002) *The War on Freedom: How and Why America Was Attacked on September 11, 2001*. Joshua Tree, CA: Progressive Press.

—— (2003) *Behind the War on Terror: Western Secret Strategy and the Struggle for Iraq*. Gabriola Island, British Columbia: New Society Publishers.

—— (2005) *The War on Truth: 9/11, Disinformation and the Anatomy of Terrorism*. New York: Oliver Branch.

Alper, L. and Earp, J. (2007) *War Made Easy: How Presidents and Pundits Keep Spinning Us to Death*. Northampton, MA: Media Education Foundation.

Associated Press (2007) The World's Top Ten Military Spenders, 11 June.

Berger, M. (2006) Zogby Poll: Over 70 Million American Adults Support New 9/11 Investigation, *PRWeb, Yahoo! News*, 22 May.

Bernays, E. (1928) *Propaganda*. New York: Horace Liveright.

Blum, W. (2003) *Killing Hope: US Military and CIA Interventions since World War II*. Monroe, ME: Common Courage Press.

Boyd-Barrett, O. (1998) Media Imperialism Reformulated, in D.K. Thussu (ed.) *Electronic Empires: Global Media and Local Resistance*. London: Arnold, pp. 155–76.

—— (2003) Doubt Foreclosed: US Mainstream Media and the Attacks of 9–11, in D. Demers (ed.) *Terrorism, Globalization and Mass Communication*. Spokane, WA: Marquette Books, pp. 3–33.

—— (2004a) Judith Miller, *The New York Times*, and the Propaganda Model, *Journalism Studies*, 5(4): 435–50.

—— (2004b) Understanding: The Second Casualty, in Stuart Allan and Barbie Zelizer (eds) *Reporting War: Journalism in Wartime*. London: Routledge.

—— (2007a) Positioning the News Audience as Idiot, in Sarah Maltby and Richard Keeble (eds) *Communicating War: Memory, Media and Military*. Bury St. Edmunds: Abramis.

—— (2007b) Recovering Agency for the Propaganda Model. Paper presented at the University of Windsor conference '20 Years of Propaganda', June.

Burke, K. (1968) *Language as Symbolic Action: Essays on Life, Literature and Method*. Berkeley: University of California Press.

Castaneda, J. (1997) *Companero: Vida y Muerte del Che Guevara*. New York: Vintage Books, Random House.

Chossudovsky, M. (2005) *America's 'War on Terrorism'*. Pincourt, Quebec: Global Research.

Cialdini, R. (1998) *The Psychology of Persuasion*. New York: Collins.

Cockburn, A. (2000) CNN and Psyops, *Counterpunch*, 26 March, www.counterpunch.org/cnnpsyops.html.

Cogan, J. (2007) Under Sustained US Pressure, Iraqi Cabinet Sends Oil Law to Parliament, *World Socialist Web Site*, 5 July, wsws.org.

Curran, J. and Park, M.J. (2000) *De-Westernizing Media Studies*. London: Routledge.

Curtis, M. (2003) *Web of Deceit: Britain's Real Role in the World*. London: Vintage.

Ellul, J. (1965/73) *Propaganda: The Formation of Men's Attitudes*. Trans. Konrad Kellen and Jean Lerner. New York: Knopf.

Entman, R.M. (2004) *Projections of Power: Framing News, Public Opinion, and US Foreign Policy*. Chicago: University of Chicago Press.

Flaherty, A. (2007) House Passes $646 Billion Defense Bill, Associated Press, 17 May.

Greenwald, R. (2004) Director, *Uncovered: The Whole Truth about the Iraq War*. Moveon.org and the Center for American Progress in Association with Artists United.

—— (2006) Director, *Iraq for Sale: The War Profiteers*. Brave New Films.

Grice, A. (2007) How Murdoch Had a Hotline to the PM in the Run-up to the Iraq War, *The Independent*, 19 July.

Griffin, D.R. (2004a) *The New Pearl Harbor: Disturbing Questions about the Bush Administration and 9/11*. Northampton, MA: Olive Branch Press.

—— (2004b) *The 9/11 Commission Report: Omissions and Distortions*. Northampton, MA: Olive Branch Press.

—— (2007) *Debunking 9/11 Debunking: An Answer to Popular Mechanics and Other Defenders of the Official Conspiracy Theory*. Northampton, MA: Olive Branch Press.

Herman, E. and Chomsky, N. (1988/2002) *Manufacturing Consent: The Political Economy of the Mass Media*. New York: Pantheon Books.

Johnson, C. (2000) *Blowback: The Costs and Consequences of American Empire*. New York: Henry Holt.

—— (2003) *The Sorrows of Empire: Militarism, Secrecy and the End of the Republic*. New York: Metropolitan Books.

Johnson, P. (2003) Amanpour: CNN Practiced Self-censorship, *USA Today*, 14 September.

Kraidy, M. (2005) *Hybridity or the Cultural Logic of Globalization*. Philadelphia, PA: Temple University Press.

Lance, P. (2003) *1000 Years for Revenge: International Terrorism and the FBI. The Untold Story*. New York: Regan.

—— (2006) *Triple Cross*. New York: Regan.

Media Lens (2007) Bush–Brown Summit: The Media Deception Continues and the Iraqi Catastrophe Deepens, *Media Lens*, 3 August, www.medialens.org.

Mitchell, G. (2007) Consider the Source: 'NYT' Reporter Targets Iran, *Editor and Publisher*, 15 July.

Moore, M. (2004) Director, *Fahrenheit 9/11*. Lions Gate Films, IFC Films and the Fellowship Adventure Group, a Dog Eat Dog Films production.

—— (2007) Director, *Sicko*. Dog Eat Dog Films production and the Weinstein Company.

New York Times (2007) The Road Home, editorial, 8 July, p. 11.

Perkins, J. (2005) *Confessions of an Economic Hit Man*. San Francisco, CA: Berrett-Koehler.

Schechter, D. (2005) Director, *Weapons of Mass Deception*. Cinema Libre Distribution and Globalvision Presentation.

Scheff, L. (2003) News You Can Abuse, *Los Angeles City Beat*, 11 December.

Sparks, C. (1998) Is There a Global Public Sphere?, in D.K. Thussu (ed.) *Electronic Empires: Global Media and Local Resistance*. London: Arnold, pp. 108–24.

Straubhaar, J. (2007) *Global Television*. London: Sage.

Tuchman, G. (1978) *Making News: A Study in the Construction of Reality*. New York: Free Press.

Tunstall, J. (2007) *The Media Were American: US Mass Media in Decline*. Oxford: Oxford University Press.

US Government (1979) *Army Field Manual 33–1: Psychological Operations*. Washington: Department of the Army.

Chapter 8

Comparative media law and policy

Opportunities and challenges[1]

Stefaan Verhulst and Monroe E. Price

Why engage in comparative media law and policy research? One might argue that all research is in essence comparative even if, as a result of the parochial urge, comparisons are subconscious or excluded. We tend towards the comparative even if it is through the desire to have greater understanding of the singular. But without the conscious effort, comparisons are mangled, inadequate, often a disservice. In this chapter, we start with the assumption that comparative research has major benefits: comparisons can lead to fresh, exciting insights and a deeper understanding of issues that are of central concern in different countries. They can identify gaps in knowledge and policies and may point to possible directions that could be followed, directions that previously may have been unknown to observers or, in the case of media law, legal reformers. Comparisons may also help to sharpen the focus of analysis of the subject under study by suggesting new perspectives.[2] Comparative media law research can give us a better understanding of how one country, or even medium, borrows from the traditions and conventions of another (such as the links between film and broadcasting, the PSB models within Europe, free speech notions in Latin American countries); how intellectual property migrates across various media over time; and where best practices exist in the world for the regulation of new communications technologies.[3] Moreover, comparative research can give us an improved knowledge as to whether specific media patterns and structures are causally conditioned by social, political, economic, historical and geographic circumstances.

Partly because of the growing internationalization and the concomitant export and import of social, cultural and economic manifestations across national borders, and partly because of political, economic, social and technological transitions, the demand for comparative research has grown. It is increasingly evident that contemporary communications structures and patterns can only be understood from a comparative perspective. Only by examining relationships across media forms, across national and regional boundaries, across cultures, institutions and environments and over time,[4] can a full picture of the processes of change and globalization be created. Hence the growth of the use of comparative research and the increased need, as well as demand, for comparisons.

Yet, despite the benefits and the growing demand, little informed discourse exists on the opportunities of comparative media law and on the potential methodological challenges of the preparation of such work.[5] This reluctance and narrowness of scope may be explained not only by a lack of knowledge or understanding of different cultures and languages, but also by insufficient awareness of the research traditions and processes operating in different national contexts. This is certainly the case in the field of comparative media law and policy, which combines the research traditions of comparative social research in general with comparative law in particular. The purpose of this chapter is to analyse the needs, possibilities, limitations and pitfalls of comparison, and to probe problems of definition, methodology and presentation.

Growing demand for comparative research

One way of thinking of the issue is environmental. What kind of context is ideal for comparative media law and policy research? One could look at the loci where this kind of work is done, or where it is attempted to be done. A principal characteristic is to have some sort of institutional commitment and something like a critical mass. Communities of scholars are built with a comparative bias. Efforts have been made at the University of Westminster, in the UK, and at the School of Business at Columbia University. We both have been engaged in trying to establish such centres (Programme in Comparative Media Law and Policy at Oxford University, 1996, and the Center for Media and Communications Studies at Central European University, 2004). Currently, one of us directs a Center for Global Communication Studies at the Annenberg School for Communication and the other continues to nourish comparativism from a perch at the Markle Foundation. MIT is another prominent university to have created a centre dedicated to comparative media research: offering a two-year course of study, the Comparative Media Studies Department allows students to study for a master's degree.

A somewhat unconventional example is offered by the Learning Initiatives on Reforms for Network Economies (LIRNE.NET), an international collaboration between four universities: the Center for Tele-Information (CTI), Technical University of Denmark; the Economics of Infrastructures Section, Delft University of Technology, the Netherlands; Media@LSE, the media and communications programme at the London School of Economics; and the LINK Centre at the University of Witwatersrand in Johannesburg. This network, which is one of the key partners in the World Dialogue on Regulation (www.regulateonline.org), has produced a number of comparative and cross-country analyses, primarily in the field of telecoms regulation. A similar, yet broader, kind of network is ORBICOM, the Network of UNESCO Chairs in Communications, which has conducted some comparative analyses.[6] The Hans Bredow Institute in Hamburg is an example of an interdisciplinary institute with comparative ambitions but rooted in a German legal context. It also is an example of a research entity funded, in the first instance, by public service broadcasters, but then branching out. One important recent entrant, Ofcom, the British regulator, has emphasized evidence-based policy-making and the need to look comparatively to understand regulatory possibilities.

Each of these units takes a different approach to comparative research. Seen together, however, they mark the growing importance of the field. Their emergence, and more generally the growth of comparative research, has its roots in a variety of forces.

Globalization, the end of the Cold War, the rise of Asian economies and the growing geopolitical importance of the Middle East are just some of the tendencies that have led to a general call for broadening of the usual scope of research to include more comparative studies. The increased transnational flow of people and information has clearly challenged the universality of Western theoretical models and concepts,[7] and has forced scholars to look beyond their borders and disciplines. Moreover, amidst a growing homogeneity and uniformity, the emphasis of research has shifted from seeking uniformity among variety to studying the preservation of enclaves of uniqueness. Anthony Giddens has, for instance, observed that 'globalization today is only partly Westernization. Globalization is becoming increasingly decentered.'[8] Indeed, while some cultural differences are diminishing as a result of globalization, others are becoming more salient. Only comparative research succeeds in capturing this richness of variety across nations, institutions and cultures.

The need for more comparative media law research clearly fits within this broader framework of globalization. In many cases, however, comparative media law has emerged in response to a more complicated mix of forces. Technological transformations, political transitions, and institutional and market restructuring are among the most important pressures. In addition, advanced telecommunications and the worldwide expansion of media markets create an urgent need to understand our emerging 'global media culture', the cross-fertilization of national and international cultural traditions, and the new styles and genres developing in this context. The world is engaged in a vast re-mapping of the relationship of governments, corporations and societies to the images, messages and information that course within and across traditional boundaries. States, governments, public international agencies, multinational corporations, human rights organizations and billions of individuals are all involved in this process. All is under construction, yielding, as it were, a thorough shaking and remodelling of media and communications systems. The result, at the moment, is a teeming experiment in reconstruction and reaction of media laws and policies. The various players are seeking a vocabulary of change and a set of laws and institutions that provide legitimacy, continued power, or the opportunity to profit from the technological prospects for change. Only with a comparative and interdisciplinary grasp of the massive changes taking place can there be a more sophisticated and nuanced understanding of the impact of media changes on democratic values and economic development.

Among the various forces driving comparative media law, technological change is, clearly, one of the most important. The introduction of a new medium is often met with both utopian visions of a more perfect society and apocalyptic anxieties about the collapse of an old order. In much the same way, the emergence of new media forces us to rethink relationships and regulatory assumptions regarding previous communication technologies. It challenges the application and value of older models of regulation to a newer environment. To understand the true complexity of technological convergence we must improve our understanding of the interrelationships among many different technologies and media environments. We must therefore compare and think across media. A fully comparative insight into the meaning of convergence and technological change across nations, its importance for regulators over time, and the different perspectives with which to assess its impact are clearly among the most important threshold issues to address, before it is possible to consider specific regulatory responses at, for instance, a pan-European level.[9]

Moreover, the massive transformations in the media sector, brought about by technological convergence, economic liberalization and globalization of manufacturing processes, have resulted in major changes to media ownership patterns throughout the world. Media ownership that was once bounded by the geographical limitations of the nation state has become transnational. Transparency of media ownership structures and guarantees of pluralism are challenges for every government and institution. The need for global mapping of media ownership and control patterns has become a major motivator behind comparative media research.[10]

These transformations, however, are more than changing the way media are controlled and analysed; they are also changing the regulatory mechanisms for the communications sector altogether. Self-regulation has, for instance, been suggested as a panacea for many of the current problems on the internet. It illustrates the move away from traditional command-and-control regulation towards more responsive and newer regulatory systems. Clearly, to analyse self-regulation on the internet the scope of study has to be transnational and comparative. Moreover, in order to examine, for instance, codes of conduct as effective response mechanisms to content concerns on the internet, the units of analysis have to be the major transnational Internet Content and Service Providers (e.g. MSN, Yahoo, Google). Cross-institutional and cross-instrument research is therefore a new and important field of comparative media law research.

In addition to these technological and institutional transitions, a growing demand for comparative data exists in transitional societies that are (re-)considering the balance between state regulatory prerogatives and the freedom of media outlets. The post-Cold War period has not only opened previously inaccessible countries for a comparative media law perspective, but also demonstrated that the shaping of media laws and the administrative agencies involved in implementing them are key determinants in the emergence of stable democracies. Much, in addition, has been learned during this period about styles of preparing laws, needs of groups involved in improving the process and entities dedicated to establishing a media sphere that includes independent newspapers, television and radio stations.[11] In some societies, there has been the challenge of inventing a media law where none existed before. In others, where a government or regime has been discredited and where control of the press was characteristic of its excesses, revision of the media law is often necessary. In a third group of societies, often in the post-Soviet transition, there are difficulties in providing technical assistance in implementing media laws and revising flaws in a first generation of legislative reforms. Problems exist because of the lack of reliable information about regulatory models, legal and societal changes within a given state, challenges of new technologies and changes in the international scheme of trading and regulation with respect to the media. Often, groups participating in the process of media law improvement (as a step towards enhancing the role of the press in a democratic society) do not have an adequate sense of the Western or neighbouring models available and how they might be interpreted and adjusted. Hence, more cross-national media law studies than ever before are being carried out and the demand for comparisons across countries is immense.

Finally, the demand for comparative media law research is also dispersed over time. It may be most intense while a statute is being drafted or debated, or a new technology is being introduced, but it is equally valuable during implementation, even though the requirement for discourse and alternatives may not be so evident. To be responsive, media law research must be able to react to these rhythms of demand.

Comparative media law research

Comparisons are an integral part of most sciences. Many scholars would therefore argue that the very nature of their method is comparative and that thinking in comparative terms is inherent to their research. In truth, no phenomenon can be isolated and studied without comparing it to other phenomena. This is certainly (or especially) the case for law as well as for media related issues, the two major strands that make up comparative media law. The question may therefore be posed whether comparative media law research presents a different set of theoretical, methodological and epistemological challenges, or whether this kind of analysis must be treated just as another variant of the (comparative) problems already embedded in traditional law and/or media research.

One could take the view that conducting comparative research across countries is no different from conducting any other kind of media and/or legal research. Another approach is to pursue comparisons without considering whether the research adds to the complexity of interpreting the results of the study. Our view is that it is necessary to be aware of the many problems of doing comparative research in a world of complex interdependencies. Without becoming paralysed in the face of these complexities, it is important to go ahead, opting for compromise and trying to use existing tools for new insights.[12] To advance our knowledge about comparative media law research it is necessary to consider some distinctive characteristics of comparative studies.

Not all comparative studies are alike. Several distinctions within comparative research can and should be made. One can, for instance, distinguish two broad types of research in comparative media law research. Exponents of *micro-comparison* analyse the laws belonging to the same legal family, within a single jurisdiction. Researchers pledged to *macro-comparison*, on the other hand, investigate laws in different jurisdictions in order to gain insight into alien institutions and thought processes.[13] For some legal scholars, concerned mainly with legal technicalities, micro-comparison holds the greater attraction, whereas macro-comparison is the realm of the political scientist or legal philosopher, who sees law as a social science and is interested in its role in government and the organization of the community. Micro-comparison appears to demand no particular preparation. A specialist in one national system considers himself or herself qualified to study the systems of various other countries of the same general family. Her main need is access to bibliographical material. But even this mechanical approach avoids certain built in problems we deal with later. With macro-comparison, no comparison is possible without identifying and thoroughly mastering the fundamentals of the legal and social systems as they differ from place to place. The scholar must, as it were, subvert her own background and seek to reason according to new criteria.

Within comparative media law, both types of investigation are often employed. In analysing regulatory responses to the changing media,[14] for instance, both micro- and macro-comparisons can be used. Micro-comparison then takes priority when a range of regulatory challenges and problems, such as data protection, competition, content control and others, are examined within a specific nation and described by a country expert. Macro-comparison follows when the research project managers compare the selected jurisdictions and their detailed descriptions.[15]

Many similar distinctions,[16] for example between heterogeneous and homogeneous comparative research, can be made. One particularly useful distinction is between vertical and horizontal comparison.[17] Vertical comparison concerns social and legal contexts showing different levels of economic and technological development, such as internet penetration or take-up of digital television. Horizontal comparison is concerned with contexts sharing a relatively similar level of economic and technological development, but largely differing in their development, their production organization, their political and legal regime, and/or other relevant characteristics.

Again, many comparative media law research projects may combine both approaches. For example, the European Commission launched a research project in 1997 called ESIS (European Survey of Information Society)[18] with the objective of comparing European data concerning new regulatory developments in the field of telecommunications and Information Society as well as presenting a mapping of the actors offering Information Society infrastructure, services and applications. The project was extended to Central and Eastern European countries and the Mediterranean countries in 1999. These two regions were compared from a vertical perspective, and within the regions it was obvious that, for example, Albania and Poland differed from each other substantially in a macro way. Tunisia and Morocco, however, were compared from a more horizontal and micro-comparative perspective. Clearly, as described below, different types of problems arise with regard to both kinds of comparison.

Another way of considering comparative media law research as a distinctive method is to look at the paradigm field in which it operates. At least four conflicting models and poles underpin most comparative media law projects.

Uniformity and diversity paradigm

Because of globalization and the creation of free markets, it is predicted that media laws and policies will present a considerable measure of similarity and uniformity, at least with respect to communications infrastructure and economic regulation. Yet, owing to the endurance of social traditions or cultural preferences that are still quite different in many parts of the world, there is and will be much less harmony between the rules dealing with content. Moreover, diversities of media law within one country may also exist on an ethnic, religious or federalist basis. Even within national borders differences still exist, for instance among the *Länder* of Germany towards media regulation.

Searching for uniformity and unearthing and explaining diversity lie at the heart of comparative media law research. Comparative media law considers the benefits and burdens of uniformity and plumbs the contexts demanding diversity and tries to establish a terminology that enables comparison. Comparative research has moved from justification for uniformity to studying the uniqueness and variety in homogeneity.[19]

Rhetoric and reality

One interesting challenge of comparative research is to face the 'grass is greener on the other side' syndrome, or, in some cases, 'dark side of the moon' comparisons. Indeed, comparisons are often used by vested interests (e.g. incumbent operators) to prove, for reasons of political or rhetorical expediency, the effectiveness or harmfulness of a specific foreign policy. Comparative data, in particular, are sometimes utilized in a deliberately muddled way to advance a particular agenda. One key task of comparative media law research, as with all methodologies, is to put legal and policy practices within their appropriate contexts to create a better understanding of reality rather than ammunition for exchanges of heated rhetoric.

Metaphors and models

During the process of comparative thinking about the global restructuring of the media and when conceptualizing regulatory responses, two specific techniques are often applied: the methods of model and metaphor.[20] First, comparing the experience of others, proponents of one system or another invoke what they deem to be a 'model' for imitation, such as looking at the BBC for public broadcasting or the 'newspaper model' for regulation. The second technique for conceptualization involves the use of metaphors to simplify the task of articulating the path of change, such as the metaphors of the 'information superhighway', 'cyberspace' or 'killer applications'. Metaphors and models are useful and common tools within comparative research and analysis. They can help guide researchers and policy-makers through uncharted territory.[21] But there are limitations. Metaphors can be poetic devices that wrap complex ideas in appealing words; they can be used to persuade even when acceptance is not wholly warranted. Both metaphors and models can be shortcuts that avoid more complex reasoning.[22]

Transfer and exclusion

Comparative media law research provides the evidence for the use of models and metaphors in policy or law transfer debates. The basic thrust of current theories of policy and law transfer[23] is the idea that law and policy diffusion is a process explained by imitation, copying and adaptation on the part of policy-makers. Comparative media law and policy play a crucial role within this process of identifying 'success policies' and best practices that can then be exported to other countries via a process of learning, interpretation and even translation. Lesson drawing,[24] as a process of interpretation and translation, is a major goal of comparative media law. In some exceptional cases, comparative media law has also been used for 'forced' policy and law transfer, by conditioning on the adoption of certain media policies financial assistance or other incentives and even to determine exclusion from membership of specific international authorities, such as the Council of Europe.[25]

Functions and aims of comparative media law

From the above, it may be obvious that comparative media law research serves multiple aims and functions. In general, and at a more epistemological level, one could define comparative research as an 'école de vérité', a methodology that seeks to supply comparative solutions and better international understanding. More concretely, at least four key uses for comparative media law research can be identified: further study of historical and cultural components, commercial application, legislative assistance, and international law and harmonization.

Historical and cultural relativism

We may view comparative media law from the standpoint of its value to the historical and cultural study of legal and policy decision-making in the field of communications (including the political economy of policy-making). Ideas regarding the place of law in society, the nature of the law itself and its relationship with new communications technologies become appreciably clearer when comparative law is joined to historical research. Indeed, to some extent, historical background may aid in forecasting the future of certain national systems and the applicability of existing law to new tendencies. A closely related consideration prompts many Western jurists, political scientists and sociologists to acquaint themselves with non-Western methods of reasoning. For example, comparative studies can reveal that sources and conceptions of free speech and its role vary widely. The notions of a rule of law and of rights of the individual – fundamental to Western civilization – are not wholly recognized by societies that, faithful to the principle of conciliation and concerned primarily with harmony within the group, do not favour excessive Western-style individualism or the modern Western ideal of legal supremacy. These differences may be used as a justification for authoritarian rule, but they also may reflect important variances in structuring the relationship of the individual and society. Comparative law may enable an improved understanding from a viewpoint of historical and cultural relativism.[26]

Commercial uses

Comparative media law may be used for essentially practical ends. Industry leaders, for instance, need to know what benefits they can expect, what risks they may run, and generally how they should invest capital or run businesses abroad. This practical aspect has encouraged the growth of comparative law in the United States, where the essential aim of law school has been usually to turn out practitioners, and one need hardly mention the strong link in Germany between big industry and the various institutes of comparative law. Sometimes it is said that studies with such a focus should not be considered a part of comparative media law, but practical considerations certainly have helped to finance and promote the development of comparative legal studies in general.[27]

Aid to legislators

The re-mapping of communications structures because of all kinds of transitions (from planned economies to free markets, from analogue to digital, from war to peace) requires an ongoing reform of legal systems. When considering new regulatory frameworks, policy-makers and legislators quite often have a desire to identify foreign models that already have been tested, instead of framing a new, revolutionary system. Seeking foreign inspiration for legal rules or institutions is a well-known phenomenon, sometimes so all-embracing that one speaks of 'reception' or 'transfer'. The study of comparative media law is therefore used by legislators to identify 'transferable models' and has found a special place among scholars in those countries where such a reception or transfer has occurred.[28]

Use in international law

Globalization of communications and the growth of the internet have led to calls for more international and regional efforts to harmonize the regulatory framework of specific transactions. Those engaging in cross-border communications, for instance, do not know with certainty which national law will regulate their content, since the answer depends to a large extent on a generally undecided factor, namely, which national court will be called upon to decide the questions of competence. The sole lasting remedy appears to be the development of a more harmonized international system. The development of the TV without Frontiers Directive in 1989 (reviewed in 1997 and 2007) was a regional answer to a similar call from transnational satellite broadcasters. Harmonization can succeed only through the medium of comparative law. Regional authorities are highly dependent on comparative material in order to identify policy issues and monitor, for instance, the implementation of existing multilateral agreements or to highlight the need for action in certain areas. An important function, therefore, of comparative law research is its significant role in the preparation of projects for the international unification of law.[29]

Methodological problems

Despite growing demand and multiple benefits, comparative media law studies are still at the pioneering stage[30] and are both difficult and risky. It is therefore necessary to examine the limitations and potential pitfalls of such studies. Comparative research in general poses certain well-known problems (e.g. accessing comparable data[31] and comparing concepts and research parameters).[32] Additionally, when comparing different jurisdictions and legal systems, researchers may be subject to further pitfalls: (1) clashing linguistic and terminological perspectives; (2) cultural differences between legal systems; (3) potential arbitrariness in the selection of objects of study; (4) difficulties in achieving 'comparability' in comparison; (5) the desire to see a common legal pattern in legal systems (the theory of a general pattern of development); (6) the tendency to impose one's own (native) legal conceptions and expectations on the systems being compared; (7) dangers of exclusion/ignorance of extra-legal rules.[33]

As for comparative media law specifically, one might observe three additional sources of limitations:[34] (1) inadequate availability of statutory and secondary material for those engaged in comparative research; (2) the quick 'expiration' of information due to the rapid and constant change of communications law (a process itself driven by rapid technological change); (3) the possibility that information, even if available and correct, may not be easily summarized, compressed, or reduced to elements that are comparable. These are questions of organization, terminology and presentation. Each of these potential difficulties is worth discussing briefly.

Limitations on availability of statutory and other regulatory sources

Despite researchers' expertise and experience in the field, the absence of ready, comprehensive and up-to-date material remains a definite limitation on the capacity to undertake meaningful comparative media law and policy research. This shortcoming restricts the way advocates and legislators can use comparative research in their process of reform. But even if the statutes and decisions are available, formal language and legal terminology within statutory or regulatory material are potentially misleading as the exclusive source of law.[35] Words alone do not convey the manner in which concepts are variously carried out and enforced. In some societies, a formal prohibition may be quite strict, but the practice may be quite lenient. A similar divergence may exist when interpreting constitutional principles, such as freedom of speech.

The speed of change of regulation and law within the communications sector

A second potential difficulty has to do with the pace of change. Comparative research usually provides only a snapshot of regulatory formations when a motion picture is required. While this is a problem of research generally, and certainly of research that depicts the way in which the world is organized as of a certain date, it is particularly true in the area of telecommunications and broadcasting, where technological innovation often outstrips legal developments. Thus the need to keep up-to-date with fast-moving technological change often muddies the waters for would-be comparatists. In particular, convergence, a favourite doctrine of regulation analysts, suggests that existing categories for regulation are being confounded.[36]

Limitations based on selection, comparability and simplification

The comparability of regulatory regimes depends on a number of factors, some constant, many transient. Some commentators[37] list the following determinative factors: the cultural, political and economic components of a society, the particular relationships that exist between the state and its citizens, a society's value system and its particular conception of the individual. Other general factors include the homogeneity of the society in question and its geographical situation, language and religion. It is indeed difficult to find countries that have achieved a similar stage of development in those areas.

Even more difficult than the problem of selection is the problem of simplification and definition: almost all forms of comparison require the articulation of similarities so that resemblance and differences can be noted. Therefore, a related problem to be addressed in any comparative study is one of context. In terms of media law and policy, for example, it is important to understand the reasons why a comparison is being made, reasons that may not have to do with the law itself but with the objectives of law. Often the goal of a broadcast regulatory structure is to increase the diversity of voices or to enhance the right of a citizen to receive or impart information. A restriction on foreign ownership may have an impact in a society rich in broadcast signals that is totally different from that in one where such signals are few and competition is just beginning.

Strategy and conclusion

If we are to overcome these stumbling blocks to comparative research, compromises and methodological strategies have to be adopted. In many cases, simply being aware of the limitations and risks may offer preventive solutions to the comparative methodological problems. In addition, according to Rosengren, McLeod and Blumler, there are three fundamental tasks that need to be carried out in all comparative studies, whether temporally or spatially oriented:

- identifying a set of basic parameters and their structural interrelationships;
- measuring the parameter values, as well as assessing the strength of their relationship; and
- comparing differences and similarities in parameter values and structural relationship over space, as well as charting the development of parameter values and structural relationships over time.

According to the authors, the first task is primarily a theoretical one, the second is an empirical one and the third represents the essence of comparative research. A successfully tested method within this set of tasks is the creation of a uniform template that indicates and defines the parameters and allows consistency and coherent comparisons, as well as flexibility and functionality. When drafting the template, parameters should clearly be theoretically justified and founded. If they are embedded in a theory, they are potentially theoretically relevant. (Indeed, in many cases, the central problem of comparative media law research is not technical but theoretical.) Moreover, experience has proven that the empirical implementation is best approached via a 'federalistic project management' by which 'native scholars' measure the parameters within their own region or country. As Rosengren *et al.* also note:[38]

> In order to be really successful, comparative research demands that – at least in the long run – all three types of tasks be solved. There is a natural order in solving the tasks and it is only in the nature of things that progress is quite differential in varied areas and fields of research.

This is just one among many possible strategies to deal with the challenges we have outlined above. The primary purpose of this chapter, as we stated at the outset, was to examine the benefits, challenges and current approaches in comparative media law studies. The demand has been growing at a dramatic rate in recent years. To an extent, some of the challenges can be attributed to this rapid growth. These are but growing pains, and in the coming years we can expect that some of the conceptual and theoretical vagueness that afflict the field will gradually solidify. Nonetheless, it is essential that researchers conduct their work while remaining aware of the bigger picture (including the challenges confronted by their field). We are not just conducting research in a vacuum, but as part of something bigger; every piece of comparative research is also an act of definition, contributing to a better understanding of the field itself.

Finally, it is worth noting that this act of definition is one of the key tasks remaining in the years ahead. As with all interdisciplinary disciplines (and particularly nascent ones), comparative media studies are always in danger of being subsumed by a sub- or parent-discipline. This can be added to the list of challenges mentioned above. Yet as we have seen in this chapter, the field has its own unique identity and its own distinctive set of contributions to make. Comparative media researchers therefore have the possibility not only of contributing to the definition of a new field; in the process, they will also sharpen that field's insights and enhance its many contributions.

Notes

1 An earlier version of this chapter was published in *International Journal of Communication*, 2 (2008): 406–20, http://ijoc.org.

2 See Linda Hantrais, Comparative Research Methods, *Social Research Update*, University of Surrey, Issue 13, Summer 1995.

3 Most examples used within this chapter are based upon the work conducted at the Programme in Comparative Media Law and Policy. For more information see http://pcmlp.socleg.ox.ac.uk/.

4 The vocabulary for distinguishing between the different kinds of comparative research may prove to be redundant and not very precise in many cases. Concepts such as cross-national, cross-cultural, cross-institutional, cross-societal, etc., are used both as synonymous with comparative research in general and as denoting specific kinds of comparisons.

5 See, for example, Else Oyen (1990) *Comparative Methodology: Theory and Practice in International Social Research*. London: Sage; Stefaan Verhulst and Monroe Price, A Methodological Perspective on the Use of Comparative Media Law, in Monroe Price and Stefaan Verhulst (1998) *Broadcasting Reform in India: Media Law from a Global Perspective*. New Delhi: Oxford University Press.

6 pcmlp.socleg.ox.ac.uk/, www.lirne.net, www.orbicom.uqam.ca, web.mit.edu/cms/index.html.

7 For a detailed description of this unease with so-called Western parochialism within media studies, see James Curran and Myung-Jin Park (eds) (2000) *De-Westernizing Media Studies*. London: Routledge.
8 Anthony Giddens, The Reith Lecture Series: New World without an End, *The Observer*, 11 April 1999.
9 For a discussion of the need for comparison of the approaches to convergence, see Stefaan Verhulst and Chris Marsden (1999) *Convergence in European Digital TV Regulation*. London: Blackstone.
10 See Monroe Price (2002) *Media and Sovereignty: The Global Information Revolution and Its Challenge to State Power*. Cambridge, MA: MIT Press.
11 See Monroe Price and Peter Krug (2000) *Media Law Enabling Environment*. Washington: USAID. See also Peter Krug and Monroe Price, A Module for Media Intervention: Content Regulation in Post-conflict Zones, Cardozo Law School, Public Law Research Paper No. 58.
12 See Else Oyen, The Imperfection of Comparisons, in Else Oyen (ed.) (1990) *Comparative Methodology*. Beverly Hills, CA: Sage, pp. 1–18.
13 One may, however, argue that a micro-comparison always implies a macro as well and vice versa.
14 See Stefaan Verhulst, David Goldberg and Tony Prosser (1999) *Regulating the Changing Media: A Comparative Study*. Oxford: Clarendon Press.
15 For examples of macro research, see Chris Dent (2004) Defamation Law's Chilling Effect: A Comparative Content Analysis of Australian and US Newspapers, *Media and Arts Law Review*, 9(2): 89–112; Michael Chesterman (1997) OJ and the Dingo: How Media Publicity Relating to Criminal Cases Tried by Jury Is Dealt with in Australia and America, *American Journal of Comparative Law*, 45(1): 109–147; Peter Klik (1988) Mass Media and Offers to the Public: An Economic Analysis of Dutch Civil Law and American Common Law, *American Journal of Comparative Law*, 36: 235.
For an example that includes both macro and micro-research, see Kati Suominen (2003) Access to Information in Latin America and the Caribbean, *Comparative Media Law Journal*, 2: 29.
16 Kohn identifies, for instance, four kinds of comparative research on the basis of the different intent of the studies. Countries can be: (1) the object of the study – the interest of the researcher lies primarily in the countries studied; (2) the context of the study – the interest is mainly vested in testing the generality of research results concerning social phenomena in the countries compared; (3) the units of analysis – where the interest is chiefly to investigate how social phenomena are systematically related to characteristics of the countries researched; (4) transnational – namely studies that treat nations as components of a larger international system. See Melvin Kohn (1989) *Cross-National Research in Sociology*. Newbury Park: Sage.
17 See Vincenzo Ferrari (1990) Socio-Legal Concepts and Their Comparison, in Else Oyen (ed.) *Comparative Methodology*, p. 67.
18 See http://www.eu-esis.org/esis2pres/esis2pres.htm.
19 See Bernd Holznagel (1999) New Challenges: Convergence of Markets, Divergence of the Laws? – Questions Regarding the Future Communications Regulation, *International Journal of Communications Law and Policy*, Web-Doc 5-2-1999. Available at www.ijclp.org/2_1999/ijclp_webdoc_5_2_1999.html; Lyombe Eko (2001) Many Spiders, One World Wide Web: Towards a Typology of Internet Regulation, *Communication Law and Policy*, 6(3): 445–84.
20 See Monroe Price (2002) *Media and Sovereignty*, Chapter 2.
21 For discussions of the uses of metaphors and models, see Stefaan Verhulst and Monroe Price, In Search of the Self: Charting the Course of Self-Regulation on the Internet in a Global Environment, Cardozo Law School, Public Law Working Paper No. 015;

Verhulst and Price (2000), Privatization and Self-Regulation as Tropes of Global Media Restructuring, Cardozo Law School, Public Law Working Paper No. 010; Monroe Price (1997) Market for Loyalties and the Uses of Comparative Media Law, *Cardozo Journal of International and Comparative Law*, 445.

22 It has also been claimed that in the case of the internet, for instance, any metaphor will fail because of its uniqueness. For a further analysis of the role of metaphors, see Raymond Gozzi, Jr. (1999) *The Power of Metaphor in the Age of Electronic Media*. Cresskill, NJ: Hampton Press.

23 For an overview of the policy transfer literature see David Dolowitz and David Marsh (1996) Who Learns from Whom: A Review of the Policy Transfer Literature, *Policy Studies*, XLIV: 343–57. The law transfer process has been described in James A. Gardner (1980) *Legal Imperialism: American Lawyers and Foreign Aid in Latin America*, 14

24 See, for instance, Colin Bennet and Michael Howlett (1992) The Lessons of Learning: Reconciling Theories of Policy Learning and Policy Change, *Policy Sciences*, 25: 275–94.

25 For a good discussion of policy transfer within the new EU accession states, see Alison Harcourt (2003) The Regulation of Media Markets in Selected EU Accession States in Central and Eastern Europe, *European Law Journal*, 9(3): 316.

26 See Richard Ross (2002) Communications Revolutions and Legal Culture: An Elusive Relationship, *Law and Social Inquiry*, 27(3): 637–84. Wei Li *et al.* (2001) The Political Economy of Privatisation and Competition: Cross-Country Evidence from the Telecommunications Sector, Discussion Paper No. 2585. London: Centre for Economic Policy Research. Available at www.cepr.org/pubs/new-dps/dplist.asp?dpno = 2825.

27 For an example of comparative legal research with business applicability, see Urs Gasser (2004) *iTunes: How Copyright, Contract, and Technology Shape the Business of Digital Media – A Case Study*, Berkman Center for Internet & Society at Harvard Law School Research, Publication No. 2004–7.

28 See Christina Spyrelli (2004) Regulating the Regulators? An Assessment of Institutional Structures and Procedural Rules of National Regulatory Authorities, *International Journal of Communications Law and Policy*, Web-Doc 1-8-2004. Available at www.digital-law.net/IJCLP/8_2004/ijclp_webdoc_1_8_2004.htm.

29 The political aim behind such unification is to reduce or eliminate, so far as desirable and possible, the discrepancies between the national legal systems by inducing them to adopt common principles of law. The method used in the past and still often practised today is to draw up a uniform law on the basis of work by experts in comparative law and to incorporate it in a multipartite treaty which obliges the signatories, as a matter of international law, to adopt and apply the uniform law as their municipal law. See Peter F. Cowhey (1990) The International Telecommunications Regime: The Political Roots of Regimes for High Technology, *International Organization*, 44(2): 169–99.

30 For some notable contributions comparing media laws, see Eric Barendt (1993) *Broadcasting Law: A Comparative Study*. Oxford: Oxford University Press; Wolfgang Hoffmann-Riem (1996) *Regulating Media: The Licensing and Supervision of Broadcasting in Six Countries*. New York: Guilford Press.

31 See Margaret Stacey (1969) *Comparability in Social Research*. London: Heinemann.

32 See Linda Hantrais and Steen Mangen (1996) *Cross-National Research Methods in the Social Sciences*. London: Pinter.

33 See Konrad Zweigert and Hein Kötz (1989) *An Introduction to Comparative Law*. Oxford: Oxford University Press.

34 See Stefaan Verhulst and Monroe Price (1998) A Methodological Perspective on the Use of Comparative Media Law, in Price and Verhulst, *Broadcasting Reform in India*.

35 A fairly extensive literature acknowledging the importance of language as a factor in comparative research and law exists. See, for example, Bernhard Grossfeld (1990) *The Strength and Weakness of Comparative Law*. Oxford: Clarendon Press, Chapter 13.

36 For two good discussions of the interaction between legal and technological change, see Uta Kohl (1994) Legal Reasoning and Legal Change in the Age of the Internet – Why the Ground Rules Are Still Valid, *International Journal of Law and Information Technology*, 7(2): 123; Lawrence Lessig (1999) *Code and Other Laws of Cyberspace*. New York: Basic Books.

37 Peter de Cruz (1993) *A Modern Approach to Comparative Law*. Oxford: Oxford University Press.

38 See Karl Erik Rosengren, Jack M. McLeod and Jay C. Blumler(eds) (1992) Comparatively Speaking: Communication and Culture across Space and Time, *Annual Review of Communication Research*, 19: 287.

Chapter 9

The labouring of international communication

Vincent Mosco and David O. Lavin

Research in international communication studies has tended to cluster around three interconnected topics: media, messages and audiences. Those who focus on media are inclined to look at power and control, including media ownership and the social, political, and economic relations involved in constructing messages and audiences. Research on messages generally focuses on content, ranging from news to propaganda to advertising, and the discursive and technological forms these messages take. Those concentrating on audiences tend to examine the way individuals and groups receive, make sense of, understand, act on, ignore or incorporate messages into daily life. The field has produced rich and varied work, but one aspect has received little attention: labour.

Intellectual and physical labour are required to produce messages and the technologies used to disseminate them. Receiving and acting on messages also requires labour. However, international communications scholars rarely address the various forms of labouring or confront the wider challenge of what Denning (1998) has called the labouring of culture. In addition, the organizations that represent media and information workers, and the presentation of labour in the media, also receive relatively little attention. This is particularly unfortunate because labour organizations are developing global strategies and making full use of media to participate in international activities (Blok and Downey, 2003; Taras, Bennett and Townsend, 2004). It is with this in mind that McKercher and Mosco have taken on a research project that aims to expand the attention scholars pay to the labouring of communication and culture. Two recent collections demonstrate that research is growing in this area (McKercher and Mosco, 2006, 2007a) and this chapter reports on how to build on this work with specific attention to the Union Network International (UNI), a Swiss-based global labour federation that specializes in media, communication, information, and service workers.

Working in different disciplines, scholars have demonstrated the importance of information and communication labour in the modern economy (Dyer-Witheford, 1999; Huws, 2003; Terranova, 2004). In an era characterized by declining trade union penetration, increasing corporate concentration, and the rise of global conglomerates that feed into – and are fed by – the spread of new communication and information technology, knowledge workers have begun to explore new ways to deepen and extend control over their labour power. This is especially the case in the communication and information sectors, which provide the equipment that makes globalization possible, and the production and distribution of the ideas that are central to its operation. Most of the literature on knowledge workers has concentrated on how the technological and institutional forces of post-industrialism structure work and worker organizations. Valuable as this research has been, it has treated labour as a largely passive category to be shaped by the dynamics of capitalism and has obscured just how labour makes itself, at work and in its organizations. This project contributes to lifting the veil on labour as an active agent, constituting itself, sometimes defensively, sometimes offensively, in the changing political economy.

For some time, Mosco and McKercher have been separately studying diverse segments of the US and Canadian communications industry, including its workers and labour organizations (Mosco and Wasko, 1983; Mosco, Zureik and Lochhead, 1989; Mosco, 2002; McKercher, 2002; Mosco and McKercher, 2006). Their joint 2004–7 project demonstrated the importance of labour convergence or the integration of labour unions and worker associations across the converging communication industries of Canada and the United States, bringing together, for example, journalists, broadcast workers, telecommunications and information specialists, among other knowledge workers, in one large organization (Mosco, McKercher and Stevens, 2008; McKercher and Mosco, 2007b; Mosco, 2005; Mosco, 2006a; Mosco, 2006b; Mosco, 2006c; Kiss and Mosco, 2005; McKercher and Mosco, 2006; McKercher and Mosco, 2007a). This research complemented the already extensive body of work which focuses on the impact of technological and industry convergence on media content, typically concluding that these forms of convergence limit content diversity and access to media (Skinner, Compton and Gasher, 2006; Kunz, 2006). This focus is justifiable but it left gaps in understanding how convergence changes the nature of work and challenges trade unions. Research is only now beginning to document the impact of media convergence on employment in the industry (DiCola, 2006; Yoo and Mody, 2000).

The results of Mosco and McKercher's 2004–7 project filled some of these gaps by documenting how major North American worker organizations have expanded their success in collective bargaining, in mobilizing membership, and in political activity. Unions such as the Canadian Communications Energy and Paperworkers Union (CEP) and the Communication Workers of America (CWA), and worker associations such as the Washington Alliance of Technology Workers (WashTech), demonstrated their success in labour actions at the Canadian Broadcasting Corporation, in organizing workers across the wireless sector, and in winning a court contest against Microsoft. On the other hand, those unions which have not been able to bring about the same level of labour convergence, for example the Screen Actors Guild, the

American Federation of Television and Radio Artists, and the Telecommunications Workers Union of Canada, are less successful, partly because they have chosen to remain focused on one particular sector of an increasingly converged industry dominated by companies that span the industry.

However, even those labour organizations that successfully achieved a measure of national or even, as in the case of the CWA, binational convergence are limited in what they can accomplish because they lack a strong international scope. For example, when the worker association WashTech, which has received strong CWA support, successfully defended information technology workers, Microsoft fought back by outsourcing the work to India and elsewhere (Brophy, 2006). Examples like this make it imperative to broaden the study of labour convergence to the international arena. In doing so, one can also respond to calls in the scholarly literature to rethink international labour federations in light of a changing global political economy (Jakobsen, 2001). But it is important to do so with research that is grounded in the complexities of a changing international division of labour that is not easily reducible to simple conclusions.

Consider the issue of outsourcing communication and information labour. Trade union organizations invariably attack it, while most businesses conclude that it is an unalloyed gain for economic growth. Basing policy, including the strategies of international labour organizations, on these simple responses is dangerous because, as research has shown, outsourcing is not without its antinomies. A large share of outsourcing in the knowledge and communication sectors is contained within the developed world, where, for example, Canada has become Hollywood North and Ireland continues to benefit from its skilled workforce and wage premium. Moreover, although India is a major source of low wage knowledge labour, its major companies such as ICICI, Tata, Infosys and Wipro are taking leading roles in the outsourcing industry. Their activities in North America suggest that place still matters and that culture continues to count. Finally, resistance is growing from labour organizations and that is one reason why the expansion of convergent unions and worker associations in the knowledge and communication sectors is particularly important (Mosco, 2006a; see also Elmer and Gasher, 2005). Research that assesses the strategies and prospects of international labour organizations needs to be grounded in a recognition that the international division of labour, particularly in the knowledge and communication sectors, is complex and not easily reduced to singularities, however attractive as political slogans or mythic symbols (Mosco, 2004).

Specifically, sensitive to these complexities, Mosco and McKercher's project examines the state of international labour organizations in the communication and information sectors, documents the relationships among them, and assesses the extent to which they enable workers to meet the challenges of informational capitalism. The research is situated in a political economy perspective which concentrates on power relationships at the institutional level and at the point of production, and addresses the extent and effectiveness of labour convergence at the international level (McKercher, 2002; Mosco, 1996; Sussman and Lent, 1998). There is an extensive body of literature on convergence in the communication and information arena that examines how technologies, companies and entire markets are coming together through the process of digitization to create new and enhanced opportunities to make communication content and the audiences for it valuable market commodities. Furthermore, convergence is increasing opportunities for companies to expand the commodity form in the labour of communication and information workers. But it also provides these workers with opportunities to mobilize effectively to challenge media corporations. To cite one example, in 2005 management at Canada's national broadcaster, the CBC, argued that the pressures of technological and industry convergence made it essential for the corporation to combine jobs across its media streams and to outsource more of its work. Workers at the national broadcaster were successful in the ensuing lockout because they were represented by a converged union, the CWA, which brought together technical workers and journalists and supported them with a large strike fund that has grown as the union has expanded its membership across the converging communication field (Mosco and McKercher, 2006). Research has documented the process of global convergence in technology, firms and markets, but we still know very little about the international dynamics of labour convergence.

It is for this reason that Mosco and McKercher are in the process of producing a global map of labour convergence by describing four primary types of international labour organization. These include international federations that remain rooted in one of the major sectors in the communication and information industries, global federations of unions that span the communication and information industries, government or public federations that represent the interests of workers, and worker associations that may be rooted in one nation but are testing new forms of organizing and are partnering with unions and federations outside the nation. In essence, it is intended to produce an assessment of the state of global labour convergence and the prospects for building international solidarity among workers and their organizations. It provides the groundwork for a set of detailed case studies that examine organizations facing a range of challenges related to convergence. These include the challenge of making use of converging technologies to meet the needs of workers and their labour organizations. In the remainder of this chapter, we identify and briefly describe the first two of the four cases and then proceed to focus on the case of UNI, including its relationship to unions in India, which form the core of our fourth case study.

The International Federation of Journalists (IFJ) provides an example of convergence that continues to focus on just one sector of the media industry. The IFJ is the world's largest organization of journalists, representing 500,000 journalism professionals who comprise its 161 member unions from 117 countries. One of the arguments made in defence of union convergence is the ability to take on broad policy issues that smaller unions cannot afford to address. The extent to which the IFJ succeeds on four of the issues to which it gives prominence – media concentration, women's rights in the media, authors' rights to control their work, and institutional attacks on press freedom – is being investigated. The IFJ also claims to bring together journalists from both rich and poor nations. This practice is particularly important because companies like Reuters have begun to outsource journalism work from wealthy nations like the UK to low-wage nations like India. Has convergence enabled the IFJ to address this practice? Finally, as technological and corporate convergence challenges traditional definitions of journalism and as some of its member unions, like the CEP in Canada, enlist workers across both the content and technical segments of the knowledge industries, can the IFJ continue to succeed by focusing on one media sector?

The project's research on the International Labour Organization (ILO) considers how labour convergence operates in a UN agency. The ILO differs from both the IFJ and UNI in that it is an arm of the United Nations and was chartered in 1919 to promote justice and human rights for workers. Formally, it produces conventions and recommendations that establish minimum standards for labour rights, including freedom of association, the right to organize, collective bargaining, abolition of forced labour, and equal opportunity and treatment. It also provides technical assistance to workers and labour organizations. This case study enables an examination of an international public institution charged with protecting workers and their unions. How does convergence affect the ILO's operation? Specifically, how has it dealt with the shift from industrial work, the main form of labour throughout most of its history, to the increasingly important category of knowledge work, as well as with the differing regional balances of those two forms of labour? The project is also assessing the extent to which the ILO has or has not been a force in building networks between first and third world information workers, between those occupying different positions in the outsourcing system and in the changing international division of knowledge work.

The chapter now considers the case of the Union Network International (UNI), a global federation that spans all sectors of the converging electronic services arena. Unlike the IFJ, UNI fully embraces convergence, calling itself 'a new international for a new millennium'. It primarily spans the newly converged electronic information and communication sectors, including workers in the postal, media, entertainment, telecommunications, and culture sectors. A driving force behind its creation was the growth of companies that span these sectors by taking advantage of converging electronic technologies. Although it is new, UNI has been in the forefront of global labour issues like outsourcing and prominent in applying pressure to global companies and global organizations like the World Trade Organization.

From its inception, a central focus of UNI was to make inroads in the high-tech and service sectors of the economy (Morgan, 2000). After two years of negotiations, the organization was founded in 2000, the result of a merger of four global unions. General Secretary Philip Jennings argues for the need for such a global organization: 'workers across the service, communications, and entertainment sector face the same employer and the same issues and are increasingly lobbying the same international organizations' (quoted in ICTUR, 2005: 408). If workers around the world labour for one employer, the most effective strategy, UNI contends, is to coordinate and act collectively on a global scale by forming global union networks to confront these multinationals. UNI is affiliated with other global union federations and is funded by fees collected from affiliated unions across the globe.

As a result of the merger and the addition of union affiliates, UNI has incorporated 15.5 million workers in 900 unions spanning 140 countries and covering twelve general economic sectors. Each sector is autonomous regarding the election of its president, vice-presidents, and committees and the determination of its policies, priorities, and structures. For example, the media, entertainment, and arts sector deals with issues such as media ownership and concentration, the structural evolution of the sector, trade policies, legal standards, technological change, copyright, and censorship. UNI's telecom sector handles the liberalization, deregulation, and privatization agendas prominent among governments today, as well as the mergers and acquisitions that are driving the restructuring of global telecommunications markets and policies. Industry-wide coordination on a global scale is seen as an effective way to build real worker power and is the underlying rationale for establishing these sectoral groups (US Newswire, 2005).

UNI is organized into four regions: Europe, Africa, the Americas, and Asia-Pacific. In many countries there are also national liaison councils. Human and trade union rights are still routinely violated in many countries, and UNI and its regional affiliates place a priority on being at the forefront of dealing with these issues. Each region is responsible for assisting in the development of independent and democratic unions and each operates under its own statutes and standing orders.

UNI also has special committees to deal with special constituents, including youth, women, and professional and managerial staff. UNI realizes that educational campaigns need to be directed towards integrating youth into the trade union movement so that they become active and informed members. Young people are often in a more precarious employment relationship than older workers and because of inexperience they are more vulnerable to employer exploitation. Each of the four regions has its own youth section to address these issues. No matter where they work, women are in a more precarious employment relationship than men due to the sexism and patriarchy that exist across the globe. Violence against women in the workplace is also still a common occurrence. In addition, working women around the globe face the double day, as the majority of family responsibilities still fall on them. Getting global employers to institute family-friendly policies, such as proper maternity leave, is a major issue for UNI. The prerogative of UNI's women's committee is to help working women deal with these issues as well as to recruit more women into the union movement so that they too become active and informed members. The UNI professional and managerial committee addresses issues facing highly qualified workers in the knowledge industries. Workers such as engineers and scientists are often referred to as professional or managerial staff, but not all occupy actual managerial roles. Job content and qualification levels distinguish them from other categories of workers, but as waged workers they also need organizational protection from their employers. To assist these workers, who often travel across borders to work on either a short- or long-term basis, UNI developed its own 'Passport'. The union claims it 'helps ensure that you take your access to trade unions with you when you move abroad to work' (UNI, 2005d).

One of UNI's more controversial policies, particularly among more militant trade unionists, is also especially relevant to communication scholars. UNI does not explicitly aim to stop economic globalization, but aims to help give it a social or human dimension. The needs, interests, and rights of workers and the communities and environment they live in cannot be sacrificed in what it perceives to be an inevitable process (Adler, 2001). Jennings (2006) notes 'the race to the bottom – where the globe is scoured for the cheapest and most exploitable labour – should be replaced by an enlightened race to the top'. One of UNI's major aims is to establish rights for workers worldwide. It contends that if globalization is to generate benefits for members and those impoverished by neo-liberal globalization, unions, like corporations, must become global players and take an active part in shaping the direction of the global economy. Specifically, it maintains that unions need to be in constructive dialogue on a global scale with business, government, and other international bodies so that labour can have a voice in shaping the global economy (UNI, 2004).

To this end, UNI has favoured Global Framework Agreements (GFAs) with multinational corporations. GFAs are intended to establish labour and union rights for workers regardless of where a corporation may operate (UNI, 2004; UNI, 2004a; UNI, 2006). These agreements are based on the International Labour Organization's *Declaration on Fundamental Principles and Rights at Work* (ILO, 2002). GFAs are seen by UNI as the most effective way to ensure decent labour standards worldwide. Over a dozen corporations have signed such agreements with the federation and, while not perfect in terms of establishing and protecting workers' rights, they mark a significant success, especially for a new international federation in very dynamic industries. At its second World Congress in 2005, UNI announced that pressuring multinational employers to sign GFAs was to be a top priority and presented a list of 100 multinational employers, highlighting Wal-Mart in particular, on which it will focus future activities (Marquez, 2006).

If UNI is going to be the 'new international' it proclaims itself to be, getting corporations to sign and abide by the GFAs will be a mark of its success. GFAs are intended to establish the groundwork for the dialogue and relationship between a multinational employer and a global trade union federation with regard to a corporation's international activities (Waterman and Timms, 2004/5). As a federation policy document puts it: 'when companies were local, unions had local agreements; when companies were national, unions had national agreements. Now in the global economy we need global agreements' (UNI, 2006a). GFAs are not a substitute for direct negotiations between a corporation and workers at a national or local level. The actual wages and terms and conditions of employment are still established through these negotiations, but the GFA is intended to be used as a basis for these discussions (UNI, 2006a).

Two notable exemplars of the GFA process involve a major telecommunications firm and one of the world's largest printing and media companies. The first is Telefónica, a global telecommunications corporation based in Spain with operations in the rest of Europe, Latin America, and the United States. For multinational corporations, signing a GFA can enhance their reputation as it demonstrates some concern for corporate social responsibility. According to the ILO, the agreement between UNI and Telefónica represented 'a historical milestone in industrial relations' (ILO, 2002: 128). Negotiations began in April 2000 and the agreement was reached in March 2001. It is binding for five years and is currently going through a review process. By signing this, Telefónica, and its subsidiaries and affiliates, pledged to respect the environment and trade union rights, and to establish minimum labour standards, which include provisions such as no child labour, no employment discrimination, a minimum wage, regulated work hours, stable employment, training opportunities, and health and safety for more than 120,000 workers in the nine countries where it operates (ILO, 2002; Sweeny, 2001; UNI, 2000).

Just because Telefónica has signed a GFA with UNI does not guarantee that it, or its subsidiaries and affiliates, will necessarily abide by it. Indeed, it is with the subsidiaries that GFAs are most difficult to enforce. For example, anti-union activity has been undertaken by management at a subsidiary call centre of Telefónica, Atento de Puerto Rico, where nineteen organizers at the call centre were fired for union activities (UNI, 2006). Ultimately the union drive was unsuccessful. In Puerto Rico, where US labour laws apply and an anti-union managerial mindset is widespread, the CWA, a UNI affiliate, met considerable resistance from local Atento management which violated both the GFA and US National Labor Relations Board (NLRB) procedures. However, in Brazil the UNI-affiliated Sindicato dos Trabalhadores em Telecomunicações (SINTETEL) has signed a collective agreement with Atento. SINTETEL noted that the GFA was paramount in its ability to successfully launch the campaign (UNI, 2006d; Howell, 2006).

When the president of the UNI telecom sector, Neil Anderson, went to Puerto Rico in October 2006 to discuss the matter with workers so that he could compile a report and make recommendations to Telefónica on how to avoid a similar scenario in the future, he expressed outrage with the way that management at Atento had dealt with the drive:

> This serious violation of the UNI–Telefónica Agreement must never be allowed to happen again and Atento must make some gesture to show they will respect the agreement in future organizing efforts by the CWA ... We cannot allow one 'rogue' company to destroy the credibility of an agreement that gives workers rights and decent jobs and is acknowledged by both unions and managers as an excellent tool for good industrial relations
>
> (UNI, 2006c)

Atento was forced by the NLRB to post notices in the workplace stating that it would not violate labour relation laws in future unionization attempts. At the UNI Telecom Global World Meeting in June 2006, a resolution was passed condemning the actions of Telefónica and Atento. The Telefónica GFA expired in 2006 and is currently being reviewed and revised by UNI and Telefónica. Since one of the main stipulations of the GFA is to allow for unionizing activity to occur, UNI is not backing down. The unionization drive at Atento de Puerto Rico remains a fundamental issue in these ongoing discussions and negotiations (UNI, 2006c; UNI, 2006d). At the UNI Global Union Telefónica Alliance meeting in Chile in January 2007, which top management from Telefónica attended, UNI reiterated that the GFA needs to be respected wherever Telefónica operates, particularly in the subsidiary companies, and it also called for Telefónica to reduce the levels of outsourcing and precarious employment. UNI also stressed that Telefónica needed to retain and further develop a skilled workforce because technological convergence demanded it. Telefónica management responded by asserting that outsourcing was the only way for the company to stay competitive, but it agreed on the need for a skilled workforce and also pledged to work harder to ensure company-wide adherence to the GFA (UNI, 2007).

In April 2007 UNI signed a similar agreement with the world's second largest printing company and a major global media conglomerate, Quebecor World, which employs 35,000 workers in more than 160 printing and media facilities worldwide. In addition to its printing operations, Quebecor World also has interests in cable television, broadcasting, telecommunications, newspapers, magazines, music production and distribution, and a variety of new media services. In their 'Joint Statement on the Respect and Promotion of International Labour Standards' Quebecor World committed to ensuring that fundamental labour rights, derived from ILO conventions, will be respected. Specifically, the company affirmed that it will not use forced, bonded or child labour, that there will be no employment discrimination, and that all workers will have equal opportunity and receive equal pay for work of equal value. It also pledged that it would not prevent workers from organizing and would not dismiss or discriminate against any employees because of union membership or participation in unionizing activities. The company also committed to respect the right of unions to represent employees and to bargain collectively on employment terms and conditions. Quebecor World has agreed that it will provide its employees with a clean, safe and healthy place to work and will develop policies aimed at creating respect in the workplace. The company and UNI have committed to ongoing cooperation and dialogue to ensure their mutual interests as well as to resolve any differences and disputes (UNI, 2007a).

UNI has made international outsourcing a central issue, particularly for the global telecommunications industry. As a global federation, UNI has members in countries that gain and lose jobs through outsourcing. Since it does not want to be accused of racism, xenophobia, or knee-jerk protectionism, the union cannot take a stance against all forms of the practice. It is the unconstrained and unregulated forms of outsourcing which UNI opposes, for example outsourcing to export processing zones where neither labour nor environmental standards exist and outsourcing that directly leads to layoffs in the country from which the work was sent (UNI, 2004; UNI, 2005). In a position paper for UNI Gerhard Rhode contends:

> While it is understandable in rational and geopolitical terms that the outsourcing countries want to fight poverty and struggle to catch up with the world-wide economy, and that it is important to create jobs in developing countries, a union cannot treat it as an abstract consequence when its own members lose their jobs.
>
> (Rhode, 2003)

The federation insists that if work is going to be outsourced, consultation with unions should occur, displaced workers should be retrained, and there should be help for them to find other comparable work (Rhode, 2003; UNI, 2004; UNI, 2005).

The second part of UNI's strategy to deal with outsourcing is to promote and support unionization and worker associations in countries where outsourced work is done. This is seen as a way to establish decent labour standards similar to those stipulated in the Telefónica GFA (UNI, 2004; UNI, 2005). The hope is that if workers are organized where the jobs are outsourced, labour standards can be raised globally (Marquez, 2006). UNI has been criticized for not paying enough attention to workers in developing countries (Moore, 2005). The federation disagrees, stating that its regional committees have substantial autonomy in how they go about organizing and recruiting workers as well as in setting its priorities. Considerable energy is directed towards projects for workers in outsourced call centres and back offices in developing countries such as India. Call centres are a special focus for UNI as these cut across industrial sectors, are growing fast, employ many younger workers and women, and often have less than favourable working conditions (UNI, no date-a).

UNI invests a lot of its organizational resources in generating solidarity among unions, especially those impacted by outsourcing and globalization (UNI, 2004; UNI, 2005). Andrew Bibby in a position paper for UNI notes:

> Reinforcing international trade unionism [includes] encouraging practical solidarity between unions in developed countries and those in developing countries working to welcome embryonic forms of trade unionism in new industries and new countries, recognizing that they may be different from traditional union structures.
>
> (Bibby, 2004)

Global support work and alliance building are therefore major components of UNI's work. This includes supporting union recruitment, organizing, bargaining, undertaking campaigns to bring global attention to specific labour issues, holding sectoral, regional, and global conferences to deal with labour issues, and participating in social activism.

But getting workers in outsourced call centres and other IT businesses to support unionization in poorer countries such as India is very difficult. As one newspaper editorial put it, these workers 'think of themselves as members of a relatively well-paid, respected professional elite in no need of union protection' (*Australian*, 2005: 4). To address this problem and the general criticism that it neglects workers in the developing world, UNI launched the IT Professional Forums, an explicit attempt to reach out to non-unionized workers. The term 'forums' is used because the use of 'trade unions' might discourage potential members who have no trade union experience. It is hoped that, through these types of organizations, Indian workers who may have some misgivings about trade unionism can be won over (Srinivasan, 2005; Bibby, 2002; Bibby, 2004). However, trade union consciousness is not absent. As a worker at one of the forums comments: 'Unity is strength – and when capitalists get collectively organized, why shouldn't we?' (quoted in Bibby, 2002). These forums are helping workers to defend their rights, for example against unfair managerial practices, and may be the first steps towards forming genuine unions (*Financial Express*, 2004).

A related UNI project, but one with a stronger unionist orientation than the forums, is the Bangalore headquartered Centre for Business Process Outsourcing Professionals that opened in 2004 and launched the Union for Information, Technology and Enabled Services Professionals (UNITES) in 2005 – a trade union that is registered with the All India Trade Union Congress. UNITES is seen as a genuine union with real potential. It presently has

9,000 members and aims to increase its membership to 20,000 by the end of 2007 (Mishra, 2007). In May 2006 it signed its first collective agreement with Excel Outsourcing Services that covers 65 workers. UNITES sees this collective bargaining agreement as modest, but it is nonetheless a major breakthrough (UNI, 2006b). If UNI-affiliated unions, such as UNITES in India, establish themselves, a constructive undertaking for the federation would be to continue to fund and support these, especially in their infancy, in order to increase the number of members with real collective bargaining rights and binding agreements.

Related to its India activities, a major UNI campaign has been directed at the growing global call centre industry. To that end, it has produced a Call Centre Charter (UNI, 2005a) as well as newsletters on global, regional, national, and local challenges, problems, and activities specific to call centre workers (UNI, no date-b). The Call Centre Charter sets out minimum standards for call centres worldwide and is intended to act as a guide for employers. It describes standards for health and safety, hours and workload, surveillance and privacy, pay and benefits, training and promotional opportunities, and the right to organize and bargain collectively. One example of a major success in its campaign resulted from a union organizing an information seminar for call centre workers in Brazil, which 100 young women attended. The seminar was meant to develop strategies to empower workers on the shop floor. Within ten days of this conference, these women went back to their respective call centres and signed up 600 workers for membership of the UNI-affiliated SINTETEL (UNI, 2004b).

Support and solidarity work is another major aspect of UNI's activity and much of this is done in conjunction with other global union federations. Solidarity work includes raising global awareness of labour issues in particular parts of the world and writing letters of protest to governments and the upper echelons of management of global corporations. UNI also undertakes corporate campaigns, which include highlighting the misdeeds of particular corporations and generating public pressure on corporations to act in a socially responsible manner. Part of the plan is to expose corporate bad behaviour through naming and shaming campaigns (Regan, 2003). But if solidarity work is going to be more than just posting articles and bulletins on the web, UNI needs to demonstrate what positive changes this work has brought about for workers who requested solidarity. Boasting, as it does, that UNI will respond to a call for solidarity assistance within 24 hours is commendable, but whether the response leads to significant action is another matter (Jennings, 2006).

UNI also supports the concept of social movement unionism as part of its strategy to expand trade union influence and relevance to workers in developing countries. It sees this as a way to supplement traditional unionism with other forms of worker and community empowerment and to establish connections with progressive elements of civil society, including cooperative movements and mutual aid societies (UNI, 2006e; UNI, 2003). UNI is also involved in global movements such as the 'Make Poverty History' campaign, focusing specifically on trade injustice throughout the world and the global fight against HIV/AIDS (UNI, 2005b; UNI, 2005c).

The federation maintains that strategically coordinated global union action is the only way to address the problems posed by multinational corporations. While some unions may be clinging to UNI in order to claim to be involved in the global labour solidarity movement, the organization itself appears to be more than just a network of affiliated unions. UNI does have a fairly well-thought-out plan of action. There is evidence of support from unions in advanced capitalist nations for establishing unions and other forms of worker organization in the developing world. Since UNI is only seven years old, its full potential is still uncertain. However, it is clear that the federation represents the global extension of a form of convergence that has received all too little attention.

In sum, research in international communication has focused a great deal of attention on media and messages and has explored various forms of technological convergence. When it concentrates on institutions, international media studies has stressed corporations, governments, and NGOs from the social movement community. Perhaps it is time to pay some attention to the labouring of international communication. Indeed, rather than asking again and again 'what will be the next new thing?' it may be time to ask a more important question: will communication workers of the world unite?

Acknowledgement

This chapter was produced with the assistance of a grant from the Canadian Social Sciences and Humanities Research Council.

References

Adler, M. (2001) German President Calls for Internationalization of Labor Movement, *Agence France-Presse*, 5 January.

Australian (2005) Cyber Coolies Baulk at Joining Trade Union, *The Australian*, 4 October.

Bibby, A. (2002) A New Union Mould, *Financial Times*, 27 February.

—— (2004) The Global Mobility Revolution, UNI (Union Network International), 17 March. Available: www.union-network.org.

Blok, A. and Downey, G. (eds) (2003) Special issue of the *International Review of Social History: Uncovering Labour in Information Revolutions, 1750–2000*, vol. 48, supplement 11.

Brophy, E. (2006) System Error: Labour Precarity and Collective Organizing at Microsoft, *Canadian Journal of Communication*, 31(3): 619–38.

Denning, M. (1998) *The Cultural Front*. New York: Verso.

DiCola, P. (2006) *Employment and Wage Effects of Radio Consolidation*. New York: Report of the Future of Music Coalition.

Dyer-Witheford, N. (1999) *Cyber-Marx: Cycles and Circuits of Struggle in High Technology Capitalism*. Urbana: University of Illinois Press.

Elmer, G. and Gasher, M. (eds) (2005) *Contracting out Hollywood: Runaway Productions and Foreign Location Shooting*. Lanham, MD: Rowman and Littlefield.

Financial Express (2004) Forum to Tackle Unfair HR Policies in BPO Industry, *Financial Times*, 28 July.

Howell, N. (2006) Global Organizing for Call Centre Workers, in F. van Leeuwen (ed.) *ILO, Labour Education 2006: Globalization and the Sectors*. Available: www.ilo.org.

Huws, U. (2003) *The Making of a Cybertariat*. New York: Monthly Review.

ICTUR (2005) *Trade Unions of the World*, 6th edn. London: John Harper.

ILO (2002) Tripartite Meeting on Employment, Employability and Equal Opportunities in the Postal and Telecommunications Services, *ILO*. Available: www.ilo.org.

Jakobsen, K.A. (2001) Rethinking the International Confederation of Free Trade Unions and Its Inter-American Regional Organization, in P. Waterman and J. Wills Place (eds) *Space and the New Labour Internationalisms*. Oxford: Blackwell.

Jennings, P. (2006) Philip Jennings' Address to LBC-NVK Congress, UNI, 24 March. Available: www.union-network.org.

Kiss, S. and Mosco, V. (2005) Trade Union Protection of Workers' Privacy: A Content Analysis of English and French-Language Collective Agreements in Canada, *Canadian Journal of Communication*, 30(4): 549–64.

Kunz, W. (2006) *Culture Conglomerates*. Lanham, MD: Rowman and Littlefield.

McKercher, C. (2002) *Newsworkers Unite: Labor, Convergence and North American Newspapers*. Lanham, MD: Rowman and Littlefield.

McKercher, C. and Mosco, V. (eds) (2006) The Labouring of Communication, special issue of *Canadian Journal of Communication*, 31(3).

—— (eds) (2007a) *Knowledge Workers in the Information Age*. Lanham, MD: Lexington Books.

McKercher, C. and Mosco, V. (2007b) Divided They Stand: Hollywood Unions in the Information Age, *Work Organization, Labour and Globalization*, 1(1): 130–43.

Marquez, J. (2006) Unions' Global End Run, *Workforce Management*, 85(2), 23 January.

Mishra, B.R. (2007) Meet the Man behind the ITES Union, *Rediff India Abroad*, 1 February. Available at: http://www.rediff.com/money/2007/feb/01ites.htm.

Moore, T. (2005) Big Labour Fights for Survival, *Winnipeg Free Press*, 4 September, p. B2.

Morgan, O. (2000) The Unions: Open Shop in the New Economy, *The Observer*, 4 September, p. 5.

Mosco, V. (1996)*The Political Economy of Communication*. London: Sage.

—— (2002) Report on Canada Industrial Relations Board File No. 22076-C re: Application Pursuant to Sections 18, 18.1 35, 44, 45 and 46 of the *Canada Labor Relations Code* between the Telecommunications Workers Union and TELUS Communications Inc. Submitted to the Canada Industrial Relations Board.

—— (2004) *The Digital Sublime: Myth, Power, and Cyberspace*. Cambridge: MIT Press.

—— (2005) Telecommunications in Canada: Technology, Industry, Policy and Labour. Report prepared for the Communications, Energy and Paperworkers Union of Canada, December.

—— (2006a) Knowledge Workers in the Global Economy: Antinomies of Outsourcing, *Social Identities*,12(6): 771–90.

—— (2006b) Citizenship Works, *Global Media Journal – Mediterranean Edition*, 1(1): 17–28.

—— (2006c) Mass Communications, in C.D. Bryant and D.L. Peck (eds) *21st Century Sociology: Reference Handbook*. Thousand Oaks, CA: Sage, pp. 549–58.

Mosco, V. and McKercher, C. (2006) Convergence Bites back, *Canadian Journal of Communication*, 31(3): 733–51.

Mosco, V., McKercher, C. and Stevens, A. (2008) Convergences: Elements of a Feminist Political Economy of Labour and Communication, in K. Sarikakis and L.R. Shade (eds) *Feminist International Communication Studies*. Lanham, MD: Rowman and Littlefield.

Mosco, V. and Wasko, J. (eds) (1983) *Labor, the Working Class, and the Media*. Norwood: Ablex.

Mosco, V., Zureik, E. and Lochhead, C. (1989) Telephone Workers' Reaction to the New Technology, *Industrial Relations*, 44(3): 507–29.

Regan, S. (2003) Corporate Governance and Social Responsibility: Building the Links, Union Network International (UNI).

Rhode, G. (2003) Jobs with No Frontiers – Global Mobility: A Challenge to Unions, UNI.

Skinner, D., Compton, H. and Gasher, M. (2006) *Converging Media, Diverging Politics: A Political Economy of the News Media in the United States and Canada*. Lanham, MD: Lexington.

Srinivasan, S. (2005) Indian Workers Resist Union for Outsourcers, *Journal Gazette*, 25 January, p. 1H.

Sussman, G. and Lent, J. (eds) (1998) *Global Productions*. Cresskill, NJ: Hampton Press.

Sweeny, J. (2001) Putting the Guidelines to Work, *Business Accounting and Finance*, 33, 1 March.

Taras, D.G., Bennett, J.T. and Townsend, A.M. (eds) (2004) *Information Technology and the World of Work*. New Brunswick: Transaction.

Terranova, T. (2004) *Network Culture: Politics for the Information Age*. London: Pluto.

UNI (2000) Telefónica and UNI Sign up on Union Rights, UNI, 24 December.

—— (2003) UNI Apro Finance Sector Committee Meeting 7–8 October 2003, Hanoi, Vietnam: Report on UNI Apro Finance Sector Activities, UNI.

—— (2004) UNI Charter on Offshore Outsourcing, UNI, 19 May.

—— (2004a) UNI Telecoms for the Long Run, UNI.

—— (2004b) Global Call Centre News, UNI, April.

—— (2005) Outsourcing and Contracting out: Failing to Deliver Quality Services, Secure Jobs and a Sustainable Telecom Industry, UNI.

—— (2005a) UNI Call Centre Charter, UNI, 25 April.

—— (2005b) Make Poverty History, UNI, 6 December.

—— (2005c) Call to Action against AIDS in Africa, UNI, 3 July.

—— (2005d) UNI Passport, UNI. Available: http://www.unionnetwork.org/UNISITE/Groups/PMS/Passport/LeafletEng.pdf (accessed 12 July 2006).

—— (2006) Telefónica under Pressure from Puerto Rico Events, UNI, 15 June.

—— (2006a) Global Framework Agreements, UNI, 31 May.

—— (2006b) UNITES India Signs First Agreement, UNI, 26 June.

—— (2006c) UNI Telecom Seeking Respect for Atento Puerto Rico Union Rights, UNI, 31 October.

—— (2006d) Opening Doors for Unions: Global Agreements, UNI.

—— (2006e) UNI-Apro Co-sponsors Asia Pacific Cooperative Conference, UNI.

—— (2007) UNI Telefónica Global Union Tells Telefónica 'No to Precarious Work', UNI, 9 January. Available: www.union-network.org.

—— (2007a) UNI Global Union and Quebecor World Reach Global Agreement on Labour Rights, UNI, 5 May.

—— (no date) About Us: Press Pack, UNI.

—— (no date-a) Call Centres, UNI.

—— (no date-b) Call Centre Newsletters, UNI.

US Newswire (2005) Global Unionism Rising to Meet the Challenge of Global Economy: Background Information on UNI Congress, Convention, *US Newswire*, 7 August.

Waterman, P. and Timms, J. (2004/5) Trade Union Internationalism and a Global Civil Society in the Making, in H. Anheier, M. Glasius and M. Kaldor (eds) *Global Civil Society*. London: Sage, pp. 175–202.

Yoo, H. and Mody, B. (2000) Predictors of Downsizing in the US Local Telephone Industry, *Information Society*, 16(1): 23–34.

Part III

Regional perspectives on internationalization

Chapter 10

Asian media studies

The struggle for international legitimacy

Indrajit Banerjee

Asian media studies emerged as an academic field of study in the 1970s and although the discipline has evolved significantly, it continues to struggle for international legitimacy. Asian media studies also continues to live in the shadow of Western models and is moulded by American and British theoretical frameworks and methodological traditions. This has to a great extent prevented Asian media studies from coming of age and establishing itself in the international arena. In recent times we have witnessed numerous debates on the prospects for 'de-Westernizing' or 'internationalizing' media studies. In my view the focus should be more on developing local perspectives and models rather than rejecting Western models and frameworks. Moreover, what is required is to extensively research local and national perspectives through the examination of local language literature across the range of disciplines that have influenced media and communication studies.

The objectives of this chapter are to highlight the difficulties faced by Asian media studies, to underline certain recent developments and to examine the challenges that lie ahead. It will argue that while Asian media studies has taken giant strides since the 1970s with the growth and expansion of media and communication schools across the region and a significant improvement in the quality of research and scholarship, the discipline continues to lack legitimacy due to numerous important obstacles and challenges. Issues of language, a lack of available resources and infrastructure, overdependence on Western paradigms and models and the lack of a culture of scholarship have constituted some of the most significant challenges to Asian media studies.

Asian media studies – the emergence of a discipline

In the 1970s, when Asian communication or media studies began to emerge as a discipline, only a handful of universities offered programmes in media and communication studies. Media and communication issues generally constituted specific areas of focus within departments of English, political science or even sociology. Media studies did not exist as a specific discipline and therefore little attention or effort was dedicated to media studies. This can be attributed to a certain extent to the fact that in many, if not most, Asian countries the media were considered as a sensitive topic, given the fact that governments generally controlled and regulated media channels and content. The media were also seen essentially as instruments for national development (and political propaganda) and, given their reach and power, governments were not inclined to promote extensive study and research on the media.

Moreover, it is important to underline the fact that in the 1970s the thrust of media or communication studies was devoted to what has been termed as 'development communication'. In this sense, 'development communication' was a precursor of media and communication studies in the Asian context. Nora Quebral (1971), who coined the term 'development communication' in the early 1970s, recently revised her definition of the field when she wrote: 'Development communication is the art and science of human communication linked to a society's planned transformation from a state of poverty to one of dynamic socio-economic growth that makes for greater equity and the larger unfolding of individual potential' (Quebral, 2001).

Thus development communication focused more on the benefits of harnessing media and communication for purposes of socio-economic development and empowerment rather than studying the workings and implications of the media themselves. Development communication was thus founded on the belief that one of the principal causes of poverty and deprivation was exclusion and that communication could be used as an instrument for enhancing people's access to knowledge and participation. In his recent review of development and participatory communication, Jakob Srampickal (2006) provides an extensive definition of development communication:

> An attempt at informing, creating awareness, educating, and enlightening the people so that they can better their lives in every way, development communication includes participatory action for learning and sharing of powers: in the social sphere through the advancement of human rights and the emergence of civil society, in the sphere of economics through the creation of an egalitarian society and in the political arena through democratization within specific cultural contexts.

Thus media or communication studies evolved gradually while development communication continued to be a major thrust of research and publication in the Asian context. In this sense, early initiatives in media or communication studies were driven by a development agenda, and one can argue that the lack of an independent and vibrant media industry in most countries also contributed to the slow progression of media studies in Asia. There was essentially nothing much to study about the media, or so it was thought. When the media did seem to be important, they were studied from a political science, sociological or even linguistic perspective. Moreover, given the growing popularity of development communication, the media or communicational processes were studied within the framework of national development and, specifically in the field of rural development, agricultural extension and education.

Asian media studies has since come a long way and has witnessed a dramatic expansion across Asia. In every Asian country there are a number of schools and departments of media and communication studies and they have become a discipline of choice for the youth. The deregulation of the media in most countries, beginning in the 1980s, led to dramatic growth of the media industry, and this development naturally highlighted key issues related to the workings of the media. A commercial media environment, marked by intense competitive pressures, brought to the fore issues relating to privacy, media independence, an excessive focus on entertainment, ethical dilemmas, human rights abuse, governance issues, gender equality and a host of other challenges.

The dramatic media explosion gave rise to a growing awareness that the media played a central role in shaping public policy and public opinion and had a powerful impact on the political and cultural spheres. Thus it was felt that the media needed to become an object of study, research and enquiry. The development of a commercial and vibrant media industry in most Asian countries also generated the need to conduct industry surveys and analysis covering, among other things, ratings, audience figures, policy and regulatory issues, and the state of the industry across all media sectors. Moreover, given the fact that the media were becoming increasingly powerful players in the political and economic spheres of nations, there emerged an urgent need to undertake political-economy analyses of the media. All these developments strengthened the rationale for the emergence of media and communication studies in Asia.

Over the past decade or more, Asian media studies has thus witnessed significant growth in both scale and scope. Some of the more prosperous nations in Asia have invested significantly in building well-equipped schools and departments of media and communication studies and have succeeded in attracting competent and well-trained Asian and Western scholars. Today, in countries like Singapore, Hong Kong (SAR) and South Korea, there are world-class schools of media, journalism and communication with faculty that are largely trained in the US or Europe. These scholars have contributed to raising the profile of Asian media studies through their scholarly publications in highly ranked international journals and their participation at the top international conferences in the field.

Why then the legitimacy crisis?

In spite of these significant developments within Asian media studies, the struggle for international legitimacy continues. Let us begin by discussing what constitutes international legitimacy in an academic discipline. However, before we take up those issues, we need to establish the foundations of the legitimization process.

Any process of legitimization requires institutions and bodies that have the authority or credibility to legitimize. In the field of media studies, given the long history and tradition of media studies in the USA and Western Europe, a handful of university departments and associations dominate the process of legitimization. These institutions organize major international conferences and publish the leading journals in the field. Any individual scholar who aims to gain respect and credibility within the field of media or communication studies has to graduate from one of these institutions, attend their conferences or publish in their refereed journals. Those institutions that have in their faculty people who have successfully accomplished any or all of these achievements gain their legitimacy. This, in a nutshell, constitutes the process of legitimization in the field of media studies and generally in all academic disciplines. It also means that these processes are well entrenched and are religiously followed as a tradition within academic disciplines, and therefore any new school or institution which tries to gain legitimacy and credibility has to follow the same path.

But academic or scholarly legitimacy also implies that the dominant theoretical perspectives and methodological frameworks are set by those institutions and associations that have already established their legitimacy in the field. Thus, in order for an academic to be recognized as a scholar in the field, she or he must have proven mastery of the theories and research methods that have been legitimized within the discipline by those very same institutions and associations. This creates a clear code and channel of conduct within any field, including media studies. However, it also prevents, in my view, the nurturing of a diversity of perspectives, theoretical frameworks and research methods as there is strict adherence to established norms of academic work.

This has been a major challenge for Asian media studies, namely the inability to conform or adhere to the established norms in media studies and to perform at the expected level of academic achievement. There are several known reasons for this. Firstly, many, if not most, Asian media academics do not have access to the English language and therefore are largely unable to either present papers at international conferences or publish in the top refereed journals. Beyond the linguistic barrier lies the inadequacy of education and training within the Asian discipline of media studies. Only a handful of Asian scholars in the past have succeeded in breaking through and establishing themselves within the discipline, and even these have been largely educated in the West. I would argue that the absence of local paradigms, perspectives and models has seriously limited the opportunity for Asian media scholars to gain legitimacy, as they have been expected to achieve standards within traditions that they have not been exposed to while having no recourse to other standards or perspectives within their local languages.

In examining the question of legitimacy, one also has to pay attention to the critical ingredients that make up legitimacy in any given field – strong academic institutions with a rich culture of scholarship, internationally acclaimed and accomplished faculty, and a tradition of publication in top international journals and conferences. How does Asian media studies fare in all these areas and what are the challenges in its quest for international legitimacy?

To begin with, until the 1990s there were only a handful of universities and colleges offering communication studies in Asia. Even those few universities or institutions that did offer media and communication studies were heavily dependent on Western scholarship and models, as the discipline had not evolved sufficiently to develop its own local ontological, epistemological and methodological frameworks. Therefore, at the outset Asian media and communication studies embraced Western models and perspectives which already had a long history and academic tradition. In Europe and North America, media or communication studies developed within the field of social sciences as early as 1910 with Max Weber's inaugural speech at the launch of the German Sociological Association, on the 'Sociology of the Press' (cited in Hardt, 1979). Other early works which helped establish the discipline of media and communication studies included Park's *The Immigrant Press and Its Control* (1922), Lippmann's (1922) seminal work on public opinion, as well as studies by Lasswell (1948), Katz and Lazarsfeld (1955) and others.

In addition, Western Europe and North America also had a much more open media environment, and the media were essentially seen as central institutions of the public sphere as well as vital instruments for democracy and good governance. The importance accorded to the media also provided media and communication studies with great significance as an academic discipline in these countries, which gave a strong thrust to the discipline and its evolution. In Asia the media were seen as potentially dangerous weapons which could destabilize national development and cohesion, and therefore media and communication studies was not given due space in both institutional and academic environments.

The only way to establish this new discipline in Asia was therefore to follow Western models and curricula and embrace the standards and traditions set by Western scholarship and institutions. In the 1960s and 1970s, and to some extent even today, most Asian scholars needed to pursue their higher education in the US or Western Europe in order to gain legitimacy. Many of these Asian scholars remained in the US and Europe after completing their education and found employment in colleges and universities. These positions were far more lucrative than those that were available in their home countries. They had succeeded and were now seen to be part of the legitimate world of media and communication studies. Interestingly, this had both positive and negative consequences on the future of Asian media studies. On the one hand, it created a brain drain of sorts as most of the best Asian scholars in media studies had emigrated (even today one can find a large number of Asian scholars in the US, UK and Australia). On the other hand, as many of these scholars focused their research on Asian media development and related issues, their publications in important journals within the discipline provided a platform for Asian media scholarship to be showcased. Soon many of the leading journals began publishing research on Asian media systems and this brought the Asian media landscape to the attention of international scholars. Moreover, once Asian scholars had broken the ground and established themselves in the US and other Western countries, it was easier for future generations of scholars to follow suit. Perhaps the irony of the situation lay in the fact that Asian media studies was gaining in prominence worldwide but was being represented mainly by Asian scholars who had settled in the West. In the meantime, Asian media and communication studies in Asia continued to remain weak until the end of the 1990s in most parts of Asia.

However, on the whole, this migration of Asian scholars to the West had serious consequences for the quality of the faculty in media and communication studies across Asia. As few scholars returned to their home countries after completing their studies, universities and colleges were faced with a severe scarcity of top-class scholars and mentors for the students. This continues to be a problem even today and, as a consequence, students prefer to go abroad to pursue media and communication studies as they feel that the standard of teaching, research and scholarship in their own countries is too weak to give them sufficient credibility in their academic and professional pursuits. Overall, a lack of quality educational institutions, weak faculty and the emigration of the best scholars have all limited the growth and development of Asian media studies since the 1970s.

Asian media studies: the turning point?

Since the beginning of the twenty-first century, Asian media and communication studies has witnessed a profound transformation, and across Asia the discipline has been gaining in prominence and importance. In my opinion, there are several reasons for this revitalization of Asian media studies. First and foremost among them is an increasing realization by both governments and the private sector at large of the critical importance of information and communication technologies as drivers of the knowledge economy and as instruments of national development. This has led to a dramatically different approach to the discipline and a new belief that media and communication studies was emerging as a key academic discipline as well as a new professional and lucrative career track.

In addition, Asia's unprecedented economic growth, led by Japan, China, South Korea and India, brought about an explosion of the media industry. Long controlled by national governments, the media were deregulated in the 1990s to benefit from the economic boom, and this produced a dramatic proliferation of print, broadcast and electronic media throughout the 1990s and into the twenty-first century. Today, China has more internet users than any other country in the world; India continues to be the largest producer of films in the world and has one of the largest number of newspapers, radio and

TV stations (not to forget that it is the fastest growing mobile telephone market in the world); South Korea leads the world in broadband penetration (and is becoming a prominent producer of TV soaps), and Japan continues to be one of the most powerful producers of media hardware and animation. This revitalization of the media industries in Asia, fuelled by unprecedented economic growth, has provided a new opportunity for media and communication studies.

Media expansion not only creates a large number of jobs for students of media and communications, but also enhances the need to research media development and its implications for society. This has been the trigger for the rise of Asian media and communication studies and has helped it to overcome the many constraints that restricted its growth in the past. Governments and the private sector have been quick to seize this opportunity, and the number of public and private institutions providing media and communication studies has mushroomed over the past decade. There has also been a significant improvement in the quality of these educational and research institutions in some parts of Asia. In Japan, South Korea, Hong Kong (PRC), China, Singapore, India and other countries, we have witnessed the emergence of centres of excellence in media and communication studies. There are a number of well-funded media and communication studies programmes in these countries with world-class faculty, infrastructure and students. Many of these programmes have managed to attract top international scholars and have enticed a number of Asian scholars settled in the West to return to Asia.

Over the past decade and more, the number of Asian scholars who have published in top-tier international journals has seen significant growth, which is essentially a reflection of the calibre of Asian media research and scholarship. In addition, in the past few years we have also witnessed the emergence of a number of quality refereed Asian journals in the field of media and communication studies. The *Asian Journal of Communication* is currently in its eighteenth year of publication and, given its track record, has attracted the attention of top international publishers and is now being published by Taylor & Francis, one of the leading publishers of journals in the field. Several other journals have also established themselves in the field of media and communication studies in Asia, including *Media Asia* (which was launched in 1974), *Asia-Pacific Media Educator, Media International Australia, Australian Journalism Review* and a number of other specialized publications. This has indeed created a vibrant publishing environment within Asian media and communication studies, which is further boosting the profile of media studies within Asia and internationally.

One must also acknowledge the role of some of the key institutions in the growth and development of Asian media studies, including Asia's premier media research, publication and resource centre, the Asian Media Information and Communication Centre (AMIC) based in Singapore. This regional Asia-Pacific media research centre not only publishes the *Asian Journal of*

Communication and *Media Asia* but also is one of the leading publishers of books on Asian media and communication studies through its series called the AMIC Asian Communication Series. AMIC also publishes the only handbook on the Asian media industry; the last edition, the *Asian Communication Handbook 2008*, was released in July 2008 (Banerjee and Logan, 2008). AMIC has been a catalyst for the development of Asian media studies for the past 38 years and has spearheaded research, publication and capacity-building initiatives in the region for almost four decades.

Thus overall there has been a marked evolution of Asian media studies in the past decade or so. Asian media studies seems to be coming of age; its increasing prominence owes much to the creation of centres of excellence, the quality of the faculty in several institutions across Asia, world-class infrastructure and a large group of students keen on excelling in the discipline both academically and professionally.

Asian media studies: the key challenge

Asian media studies has come a long way since its inception, with a large number of Asian scholars who have attained international recognition for their scholarship, with strong schools and institutions teaching media research and professional skills, and with the growth of top-level Asian journals and publications. However, a key feature of Asian media studies has been its inability to develop local theories and conceptual frameworks. Even today, Asian media studies is dominated by Western models, theories and paradigms. Wimal Dissanayake summarizes the challenge when he states:

> If Asian communication scholars are to come up with models of communication which bear the imprint of their own cultures and which will enable them to comprehend better and conceptualize more clearly the complexity of human communication, it is indeed imperative that they shake off the influence of the mechanistic Aristotelian model. They need to address their mind to the task of finding out how best they can draw upon the cumulative wisdom of Asian human sciences as a means of formulating theories and models of communication.
>
> (Dissanayake, 1988: 6)

Asian media scholars have learnt how to play the academic game better by appropriating Western theoretical constructs and methodologies. They have learnt how to publish in top international journals, but are they making any difference if they are not bringing to these journals new perspectives and new epistemological and theoretical contributions that are extracted out of their local experience?

The community of media scholars around the world has missed out on the opportunity of learning from different local contexts and experiences. Imagine how much richer media studies would be if scholars from Latin America, Africa and Asia brought new ontological, epistemological and methodological perspectives into the world of media studies. What we have seen so far in the history of the discipline has been a one-way process whereby everyone is trying to appropriate Western models and perspectives rather than everyone contributing to the body of knowledge in the field through their own experiences. This has significantly reduced the range, scope and wealth of media studies around the world.

Indeed, there are several important obstacles to attempts to internationalize media studies, including linguistic barriers, access to information and a hierarchy of institutions and processes of legitimization. However, the single most important barrier lies in the fact that as most media studies scholars are educated using Western models and frameworks, there has been an absolute vacuum when it comes to developing teaching and research methods that are locally developed. This has created a vicious circle where everyone gets co-opted into the same framework, while no attempt can be made to develop alternative or local models and methods.

Yoshitaka Miike (2006) aptly summarizes the handicap of media and communication studies when he writes: 'Forms and functions of communication differ from culture to culture. Therefore, we will never gain a rich and profound understanding of the subtleties and pluralities of human communication until we take culture into due consideration.' Goonasekera and Kuo (2000) also argue that it is time to question the validity of mainstream communication theories when applied to vastly different contexts. It is time also to ponder how Asian communication research can provide new resources and findings to enrich communication theories and models around the world.

References

Banerjee, I. and Logan, S. (eds.) (2008) *Asian Communication Handbook 2008*. Singapore: Asian Media Information and Communication Centre.

Dissanayake, W. (1988) *Communication Theory: The Asian Perspective*. Singapore: Asian Media Information and Communication Centre.

Goonasekera, A. and Kuo, E.C.Y. (2000) Foreword, in A. Goonasekera and E.C.Y. Kuo (eds) Towards an Asian Theory of Communication?, *Asian Journal of Communication*, 10 (2): 1–123.

Hardt, H. (1979) *Social Theories of the Press: Early German and American Perspectives*. Beverly Hills, CA: Sage.

Katz, E. and Lazarsfeld, P.F. (1955) *Personal Influence: The Part Played by People in the Flow of Mass Communications*. New York: The Free Press.

Lasswell, H.D. (1948) The Structure and Function of Communication in Society, in Lyman Bryson (ed.) *The Communication of Ideas*. New York: Institute for Religious and Social Studies, p. 37.

Lippmann, W. (1922) *Public Opinion*. New York: Macmillan.

Miike, Y. (2006) Non-Western Theory in Western Research? An Asiacentric Agenda for Asian Communication Studies, *Review of Communication*, 6(1–2): 4–31.

Park, R.E. (1922) *The Immigrant Press and Its Control*. New York: Harper and Brothers.

Quebral, N.C. (1971) Development Communication in the Agricultural Context. Paper presented at UPCA symposium in honour of Dioscoro Umali, cited in J.F. Jamias (1975) *Development Communication: Readings in Development Communication*. University of the Philippines, Los Baños: Department of Development Communication.

—— (2001) Development Communication in a Borderless World. Paper presented at the 'New Dimensions, Bold Decisions' conference, Department of Science Communication, University of the Philippines, Los Baños.

Srampickal, J. (2006) Development and Participatory Communication, *Communication Research Trends*, 25(2).

Chapter 11

Rethinking Chinese media studies

History, political economy and culture

Yuezhi Zhao

The agenda of 'internationalizing media studies' has been pursued by scholars of Chinese media and communication from a variety of angles. A growing body of literature has addressed different aspects of Chinese media institutions and communication processes from analytical frameworks ranging from the liberal conception of power to the Foucaultian notion of governmentality. Some of the main lines of enquiry have included: the Chinese system of propaganda and media control, especially internet control (e.g. Qiu, 1999; Tsui, 2003; Shambaugh, 2007; Brady, 2008); the fusion of party-state power and market rationality in the Chinese media (e.g. Barme, 1999; Lee, 2000; Bai, 2005; Lee, He and Huang, 2006; Zhao, 1998, 2000a); the prospects or lack thereof for political democratization, along with the localization of Western-style media professionalism and the emergence of Chinese 'public sphere' and 'civil society' in the context of media commercialization, globalization and the explosion of new technologies (e.g. Chan, Pan and Lee, 2004; Lynch, 1999; Pan and Ye Lu, 2003; Pan and Chan, 2003; Tai, 2006; Yang, 2003, 2007; Zhao, 2000b, 2001, 2005).

The past few years have also witnessed the emergence of analyses that link developments in the Chinese communication industries with the structural logic of transnationalizing capitalism, which, until the global financial crisis of 2008, had encompassed China and the broad terrain of information and communication as its 'two poles of growth' since the 1980s (Schiller, 2005), as well as studies that examine the accommodations and tensions between transnational capital and the Chinese state at the national and local levels in the transformation of media and communication industries (e.g. Chin, 2003; Fung, 2006; Lee, 2003; Xin, 2006; Zhao, 2003a, 2004; Zhao and Schiller, 2001).

Building upon this literature and drawing on my own more recent work (Zhao, 2007a, 2007b, 2008a, 2008b; Zhao and Duffy, 2007; Chakravartty and Zhao, 2008), this chapter explores potentials for broadening and deepening Chinese media and communication research in the process of internationalization. Rather than focus on obvious 'internationalizing' issues centring on the transnational flows of media capital, forms, contents, and influences, including China's recently accentuated efforts in projecting its own 'soft power' abroad, I foreground issues pertaining more closely to domestic Chinese social processes by arguing that there is an imperative for this area to re-root itself in history, re-embed itself in the Chinese social terrain, redefine agency, reengage with meaning and community, and, finally, reclaim utopian imaginations. I believe that these five 'R's – which are by no means mutually exclusive – will enable researchers not only to broaden and deepen the analysis of Chinese media and communication, but also to make theoretical contributions to the broader field of global media studies, enabling it to have a more productive dialogue with Western-centric conceptual frameworks, and also potentially enrich them and transcend their limitations.

Re-root the area in history

I am not merely calling for historical studies in Chinese media and communication, which are not only badly needed in their own right but also have demonstrated their value in illuminating contemporary developments, from online activism to telecommunication developments (Zhou, 2006; Winseck and Pike, 2007). Rather, I argue for a reorientation of the area that is mindful of China's revolutionary history and the ways this history casts a long shadow over today's reality. This entails two considerations.

First, as Lin Chun (2006) has argued, it means a serious reengagement with China's post-colonial and socialist legacies. More specifically, this entails the recognition of the Chinese state as one forged in an anti-imperialist and anti-capitalist social revolution, with a historically grounded popular base of legitimacy, not a simple absolutist state that the Western European bourgeoisie fought against historically. This historical legacy not only continues to shape the political economic and discursive transformations of the Chinese communication system, but also continues to define the parameters of control and resistance in Chinese communication politics.

Second, re-rooting studies in this area in history implies a recognition that China (and the world) have not yet arrived at 'the end of ideology' and 'end of history', and that the struggle between left and right, and between capitalism and socialism, is not over. The peculiar situation of a communist party supervising a capitalistic revolution in China means that the party-state has been compelled, on the one hand, to suppress what it calls 'bourgeois liberalization', i.e. an open embrace of liberal democratic capitalism in politics and ideology, and, on the other, to contain the haunting 'spectre' of communism, more specifically leftist critiques of 'capitalist restoration' and the independent communication activities of Chinese social forces that have contested the terms and negative consequences of capitalistic developments. In the words of Deng Xiaoping, while continuing to proclaim allegiance to the 'socialist road', the party 'must guard against the right, but guard primarily against the left' as it adopts neo-liberal developmental strategies and negotiates the terms of China's reintegration with global capitalism. The study of Chinese media censorship and the resistance to it, which has commanded much English-language scholarly attention, needs to be placed not only within the context of the Chinese state's role in containing popular and anti-imperialist nationalistic sentiments and disciplining Chinese labourers for transnational capitalistic production, but also within the context of the unfinished ideological struggle between capitalism and socialism – that is, beyond a liberal condemnation of a repressive state and its pure will to power or the actualization of the Foucaultian panopticon.

Two censorship cases in early 2006 dramatized the ideological parameters that define the party-state's regime of control and its structured asymmetries vis-à-vis competing ideological positions and divergent social forces in its actual application.[1] On 25 January 2006 *China Youth News' Freezing Point* weekly was suspended because of its publication of an article by Yuan Weishi on 11 January 2006. In his article, Yuan, a philosophy professor, repudiated official history for its anti-imperialist narrative. In particular, Yuan faulted the official depiction of the armed resistance of the Taiping rebels and the Boxers against foreign invaders in the nineteenth century as patriotic precursors of the party's own anti-imperialist struggles. In language reminiscent of 'reverse Orientalism' (Pickowicz, 1995: 212), Yuan charged the Boxer Rebellion of 1900 for being 'against civilization and humanity', maintaining that the Boxers' 'evil deeds' 'brought greatest tragedy to the country and the people'. In response, the Central Committee of the Chinese Communist Youth League, the authority responsible for the newspaper, suspended the weekly's publication and forced a 'rectification'.

The suspension gained broad publicity and was loudly protested both within and outside China. Li Datong, *Freezing Point*'s editor, posted an open letter on the internet condemning the 'unconstitutional' and 'illegal' suspension of the paper. An influential group of liberal-minded, retired high-ranking party officials, academics as well as former media and propaganda chiefs, issued an open letter condemning the censorship acts as 'ridiculous, rude and totally beyond the boundaries of law' (Associate Press, 2006). However, what was lost in the domestic and international drumbeat against censorship and the seemingly universalistic defence of press freedom was the fact that *China Youth News*, the Communist Youth League organ, should have published a piece that so explicitly challenged the official party view in the first place. Behind the liberal invocation of constitutional authority is the struggle between competing forces within the Chinese party-state over historical truths and the control of a party organ.

The party-state's censorship regime capitulated in the face of domestic and foreign outcries against censorship. However, as liberal forces celebrated their victory over the party's decision to allow *Freezing Point* to resume publication on 1 March 2006, a different arm of the state issued a censorship order of a very different nature. On 22 February 2006 the Internet Propaganda Management Division of the Beijing Government Information Office ordered the closure of two grass-roots leftist websites, *China Workers Net* (established on 1

May 2005) and *Communists Net* (established on 26 December 2005), and the latter's bulletin board, Worker-Peasant-Soldier BBS (established on 20 January 2006). The reason given was that these websites did not have a registered capital of 10 million yuan ($1.2 million) and thus were 'illegal'. According to a September 2005 government regulation on internet news and information services, a business entity that is engaged in the provision of such services must have a registered capital of no less than 10 million yuan.

The party had shut down many websites before on political grounds, and many existing ones continue to operate without the required amount of capitalization. However, this was the first time the authorities invoked this requirement to shut down autonomous workers' and communist websites. What had made these websites so dangerous to the party was that they provided 'uncensored news about worker unrest' (*Economist*, 2006) and had gained influence as leftist websites and as the opinion forums of workers and farmers. Even more threatening to the party, these websites dared to claim to be 'communist' outside the party.

That Yuan's article appeared in an official newspaper while leftist websites could only carve out an existence at the margins of Chinese cyberspace is itself highly indicative of the asymmetric access to venues of public discourse by proponents of 'antigovernment' views of the right and the left in China. Moreover, contrary to the outburst of anger and protest from leading party editors, intellectuals and former party officials, who mobilized their domestic and international communication networks to defend *their* right to present *their* views as the official view in a party organ as a *constitutional* right and condemn the party's censorship as ridiculous, editors at these marginal websites could only express a sigh of resignation in the face of legalized repression. Significantly, none of the individuals who protested against the party-state's censorship regime in the *Freezing Point* case rose to defend these leftist websites within the terms of constitutionalism and the universalizing language of press freedom, let alone to condemn the blunt capitalistic bias of the government regulation in a state that is still ruled by a Communist Party.

Re-embed the area in the social terrain

The argument for a contextualized understanding of the party-state's censorship regime and domestic and international protests against it lays the ground for my second 'R', that is, to re-embed Chinese media and communication studies in the totality of Chinese social relations. Following Golding and Murdoch (1978: 253), who wrote with reference to advanced societies in the West and East before the collapse of East European communism and capitalism's neo-liberal turn, I argue for an integrative political economic approach that is capable of 'relating the various levels of the mass communication processes, both to each other and to the central dimensions of social structure and social processes'. As these two scholars noted, this entails three concerns: the relations between the unequal distribution of control over systems of communications and wider patterns of inequality in the distribution of wealth and power, particularly between the media and the class structure, the processes of legitimation, and, finally, the sources of social dissent and political struggle, and the dialectical relations between challenge and incorporation (Golding and Murdoch, 1978: 353).

All these concerns are of paramount importance in the case of China, where accelerated capitalistic developments have not only accentuated preexisting inequalities but also engendered rapid processes of class polarization, and where the installation of capitalistic social relations by a party-state that still calls itself 'socialist' has posed profound challenges of legitimacy. Furthermore, China's social transformation is boiling with – even constituted by – political economic contradictions, social conflicts, and ideological and cultural tensions. In the area of communication politics, there have been three major waves of overt and covert debates and conflicts on the direction of the reform process since its inception in 1978, including the 'first debate' between 1982 and 1984, the June 1989 bloodshed and the 'second debate' before and after it, which ended with Deng's imposition of a 'no debate' curse in 1992 – that is, there should be no debate about the capitalist or socialist nature of the economic reforms – and the 'third debate' between 2005 and 2007, which I will discuss further in the next section. Within Chinese society, as Perry and Selden (2003) have observed, the reform process has engendered multifaceted conflicts and myriad arenas of resistance at every stage, from tax riots, labour strikes and interethnic clashes to environmental, anticorruption, and gender protests, legal challenges, pro-democracy demonstrations, local electoral disputes, religious rebellions, and even mass suicides. Moreover, the emerging patterns of conflict and resistance have stimulated and shaped significant dimensions of the reform programme itself (Perry and Selden, 2003: 1–2).

As the processes of social stratification, class polarization, and cultural displacement have accelerated in a rapidly globalizing context since China's WTO accession in 2001, the frequency and velocity, as well as the breadth and scope, of these 'hydra-headed' conflicts and resistance have also intensified at both elite and popular levels. Whether it is the debate over the relative powers of state and market, or the search for the Chinese public sphere or the prospects for media professionalism, it is important to relate these analytical categories to the processes of class formation and social conflict. Moreover, China's deepening integration with the global economy and the prominent role foreign capital plays in the domestic Chinese economy have meant that the central axis of social stratification and the processes of class formation have taken on a strong transnational dimension, turning the media and communication field into a key site for the unfolding politics of class formation and legitimation within and beyond China's borders.

Again, let me illustrate this point with two contrasting case studies on the class bias of China's emerging media and internet public sphere, and the complicated intersection between class politics, media professionalism, and media and internet-based urban middle-class reformism. In the first case, Sun Zhigang, a 27-year-old university graduate, who worked as a graphic designer in Guangzhou, was beaten to death in 2003 by the local police under the state's draconian detention regime against rural migrants – that is, rural migrants who were unable to produce authorized papers in the cities would be arrested and sent back to the countryside. Sun was born into a rural family, but he had crossed the rural–urban divide through university education. He was not meant to be the target of the detention regime, but he became one because he did not carry his personal identification card and was in the wrong place at the wrong time. Although the police tried to cover up the case, Sun's socio-economic status as a university graduate made his victimization by the detention regime and police brutality newsworthy. Through Sun's urban-based classmate networks, the *Nanfang Metro News* (a market-based subsidiary of the Guangdong Province party organ *Nanfang Daily*) uncovered the story. This is journalistic autonomy vis-à-vis the state at its best; the newspaper went all the way to establish the facts – i.e. helped Sun's family to obtain an independent autopsy report proving that Sun died of physical injuries, rather than a heart attack, as the police had alleged.

News coverage made explicit efforts to place Sun's death in the broad social context, linking his case to universal citizenship rights, the ending of the arbitrary power of the state, and the establishment of liberal constitutional governance. The reporter even went on a major liberal internet website to issue a call for Chinese intellectuals to crusade on behalf of Sun and citizenship rights. In the subsequent media and internet mobilization, 'Detainee Sun' became 'University Graduate Sun' and eventually 'Citizen Sun', the symbol of individual liberal rights – i.e. negative freedoms, that is, freedom from the arbitrary power of the state. Sun became a symbol that the urban middle class could identify with, while the *Nanfang Metro News* emerged as symbol of an incipient independent professional journalism engaging in a heroic battle against state censorship and police cover-up. Here professionalism means advocacy on behalf of the weak, placing a story in a broader social and political context, and, if required, establishing the facts in the first place.

In contrast, in the Wang Binyu case in 2005, professionalism had come to mean something quite different. In China, migrant workers, 150 million strong, are not only denied urban citizen rights but also often their pitiful salaries – their employers often fail to pay them. Thus, their economic and social rights are seriously violated. Wang Binyu was also a 27-year-old man. However, unlike Sun, Wang had to quit school at grade four due to poverty and became a migrant worker. After exhausting all administrative and legal means to collect his unpaid salary and being verbally and physically abused by his foremen, and others, Wang ended up killing four people and then immediately turned himself in to the police. Wang was on death row when the Xinhua News Agency publicized his story and attempted to use the case to dramatize the need for the whole of society to pay more attention to the economic rights of migrant workers.

The story immediately stirred up a media and internet controversy. Internet opinion overwhelmingly sympathized with Wang, arguing that Wang's action was an understandable reaction to the social injustice he faced. A campaign to save Wang from the death penalty soon developed. Drawing on a broad notion of justice, arguments against the death penalty refused to treat the case as an isolated criminal act but to place it within a wider social context of class exploitation. The internet crusade on behalf of Wang thus threatened to shake a criminal justice regime based on liberal individual rights. Yes, Wang needed to be brought to criminal justice, but what about the class-based social justice of the 100 million migrant workers that Wang symbolized? 'Wang the Murderer' threatened to become 'Wang the Symbol of a Repressed and Betrayed Social Class'. More specifically, leftist online discourses seized the opportunity to criticize the party's betrayal of its working-class constituency and link the pending prosecution of Wang with the death of the Chinese communist state itself. Feeling threatened, the party-state ordered a media blackout on the case. Wang was secretly executed. But even before the party's iron fist did its work, a very different version of professionalism had been mobilized by the market-oriented urban press to contain an emerging discourse on class conflict.

In particular, *Nanfang Metro News*, the crusading hero in the Sun Zhigang case, issued an editorial entitled 'Compassion Should Not Cover up True Facts, Sympathy Must Return to Professional Principles'. In the editorial, the paper implicitly criticized the Xinhua News Agency story and subsequent media stories about the case for violating the principle of 'journalistic professionalism', that is, for not sticking to the immediate 'facts' of Wang's brutality as a murderer, for bringing in too much social background, and for dramatizing the social significance of Wang. *China News Weekly*, a market-oriented current affairs magazine, echoed this view by calling for 'Vigilance against Public Opinion Bias'.

Thus, although media professionalism, along with some form of a Chinese 'public sphere', is emerging, it is a multifaceted regime and it is implicated in the politics of class containment. As market-oriented media proliferated in China, China's rising urban middle class – the favoured customers of these media outlets – have managed to project their voices and steer state policies to their advantage. However, many disenfranchised social groups are not able to do this, and state censorship has often reinforced the social biases of the media market. It is less interesting, therefore, to measure the Chinese 'public sphere' against some idealized form than to analyse the substantive dimensions of Chinese communication politics and its relationships with the processes of state transformation and the reconstitution of class and other forms of social relations.

As Nancy Fraser (1992) has noted, revisionist historiography has called into question not only the exclusive nature of the bourgeois public sphere, but also its conflicts with other counter-publics, such as nationalist publics, popular peasant publics, elite women's publics, and working-class publics. These 'subaltern counter-publics', as Fraser calls them, were contesting the exclusionary norms of the bourgeois public sphere from the very beginning. Consequently, the emergence of a bourgeois public was never defined solely by the struggle against absolutism and traditional authority, but by the problem of popular containment as well. Thus, one can no longer assume that the bourgeois conception of the public sphere was simply an unrealized utopian ideal. Instead, it is the institutional vehicle for a major historical transformation from political domination based primarily on acquiescence to superior force to rule based on consent supplemented with some measure of repression.

Fraser's discussion of the bourgeois public sphere's antagonistic relationship with subaltern publics is useful in helping us to see through any universalistic claims of an emerging bourgeoisie which wishes to replace the party to establish hegemonic rule over Chinese society. The peculiar situation in China, of course, is that a state that claims to represent a variety of counter-bourgeois publics – peasants, workers, women, ethnic groups, nationalists – is simultaneously engendering a bourgeois class. The contradictory formation of the Chinese state and the balance of power in Chinese society has meant that popular containment, rather than struggle against an authoritarian state, has become the political priority of the Chinese bourgeoisie, which as a class has yet to cut its umbilical cord with the party-state.

Still, both Habermas' original concept and Fraser's reformulation of a post-bourgeois public sphere are specific to modern societies in the West. As China scholar Philip Huang asks: 'When we substitute segmented and largely rural local communities for Habermas's integrated and urban public sphere … what is left of the concept of public sphere to warrant retention of the term?' (1995: 122). Internationalizing media studies in the Chinese context not only requires recognition of the specific articulation of state and society relations in the Chinese media and communication system, but also requires that attention is paid to the ways Chinese society is different from Western societies and the ways inequalities and injustices in Chinese society are structurally connected to today's transnationalized processes of capitalistic accumulation, from the low wages of China's industrial workers as China's 'comparative advantage' in the global economy to rural economic depression and environmental degradation. Despite its theoretical limitations and its connections with the Cold War project of containing the Third World, one of the legacies of the modernization paradigm in international communication research has been its attention to the peasantry, the mythic Ifes and Bvanises whom Schramm (1964) viewed as potential human resources to be mobilized through the mass media, and whose traditional values and practices needed to be replaced by 'modern' ones. It is unfortunate that the shift from the modernization paradigm to the democratization paradigm should have led to a heavily urban middle class-oriented research agenda. This leads to my third 'R', which concerns the agency of China's different social forces.

Redefine agency

Once again, the extraordinary situation in China is that a state that was forged in a communist revolution and still claims to be building socialism has been pursuing a paradigm of development that was the product of capitalism, thus turning socialism into a cover for policies of development inspired by capitalism (Dirlik, 2005). Such a unique condition has meant that the objective processes of neo-liberal 'accumulation by dispossession' (Harvey, 2003) and the consequences of rapid class polarization and cultural dislocation resulting from 'neo-liberalism with Chinese characteristics' (Harvey, 2005) have been subjectively experienced by a population that has been educated in the socialist ideology of economic equality, social justice, and the rightness, if not the liberal legal right, of rebellion. Despite official blackouts of news on various forms of social protest and the media's relentless promotion of economic prosperity and cultural festivity, China's different social classes experience and feel an acute sense of class conflict in their everyday consciousness.

As an unusually candid survey conducted by the Chinese Academy of Social Sciences revealed, China's urban population expressed a strong sense of social conflict along major political economic cleavages. The survey revealed that 79 per cent feel there are various degrees of conflicts between capital and labour, 78 per cent feel conflicts between officials and the ordinary people, and nearly 76 per cent feel conflicts between the rich and the poor (Li *et al.*, 2005: 136–8). Moreover, the population groups that identify themselves as either at the top or at the bottom of the class structure tend to perceive stronger social conflicts along these dimensions. Not only does there exist 'apparent mutual hostility between the rich and the poor', but 'a significant proportion of those who self-identify as being at the top of the social structure are unwilling to shoulder the responsibility of helping the poor' (Li *et al.*, 2005: 171, 174–5). Considering the urban bias of the survey, which was conducted in metropolitan centres and provincial capitals, the actual sense of class division among the national population is probably much sharper.

This heightened level of sensitivity towards social division and injustice on the part of the lower classes, as well as the arrogance of the rich and the powerful, are precisely what explains why a traffic incident involving a BMW driver and a peasant in Harbin turned into the explosive 'BMW incident' in the Chinese media and cyberspace in 2003. The same reasons also explain why an ostensibly 'purely pedestrian' encounter between a self-proclaimed ranking government official and a lowly porter in Sichuan Province turned into the 'Wanzhou uprising' of 28 October 2004, in which tens of thousands of ordinary people stormed the city square and set fire to the city hall (Kahn, 2004). Despite Deng's 'no debate' edict, by the summer of 2005 the 'third debate on reform' about the stakes of China's different social classes in the ongoing social transformation had broken out in the Chinese media and ideological field. Moreover, unlike the debates in the 1980s and 1990s, which were confined to domestic elites, this one was ignited by Lang Xianping, a US-trained and Hong-Kong based, transnational intellectual voice, and driven more robustly by grass-root critiques of the neo-liberal reform orientation. Most importantly, this debate brought into sharper focus conflicting class interests and the instrumental role of media and communication in the formation of class consciousness.

In light of the drastically widening social divisions in Chinese society and the conflicting interests of China's different social classes, analysis of Chinese communication needs to move beyond undifferentiated constructions of 'the media consumer', 'the public' and 'the audience'. These formulations simply turn the party's formulation, that is, the identification of the party with 'the people', on its head, without breaking away from its totalizing logic. As Mosco argues, the term 'audience' is 'not an analytical category, like class, gender, or race, but a product of the media industry itself, which uses the term to identify markets and to define a commodity' (1996: 262). The use of 'audience' or 'the public' as a privileged and undifferentiated analytical and existential category vis-à-vis the state can potentially serve to mystify the media's role in the construction of social classes, gender, ethnicity and other categories of difference, and conceal the role of the media and processes of communication in mediating social relations.

In short, a media study that continues to critique the fusion of party-state and market power in the Chinese media without a detailed analysis of the processes of social stratification and class formation is no longer adequate, if it ever was. Nor is it enough to focus merely on the agency of Chinese liberal intellectuals in challenging party-state power, or the agency of Chinese state officials and media producers in negotiating with transnational capital in the process of growing China's own communication industries and increasing their stakes in the global market system. It is important to pay attention to the everyday communicative practices of China's subaltern social classes, and the ways these subaltern Chinese social forces have managed to communicate their struggles with, and often without, the state-controlled, market-driven, and increasingly globalized media system. Since 2003, these struggles, along with other factors, have compelled the party state under the Hu Jintao leadership to readjust the reform agenda to embrace the ideals of social justice and a more human-centred developmental course.

The young fans of the *Supergirls* – the Chinese version of *American Idol* – as the interactive 'audience commodity' of the synergized Chinese television and mobile phone industries, are cool, and the cultural politics surrounding them and China's youthful urban consumers are extremely important.[2] However, do scholars of Chinese media know how to translate the English term 'trade union' into Chinese both literally and metaphorically? This is not a rhetorical question. Rather, it was provoked by my actual reading experience in China in summer 2005. I was giving lectures at Shanghai's Fudan University on the political economic and cultural approaches to communication studies. At the local bookstore I was thrilled to discover a newly published cultural studies journal, which contained a translation of Stuart Hall's well-known text 'The Rediscovery of "Ideology": Return of the Repressed in Media Studies'

(1982). However, I was astonished to discover that, in the article, the term 'trade union' was translated to mean a business association (*maoyi lianghehui*) rather than a union of workers. Although the party does not allow workers to organize independent trade unions, there are still official trade unions and the party's central propaganda department has not gone so far as to ban the use of the term 'trade union' altogether. Rather, in an illustration of precisely the kind of hegemony that Hall's article explicates, the agency of Chinese workers and the term 'trade union' seldom register in the consciousness of scholars of Chinese media and culture as they translate British cultural studies, with its strong initial concern with working-class agency, into Chinese and apply this approach to the analysis of Chinese media and popular culture.

If internationalized Chinese media studies are to do more than provide intelligence and legitimacy to the globalizing media and high-education industries in the West in the so-called 'era of China', there is an imperative for researchers to transcend their elitist and class biases, and to start to engage with the subjectivity of not only China's rising urban middle class as consumers and citizens in a globalizing market liberal discourse, but also Chinese workers and farmers – the two social classes that make up the numerical majority of the Chinese nation, and whose alliance is still nominally the power base of the Chinese socialist state. With a few very encouraging recent exceptions (e.g. Cartier *et al.*, 2005; Qiu, 2009; Harwit, 2004; Lu, 2005; Zhao and Duffy, 2007; Hong, 2008; Sun, 2009) and in contrast to area studies scholars in sociology, anthropology, and political science, scholars of Chinese media and communication have largely neglected the topic of class formation and class consciousness in general and, more specifically, the agency, subjectivity, and communicative needs and practices of Chinese workers and farmers; and to reemphasize, state censorship is not an adequate explanation for this blind spot. Given how Chinese workers are instrumental to the maintenance of transnational capitalist production and increases in the salaries of Chinese workers can translate into a surge in the prices of consumer goods at Wal-Mart, this is no insignificant topic. As Dan Schiller (2008: 413) has highlighted, the making of a gigantic Chinese working class of perhaps 200 million wage-earners during a compressed period of just three decades and with significant linkages to transnational capital formation is a process that has world historical importance for the development of politics, culture and social policy. Similarly, there is an imperative for communication scholarship to explore the subjectivity and communicative practices of China's vast rural population, at a time when social instability in the rural areas has become a major political concern and the 'agrarian question' has once again come to the fore of the Chinese political economy.[3]

Reengage with meaning and community

Yet class consciousness is not the only dimension in a broadened redefinition of agency and subjectivity. Concepts such as 'civil society' and 'public sphere' are not just socio-political categories. They concern not only the organization of society and politics, but also a form of life. As sociologist and China scholar Richard Madsen notes, a concept of modern civil society based solely on utilitarian contractual relations and self-interest is inherently unstable. Classic social theorists from Durkheim to de Tocqueville emphasized the importance of pre-modern religious and political traditions for importing stability, solidarity, and moral discipline to modern civil society. Indeed, 'modern Western social theory has never resolved the issue of how to reconcile the modern market with the pre-modern moral traditions that have somehow made it function' (Madsen, 1993: 188). Similarly, Karl Polanyi ([1944]1957) emphasized the embeddedness of markets in society. Thus, '[f]or markets to be sustainable they must also be capable of at least staking a claim to furthering the ethical basis of social life' (Jenkins, 2004: 307). In the aftermath of the spectacular collapse of the global financial system in 2008, when even the architects of neo-liberalism have had to reckon with the devastating consequences of their own excesses in promoting unregulated financial markets and reckless financial speculation, Polanyi's attention to the symbolic legitimacy of market transformation seems especially prescient. Likewise, democratization is not simply a political process, but also a cultural one, involving the media in a process of identity formation much broader than the provision of political information (Zhao and Hackett, 2005: 25–6). In fact, the question of the cultural role of media and communication has become increasingly salient at the current historical juncture, as witnessed by the eruption of ethnic, religious and other identity-based conflicts and movements since the 1980s both within and beyond nation-state boundaries.

In the context of this discussion, it is possible to see in a different light the Chinese student protesters' notorious failure to come up with a concrete definition of democracy in Tiananmen Square in 1989. While some may have indeed simply wanted capitalism and liberal democracy, we may assume that many of those camping at Tiananmen Square in 1989 wanted a new form of life that neither state socialism nor Western capitalist modernity has been able to provide. This is partly why, power struggles and hypocrisies among the protesters notwithstanding, the sense of community, common purpose, fraternity, and morale that was forged out of that lived experience (even the thieves stopped stealing during the height of the pro-democracy movement in 1989, so the story went) is so valuable and memorable to both the participants and their outside observers. The issues of community, ethics and morality have returned with a vengeance in post-1989 China and found expression in different forms, including the massive subjective revolution of Falun Gong. Though the party denounces Falun Gong as a cult, and a liberal analytical framework may treat it as an issue of religious freedom (thus assigning it to the domain of private conscience), this kind of cultural backlash and identity formation challenges any linear notion of liberal democratic cultural development in the era of market liberalization and globalization (Zhao, 2003b).

Just as the resurgence of online leftist activism since 2003 challenges Chinese media and communication scholars to take the history of China's socialist state formation seriously (Hu, 2006), so the upsurge of nationalistic sentiments both online and offline (Gries, 2004; Sun, 2002; Qiu, 2006; Zhou, 2006), the revival of traditional cultural values and practices in both the official and vernacular realms, and the rise of the transnational Falun Gong movement challenge the narrowness of a modernistic, rationalistic, and Western-centric project promoted by the Chinese 'new enlightenment' narrative of modernity in the 1980s, which continues to have considerable impact on the field of Chinese media and communication studies. Within this narrative, anything that does not fit into a modernist rationality is feudal and banished to the realm of cult – from the Mao cult to the Falun Gong cult – while the rising tide of nationalism is blamed primarily on the manipulation and fanning of the Chinese state for the purpose of its own preservation. One can dispute the intensity and the specific political and cultural orientation of these identities, but more modernization and globalization will not do away with the human need for collective belonging and 'communities of memory' that allow people to make sense of their history, their place in the world, and their future.

It is important, as some media scholars have argued, to correct the rationalism and cognitivism of most theorizing about the public sphere, and to 'recognize the likely importance of the affective dimensions of collective belonging and social cohesion' (Schlesinger, 1999: 270). Furthermore, while it is important to account for the inspirational logic of modernization and modernity, the lures and promises of the globalized media and communication industries, as well as the emancipatory potentials of civil society formations outside the state, it is necessary to draw from post-colonial critiques of imperialism and empire to develop analyses that account for the complicated politics of class and nation, inequalities and exclusions within civil society (Chakravartty and Zhao, 2008), as well as competing counter-narratives of Chinese modernity (Yu, 2006).

If a critique of problematic assumptions in Habermas' original formulation of the public sphere opened up the possibility for imagining a 'post-bourgeois' public sphere based on the transcendence of economic inequality (Fraser, 1992), a less rationalist and a 'more abstract' understanding of the concept, together with post-colonial challenges to the Eurocentric conflation of capitalism and modernity, open up the possibility for imagining non-Western public spheres, alternative modernities, and different forms of democracy. For example, as Madsen (1993: 187) argues, if the public sphere is defined at the more abstract level of a form of life, then:

> The concept of the public sphere is not wedded to a particular Western set of economic and political structures. It presumes that there may be different concrete forms of democracy. Far from presuming that a society like China must become like the West, it assumes that the West itself needs to search for new ways to revitalize its public spheres. The search for new ways to institutionalize a public sphere under modern (or postmodern) circumstances brings China and the West together in a common quest.

Recovering utopian imaginations

Although China's neo-liberal reformers have long projected a utopian market society as 'a wonderful order' which features 'clearly delineated property rights, fair exchange, legal justice, and a harmonious society' (Zhang, 2004), it remains politically dangerous to discuss utopia in the Chinese context, because it can easily provoke accusations of a 'totalitarian nostalgia'. Still, no amount of symbolic violence against the critics of the transnationalized process of 'accumulation by dispossession' will deflect the popular quests for social justice in China, as it is elsewhere in the world. By recovering utopian imaginations, I mean to reemphasize a more radical critique of 'cultural imperialism', initially articulated against the backdrop of international socialist and decolonization movements, and one that is predicated upon the possibility of transcending capitalistic social relations (Schiller, 1996). This entails a scholarship that insists on the relevance of 'the ongoing struggle between the drive to realize self-social value in human labor and the drive to reduce labor to a marketable commodity' (Mosco, 1998: 16), and one that moves beyond abstract categories and depopulated processes such as 'Chinese culture' and 'China's rising' in frameworks that either essentialize cultures and reduce cultural differences to variations within global capitalism or project 'China's rising' in a zero-sum game of inter-capitalist rivalry with the United States as the current global hegemon. It also entails a focus not only on media institutions and industries, but also on historically located human subjects, their lived experiences, communication practices, social imaginaries, as well as their struggles in the context of a profound crisis in the global capitalist order in which China is playing an increasingly important part. Specifically, I subscribe to Pierre Bourdieu's (1998: 129) notion of a 'reasoned utopia', articulated in the context of the struggle against neo-liberal 'economic fatalism' in the 1990s. Now that neo-liberalism has suffered a fatal blow with the implosion of the global financial order in 2008, this entails a commitment to practical projects aiming to reconstruct a humane and sustainable post-neo-liberal global social order in a way that differs from an 'objectivist automatism' that counts on the world's objective contradictions to revolutionize the world, on the one hand, and a 'pure voluntarism based on an excess of optimism' on the other.

I propose such an ethical-political commitment not merely because the Chinese Communist Party has refused to surrender the banner of socialism, although it is true that, as the social contradictions of capitalistic developments intensify, the party has been compelled to reclaim the ideals of social justice and human-centered development. Nor it is because, as Lionel Barber (2009), editor of the *Financial Times* told Chinese Premier Wen Jiaobo in a February 2009 interview about China's role in managing the ongoing global financial crisis 'for 30 years some people have said capitalism will save China, and now maybe people are saying China must save capitalism'. Rather, and to build upon my first 'R', that is, my argument about the importance of a historical perspective, it is because of the continuing resonance of the Chinese anti-capitalist and anti-imperialist social revolution among segments of the Chinese population, and furthermore because of the ongoing appeal of communistic ideals in a Chinese society that once again bears all the evils of the 'old society', that the communist revolution sought to turn upside down.

Again, let me illustrate my point with an unexpected encounter in the empirical field. On Christmas Eve 2004 I found myself in a meeting room at Guangzhou's Guangdong Film Distribution Corp., participating in a discussion about the difference between a 'communist' and a 'party member' with the producer, director, cinematographer, and distributor of the independent documentary *Soul of the Nation* (*Guohun*), which tells the stories of China's nationalist and communist revolutionary heroes by touring their tombs and memorials throughout the country. Zhao Jun, the producer, recalled that his elementary school teacher had explained that whereas a communist was a true believer in communist ideals, a party member was somebody who had joined the Communist Party as an organization. Although I was interested in researching independent media production outside the party-state and I have read quite a lot about independent documentaries that exposed the dark sides of the party's history in the Western and Diaspora Chinese media, I did not expect to meet a group who jokingly self-identified themselves as 'Bolsheviks outside the party' in 2004, making and distributing a 'red theme', independent documentary in Guangzhou, the frontier of China's 'reform and openness' and globalized commercial popular culture.

Furthermore, the four individuals – Zhao Jun, Zhong Luming, Chen Shuisheng and Gao Ning – are neither bitter 'old leftists' nor 'angry youth'. Rather, they are very 'urban middle class' – successful media professionals in their forties and the indisputable winners of the reform era. Zhao is the manager of the Guangdong provincial film distribution bureau. Zhong is a popular DJ at a Guangzhou radio station. Chen is a director of photography at the Zhujiang Film Studio. Gao, the distributor, formerly worked as a reporter for a local party organ. None of them are party members. But they each have a strong sense of idealism, sharing a concern about social injustice and rising inequality, about the lack of democracy in China, and about what they see as the corrosive impact of a hyper-commercialized media culture on popular consciousness. Most importantly, contrary to the neo-liberal marginalizing strategy of portraying anybody who is critical of the reforms as 'wanting to return to the past', these individuals made it clear that their work was about the future. Precisely for this reason, their targeted audience is the youth. In fact, the impetus for the documentary came from Zhong's experience as a DJ in Guangzhou radio and his realization that his popular culture and celebrity-obsessed youthful audience had little sense of Chinese history – in 1999, when he asked his audience about two important dates in Chinese modern history, they phoned in to say that they were the birth dates of a pair of pop culture stars. His idea for making a documentary about China's nationalist and revolutionary struggles resonated with his friends, and so began the five-year process of making a 'red' educational documentary about nationalism and communism from outside the system. For these individuals, the 'dialectic of the Chinese revolution', which for Jiwei Ci (1994) has gone from 'utopianism to hedonism', seems to have reached its opposite: from hedonism to utopianism.

The group raised two million yuan from their own pockets, their circles of friends, and Hong Kong sources and went through all kinds of ordeals and humiliations, including having to stalk a film bureau official from the State Administration for Radio, Film and Television (SARFT) in a washroom, in their efforts to secure a production permit. Without official status, they had to rely on persuasion to secure access to some of the closely guarded memorial sites. Some of their families and colleagues did not understand them. Custodians of revolutionary memorials in affluent areas such as Shanghai and Guangzhou reminded them that even the Communist Party itself has turned away from such a subject. The crew's Guangdong origin was also frequently the source of suspicion as they travelled the country in search of China's revolutionary and heroic souls. 'Aren't you Cantonese interested only in money-making?' they were often asked. But Zhao Jun believed otherwise: 'Communist ideals aren't obsolete as long as there are injustices in society.' They not only reminded people about Guangdong's revolutionary credentials in modern China, but also explained to me that Guangdong's economic development is precisely what has made it possible for them to raise the necessary funds to pursue the project. Responding to my query about the relationship between nationalism and communism and the film's foregrounding of nationalism, Zhao Jun argued that the nationalism they celebrate is anti-imperialist, not chauvinistic. He also insisted that communist ideals have long had a Chinese grounding and are both universal and national.

The crew also found many sources of encouragement and discovered many 'resources of hope', as Raymond Williams (1989) would say, during the process. One film bureau official, moved by their determination, ended up strategizing with them about how best to approach a higher-level SARFT official. Propaganda officials and custodians of memorials in poor and old revolutionary base areas welcomed them with open arms. In Guangdong's Pearl River delta, Gao Ning recalled with great admiration how the director of a township cultural centre, who was also the township's film exhibitor, assumed the duty of looking after the bicycles of the film's student viewers, saying that, as a party member, the least he could do was to ensure that the student viewers' bikes were not stolen while they were watching the film.

When I met Gao Ning in Guangzhou, she was busy promoting the film through Guangdong's school system. However, she realized that the most relevant audience would be party officials, and a perfect window of opportunity had opened up for her to reach them. Although they had started the project in 1999, by the time it was completed in 2004, the Hu Jintao leadership had launched the ideological education campaign to 'preserve the advanced nature of communist party members'. Consequently, this group of independent cultural producers and 'autonomous communists' were hoping to use the documentary to reeducate party members about communist ideals. As Gao explained, this was a formidable task because it meant obtaining the approval of the party's propaganda department and organizational department. She said that somebody had even given her a multimillion-yuan quote about the 'cost' (i.e. the bribery needed to grease the wheels of the party machine) of getting the documentary listed as the party's recommended study material. Of course, this was antithetical to the very ideals of the film, and Gao was not optimistic about the chances of success on that Christmas Eve.

Yet shortly after I left China in January 2005, I read a news story on the internet reporting that the film had indeed become a designated study piece for the party's education campaign, and Zhang Dejiang, the Guangdong provincial party secretary, widely condemned for his media censorship acts in China's liberal media circles, had specifically instructed provincial party leaders to watch it (*Nanfang Daily*, 2005). Thus, a genuinely independent cultural production ended up feeding into the party's ideological education campaign. The communist commitment of a group of urban media professionals outside the party reportedly moved more than a thousand party members in party-state organs to tears in a collective viewing of the documentary on 6 February 2005 (Nanfang Net, 2005). Although this particular dynamic of intersection between agency and structure, official and 'unofficial', as well as the past, present and future, is perhaps not 'representative' of 'what truly happens' in China, it is hard to ignore how this story underscores the ironic twists and turns of the developmental logic of media and communication in contemporary China.

A concluding remark

Herbert Schiller (1983: 257) once wrote:

> Instability, guerrilla warfare inside and outside corporate boardrooms, and crisis overall constitute rough terrain for independent, critical researchers ... The stakes are enormous and the perils formidable. But, most important, the agenda of communications research ultimately is bound to be determined by the articulated needs of oppressed nations, classes, races, and people. In this setting, what better incentive is there than to be of use to those struggling for new and more human social forms?

In the midst of a deepening global economic recession, a protracted 'war on terrorism', and mounting environmental crises, and as the realities and discourses of 'China's rising' provoke both hopes and fears, Schiller's remarks remain more relevant than ever for independent and critical scholars of Chinese media and communication.

Notes

1 For more detailed discussions of these two cases, as well as the two cases in the next section, see Zhao (2008b), chapters 1 and 5.
2 For an insightful study of the intersection between transnational marketing and urban youth sub-culture, see Jing Wang (2008).
3 Weber and Cui (2007) have begun to address the issue of the urban/rural divide with regard to online civil engagement in a recent conference paper.

References

Associated Press (2006) Communist Party Elders Slam Media Controls, *Vancouver Sun*, 16 February, A11.

Bai, Ruoyun (2005) Media Commercialization, Entertainment and the Party-State, *Global Media Journal*, 4(6), http://lass.calumet.purdue.edu/cca/gmj/OldSiteBackup/SubmittedDocuments/spring2005/pdf_files/BaiSp05.pdf.

Barber, Lionel (2009) Transcript: Wen Jiaobo. *Financial Times*, http://www.ft.com/cms/s/0/795d2bca-f0fe-11dd-8790-0000779fd2ac.html. Accessed February 4, 2009.

Barme, Geremie (1999) *In the Red*. New York: Columbia University Press.

Bourdieu, Pierre (1998) A Reasoned Utopia and Economic Fatalism, *New Left Review*, 1–227 (January/February): 125–30.

Brady, Anne-Marie (2008) *Marketing Dictatorship: Propaganda and Thought Work in Contemporary China*. Lanham: Rowman & Littlefield.

Cartier, Carolyn, Castells, Manuel and Qiu, Jack Linchuan (2005) The Information Have-Less: Inequality, Mobility, and Translocal Networks in Chinese Cities, *Studies in Comparative International Development*, 40(2): 9–34.

Chakravartty, Paula and Zhao, Yuezhi (2008) Introduction: Toward a Transcultural Political Economy of Global Communications, in Paula Chakravartty and Yuezhi Zhao (eds) *Global Communications: Toward a Transcultural Political Economy*. Lanham, MD: Rowman and Littlefield, pp. 1–19.

Chan, Joseph Man, Pan, Zhongdang and Lee, Francis L.F. (2004) Professional Aspirations and Job Satisfaction: Chinese Journalists at a Time of Change in the Media, *Journalism and Mass Communication Quarterly*, 81(2): 254–73.

Chin, Yik-Chan (2003) The Nation-State in a Globalising Media Environment: China's Regulatory Policies on Transborder TV Drama Flow, *The Public/Javnost*, 10(4): 75–92.

Ci, Jiwei (1994) *Dialectic of the Chinese Revolution: From Utopianism to Hedonism*. Stanford, CA: Stanford University Press.

Dirlik, Arif (2005) *Marxism in the Chinese Revolution*. Lanham, MD: Rowman and Littlefield.

Economist (2006) China and the Net: The Party, the People and the Power of Cyber-Talk, 27 April.

Fraser, Nancy (1992) Rethinking the Public Sphere: A Contribution to the Critique of Actually Existing Democracy, in Craig Calhoun (ed.) *Habermas and the Public Sphere*. Cambridge, MA: MIT Press, pp.109–42.

Fung, Anthony (2006) Thinking Globally, Act Locally: China's Rendezvous with MTV, *Global Media and Communication*, 2(1): 71–88.

Golding, Peter and Murdoch, Graham (1978) Theories of Communication and Theories of Society, *Communication Research*, 5(3): 339–56.

Gries, Peter Hays (2004) *China's New Nationalism: Pride, Politics, and Diplomacy*. Berkeley: University of California Press.

Hall, Stuart (1982) The Rediscovery of 'Ideology': Return of the Repressed in Media Studies, in Michael Gurevitch, Tony Bennett, James Curran and Janet Wollacott (eds) *Culture, Society and the Media*. London: Methuen, pp. 56–90.

Harvey, David (2003) *The New Imperialism*. Oxford: Oxford University Press.

—— (2005) *A Brief History of Neoliberalism*. Oxford: Oxford University Press.

Harwit, Eric (2004) Spreading Telecommunications to Developing Areas in China: Telephones, the Internet and the Digital Divide, *China Quarterly*, 180: 1010–30.

Hong, Yu (2008) *Class Formation in High-Tech Information and Communications as An Aspect of China's Reintegration with Transnational Capitalism*, Ph.D. Dissertation, University of Illinois, Urbana-Champaign.

Hu, Andy (2006) 'Swimming against the Tide: Tracing and Locating Chinese Leftism Online', MA thesis. School of Communication, Simon Fraser University, Canada.

Huang, Philip C.C. (1995) Rural Class Struggle in the Chinese Revolution, *Modern China*, 21(1): 105–43.

Jenkins, Rob (2004) The Ideologically Embedded Market: Political Legitimation and Economic Reform in India, in Mark Bevir and Frank Trentmann (eds) *Markets in Historical Contexts: Ideas and Politics in the Modern World*. Cambridge: Cambridge University Press, pp. 305–35.

Jing, Wang (2008) *Brand New China: Advertising, Media and Commercial Culture*. Cambridge, MA: Harvard University Press.

Kahn, Joseph (2004) China's 'Haves' Stir the 'Have Nots' to Violence, *New York Times*, 31 December.

Lee, Chin-Chuan (ed.) (2000) *Power, Money, and Media: Communication Patterns and Bureaucratic Control in Cultural China*. Evanston, IL: Northwestern University Press.

—— (2003) *Chinese Media, Global Contexts*. New York: RoutledgeCurzon.

Lee, Chin-Chuan, He, Zhou and Huang, Yu (2006) Chinese Party Publicity Inc. Conglomerated: The Case of the Shenzhen Press Group, *Media, Culture and Society*, 28(4): 581–602.

Li, Peilin, Yi, Zhang, Yandong, Zhao and Dong, Liang (2005) *Shehui chongtu yu jieji yishi* (Social Conflicts and Class Consciousnesses). Beijing: Shehui kexue wenxian chubanshe.

Lin, Chun (2006) *The Transformation of Chinese Socialism*. Durham, NC: Duke University Press.

Lu, Xinyu (2005) Ruins of the Future: Class and History in Wang Bing's Tiexi District, *New Left Review*, 2–31 (January/February): 125–36.

Lynch, Daniel (1999) *After the Propaganda State*. Stanford, CA: Stanford University Press.

Madsen, Richard (1993) The Public Sphere, Civil Society, and Moral Community: A Research Agenda for Contemporary Chinese Studies, *Modern China*, 19(2): 183–98.

Mosco, Vincent (1996) *The Political Economy of Communication*. Thousand Oaks, CA: Sage.

—— (1998) Political Economy, Communication, and Labor, in Gerald Sussman and John Lent (eds) *Global Productions: Labor in the Making of the 'Information Society'*. Cresskill, NJ: Hampton Press, pp. 13–38.

Nanfang Daily (2005) Zhang Dejiang jianyi kan jilupian Guohun (Zhang Dejiang Suggested Viewing Documentary *Soul of the State*), 25 January. www.southcn.com/news/gdnews/xcrc/lxgz/gd/200501250063.htm (accessed 20 February 2005).

Nanfang Net (2005) Shengzhi jiguan 1000 duoming dangyuan hanlei kan dianying jilupian Guohun (More Than One Thousand Party Members in Provincial Organs Watched *Soul of the State* in Tears), 7 February. www.southcn.com/news/gdnews/nanyuedadi/200502070055.htm (accessed 5 December 2005).

Pan, Zhongdang and Chan, Joseph Man (2003) Shifting Journalistic Paradigms: How China's Journalists Assess 'Media Exemplars', *Communication Research*, 30(6): 649–82.

Pan, Zhongdang and Ye Lu (2003) Localizing Professionalism: Discursive Practices in China's Media Reform, in Chin-Chuan Lee (ed.) *Chinese Media, Global Contexts*. New York: RoutledgeCurzon, pp. 215–36.

Perry, Elizabeth J. and Selden, Mark (2003) Introduction: Reform and Resistance in Contemporary China, in Elizabeth Perry and Mark Selden (eds) *Chinese Society: Change, Conflict and Resistance*, 2nd edn. London: RoutledgeCurzon, pp. 1–19.

Pickowicz, Paul (1995) Velvet Prisons and the Political Economy of Chinese Filmmaking, in Deborah S. Davis, Richard Krause, Barry Naughton and Elizabeth J. Perry (eds) *Urban Spaces in Contemporary China*. Cambridge: Woodrow Wilson Center Press and Cambridge University Press, pp. 193–220.

Polanyi, Karl ([1944]1957) *The Great Transformation*. New York: Beacon Press.

Qiu, Jack Linchuan (1999) Virtual Censorship in China: Keeping the Gates between the Cyberspaces, *International Journal of Communications Law and Policy*, 4: 1–25.

—— (2006) The Changing Web of Chinese Nationalism, *Global Media and Communication*, 2(1): 149–52.

—— (2009) *Working-Class Network Society: Communication Technology and the Information Have-Less in China*. Cambridge, MA: MIT Press.

Schiller, Dan (1996) *Theorizing Communication: A History*. New York: Oxford University Press.

—— (2005) Poles of Market Growth? Open Questions about China, Information and the World Economy, *Global Media and Communication*, 1(1): 79–103.

—— (2008) China in the United States. *Communication and Critical/Cultural Studies*, 5:4, pp. 411–415.

Schiller, Herbert (1983) Critical Research in the Information Age, *Journal of Communication*, 33(3): 249–57.

Schlesinger, Philip (1999) Changing Spaces of Political Communication: The Case of the European Union, *Political Communication*, 16(3): 263–79.

Schramm, Wilbur (1964) *Mass Media and National Development*. Stanford, CA: Stanford University Press.

Shambaugh, David (2007) China's Propaganda System: Institutions, Processes and Efficacy, *China Journal*, 57: 25–58.

Sun, Wanning (2002) *Leaving China*. Lanham, MD: Rowman and Littlefield.

—— (2009) *Maid in China: Media, Morality, and the Cultural Politics of Boundaries*. London: Routledge.

Tai, Zixue (2006) *The Internet in China: Cyberspace and Civil Society*. New York: Routledge.

Tsui, Lokman (2003) The Panopticon as the Antithesis of a Space of Freedom: Control and Regulation of the Internet in China, *China Information*, 17(2): 65–82.

Weber, Ian and Xi, Cui (2007) Social Differentiation and Online Civic Engagement in Urban-Rural Communities: Tensions, Stresses, Implications. Paper presented at *Beijing Forum 2007*, Beijing, 2–4 November.

Williams, Raymond (1989) *Resources of Hope: Culture, Democracy, Socialism*. London: Verso.

Winseck, Dwayne and Pike, Robert (2007) *Communication and Empire: Media, Markets, and Globalization, 1860–1930*. Durham, NC: Duke University Press.

Xin, Xin (2006) 'Xinhua News Agency and Globalization: Negotiating between the Global, the Local, and the National, in Oliver Boyd-Barrett (ed.) *Communications Media Globalization and Empire*. Eastleigh: John Libbey, pp. 111–28.

Yang, Guobin (2003) The Co-evolution of the Internet and Civil Society in China, *Asian Survey*, 43(1): 405–22.

—— (2007) How Do Chinese Civic Associations Respond to the Internet: Findings from a Survey, *China Quarterly*, 189: 122–43.

Yu, Haiqing (2006) Chinese Media Spectacles in the New Millennium: Counternarratives of Chinese Modernity, Ph.D. dissertation, University of Melbourne, Australia.

Zhang, Tianwei (2004) Cong lingyige jiaodu kan jingji renwu pingxuan zhong Lang Xianping luoxuan (Another Perspective on the Failure to Select Lang Xianping as an Economics Figure), *Jiangnan shibao*, *news.sina.com.cn/o/2004-12-s.shtml* (accessed 25 May 2005).

Zhao, Yuezhi (1998) *Media, Market, and Democracy in China: Between the Party Line and the Bottom Line*. Urbana: University of Illinois Press.

—— (2000a) From Commercialization to Conglomeration: The Transformation of the Chinese Press within the Orbit of the Party State, *Journal of Communication*, 50(2): 3–26.

—— (2000b) Watchdogs on Party Leashes? Contexts and Limitations of Investigative Journalism in Post-Deng China, *Journalism Studies*, 1(2): 577–97.

—— (2001) Media and Elusive Democracy in China, *The Public/Javnost*, 8(2): 21–44.

—— (2003a) Transnational Capital, the Chinese State, and China's Communication Industries in a Fractured Society, *The Public/Javnost*, 10(4): 53–73.

—— (2003b) Falun Gong, Identity, and the Struggle over Meaning Inside and Outside China, in Nick Couldry and James Curran (eds) *Contesting Media Power: Alternative Media in a Networked World*. Lanham, MD: Rowman and Littlefield, pp. 209–23.

—— (2004) The Media Matrix: China's Integration into Global Capitalism, in *Socialist Register 2005: The Empire Reloaded*. London: Merlin Press, pp. 197–217.

—— (2005) Who Wants Democracy and Does It Deliver Food? The Evolving Politics of Media Globalization and Democratization in China, in Robert Hackett and Yuezhi Zhao (eds) *Democratizing Global Media: One World, Many Struggles*. Lanham, MD: Rowman and Littlefield, pp. 45–67.

—— (2007a) After Mobile Phones, What? Re-embedding the Social in China's 'Digital Revolution', *International Journal of Communication*, 1: 92–120, http://ijoc.org/ojs/index.php/ijoc/article/view/5/20.

—— (2007b) Marketizing the 'Information Revolution' in China, in Graham Murdoch and Janet Wasko (eds) *Media in the Age of Marketization*. Cresskill, NJ: Hampton Press, pp. 189–217.

—— (2008a) Neoliberal Strategies, Socialist Legacies: Communication and State Transformation in China, in Paula Chakravartty and Yuezhi Zhao (eds) *Global Communications: Toward a Transcultural Political Economy*. Lanham, MD: Rowman and Littlefield, pp. 23–50.

—— (2008b) *Communication in China: Political Economy, Power, and Conflict*. Lanham, MD: Rowman and Littlefield.

Zhao, Yuezhi and Duffy, Robert (2007) Short-Circuited? The Communication and Labor in China, in Catherine McKercher and Vincent Mosco (eds) *Knowledge Workers in the Information Society*. New York: Lexington Books, pp. 229–47.

Zhao, Yuezhi and Hackett, Robert (2005) Media Globalization, Media Democratization: Challenges, Paradoxes, Issues, in Robert Hackett and Yuezhi Zhao (eds) *Democratizing Global Media: One World, Many Struggles*. Lanham, MD: Rowman and Littlefield, pp. 1–28.

Zhao, Yuezhi and Schiller, Dan (2001) Dances with Wolves? China's Integration with Digital Capitalism, *Info*, 3(2): 137–51.

Zhou, Yongming (2006) *Historicizing Online Politics: Telegraphy, the Internet, and Political Participation in China*. Stanford, CA: Stanford University Press.

Chapter 12

Media and cultural studies in the Arab world

Making bridges to local discourses of modernity

Tarik Sabry

> We often borrow from the western cultural repertoire its results and fruits, ignoring its principles and *ussus* (bases). We import from it to consume only and not to plant and create, and the latter requires a fertile ground, which cannot in turn be imported.
>
> (Jabri, 1989: 35)

> Nowadays, it is verging on intellectual blasphemy to talk of 'Arab modernity'. But the fact remains that denying the success of this experiment, even if we must consider it now predominantly to be over, implies a contempt for Arab cultural and real – that's to say lived – history.
>
> (Kassir, 2006: 44)

The events of 9/11 have had major effects on global and local politics; triggering two wars, regime toppling and an all-illusive and as yet undefined and timeless war now known to everyone as the 'global war on terror'. Some have even dared to define our world and age through two prefixes: pre-9/11 and post-9/11. In my field of interest, Arab media, culture and society, the effects have not gone unnoticed: 9/11 has certainly rekindled the West's interest in the Arab and everything Arab: media, culture, society, politics, etc. If fields of enquiry are indeed, as we learn from Scannell (2007), the product of *endogenous* and *exogenous* events, then 9/11 (as an external historical event) has certainly played a part in the morphing of Arab media, culture and society from an area of negligible interest to a hot topic. Evidence of this is visible in the plethora of academic publications, courses, seminars and conference panels dedicated to the study of the subject. The outcome is a rather rich and varied scholarship covering a range of areas, including, but not limited to, the political economy of Arab media, media and democratization, Arab satellite broadcasting and Arab popular culture. Notwithstanding the importance of this work, a lot of which is, incidentally, concentrated in British and US academe, little attention has been given to either the epistemological problematics that usually come with the development of new fields of enquiry or the dreaded burden of representation from which Orientalists have yet to recover.

A key question that has yet to be rehearsed is: how does the implosion of the recent literature on Arab media, culture and society relate to or, even better, inform Arab contemporary thought and vice versa? To use Taha Abdurrahman's terminology (2006), I contend that the creative process marking the compendium of research into Arab media, culture and society (to which both Arab and Western scholars have been contributing) has largely been one of *ebda' mafssul* ('disconnected creativity') rather than *ebda' mawassul* ('connective creativity').[1] In other words, the debates on the subject of Arab media, culture and society have largely been uncritically contextualized within readily available, and often borrowed, conceptual frames of analysis that are detached from argumentations and debates inherent to Arab thought and its problems. And even where the creative process has begun to show aspects of connectivity to the Arab-Islamic cultural repertoire, discourses of *ta'sseel* (authentication) seem to have, unfortunately, overtaken as the main intellectual objective, leaving little space for self-reflection and critique. This chapter is an attempt to rehearse different ways and means of bridging this gap. Here, I situate my argumentation on Arab media studies/cultural studies[2] within the intellectual process of 'de-Westernization', described by Curran and Park as the 'growing reaction against the self-absorption and parochialism of much Western media theory' (2000: 3). I contend that the de-Westernization of media and communication theory in the Arab/Islamic context is better understood when reconnected with contemporary Arab philosophical discourses of modernity. Using examples from work by mostly Maghrebi thinkers and philosophers, this chapter demonstrates how the 'de-Westernization debate' in Arab scholarship originates in problematics inherent to contemporary Arab thought, especially in the duality problematic of *assala* (originality/authenticity) and *mu'assara* (contemporaneity). It also critiques 'de-Westernization' as discourse and argues for a 'dialogic' approach (between Arab and Western scholars) that operates within a double-critique structure, where 'de-Westernization' processes can too become objects of critique and subversion.

'De-Westernization' as discourse

The media theory 'de-Westernization' debate can easily be traced back to the late 1980s, a decade after the inception of British media studies and cultural studies. Terms commonly used to describe the debate included intellectual concerns such as 'appropriation', 'translation', 'localization', 'authentication', and so on (see Ang and Morley, 1989; Stratton and Ang, 1996; Sparks, 2000; Morley and Chen, 1996; Curran and Park, 2000; Abbas and Erni, 2005). Since this chapter concentrates primarily on the Arab case, it is important to note that the development of Mass Communication theory in the US in the 1930s and 1940s had also triggered heated discussion on 'de-Westernization' in Arab academe, mainly in Egypt where the first mass communication department was established as early as 1939. Glass traces this debate to the

1950s at the University of Cairo. In his article 'The Global Flow of Information: A Critical Appraisal from the Perspective of Arab Islamic Information Sciences', Glass (2001: 220–2) stratifies Arab media and communication scholars into five different intellectual traditions:

Group 1: (1950s–96) Their work was concerned with public opinion and the social functions of communication and was largely influenced by American communication models.
Group 2: Also established in the 1950s, this group worked hard to institutionalize the teaching of media practice.
Group 3: Established in the 1960s and was mainly concerned with classical Islamic theories of communication.
Group 4: Established in the 1970s and called for the re-Islamization of Arab information.
Group 5: Described as the product of the 1980s, advocated an 'Arab conceptualisation of information'.

The 'de-Westernization' debate is also part of a much older and broader intellectual tradition that questioned the universality of the values and grand narratives of the Enlightenment. This critical tradition, reaching as far back as Nietzsche, has resulted in a whole body of work, since embraced by subsequent generations of scholars to unpick and critique frames of knowledge and thought that assumed the universality, and thus the superiority, of the Enlightenment and its ideas. Abdullah Laroui's *Histoire du Maghreb* (1970) and Edward Said's *Orientalism* (1978) are two good examples of such critical work.

'De-Westernization' in the field of media/cultural studies is rapidly becoming an intellectual project in its own right. It is also emerging as a 'discourse' with layers of meanings that require ceaseless troubling and subverting. Discourses of 'de-Westernization' have been driven by both endogenous and exogenous elements. The former are manifest in articulations and debates emerging from within the discourse in relation to problematics of translation, appropriation and localization (as intellectual processes). The latter are concerned with a number of external elements, inextricably linked, that resulted from changes in the world (globalization being a key factor), the demands of the education market and the changing nature of student intake. I choose to call this 'growing reaction' of 'internationalization' and 'de-Westernization' a discourse, and not merely a framework or debate, because of its heterogeneous nature – the discourse of de-Westernization is multilayered – and also because attempts at de-Westernization are driven by a multiplicity of processes, including the intellectual, the pedagogic, the demagogic and the economic.

Economic development, especially in China, South Korea and Japan, has encouraged the middle classes of these countries to invest large sums of money so that their offspring can continue their higher education in the US or the UK. For some British universities offering undergraduate and graduate courses in the fields of media/cultural studies, the intake of international students has increased exponentially, so much so that in certain MA courses the number of international students outnumbers that of British students. It has now occurred to academics teaching media and cultural studies in Britain that the changing nature of the student intake dictates a fundamental change in (a) the content of their taught courses (which had hitherto focused mainly on British and American media) and (b) how such content is delivered pedagogically. A number of media and communication departments in British universities, for example, have, as a consequence, sought globalizing/internationalizing as a survival strategy for both intellectual and economic reasons. The dictum now is: internationalize or perish. How much of this, however, is driven by intellectual concern (which we see in the development of international media centres and changes in teaching content), the logic of the market, or both, is unclear.

Why study Arab media?

Access to media technology in the Arab world has grown exponentially over the last decade. Arab satellite channels have mushroomed, private radio stations are on the increase and the private press market is growing daily. Also more and more Arabs have access to the internet, including hundreds of blogs dealing with a myriad of themes ranging from popular jokes, pornography and religion to local politics. The recent move towards media deregulation by a number of Arab governments is likely to extend the number of private media players and therefore the number of media outlets. Although the Arab media's implosion never amounted to any real political change, and although media deregulation, as we know from other cases, tends largely to favour rich and big media players, it is fair to say that Arab audiences have never had so much choice (be it in entertainment or news), and at no other time did we witness such a scramble for Arab audiences' minds and disposable incomes. The outcome is a confluence of competing institutions (including advertisers) and discourses: 'local' and transnational, imperialist and anti-imperialist, liberal and extremist, populist and elitist, pan-Arabist and anti-pan-Arabist, all jostling for the attention of Arab audiences. This substantial change in the Arab media map, brought about by modernity and its institutions, has not, however, been equalled in academic research.

Arab academe, which should be most concerned with this development, has been very slow in accepting the study of media as a scientific subject of enquiry (Talal, 1999)[3] and when it did, it occupied a large epistemic void with uncritical facile empiricism imported, just like the media technology, from 'uncritical regions' of Western academe and taught or, shall I say, force-fed en masse to Arab students. What's more, Arab universities, with few exceptions, are heavily policed and remain part of the state apparatus par excellence. The hierarchy of the Arab university is answerable to the authoritarian state and plays a major role in maintaining the status quo. Critical rationality is discouraged. This 'lack of autonomy has resulted in a situation where universities are run according to the requirements of the governing political logic, and not a plan or wise educational policy' (AHDR, 2003: 56). The question, however, as I argue elsewhere, is not only one of subject; it is also one of methodology (Williams, 1961). What should we teach in Arab media and cultural studies, and how do we teach it? The success and credibility of a field such as that of Arab media and cultural studies, I argue, will depend not only on its ability to articulate and assess the dynamics of power as they emerge from the cultural text (both written and visual), and how the latter is communicated and received, but also on its articulation and examining of the economic and political structures that govern and influence cultural production in the Arab world (Sabry, 2007).

Towards de-Westernization as double-critique

In their book *De-Westernizing Media Studies*, rather than tracking 'particular aspects of media globalization' through descriptive methods followed in 'American textbooks', Curran and Park, who are more interested 'in extending communication theory', opted for a more 'interpretive orientation' and so decided to organize their edited collection around comparative perspectives of different 'national media systems' (Curran and Park, 2000: 12). To achieve this, they set their contributors a 'global' exam paper made up of four key questions, which I quote below in full (ibid.):

1 How do the media relate to the power structure of society?
2 What influences the media, and where does control over the media lie?
3 How has the media influenced society?
4 What effect has media globalization and new media had on the media system?

There is no doubt that the answers to this set of 'imposed' questions made for a huge improvement over the conventional or the rather descriptive American-textbook style, criticized by Curran and Park. In this case, it is fair to say that the book not only provides a comprehensive account of different media systems from different cultural contexts, but is also an important contribution to the growing discourse of 'de-Westernization'. In setting the agenda, however, the editors unwittingly reproduced the very kind of 'self-absorption and parochialism' from which they intended to steer away, for, in dictating the parameters of discussion, no matter how good the intentions were, the editors have limited what could be said about the media in different cultural contexts to a set of questions which they (as scholars from the centre) thought were relevant and important. Framing the questions within presupposed hermeneutical categories such as the 'social' and 'power structure' (again regardless of their importance) is a way to police the debate. What is more, the editors also assume that the hermeneutical and methodological tools necessary for the articulation of such important questions are there at hand and already available, for all contributors. The discourse of de-Westernization, I am afraid, has to dig deeper than this. If the media constitute the 'modern' phenomenon par excellence and if their study has largely been a way of coming to terms with 'modernity's pathologies' (Scannell, 2007), then, surely, their study has to be informed by and be answerable to the philosophical discourses of modernity in different local cultural contexts. In this way, the study of media is relocated within and is joined to a cultural repertoire that it can enrich and from which it can learn. The study of the media in the West does not stand alone; it is interdisciplinary and part of a linear philosophical argument and critical tradition that can be traced from Hegel to Habermas. The relocating and reconnecting task is fundamental. It is the basis upon which our thinking about media and communication should be built.

'De-Westernization' of media and communication theory are better understood in terms of a discourse because the claims to 'authenticity' that often accompany such an intellectual process are themselves encrusted in discourses that require unpacking and subverting. In this case, the discourse of 'de-Westernization' would be far more effective were it to function through a 'double-critique' structure,[4] to use Abdelkabir Khatibi's terminology (Khatibi, 1980), one which is mechanized through a dual intellectual exercise that is able to oscillate between de-Westernization and de-de-Westernization, authentication and de-authentication. However, the discourse of de-Westernization, as it stands, is still in its infancy, at a stage where more intellectual effort is channelled towards authentication than to the questioning and subverting of the claims that come with such a process. This causes disequilibrium in the structure of the 'de-Westernization' discourse, making it less critical.

De-Westernization or 'dialogism'

Is it possible to have an Arab media and cultural studies without an Arab critical theory? In other words, is it enough to rely on Western critical theory as a knowledge frame for the articulation of a whole field of enquiry into media, culture and society in the modern Arab world? The point of asking such a question is not an attempt at authentication. Rather, the question I pose is more concerned with highlighting the necessity for thinking about a localized form of critical theory that is conscious of its time, its cultural and historical specificities and the philosophical problematics it poses. Looking at the philosophical discourse of modernity in the West from Hegel to Habermas, one is struck by the linearity of argumentation on modernity, especially the problematic of time-consciousness and self-reassurance. The question of time-consciousness was paramount to the articulation of European modernity as a concept and modern time-consciousness was constantly revitalized by

Western thinkers including Hegel, Nietzsche, Adorno, Benjamin, Heidegger, Baudelaire and others (see Habermas, 1987). In the Arab case, and with the vantage point of hindsight, the intellectual task of coming to terms with modernity's 'self-reassurance' and 'time-consciousness' must not be left solely to philosophical analysis. This exercise has to be complemented by a culturalist approach, which, in my view, is (without meaning to belittle the role of philosophy) more equipped to deal with the nowness, or the present tense, of everyday Arab cultures in all their 'ordinary' and artistic manifestations.

In his book *Contemporary Arab Thought*, Abu-Rabi' accentuates the importance of Western critical theory and the social sciences in making sense of modernity in the Arab-Muslim region, arguing that since 'the Muslim and Arab worlds have for the last two centuries been shaped by two main forces: colonialism and global capitalism … a theorization of social life in the Arab-Islamic worlds cannot take place outside Western critical theory and its critique of capitalism' (Abu-Rabi', 2004: 3). Abu-Rabi' also advances the notion that 'neither the intellectual nor social nor economic history of the modern Arab world can be understood in isolation from the totality of world processes in the economic, political, and intellectual fields' (ibid.: 3). Whilst I share Abu-Rabi's view that the Arab situation, and indeed any other situation, can no longer be examined through the prism of the local alone, I think relying solely on Western critical theory to make sense of what it is to be modern in the Arab world today is somewhat problematic. Is it possible to speak of, or imagine, a quintessentially 'Arab' critical theory, when most Arab philosophers and thinkers who have led the debate on modernity have done so through their encounters with the West and Western frames of thought? The cultural and historical affinities shared between the West and the Arab world (especially vis-à-vis cultural exchange) can be traced back to Andalusia, and to Arab philosophers' incorporation of Greek aesthetics and modes of reasoning. It is also important to add here that even in the Arab *Nahda* (Renaissance) of the late nineteenth and early twentieth centuries, Arab culture reconstructed itself on the basis of the discovery of European culture. 'Far more than Japan,' argued Kassir, 'where modernization concentrated on reproducing the technological, military and financial mechanics of the West's supremacy, the Arab world, nowadays described as inherently closed, embraced all the intellectual debates that came from Europe' (Kassir, 2006: 49). Today most Arab philosophers and thinkers are not unaware of the Western episteme; in fact the majority have incorporated it in their work as a methodological tool. The Arab world's historical and cultural affinities with the West make it naïve, if not misleading, for us to engage in a facile discourse of authenticity. This is why I tend to favour a 'dialogical' approach (to use Bakhtin's term) that goes beyond the one-way, monologic frames of thought, and where one is able to acknowledge and, most importantly, learn from the other's modalities and ways of interpreting the world. 'De-Westernization', as a term, is also inherently negative, since it is based on the elimination and exclusion of the other and does nothing but reproduce suzerain orientalist oppositional discourses of 'us' and 'them'.

To situate this 'dialogical' approach within the double-critique structure, articulated earlier, as a prerequisite for a critical discourse of de-Westernization/internationalization, it is imperative that Arab/Western 'dialogism' too becomes a constant object of critique and reflection. Since the development of academic fields is partly shaped, as we learn from Scannell (2007), by intellectual formations that are in turn affected by certain historical 'moments', then how is this going to affect the structural and methodological development of a field such as Arab media and cultural studies, to which both Western and Arab scholars have been contributing not only from different geographies but also from different historical moments? How will the confusion caused by arbitrariness between the cultural temporality and the historical 'moment' within which knowledge is produced about Arab media, culture and society affect the development of Arab cultural studies and media studies (Sabry, 2007)? The 'dialogical approach' may present us with a better alternative to one-way asymmetrical discourses of de-Westernization, but this must not put it above critique or reflection. The 'dialogic' must also be constantly subverted and troubled.

In the Arab context, what we need to ask is: in what ways will the field of media and cultural studies help answer, or at least deal with, questions inherent to the contemporary philosophical discourse of modernity, as conceived by Arab thought? This question has so far been downplayed, if not ignored, for two main reasons. On the one hand, the philosophical discourse of modernity, as conceived and thought by contemporary Arab philosophers and thinkers, has yet to consider the media and their role in society as the subject of serious academic enquiry. On the other hand, the media theory de-Westernization discourse, as it appears thus far in Arab-Islamic scholarship, has yet to recognize the epistemological significance in reconnecting the discourse of de-Westernization with the Arab or local philosophical discourses of modernity. In previous work (Sabry, 2007) I began to deal with these two interrelated 'unthinkables', to use Arkoun's (2006) term, by attempting to reconnect the influential treatise of the Arab philosopher Mohammed Jabri, namely his *Critique of Arab Reason*, to the question of Arab media, culture and society. I showed how Arab media and cultural studies may provide an answer to the deficits Jabri has identified in Arab modes of reasoning, especially those dealing with confusion in Arab cultural temporality. What follows is a continuation of the same task, but here I hope to broaden the debate to include other argumentations from within the Arab philosophical discourse of modernity (to which Jabri has been a prominent contributor), and to demonstrate how these, as they enter a dialogical relationship with Western critical theory, may not only form the body of critical work necessary for localizing media and communication theory in an Arab context, but also help to unveil the epistemological problematics from which the Arab/Islamic discourses of 'de-Westernization' originate.

The struggle for authenticity

How can we then, with the help of this 'dialogical' approach to knowledge, make the field of media/cultural studies relevant to the Arab world, assuming, of course, that there are shared historical and cultural commonalities that make it possible for us to speak of one Arab world? To engage with this question, it is vital to examine key debates and problematics in contemporary Arab thought. If most of what has been written in the last three decades within this repertoire has, in the main, been either directly or indirectly about 'modernity', its meanings, challenges and pathologies,[5] then it is only logical, since the media are the modern institution par excellence, to investigate the role they play in the process of modernization.

Debate on modernity in contemporary Arab thought is multi-faceted and occupies different cultural temporalities. It is framed and discussed within different stages of Modernity's development (as a philosophical concept) and, as such, is at once Hegelian, Heideggerian, neo-Marxist and Foucauldian, modernist and postmodernist. The 'West', because of its dual nature as 'model' and 'enemy', is presented in contemporary Arab thought not merely as a civilizational alternative, but also as a kind of *assl* (originality), belonging to the future rather than the past. From this a different kind of struggle for authenticity within the Arab renaissance has resulted, one that continues today in the contemporary Arab discourse of modernity (and also, as I will show later, in the discourse of media theory de-Westernization itself).

The Arab philosophical discourse of modernity is polarized by a struggle for *ussul* (origins) and models. The outcome is a binary structure within the Arab discourse of modernity, with one group adhering to the *ussuleyat* (originations) inherent to the Arab-Islamic heritage, and the other to *ussuleyat* inherent to Western modernity (Jabri, 1989: 21). This *duality* has also been reinforced by debate on heritage and contemporaneity.[6] The perpetual oscillation between heritage (*mawruth thaqafi*) and contemporaneity (*mu'assara*) is a key aspect of the Arab philosophical discourse of modernity and is largely what motivates discourses of Arab-Islamic authenticity. Jabri traces the struggle for authenticity to the Arab *Nahda* (Renaissance) of the late nineteenth and early twentieth centuries:

> Duality of the exogenous (the West) into a threat as well as a civilisational model (the enemy and the model at the same time) has led to the dualization of the modern Arab Renaissance's position towards the past and the future. This also resulted in an overlap in the Renaissance mechanism between return to the *roots* and departure from them to the future … This

> made the Renaissance of Arab thought problematic. It is also what we have been used to calling the *assala* and *mua'ssara* problematic.
>
> (Jabri, 1989: 20; author's translation from Arabic)

The struggle for Arab authenticity in contemporary Arab thought continues and is characterized by at least three key positions:

1. the historicist position: progress and development in the Arab and Islamic worlds can only be maintained if and when a decisive break with the past and its heritage takes place;
2. the *turatheya*[7] position: Arab-Islamic heritage is a key component of Arab culture and makes for the best, if not the only, possible and most coherent civilizational model;
3. the rationalist position: cultural heritage is important, but rather than breaking with it – aesthetically, ethically, epistemologically – we need to modernize it from within using modern (Western) methodology so that it is reconciled with our present cultural temporality.

These positions are not static, of course, since they all overlap. The historicist position, which can be encapsulated by Abdullah Laroui's cultural project, especially his call for a decisive break with the past (Laroui, 2001), must not be confused with an outright rejection of *ussul* or cultural heritage. For Laroui, these remain very important objects of enquiry. What he rejects, however, are their value systems.[8] Also, the rationalist position (mainly Jaberism) does not make the historicist or *turatheya* positions less rational. In other words, these positions are not anti-rationalist. It is the insistence of the *Turatheya School* on finding solutions for the present using lessons from the past, and its critical stance towards modalities of Western rationality, that position it within the discourse of *turatheya*. Argumentations on the Arab-Islamic cultural heritage (by which the Koran, the *Sunnah*, and all that which we could classify under Lalande's *raison constituée*, from *fiqh*, language and aesthetics to political reason and the sciences, are often meant) and how the latter is dealt with[9] make up a very important part of Arab modernity's philosophical discourse. These ongoing argumentations, however, are not specific to the Arab world or to the Arab philosophical discourse of modernity, as they also formed part of a debate in the West, engaging philosophers from Hegel to the Frankfurt School. Dealing with the issue of heritage (religion) in the Western philosophical discourse of modernity can be traced to Hegel, who was against both religious orthodoxy and the religion of reason (Habermas, 1987: 25). Hegel observed in *The Difference* that:

> The further the culture advances and the more manifold becomes the development of the expressions of life within which the diremption can entwine itself, the greater becomes the power of diremption … and the

> more meaningless and alien to the whole of culture become the strivings of life (once sublimated in religion) to again give birth to itself in harmony.
>
> (Hegel in Habermas, 1987: 20)

To give another example, Baudelaire's answer to harmonization between modernity's 'fleeting transient' and the 'immovable' sacred is to 'extract from fashion the poetry that resides in its historical envelope, to distil the eternal from the transitory' (Baudelaire in Habermas, 1987: 10).[10]

To go back to the Arab case, and the focus of this chapter, it is odd how the *turatheya* schools and their authenticators accept contemporaneity – a product of modernity – when it comes to technology, the economy and other spheres of life, but not when it comes to other spheres such as the intellectual. As Jabri put it succinctly:

> The problem that faces us does not lie in choosing which civilisational model to opt for: modernity, or *assala*, or reconciling the two, but the problem, in truth, lies in the duality of our position towards this duality. We accept this duality at the level of modernisation and the need to modernise economy, and other contemporary sectors, political, social, and educational. We also spend a lot of money on the traditional sectors, safeguarding them in the name of heritage and *assala*: one group adheres to modernity as a civilisational model, the other to *assala* alone. A third party tries to reconcile the two, but only by trying to make this duality more bearable and less heavy. However, we at the same time refuse this duality on other levels: spiritual and intellectual life.
>
> (Jabri, 1989: 13; author's translation from Arabic)

Aziz al-Azmeh tackles the duality problematic further by pointing out that debates on authenticity (*assla*) and contemporaneity (*mu'assara*) take it for granted that authenticity is monolithic, when it is, in fact, a discourse with different and competing voices (al-Azmeh, 1992: 18–21). Al-Azmeh provides a nuanced critique of authenticity in contemporary Arab thought by calling into question not only claims to authenticity, but also the nature and structure of the claimed authenticity. Here, authenticity is unpicked as a discourse that cannot be tied to one meaning or paradigm, but to a multiplicity of complex and, at times, conflicting voices. Al-Azmeh thus objectifies *assla* as discourse and calls for its deconstruction and subversion. *Assala* (originality) in its twentieth-century pan-Arab and Islamic sense, al-Azmeh observes, finds its origin not in the Arab-Islamic tradition, but in the Western repertoire, particularly in its meanings of *dialectics* (al-Azmeh, 1992: 24). So, what often presents and defines itself as *assil* (original and authentic) camouflages the very identity of the *assala* it advances. The opposite of contemporaneity, argues Abu al-Majd, is not *assala* but *Salafiya* (see Salafism)[11] and *turatheya* (Abu al-Majd in al-

Azmeh, 1992: 26). Al-Azmeh also demonstrates how authentication as Islamization often takes place within a discourse that largely serves the telos of the authenticator rather than Islam. In this case, it is not Islam that determines the particularity of a certain institution or history. Rather it is the history and institution that determine Islam and its culture (al-Azmeh, 1992: 28). Gholam Khiabany's critique (2006) of Hamid Mowlana's 'Islamization' of communication theory provides a good insight into how discourses of authentication can serve ideological ends. However, to frame all attempts at authentication as *Salafist*, or purely ideological, would be misleading. Taha Abdurrahman (2002), the Arab philosopher who advocated the Arab right to philosophical difference, provides a more nuanced discourse of authenticity which privileges the spirit of modernity over that of Western modernity. According to Abdurrahman, the spirit of modernity has three main aspects that can be summarized in three principles: *Rushd* (which he bases on independence or liberation and creativity), *critique* (based on the transition from belief without evidence to critique based on evidence) and *Shumul* (moving from the particular to the general).

The reality of modernity, argues Abdurrahman, is not the same as its spirit, even if this reality results from the practice of this spirit. Rather, the reality of modernity is specific to a choice from different possibilities or modalities of the spirit of modernity (Abdurrahman, 2006). Reason, he argues, is not static; it is fluid and constantly changing. There is not just one kind of rationality, advances Abdurrahman, but different rationalities.[12] In line with Khatibi's concept of double-critique (1980), Abdurrahman also critiques the limitations of Western rationality in privileging physical, worldly, objective phenomena over ethics or values. His call for the 'ethicization' of modernity is a double-edged critique, directed at both the Western rationalist project and voices from within the Arab philosophical discourse of modernity (known as the rationalists) that propagate Western discourses of modernity, without much care for critiquing its limitations. What Abdurrahman calls for is not merely a rational society, but a rational-ethical society. For him, there is no ethics without religion and no religion without ethics.

Reconciling thought and reality: for modernity as a consciousness and a lived experience

What the Arab discourse of modernity is not about, as yet, however, is humans and lived experience. We simply cannot make sense of modernity in the Arab world today without making sense of what it means to be modern, and if living in a mass mediated world is part of modern experience, then a philosophical discourse that ignores this is surely lacking in contemporaneity, a key component of modernity. The cultural time-consciousness of Arab modernity cannot be reassured of its time and consciousness solely through Cartesian doubt or through its historicist/rationalist schools, and if we are to make use of the Arab discourse of modernity as a bridge to understanding contemporary Arab media, culture and society, we will then have to begin by removing it from its discourse, making it an object for critique before it can become a tool of critique. As the Arab discourse of modernity is heavily influenced by Western thought and methodology (especially the rationalist and historicist positions), it has unwittingly inherited a much debated problematic in modern Western epistemology, which can be traced to Descartes. As Scannell observed:

> Descartes exemplifies the problem of modern epistemology whose default position is scepticism. What can I be certain of? The only thing I know for sure, when I come to think of it, is that I exist. I exist in my head. I can't be sure that anything exists outside my own self-consciousness. Kant said that the scandal of philosophy was that it could not furnish conclusive proof, starting from subjective self-consciousness, of an external world. And Heidegger's response in *Being and Time* is that the real scandal is that academics go on trying to come up with a proof, over and over again. His own starting point is with the facticity (the actual matter-of-factness) of the actually existing living world and not the contents of his own mind, which is where an awful lot of modern philosophers and others start.
>
> (Scannell, 2007)

The Arab philosophical discourse of modernity has yet to ontologize or humanize its take on modernity, that is, to deal with modernity as real and lived experience rather than merely a conceptual thought that takes place in consciousness. In an article entitled 'How Should We Write the History of the Middle East?', Hourani (1991) argues that popular discourse in the modern Arab world unveils more about the realities of the Arab world than it does about intellectual discourse. Bridging the gap between thought and reality in Arab discourses of modernity will make for a braver and more realistic understanding of what it means to be modern in the Arab world, and this, as I argue elsewhere (Sabry, 2007), is not the task of philosophy alone, but also one for Arab sociology, media studies and cultural studies.

Manifestations of the duality problematic in recent discourses of media theory de-Westernization

The old/new dual debate on *assala* and *mu'assara* is not unrelated to ongoing attempts, by some Arab-Muslim scholars, at de-Westernizing media and communication theory. In fact, this discourse of authentication is nothing but a reflection of the duality problematic described earlier. It is essential that the Arab discourses of the 'de-Westernization' and 'internationalization' of media theory are understood and articulated within the *assala* and contemporaneity problematic, and the broader discourse of Arab modernity. No serious discussion on Arab media, culture and society can ignore such debate, for I see the de-Westernization discourse as an extension of this debate. Two relatively recent pieces of work – one by Mohammad Ayish entitled 'Beyond Western-Oriented Communication Theories: A Normative Arab Islamic Perspective' (2003), the other, by Basyouni Hamada, entitled 'Islamic Cultural Theory' (2001) – are attempts at de-Westernization which also reflect the duality in Arab thought articulated by Jabri.

On the one hand, Ayish provides us with an interesting and insightful analysis that theorizes Arab-Muslim communications and their audiences, while tracing and making use of characteristics inherent to Arab heritage that date back to the *jahiliya* (the period predating Islam). Hamada, on the other hand, adduces what he considers to be a coherent set of Islamic cultural principles, which he recommends as a normative framework for governance of the media in a 'just' and democratic Islamic society. Hamada's point of reference is Islam, and particularly the Koran, a text that satisfies (and in fact preaches) all the prerequisite elements recommended by the author to guarantee a democratic Islamic 'public sphere'. Both authors' attempts to de-Westernize media and communication theory – and, in Hamada's case, to formulate an Islamic *Shura*-based public sphere – are useful (see Sabry, 2007: 157–8). Notwithstanding the importance and relevance of Ayish's and Hamada's attempts at authentication, a process of de-authentication and de-de-Westernization is necessary, were we to stay faithful to Khatibi's proposed double-critique structure. Although the hermeneutics upon which we rely to interpret media, culture and society in the Arab world ought to be broadened to include a category that precedes both the 'social' and the 'cultural', namely the existential, the latter category should be articulated in ways that do not put it above debate or critique. The category 'Islamic culture', as it appears in Ayish's and Hamada's work, is a taken-for-granted category. It is articulated as a thinkable, and part of a closed, process when, if anything, conceptualizations of 'Islamic culture theory' are only possible if and when we are prepared to objectify 'Islamic culture', making it open to an ongoing process of rearticulation and reinterpretation. A reworking of the idea of Arab and Islamic culture is fundamental and should precede all attempts at theorizing media, culture and society in the Arab and Islamic worlds. However, the rearticulation of Arab cultures within the category of the 'existential' must not necessarily lead to the latter's Islamization, as this would limit analysis of culture to the realm of the sacred, alienating its ontological structure. Religion must be allowed to shape culture, to be part of its fabric, but culture, any culture, must not be defined or determined solely through religiosity.

The task ahead

The post-colonialized subject lives in different cultural temporalities simultaneously. He has no choice in the matter. He lives in his time, the time of his colonizer, and also in a 'third space', constantly in flux, perpetually in a struggle to be born. It is only through working out what this third space is, and how it operates (not metaphorically but empirically), that the 'new man', about whom Albert Memmi so famously talked, can emerge. This third space, with all its ambiguities, is nothing other than a consequence of, and a reaction to, modernity's disorders. Working out what this third space is, is about coming to terms with what it means to be modern in the world. Transnational media have amplified the problematic of overlap in Arab cultural temporality, as the confusion now is not only between the old and new within the Arab cultural repertoire, but also between a multiplicity of travelling cultural temporalities. Understanding this three-dimensional overlap in Arab cultural temporality is a prerequisite for making sense not only of the structure of feeling of the contemporary Arab, but also of Arab popular cultures and their audiences.

Reworking the idea of Arab-Islamic cultures requires us to record their present expressive powers in their sacredness and imperfections, and let us also add in their 'dialectical deformations' (Berque, 1983: 24). The 'quest for an original approach' to Arab modernity, argued Berque, cannot be abstracted or removed from 'the contemporary culture the Arabs are already constructing for themselves' (Berque, 1983: 69). An anthropological/ontological articulation of culture as lived experience is vital to this quest. This, as I see it, is a role for a hermeneutically flexible and open Arab cultural/media studies and its future advocates. The task that lies ahead, however, is greater than 'de-Westernization' or internationalization: it is one of creativity. It is, to use Lalande's distinction again, to be able to think of and rehearse different ways of activating '*la raison constituante*' (the mental activity that creates knowledge, constructs meanings and decides on rules and principles) in the Arab cultural repertoire. This intellectual task is only possible through troubling and substituting outmoded modalities of Arab thought inherent to its *raison constituée* (that part of reason that is already constituted) with new modalities that are answerable to the present tense of Arab cultures and not their past. This process has already begun. Fatema Mernissi's troubling of male/female dynamics in Arab-Islamic societies, Abdullah al-Ghadhami's revolt against Arab poetic aesthetics and call for a transition from literary criticism to cultural criticism (2000), and let us also add Moustapha Safouane's championing of the vernacular as a liberating force from the dictatorship of classical Arabic and 'those it serves' (Safouane, 2007), are all intellectual projects that operate exactly where cultural activity and creativity are required. Their work is a step in the right direction.

Notes

1 Author's translation from Arabic.

2 This chapter serves as a continuation of the discussion I started in a recently published work, namely 'In Search of the Present Arab Cultural Tense' (2007), where I articulated the necessity for an epistemic space through which the study of Arab cultures (media and other new forms of artistic expression included) could become central objects of scientific enquiry, arguing that a field of Arab media/cultural studies

would be far more useful were it informed by, and reconnected with, sociological and philosophical problematics raised by contemporary Arab thought. I also made the case for a supple hermeneutics that would allow for less deterministic interpretations and theorizations of Arab media and cultures, and stressed the importance of reworking or broadening the idea of Arab 'cultures' in such a way that our reference points are informed not merely by the sacred and the timeless, but also by the grittiness and ordinariness of culture as it unfolds in its everyday ontological time-based-world-structure.

3 Interview with Dr Mohamed Talal, from the Superior Institute of Journalism, Rabat, May 1999.

4 Khatibi's double-critique is influenced by Derrida's concept of double-take.

5 To give but one example, all the concepts that the Arab philosopher Abdullah Laroui articulates in his books: Mafhum al-ideolujeya (*The Meaning of Ideology*) (1980), Mafhum al-Hurreya (*The Meaning of Freedom*) (1981), Mafhum Addawlat (*The Meaning of the State*) (1981), Mafhoum attarikh (*The Meaning of History*) (1992) and Mafhoum al-Aql (*The Meaning of Reason*) (1996, 2001) were, in many ways, dealing with modernity. As Laroui put it in *Mafhoum al-Aql* (*The Meaning of Reason*): 'All I have written so far can be considered as parts in one volume, on the meaning of modernity' (2001: 14). Laroui's call for an epistemological break with the past (the content of the old Arab-Islamic cultural heritage) and what he termed *hassm* (decisive break with the past) has been one of his key and decisive contributions to the Arab philosophical discourse of Modernity. Other key Maghrebi philosophers/thinkers whose intellectual projects have been dedicated to writings on Arab-Islamic modernity include Mohamed Abed Jabri, Mohammed Sabila, Taha Abdurrahman, Abdelkabir Khatibi and Mohamed Arkoun.

6 For a comprehensive guide to key debates dealing with the *assala* and *mu'assara* problematic in Arab thought, see a book (in Arabic) entitled *Aturath wa tahadeyat al-a'ssr fi al-Watan al-Arabi: al-Assala wa al-mua'ssara*, Beirut: Centre for Arab Union Studies (1985). The book, based on a conference organized by the same Centre, is 872 pages long and offers very useful interventions on the problematic of *assala* and *mu'assara* by key philosophers and thinkers from different parts of the Arab world.

7 The term *turatheya* comes from *turath*, meaning heritage. In this sense *turatheya* refers to schools of thought that privilege *turath* as a civilizational model and reference point.

8 See Mohamed Sheikh (2007: 53).

9 To give two examples: Taha Abdurrahman divides cultural heritage '*turath*' and its past into two elements: the past events and the past of values. Abdelkarim al-Khatibi uses a more nuanced interpretation, making a distinction between *originalié* (authenticity) and *originarité* (source). Khatibi favours dealing with heritage as a source rather than as that which is authentic, as sources are continually in flux (Khatibi).

10 See Baudelaire's 'the painter of modern life' in *Selected Writings on Art and Artists* (1972).

11 Salafism is 'an Islamic movement associated with Wahhabism that in its radical form emphasizes strict interpretation of religious texts and opposition to non-Islamic influences' (see *Encarta Dictionary*).

12 Abdurrahman, *The Question of Ethics*, 179, in Sheikh (2007: 143).

References

Abbas, Ackbar and Erni, John Nguyet (2005) General Introduction, in A. Abbas and J.N. Erni (eds) *Internationalizing Cultural Studies: An Anthology*. Oxford: Blackwell.

Abdurrahman, Taha (2002) *al haqu al-Arabi fi al-ikhtilaf al-falsafi*. Casablanca: Arab Cultural Centre.

—— (2006) *Ruh al-Hadatha: al-Madkhal ela ta'ssis al-hadatha al-Islamiya*. Casablanca: Arab Cultural Centre.

Abu-Rabi', I. (2004) *Contemporary Arab Thought: Studies in Post-1967 Arab Intellectual History*. London: Pluto Press.

AHDR (2003) *Building a Knowledge Society*. Arab Human Development Report, United Nations Development Programme.

Al-Azmeh, Aziz (1992) *al-Assala aw siyassat al-hurub mina al-waki'*. London: Dar al-Saki.

Al-Ghadhami, Abdullah (2000) *Qiraa' fi Annaqd Athakaafi*. Casablanca: Arab Cultural Centre.

Ang, Ien and Morley, David (1989) Mayonnaise Culture and Other European Follies, *Cultural Studies*, 3(2): 135.

Arkoun, Mohammed (2006) *Islam: To Reform or to Subvert*. London: Saqi Books.

Ayish, Mohammad (2003) Beyond Western-Oriented Communication Theories: A Normative Arab-Islamic Perspective, *Javnost/The Public*,10(2): 79–92.

Berque, Jacques (1983) *Arab Rebirth: Pain and Ecstasy*. London: Saqi Books.

Centre for Arab Union Studies (1985) *Aturath wa tahadeyat al-a'ssr fi al-Watan al-Arabi: al-Assala wa al-mua'ssara*. Beirut: Centre for Arab Union Studies.

Curran, James and Park, Myung-Jin (eds) (2000) *De-Westernizing Media Studies*. London: Routledge.

Glass, Dagmar (2001) The Global Flow of Information: A Critical Appraisal from the Perspective of Arab Islamic Information Sciences, in Kai Hafez (ed.) *Mass Media, Politics and Society in the Middle East*. Cresskill, NJ: Hampton Press, pp. 217–40.

Habermas, Jürgen (1987) *The Philosophical Discourse of Modernity*. Cambridge, MA: MIT Press.

Hamada, Basyouni (2001) Islamic Cultural Theory, Arab Media Performance, and Public Opinion, in Slavko Splichal (ed.) *Public Opinion and Democracy: Vox Populi-Vox Dei*. Cresskill, NJ: Hampton Press, pp. 215–39.

Hourani, Albert (1991) How Should We Write the History of the Middle East?, *International Journal of Middle East Studies*, 23(2): 133.

Jabri, Mohammed (1989) *Ishkaleyat al-Fikr al-Arabi al-Mua'ssir*. Casablanca: Banshra.

—— (2000) *Naqd al-aql al-Arabi*. Casablanca: Arab Cultural Centre.

Kassir, Samir (2006) *Being Arab*. London: Verso.

Khatibi, Abelkabir (1980) *Annakd al-Mujdawaj*. Beirut: Dar al-Awdah.

Khiabany, Gholam (2006) Religion and Media in Iran: The Imperative of the Market and the Straitjacket of Islamism, *Westminster Papers in Communication and Culture*, 3(2): 3–21.

Lalande, André (1948) *La Raison et les Normes*,. Paris.

Laroui, Abdullah (1970) *L'histoire du Maghreb*. Paris: Maspero.

—— (1980) *Mafhoum al-Hurreya*. Casablanca: Arab Cultural Centre.

—— (1981) *Mafhoum Adawlat*. Casablanca: Arab Cultural Centre.

—— (1992) *Mafhoum Attarikh*. Casablanca: Arab Cultural Centre.

—— (2001) *Mafhoum al-Aql*. Casablanca: Arab Cultural Centre.

Morley, David and Chen, K. (eds) (1996) *Stuart Hall: Critical Dialogues in Cultural Studies*. London: Routledge.

Sabry, Tarik (2007) In Search of the Present Arab Cultural Tense, in N. Sakr (ed.) *Arab Media and Political Renewal: Community, Legitimacy and Public Life*. London: IB Tauris, pp. 154–68.

Safouane, Moustapha (2007) *Why Are the Arabs Not Free?* Oxford: Blackwell.

Said, Edward (1978) *Orientalism*. London: Routledge.

Scannell, Paddy (2007) *Media and Communication*. London: Sage.

Sheikh, Mohammed (2007) *Al-Maghaareba wa al-Hadatha*. Rabat: Ramsis.

Sparks, Colin (2000) Media Theory after the Fall of European Communism: Why the Old Models from East and West Won't Do Anymore, in James Curran and Myung-Jin Park (eds) *De-Westernizing Media Studies*. London: Routledge, pp: 35–50.
Stratton, Jon and Ang, Ien (1996) On the Impossibility of a Global Cultural Studies: 'British' Cultural Studies in an International Frame, in D. Morley and K. Chen (eds) *Stuart Hall: Critical Dialogues in Cultural Studies*. London: Routledge, p. 362.
Williams, Raymond (1961) *The Long Revolution*. London: Penguin.

Chapter 13

De-Sovietizing Russian media studies

Elena Vartanova

Understanding changes in Russian media would be incomplete without reflection on changes in the theoretical frameworks in which contemporary Russian media studies exists. And vice versa, without identifying the dominant or at least the most widespread theoretical concepts, analysis of the Russian media would be incomplete. This chapter attempts to identify the main stages of change in Russian media studies, to describe the principles of media/journalism studies in the Soviet Union, their transformation in post-Soviet Russia and the impact on present research, to assess the role played by foreign concepts on media research in Russia, and to summarize the main trends of change in Russian academic thinking.

Re-framing media studies in Eastern Europe

Re-framing media studies in Russia and, more broadly, in all the post-socialist countries of Eastern Europe has been a very complex and dramatic process for many reasons. The core problems here are not only the complexity and multidimensionality of the two concepts of 'Eastern Europe' and 'post-socialism', but also the different relationships between Marxist-Leninist ideology, national media and journalism practice and theoretical approaches.

Media studies in socialist countries has traditionally been considered a discipline based on Marxist-Leninist theory, although neither Marx nor Lenin elaborated any holistic media theory. However, they did produce many articles and statements that set out the basic principles of Soviet normative media/journalism theory. This perhaps partly explains why there are noticeable differences in the treatment of media concepts in different socialist countries. Despite common ideological and theoretical foundations, the variety and diversity of national versions of 'Soviet' media theory were quite substantial. Not only language, but economic, demographic, ethnic, cultural and even religious-based differences influenced approaches to media/journalism theory, which varied between different national contexts although they shared an understanding of the propaganda function. By the 1970s sociological audience research in Russia, Poland and Hungary was carried out outside mainstream

'Soviet' journalism theory and showed different attitudes to media. From the 1960s to the 1980s, approaches to TV, cinema and popular music were clearly influenced by different national traditions in cultural studies, defined by diverse aesthetic and ethical values (see, for instance, Sappak, 1963).

With the series of 'revolutions' in Eastern Europe in the late 1980s and the disintegration of the USSR in 1991, the fall of the old Marxist-Leninist ideology became inevitable; this was especially true of media theory. Theories imported from Western discourses became the most influential factor in changing the media landscape of Eastern European media studies up to the mid-1990s. Clear and often oversimplified concepts such as the 'fourth estate' or 'watchdog' concept and such US-centric academic books as *Four Theories of the Press* became popular. There was also a move to de-nationalize media theory, which was more of a denial of 'Soviet' theory than a negation of national traditions. The second stage, in the late 1990s, resulted in a national contextualization of imported concepts and methodologies and was characterized by the growing importance of applied research inspired by the growth of media and advertising markets and policy research, especially in the EU candidate member states. In many countries media systems were studied through the prism of the political economy tradition, due to the introduction of market relations. At the millennium, new concepts such as public sphere, information/network society, globalization theory, media economics, media psychology, cultural studies, anthropology, etc., entered media discourse. There was a noticeable increase in the number of publications in national languages, which nevertheless demonstrated the strong influence of imported ideas.

From the early 2000s, national schools in media studies began to combine 'Western' influences with more local reflections and empirical data, not only in terms of language but also in terms of concepts and research methods. Perhaps we are entering a phase of creating a new form of national media studies by integrating global and local/national, new and old, with a special focus on media criticism. The real ground for this is the institutionalization and maturation of the national media systems, which is bringing about this transition.

The slow transformation of theoretical paradigms might be explained in several ways. Certainly, theories change slower than reality, and this is one of the most obvious explanations. A less obvious, but still important, reason is the survival of 'old players' in Russian media studies and academic publishing. Media studies is carried out in various Russian regions. In most cases it is based at faculties/departments/chairs of journalism at universities, and the majority of these were established before 1991. Although in many places departments of mass communications, mass media and sociology, with a particular focus on media, have emerged, their role is rather limited. This is partly because universities still control the publishing of textbooks, research monographs and journals. Today the market has essentially changed the priorities, and textbooks have become the preferred and most profitable type of academic content. Consequently, the opportunity for new research centres to publish research monographs is limited. Private publishers, though active, are even more profit oriented and, in terms of publishing research, are very selective and restrictive. Another key problem for media studies, as well as for media in general, is the continuing media subordination/servility to politics and/or the market, resulting in a continuous flow of applied and commissioned research that clearly lacks any critical thinking.

Soviet media theory: theoretical foundations

Soviet media theory is based on numerous writings and statements by Marx, Engels and Lenin describing the role of the press in political and social life. They often emphasized the partisan nature of journalism, and its role was to debate actual issues of political life, supporting and defending positions of the party to which it was affiliated. Thus, the essentials of Soviet media theory arise from:

- the proletarian partisanship described by Lenin in 'Party Organization and Party Literature' in 1913 (Lenin, 1979);
- press subordination to the tasks defined by the ruling party, in this case the Communist one;
- the ideological and instructive role of the media, which should educate the audience by actively forming its tastes and wishes (article 'On Svoboda Magazine' of 1901 in Lenin, 1979);
- a Party newspaper as a cornerstone, a backbone infrastructure of the Communist Party (article 'Where to Begin' of 1901 in Lenin, 1979): 'a party as an organization disseminating the ideas advocated by a newspaper';
- media having not only 'propagandist' and 'agitator' functions, but also that of organizer: 'But the whole point is that *there is no other way* of *training* strong political organizations except through the medium of an all-Russia newspaper' (article 'What Is to Be Done' of 1902 in Lenin, 1979).

Soviet journalism theory originated in an intellectually challenging context. Before the Bolshevik Revolution of 1917, Russian journalism as a profession and area of research had not yet matured, which was also true of many other countries. In their efforts to construct a new social reality, the leaders of Soviet Russia faced the emergence and growth of new media technologies, such as radio and cinema, that opened up possibilities for a manipulative, but also educational, role for journalism. The complete integration of the press (and later radio and TV) into the system of political and cultural management of Soviet Russia provided a unique chance to test new concepts of journalism, its functions and effects in a society that was consciously constructed to support the Communist Party in its struggle for power.

Soviet media theory defined journalism as 'a social activity of collection, transmission and periodical dissemination of information through mass communication channels aimed at propaganda and agitation' (Ovsepyan, 1979). Accordingly, the principles of Soviet journalism declared by Soviet scholars included partisanship ('*partijinost*'), proletarian internationalism, socialistic patriotism, humanism, and people belonging ('*narodnost*'). Although the two latter principles attempted to introduce the importance of universal values, Soviet media theory emphasized that journalism in a socialist society had to prioritize the interests of only one dominant class, the proletariat; therefore the principle of people's belonging might be applied only to friendly social forces. Among the tasks of journalism, the key one was that of upbringing and education, although in a spirit of ideological correctness. Journalism as a social activity was also considered as one of the ways to accomplish Socialist democracy. For this purpose a vast group of voluntary correspondents (*rabsel'kor*) was maintained across the country to provide feedback from audiences to media outlets, as were letters to editors. However weak, this type of relationship signified the importance of both audiences' response and media effects analysis to those in power.

Empirical studies therefore were centred around descriptive and qualitative methods of research, and the use of sociological methods was at first fairly limited. However, the sociology of journalism began to mature in the 1960s with the research of media uses in big industrial cities (Taganrog). For the first time in the history of the Soviet media, audiences and their interests, needs and wishes came into the focus of research. From then on the discipline of mass media sociology acquired strong methodological tools and managed to occupy a distinctive niche in the field of Soviet media research. Another valuable component of Soviet journalism theory was represented by the concepts of socialist journalism ethics, which was deeply rooted in the normative ethics of a socialist citizen.

Summarizing the basic concepts of Soviet media/journalism theory, we need to emphasize that it had a clear normative character. Media professionals had to be Communist Party affiliated, people-oriented (in terms of interest in their social needs), ethical, truthful and educating. Normative professional values important to the work of journalists were:

- priority of correctness over topicality and timeliness; therefore news and reporting were much slower than in 'Western' commercial media, partly because facts had to be double-checked – in terms of ideological correctness as well as accuracy;
- feature and polemic genres involving personal judgements and opinions were of higher professional importance for journalists, and therefore the issue of creativity in journalism was of high priority;
- 'publicistics' (political or moral essays with moral and ideological reasoning) as the core and top-professionalism of journalists' linking journalism to politics and ideology;
- a social obligation for a journalist to be an active citizen.

The last theoretical point had an apparently normative character, but this also made Soviet media theory practice-oriented. Soviet journalists had to comply with several 'musts' and in many respects these 'musts' were mostly of an ideological and political, and less of a professional, nature. The last requirement together with loyalty to the Communist Party, ideological accuracy and a missionary vision of professional duties made Soviet journalism theory extremely normative and binding.

It would be unfair to say that there were no conceptual alternatives to Soviet media theory. Opposed media concepts came from the dissident movement that saw the media as free and unrestrained by the Communist Party propaganda voice of intellectuals (intelligentsia). Since on politically sensitive issues the dissident media could not provide any alternatives to ideological censorship, they focused on cultural issues, thus supporting alternative cultures in various artistic forms (rock music, *chansons*, elitist cinema). A theoretical point here was the importance of political metaphor, which stimulated the work of imagination and created specific skills to read 'between the lines'. Close to the strong tradition of cultural studies in film and cinema research, this approach valued media as a channel for aesthetic genres for a minority audience, compared to the official news, analysis and comments that had a purely ideological character. In a certain sense, the popularity of the dissident media among intellectuals created a bridge to glasnost and the investigative journalism campaign with regard to unearthing Soviet history.

In conclusion, it should be pointed out that there are distinct differences between Soviet theory as presented by Siebert *et al.* (1956) and the concepts used in Soviet media studies. In the context of the USSR, the theory had at least recognized the role of audiences.

'Winds of change': new concepts

Breaking with the past and with the old theory has inspired Russian scholars to look for entirely different approaches and to make use of the most popular, often populist, 'Western' media concepts, however simplistic and irrelevant they might be. Western concepts of media became the first and, until now, the most influential factor in changing the landscape of Russian media research. *Four Theories of the Press*, translated into Russian in 1998, became the founding text for media/journalism theory, with such concepts as the 'fourth estate' and the 'watchdog of democracy' shaping public debate. Russian scholars appeared to analyse Russian media by simply transferring Western concepts into the Russian context (Androunas, 1993). It took several years before Russian media studies managed to interpret the changes in Russian media by considering intellectual tools from the 'Western' theories to interpret media changes in their own way.

In the post-Soviet era, journalists too used popular Western concepts in their debates on the nature and roles of evolving Russian media to emphasize the processes of liberation and openness in the press and TV and to highlight the increasing influence of media on political processes and audiences. By the mid-1990s minor attempts were being made to conceptualize the changes, while the bulk of analysis was produced by such media critics as Alexey Pankin and Irina Petrovskaya. Increasingly, media researchers were contextualizing Western theories to suit Russian media realities, including research in new fields such as advertising, public relations and media consumption. Other fields of academic enquiry included political communication, media sociology and media psychology.

The process of de-Sovietizing Russian media studies was a complicated and uneasy one, requiring the re-conceptualization and modernization of key definitions and new theories in order to incorporate global and national, innovative and inherited approaches.

Russian media theories after 1985

Glasnost and libertarian theory

Changes in the Soviet media began after Mikhail Gorbachev, the new leader of the Communist Party, started to promote a new politics of acceleration (of economic development), perestroika (reconstruction) and glasnost (openness). This also signified the first attempts to revolutionize Soviet media theory because both in the Soviet Union and in the West the concept of glasnost was considered as a challenge to previous theories (Nordenstreng *et al.*, 2002). This was certainly true, and in the mid-1980s to early 1990s the level of openness and social criticism as compared to Soviet journalism was extremely high. This gave some Western scholars grounds to say that Soviet theory was obsolete and remained only of historical interest. Media scholars consider that from the mid-1980s, and after the fall of the Soviet Union, Russia adopted a mass media model closer to the social responsibility principle (Mickiewicz, 1988; McNair, 1989, 1991). This was certainly true in relation to libertarian/social responsibility concepts.

Although in the 1990s critical attitudes to the *Four Theories of the Press* became common in Western media studies (Nerone, 1995), in new Russian circumstances the book became very popular because it addressed the most up-to-date issues in Russian political life, i.e. the freedom of speech concept, based on ideals of the 'free' market, was the complete opposite of Soviet theory that viewed the media as purely instruments of politics and ideology. After the abolishment of censorship by the Law on Mass Media (1991), there emerged a clear need to replace outdated practices of surveillance and control with more liberal concepts of the freedom of the press.

Not surprisingly, the first attempts to conceptualize glasnost as an independent media strategy used by Gorbachev and the leadership of the Communist Party were made by foreign scholars. Reimo Paasilinna (1995) argued that glasnost was the process of systematic, continuous and complete informing of people on all spheres of life both in the USSR and abroad, except for state or other legally protected information or anything violating generally accepted social, moral and ethical norms. Nevertheless, he underlined that it was an instrument for the leadership in carrying through political reforms. In his view, the concept of glasnost was not an independent one, but rather the upgraded policies of the Communist Party and the socialist state to promote and support other initiatives started by Gorbachev. This slightly differed from the approach of Brian McNair, who described it as 'a political culture of debate and difference, rather than uniformity and regimentation' (1993: 57), but was close to a point made by Karol Jakubowich (1990), who considered the concept instrumental in relation to the existing political structures.

Russian scholars have enthusiastically used the concept of glasnost to prove the changes and transformation in Russian media. Yassen Zassoursky argued that glasnost was an effort to adapt the administrative-bureaucratic model of the Soviet media to Western ideals of a free and open society, stressing that it was a policy of liberation of the media 'from the top down' (Zassoursky,1997). Ivan Zassoursky has pointed to the restricted character of glasnost as an autonomous concept in terms of its relations to 'freedom of speech theory' by saying that the partly liberated press was Gorbachev's only ally in his struggle with conservative forces in the Communist Party (Zassoursky, 2001, 2004).

Concluding, we might say that glasnost, although resulting in revolutionary changes in the Russian media, did not represent a structured and well-elaborated theory, but rather was a variation of late Soviet media policy with a clear instrumental character. This may also explain why current media studies use this concept very sparingly.

Public sphere

For Russian media studies, the concept of the 'public sphere' developed by Jürgen Habermas has become extremely important for two reasons. First, it put forward the separation and even the opposition of the 'state' and the 'public', which was considered to be comprised of individuals – 'private' people. In relation to Russian media, this was a completely revolutionary point, since, in terms of both control over content, news flows and ownership structures, media were always in the domain of the state. In fact, throughout its history, even in imperial Russia, media were always closely associated with the state. The public-sphere concept also proposed the idea of 'private' individuals, who might or might not be organized in parties or in other types of communities. Second, it introduced the idea of public debate, negotiations between state/power structures and media/public with a definite emphasis on the responsibilities of all who take part in the debate (Habermas, 1989).

The concept of the public sphere in the context of Russian media involved the conceptualizing of public debate truly mediated by mass media. The media are viewed as a factor in creating the conditions for dialogue between the state and citizens, for better feedback from the electorate, and for multidimensional societal mass communication (Prokhorov, 2001; Resnyanskaya, 2001, 2003). However, attempts by the state to formalize conditions for 'information security' and to dominate the creation of national media policy led to Russian scholars calling for the introduction of the concept of 'information order', in which various interests presented in the mass communication landscape could be taken equally into consideration. In Prokhorov's view, 'dialogical collaboration of diverse media aiming at formation of monoplural core of the public on the basis of ideological consolidation and mobilization is the major constructive force of the public sphere' (Prokhorov, 2001). Recently, research has expanded the concept of the public sphere by introducing the notion of 'public interest' as a basic/core component of journalism, viewing mass media as an essential part of the public sphere (Svitich, 2000; Korkonosenko, 2004; Lozovsky, 2006).

However, the preconditions for the emerging public sphere, as viewed by Russian media scholars, include not only the activities of the mass media themselves, but also a certain level of political culture in a society that should ensure and stimulate participation in debate in the public sphere. Therefore, some clarification of the roles played in the public arena by actors in the political communication process is needed, thus diminishing the influence of established structures of power and increasing the authority of individuals and civil society. The 'fourth power' should not be at the service of the state (Zassoursky, 1997).

Open society

The concept proposed by Karl Popper (1945) of an open and market-driven society as an antithesis to the socialist command economy and closed society was key to the process of defining the nature, functions and social role of modern Russian media as both an agent and a subject of transformation. Popper's powerful defence of democratic liberalism as a social and political philosophy and his devastating critique of the principal philosophical presuppositions underpinning all forms of totalitarianism were welcomed by Russian scholars. This happened mostly because Russian society was turning away from strong censorship and ideological surveillance in media (characteristics of a closed society) to a more free, pluralist and market-oriented media model, seen as an important element of an open society.

The importance of the 'open society' concept in relation to media studies research has been proved by an extremely productive cooperation between Russian and Dutch media scholars. A particular interest has been given to such issues as open access to information and mass media, media accountability to the public prior to media accountability to the state, new levels of freedom and responsibility of media in the age of global communications, media diversity, the social roles of participatory media, and the interrelations of mass media, state and private business (Zassoursky and Vartanova, 1998). The growth of the internet and new media posed theoretical challenges to researchers with a special focus on new media, concepts of public service vs. universal service, and tolerance in mass media (Zassoursky and Vartanova, 1999).

Theorizing on media and the open society has extensively used the concept of glasnost as a starting point. A direct link from the abolishing of censorship (to which glasnost had led) to the emergence of an open society in Russia can be seen in much of the research. However, the joint Russian–Dutch research ended in the early 2000s just before some trends towards 'closing' society and subsequent changes in media became evident.

The concept of an open society has fitted well into the general context of the liberalization of journalism as a profession and the liberation of journalists from previous ideological pressures coming from power elites. Early dreams of 'unrestricted' press freedom and a 'borderless' open society were chased away, however, by evolving ownership systems controlled by 'oligarchs', by the process of media commercialization, and by a return to a certain political manipulation by the political elite. In this case, the political economy model of media became useful, producing one of the most interesting areas of Russian media studies. Another crucial aspect of the 'open society' concept, issues of media responsibility or accountability, were not widely debated among scholars.

The political economy of Russian media

The increased power of a few oligarchs in the Russian media has been the focus of much research both in Russia and abroad (McNair, 1991, 1994, 2000; Mickiewicz, 1997; Zassoursky, 2004). Foreign studies often grouped together several countries of Eastern Europe, attempting to generalize the effects produced by the introduction of market relations into media operations on journalism and audiences, although this was not easy to do. Specific forms of privatization in Russia and, as a particular case of this process, the growth of media empires as part of the Russian system of political management in the1990s caused a lot of attention to be given to the political economy of the media. Foreign scholars analysed the development of post-socialist media systems in the frame of global political and economic contexts that had impacts on emerging media models (Pietiläinen, 2002). The process of the *Balkanization* of media models in the post-socialist area has been described in terms of heavy state control, a high degree of mass media partisanship, and the integration of TV and illegal business, through advertising (Splichal, 1994; Sparks with Reading, 1998).

With their own perspective on this, Russian researchers actively explored how political influences gained by media companies were transformed into economic profits. This Russian approach concentrated on the emergence of media-political capital as an institution of corruption, arguing that media were not only a business but a source of political influence and integration into dominant political elites, without any consensus among media professionals or acceptance of common professional ethics (Becker, 2004; Zassoursky, 2004). Only recently have some research centres started to look at issues of media economics, management and marketing, countering the critics of political economy by moving into practical research (Gourevish, 2004; Tulupov, 2000; Vartanova, 2004a).

Applied research

The new 'partnership' of journalism and sociology has emerged as a response to the introduction of market relations into the everyday practice of Russian media. With the rise of advertising as the main source of revenue for media companies, the sociological tradition has been actively revived. Russian media studies has been deepened due to the extensive use of sociological research instruments, used both to conceptualize the change in media habits and behaviour and to predict new trends in the transformation process (see, for instance, Resnyanskaya and Fomicheva, 1999). Deepening the sociological tradition in media studies, scholars came to newsrooms to interview journalists and managers not only to study the field but also to provide practitioners with relevant and reliable data (Koltsova, 2001; Juskevits, 2002). Media sociology became increasingly practical and therefore required by media professionals, although it has introduced and adapted to Russian circumstances a number of theoretical concepts (Fomicheva, 2005)

Another research area which has produced considerable practical effects for media professionals is research in media law. The usefulness and importance of conceptual work in the area became obvious when journalists and other media professionals began to feel a need for legal and juridical knowledge and also for practical assistance for media law experts (Richter, 2002).

Information/network society

The role of technology in the development of mass media has traditionally attracted a lot of attention from Western media scholars. However, Soviet media theory left this issue almost untouched. With the rise of the internet and new media, Russian scholars have opened up a completely new area of research that was almost non-existent in Soviet media theory. Based on Castells' assumption that the emergence of an informational society is supported by network structures which grow from capitalism, and its support for technology and social flexibility, the Russian approach explores the idea of a network structure dominating social relations and communications practices, thus substituting or at least challenging the tradition of a vertical hierarchy in Russian political and communicative practices (Vartanova, 2004b). This research area also involves thinking about the future of media systems in both Russia and worldwide (Vartanova and Zassoursky, 2004).

Globonationalization

The most important attempt to analyse Russian media through the prism of the globalization concept was made by Terhi Rantanen (2002). She has shown that Russian media are subordinate to the major trends of development which shaped the dynamics of media systems in many countries worldwide. One of the crucial points concerning globalization and media in general and Russia in particular was the idea that the process of globalization always combines global with national, general with particular, supranational with local.

Therefore, it is argued, globonationalization has taken place in Russian media through the adaptation of Western formats (programme genres, the structure of TV programming, growing homogenization of entertainment content) and by absorbing global elements and transforming them into national content. Although Rantanen's book was published before the industrial logic of the Russian media industry became clearly visible, the variety of adaptation strategies – in the market activities of media companies, in formatting and distributing content, in broadcast programming – demonstrates these globalization tendencies.

A useful matrix of analysis was proposed by de Smaele (1999), who put the development of Russian media not only in the context of Western European media culture, but also in the context of Asian media and traditions. This has posed an exciting research question: how to identify the relevant elements for the description of national media systems and to correlate media with socio-economic and cultural traditions and national models as well. Continuing this line, Russian researchers aimed at the identification of trends of global development, especially in analysing the economy of the Russian commercial media system, which falls under general market laws: decreasing interest of young people in print media, regionalization of the press markets, tabloidization, and the growing importance of national TV as a part of the leisure industry (Nordenstreng, Vartanova and Zassoursky, 2002). On the other hand, the peculiarities of the Russian journalism culture and media-politics relations place the Russian media model closer to the Eurasian context, illustrating a paternalistic pattern of relationships (political elite often playing the role of a decision-making father vs. journalists as obedient children) inherited from the early days of Russian journalism in Imperial Russia (Vartanova, 2007).

Conclusions

Concluding the overview of the transformation in Russian media studies, we need to question how in the past decade the research agenda in Russian media studies has been framed, by whom and with what results. This is especially important in the present circumstances of modern Russia, when the evolving Russian media business criticizes journalism education and media research for their inability to respond to the needs of the market, while the Russian public complains that the media are failing to fulfil their public-service obligations. A number of surveys in 2005–6 showed a desire for 'moral' censorship, thus reflecting the audience distrust of the media and journalism. This actually demonstrates that the negation of normative approaches to the cultural and educational roles of journalism/media and the lack of media ethics have created serious tensions in the relations between Russian media, journalists and the public.

There is a growing need to encourage the development of more structured media theory. Although the general socio-economic framework has radically changed, media theory has not yet formulated new roles for media professionals, and therefore many issues have remained unclear. While the practical character of Russian media research has become evident, we still need to comprehend the changes in media with more critical and analytical tools.

To distinguish the 'Soviet' component in contemporary media studies in Russia is still a complex task. There are of course numerous features of previous concepts and values that until now have shaped academic discourse and produced a number of normative and politically engaged studies. In many cases this seems to happen rather unconsciously. On the other hand, the influence of foreign theories and concepts has not deprived Russian media study of its clear national character. Although the use of foreign, mostly Western European and American, academic literature has become almost a norm, Russian authors do not accept Western concepts uncritically. The integration of foreign theories is not only an issue of adaptation; it is rather a process of creating synergetic concepts by combining the global and the national. The only problem which is still not completely solved is the negation, even disregard, of the recent history of research. Its assessment is still needed.

References

Androunas, E. (1993) *Soviet Media in Transition: Structural and Economic Alternatives*. Westport, CT: Praeger.

Becker, J. (2004) Lessons from Russia: A Neo-authoritarian Media System, *European Journal of Communication*, 19(2): 139–63.

de Smaele, H. (1999) The Applicability of Western Media Models on the Russian Media System, *European Journal of Communication*, 14(2):173–89.

Fomicheva, I. (2005) *Vvedenije v mediametriju* (Introduction to Media Metrics). Moscow: Aspekt Press.

Gourevish, S. (2004) *Ekonomika otechestvennikh SMI* (Economics of Russian Mass Media). Moscow: Aspekt Press.

Habermas, J. (1989) *The Structural Transformation of the Public Sphere*. Cambridge: Polity.

Jakubowich, K. (1990) Between Communism and Post-Communism: How Many Varieties of Glasnost, in Slavko Splichal, John Hochheimer and Karol Jakubowicz (eds) *Democratization and the Media: An East West Dialogue*, Ljubljana: Faculty of Sociology, Political Science and Journalism, pp. 40–55.

Juskevits, S. (2002) *Professional Roles of Russian Journalists at the End of the 1990s: A Case Study of St. Petersburg Media*. Tampere: Tampere University Press.

Koltsova, O. (2001) News Production in Contemporary Russia: Practices of Power, *European Journal of Communication*, 16(3): 315–35.

Korkonosenko, S. (2004) *Prepodavaya zhurnalistiku* (Teaching Journalism). St Petersburg.

Lenin, V. (1979) *Lenin o pechati* (Lenin about the Press). Moscow: Progress.

Lozovsky, B. (2006) *Zhurnalistika kak spectificheskaya forma representazii deistvitelnosti* (Journalism as a Specific Form of Reality Representation). Izvestiya Uralskogo Gosudarstvennogo Universitets. ?No. 40: 27–37.

McNair, B. (1989) Glasnost, Restructuring and the Soviet Media, *Media, Culture and Society*, 11(3): 327–50.

—— (1991) *Glasnost, Perestroika and the Soviet Media*. London: Routledge.

—— (1993) Reform and Restructuring in the Soviet Media: Before and after the August 1991 Coup, in J. Eldridge (ed.) *Getting the Message*. London: Routledge, pp. 53–72.

—— (1994) Media in Post-Soviet Russia: An Overview, *European Journal of Communication*, 9(2): 115–35.

—— (2000) Power, Profit, Corruption, and Lies: The Russian Media in the 1990s, in James Curran and Myung-Jin Park (eds) *De-Westernizing Media Studies*. London: Routledge, pp. 79–94.

Mickiewicz, E. (1988) *Split Signals: Television and Politics in the Soviet Union*. New York: Oxford University Press.

—— (1997) *Changing Channels: Television and the Struggle for Power in Russia*. New York: Oxford University Press.

Nerone, J. (ed.) (1995) *Last Rights: Revisiting Four Theories of the Press*. Urbana: University of Illinois Press.

Nordenstreng, K., Vartanova, E. and Zassoursky, Y. (eds) (2002) *Russian Media Challenge*. Helsinki: Kikimora, second edition.

Ovsepyan, R. (1979) *Sovetskaya zhournalistika i kommunisticheskoye vospitaniye trudyashihsya*. (Soviet Journalism and Communist Upbringing of Workers). Moscow: Izd-vo Mosc. Un-ta.

Paasilinna, R. (1995) *Glasnost and Soviet Television*. Helsinki: Yleisradio.

Pietiläinen, J. (2002) *The Regional Newspaper in Post-Soviet Russia*. Tampere: Tampere University Press.

Popper, K. (1945) *The Open Society and Its Enemies*, 2 volumes. London: Routledge.

Prokhorov, Ye. (2001) *Journalism and Democracy*. Moscow: RIP-Holding.

Rantanen, T. (2002) *The Global and the National: Media and Communications in Post-Communist Russia*. Lanham, MD: Rowman and Littlefield.

Resnyanskaya, L. (2001) *Dvukhstoronnaya kommunikatsija: metodika organizaysii obshestvennogo dialoga* (Two-Way Communication: Methods to Organize Public Dialogue). Moscow: Pulse.

—— (2003) *Obshestvennyi dialog i politicheskaya kultura obshestva* (Public Dialogue and Political Culture in Society). Moscow: Pulse.

Resnyanskaya, L. and Fomicheva, I. (1999) *Gazeta dlya vsei Rossiji* (Newspaper for the Whole of Russia). Moscow: Facultet zhurnalistiki.

Richter, A. (2002) *Pravovyje osnovy zhurnalistiki* (Legal Basis of Journalism). Moscow: izd-vo Mosk. Un-ta.

Sappak, V. (1963) *Televideniye i my* (Television and Us). Moscow: Iskusstvo.

Siebert, F.S., Peterson, T. and Schramm, W. (1956) *Four Theories of the Press*. Urbana: University of Illinois Press.

Sparks, C. with Reading, A. (1998) *Communism, Capitalism and Mass Media*. London: Sage.

Splichal, S. (1994) *Media beyond Socialism: Theory and Practice in East-Central Europe*. Boulder, CO: Westview Press.

Svitich, L. (2000) *Fenomen zhuralisma* (Journalism as Phenomenon). Moscow: Faculty of Journalism, ICAR Publisher.

Tulupov, V. (2000) *Design i reklama v marketinge rossijskoi gazety* (Design and Advertising in Newspaper Marketing). Moscow: Voronesh.

Vartanova, E. (2004a) *Mediaekonomika zaroubezhnykh stran* (Media Economics in Foreign Countries). Moscow: Aspekt Press.

—— (2004b) The Russian Network Society, in Manuel Castells (ed.) *The Network Society: A Cross-Cultural Perspective*. Cheltenham: Edward Elgar, pp. 84–98.

—— (2007) Russian Media Economy: Eurasian Model, in Elena Vartanova (ed.) *Media and Change*. Moscow: MediaMir, pp. 103–21.

Vartanova, E. and Zassoursky, Y. (2004) *Shaping Tomorrow's Media Systems*. Moscow: Faculty of Journalism/UNESCO.

Zassoursky, I. (2001) *Rekonstrukzija Rossii: Media i politika v 90ye*. (Reconstruction of Russia: Media and Politics in the 1990s). Moscow: izd-vo Mosk. Un-ta.

—— (2004) *Media and Power in Post-Soviet Russia*. Armonk, NY: M.E. Sharpe.

Zassoursky, Y. (1997) *Media in Transition and Politics in Russia*, in Servaes Jan and Lee Rico (eds) *Media and Politics in Transition*. Leuven and Amersfoort: Acco, pp. 213–21.

Zassoursky, Y. and Vartanova, E. (eds) (1998) *Changing Media and Communications*. Moscow: Faculty of Journalism, ICAR Publisher.

—— (1999) *Media, Communications and the Open Society*. Moscow: Faculty of Journalism, ICAR Publisher.

Chapter 14

Citizens' media as political subjects

The case of community radio in Colombia

Jair Vega and Clemencia Rodríguez

The intent of this chapter is to shed light on how citizens' media play roles as political subjects. Framed by Chantal Mouffe's (1988, 1992) theories of radical democracy, 'citizens' media' have been defined as media which help trigger processes leading to the transformation of individuals into citizens (Rodríguez, 2001). From a communication perspective, citizens' media act as catalysts for processes of symbolic appropriation and re-coding of the environment and individuals. These processes help people develop identities strongly tied to local realities and deeply committed to new approaches to shaping the collective future of their communities. Citizens' media open up communication spaces where individuals can use their own languages, signs and codes to re-name the world in their own terms. This appropriation of the naming process is fundamental to the transformation of individuals into citizens who shape their own futures (Rodríguez, 2001). Thus, in this sense, not all community media are citizens' media; the term citizens' media applies only to those media which facilitate the processes described here.

In this chapter we aim to further develop the concept of 'citizens' media' to better reflect how, in certain cases, the *medium itself* becomes a political subject with agency. In addition to the role of these media as tools used by citizens to exert citizenship, the medium also becomes a social subject in itself. In other words, we try to see media as entities, or citizens, having the power to intervene in their communities' political and cultural everyday life. We seek to present citizens' media as social subjects participating in decision-making processes at local, regional and national levels, and as subjects playing a significant political role.

With this purpose in mind, we will first describe the current Latin American citizens' media scene and then propose an elaboration on the concept of citizens' media. We intend to emphasize the ways these media become social subjects by weaving their own networks of relationships. Finally, we will discuss a study exploring the way in which fifteen Colombian community radio stations practised this, weaving relationship networks to become citizen-like subjects.

The struggle for democratization of communication in Latin America

It has been suggested that since the 1970s Latin America has been the region of the world where alternative, community, and citizens' media have made the greatest impact (Gumucio-Dagrón, 2005). Why do we see such a proliferation? Factors include the emergence of theories such as those of Paulo Freire and Antonio Pasquali emphasizing the importance, since the 1960s, of true communication in the consolidation of democratic political subjects. In his *Pedagogía del Oprimido* (Freire, 1980, 2005), Paulo Freire argues that education based on dialogue is a prerequisite for 'concientization', a term he defines as the process through which individuals appropriate themselves, their place in the world, their right to determine their own future, and their role in history.

In *Comprender la Comunicación*, Pasquali (1979) establishes the difference between information and communication, and warns of the danger of confusing the two. According to Pasquali, communication is a dialogue in which individuals interact, thus becoming social and cultural subjects. For Freire and Pasquali, the key characteristic of strong democracies is the participation of social subjects capable of using their voice in the public sphere to express and name the world in their own terms.

In the late 1980s these theoretical approaches gave rise to the New World Information and Communication Order (NWICO) (UNESCO, 1980).[1] For the next twenty years, NWICO was considered the framing and inspiration for initiatives that pursued the dialectical utopia of Freire and Pasquali.[2] In Latin America such initiatives included information, communication and cultural national policies (most of them banished today by the International Monetary Fund and its structural adjustment policies); South-to-South communication projects (such as the Inter Press Service); and thousands of attempts to use media for communication (in the sense proposed by Pasquali) and for 'concientization' (Rodríguez and Murphy, 1997). This age marks the start of Latin American communication academia's commitment to progressive social movements struggling for democracy and social justice in the region.

The progressive Catholic Church in Latin America, led by the Liberation Thelogians, promoted the development of alternative and community media. Liberation Theology assumes the mission of all Catholics to be one of making the world a better place by combating poverty. This mandate requires a struggle against the evils of external domination and internal colonialism. Liberation Theology understands this mission to be achievable only through strong political activism, sometimes even including revolutionary activity and violent conflict. The ultimate goal in this struggle is human redemption, which 'involves not only cleansing from individual sin, but liberation from oppressive structures of the world of today'.[3] In the field of communication and media, Latin American Liberation Theology made two important contributions during the 1970s and 1980s. First, the movement created an awareness of the need for a model of communication that was distinct from the commercial media model. Second, Liberation Theology promoted a belief in small, participatory, horizontal media as alternatives to the exclusionary nature of commercial media. As a result, in the 1970s hundreds of Catholic collectives, from Patagonia to the Rio Grande, developed their own citizens' media. Using techniques as diverse as theatre, dance, puppets, murals, printed materials, video, radio, cassettes and loudspeakers, churches and Catholic community groups embarked on a myriad alternative communication projects (Rodríguez, 2003).

Colombia is a good illustration of the Latin American position. In this country, communication and media policies have somehow prevented the comprehensive commercialization of mass media. The progressive Colombian Catholic Church and other progressive social justice movements invested resources, work and creativity in the consolidation of alternative media, ranging from barrio loudspeakers and alternative presses to community radio programmes that were broadcast in city buses.

In Colombia, citizens' media have evolved to the point where communication is seen as a political project which is an end in itself. During the 1970s and 1980s, Colombian media activists struggled to establish and cultivate alternative media aimed at satisfying the information and communication needs of social movements. At that time, alternative and community media were seen as 'loudspeakers' at the service of social movements. However, since 1995 a group of pioneers has emerged from the country's first generation of community media. This new generation has undertaken an in-depth reflection on the role these media play in a country like Colombia. Based on their own praxis as community media producers/activists, this group of organic intellectuals has redefined community media. These pioneers began articulating an idea of community media as being more than mere instruments for mobilization. According this new vision, community media became communication spaces in and of themselves. After this re-visioning, citizens' media ceased to be 'loudspeakers' for social movements and became communication spaces that feed a public sphere where various identities within a community can meet, recognize one another, talk, and agree on a shared future. Thus, communication per se became the political goal.

From alternative media to citizens' media

Both media activists and scholars use several terms to refer to non-profit media managed by local community entities. These terms include: community media, popular media, radical media, grass-roots media, alternative media, citizens' media, and the French term *médias libres*. Each of these terms emphasizes a particular aspect of media and is related to different theories on the democratization of communication. For instance, the term 'alternative media' highlights the difference between these media and commercial media. While the latter are vertical and exclusive, alternative media are defined as horizontal and inclusive. In other words, alternative media are not defined in terms of what they are, but of what they are not. The term 'alternative media' is associated with the instrumentality of resistance to media concentration in the establishment of democratic communication.

The term 'citizens' media' (Rodríguez, 2001) is based on the concept of radical democracy proposed by feminist scholar Chantal Mouffe (1992, 1988). The main component of Mouffe's theory is the necessity of redefining the concept of citizenship. Theories of liberal democracy define citizenship as 'membership in a polity' (Kivisto and Faist, 2007: 1), a status granted by the central state, which acts as the cornerstone of democracy (without citizenship, individuals cannot participate in the democratic process). Mouffe questions whether a formal institution should govern the granting or denying of citizenship status, upon which participation in the democratic process depends. Mouffe suggests a redefinition of the terms 'citizenship' and 'citizens' and maintains that 'citizenship' should not be a formal and legal term, but rather a condition determined by individual experience.

For Mouffe, a citizen is a political subject because he/she has been defined not as an individual with his/her own rights and duties, but as a person whose existence is located in a specific social place (Mouffe, 1992, 1988; McClure, 1992). A citizen exists insofar as he/she participates in interactions that are rooted in local everyday life, including relations with family, friends, neighbours, work colleagues, church members, etc. It is from these relationships that each citizen does (or does not) extract portions of economic and/or cultural power. These portions of power, each one having its own texture, are the raw material of democracy. They allow people to influence the future of their social community. Therefore, for Mouffe, a citizen has a clear idea of his/her own future; citizens generate power through their relationships every day, and use this power to shape their communities.

Based on Mouffe's redefinition of citizenship, 'citizens' media' become those media which facilitate the transformation of individuals into citizens. Citizens' media activate the appropriation of symbols and the re-coding of people and their environment-processes of identity construction strongly rooted in local relations. It is from these processes and relations that the future can be redesigned.

Until now, Rodríguez (2001) has defined citizens' media as community media that have the potential to transform individuals into citizens. This definition highlights the role of citizens' media as 'instruments' in processes of citizenship consolidation. Here, we propose to advance this theory by looking at the medium itself as a political subject. If we apply Mouffe's redefinition of citizenship to community media, we can begin to see that defining community media as a legislated status conferred by the state is not enough. A genuine citizens' medium is one that actively intervenes in its social and cultural environment with clear proposals for shaping the community's future. In other words, in addition to politicizing those actively involved in media production, citizens' media can be defined as entities that in themselves act as political subjects in their own local context. The medium itself enacts political agency, participates in local decision-making processes, intervenes in re-creating the local, social and cultural environment.

Citizens' media live in constant relations and interactions with the environment in which they exist. These relations occur between the medium and all kinds of different entities, including community organizations, local or national government entities, church groups, universities, the business sector, international cooperation agencies, and other media. Just as we have seen that individual citizens produce portions of power through their daily relationships and interactions, so citizens' media produce portions of power that can be symbolic, material or cultural out of their daily relationships. This power enables the medium to publicly articulate specific policies and proposals and to become an active participant in its community.

In this sense, the evolution from community media to citizens' media depends upon the medium's interactions with other social subjects and local political forces, the ways in which it builds its legitimacy in a social context, and the extent to which the medium is able to maintain autonomy vis-à-vis all the other political subjects with which it interacts.

Citizens' media establish (or fail to establish) their autonomy in the course of daily interactions with other organizations. Thus, observing the tensions that emerge in these power-permeated relationships, we can ascertain the extent to which a community medium has established the identity of a citizens' medium. These tensions derive from the intersections and conflicts between the medium's own political agenda and agency and the interests and demands of community groups and institutions with which the medium interacts.

Community radio in Middle Magdalena, Colombia

The region of Magdalena Medio (Middle Magdalena) (MM) lies in the centre of Colombia, covering an area of 30,000 square kilometres that includes territories from four provinces (Antioquia, Bolívar, Santander and Cesar), and is home to approximately 800,000 Colombians. The region has one of the highest rates of violence in the country: in 2002 the homicide rate was at 250 homicides per 100,000 inhabitants[4] (Katz García, n.d.). There is widespread violence in both rural and urban areas of the region, including guerrilla and paramilitary activity, drug trafficking, oil mafias, and common delinquency.

In this context of violence and unrest, the Programa de Desarrollo y Paz del Magdalena Medio (PDPMM; Peace and Development Programme for Middle-Magdalena) was born in 1995 as an attempt to decrease levels of violence and improve the quality of life in local communities. The PDPMM was developed through the cooperative efforts of several institutions, including

ECOPETROL (the largest oil-processing corporation, until recently publicly owned), the Diocese of Barrancabermeja, and CINEP – a well-known Colombian NGO. Their concern about the proliferation of armed conflict led them to collaborate on a comprehensive development project for the entire region.

In the early 1990s media activists had begun developing citizens' radio initiatives throughout Colombia. In 1995 the PDPMM discovered there were five community radio stations run by citizens' groups and collectives in Magdalena Medio. Through these stations collective groups were able to strengthen their capacity to participate in local governance, monitor public institutions, and express local concerns. Participants in these citizens' media ventures included parent–teacher associations, teachers' collectives, cultural groups, religious organizations and churches, community leaders, and local authorities.

The PDPMM decided to support the community radio stations of Magdalena Medio. Between 1995 and 2005, with the help of the PDPMM, five more radio stations were able to secure community broadcasting licences and obtain the necessary technical infrastructure for broadcasting. Today ten community radio stations and five communication collectives, covering fifteen municipalities within Magdalena Medio, are organized as the Asociación Red de Emisoras Comunitarias del Magdalena Medio (AREDMAG; Network of Community Radio Stations of Magdalena Medio).

AREDMAG's leaders welcomed our offer to collectively design an evaluation methodology informed by their questions about the impact of these community media on the local social fabric of the region. AREDMAG told us they wanted to know about the role of its fifteen community radio stations in cultivating a strong and diverse public sphere, strengthening a culture of peaceful coexistence, and facilitating local and regional decision-making processes. The following narrative documents the results of our attempt to answer one of AREDMAG's questions through an evaluation study.

The AREDMAG evaluation study

In 2004 Clemencia Rodríguez (The University of Oklahoma in the USA), Amparo Cadavid (Universidad Javeriana in Bogotá, Colombia) and Jair Vega (Universidad del Norte in Barranquilla, Colombia) created an academic team to research the impact of citizens' media. The team designed a participatory citizens' media evaluation methodology. An agreement was reached with AREDMAG to evaluate the impact of its fifteen community radio stations in the Middle Magdalena region. One of AREDMAG's questions about the role of its radio stations was: to what extent are AREDMAG's community radio stations political subjects with decision-making power in each of their municipalities and in the region as a whole?

The core research question for this study emerged from the efforts of AREDMAG's leaders to understand what they had achieved since 1995, and how to set a course of action for the future of their community radio stations. Thus, our point of departure was the need to design a methodology that would allow the protagonists of community radio to reflect upon their own experiences. As academics, we placed our know-how at the service of AREDMAG's needs and concerns. In this sense, we continued the legacy of Latin American communication academia, which since the 1980s has been strongly committed to social justice and thus tightly connected to progressive social movements and grass-roots organizations.

In order to answer AREDMAG's question we used mnemonic mapping – a data-gathering technique developed by Pilar Riaño-Alcalá (2006, 2000a, 2000b, 1999, 1998) – to trigger discussions about individual and collective experiences. Riaño-Alcalá's methodologies are based on understanding collective memory as a space where the identity markers of a collectivity are expressed. Mnemonic mapping allows people to identify and locate places and relationships that have special meaning for their group on a collectively produced map. In this particular case, we asked community radio producers to identify, locate and map all the relationships their community radio stations held with other organizations. Each map produced reflects the radio producers' perceptions of the network of relationships each of their radio stations inhabits. This work went beyond mapping exact networks to mapping perceived networks.

A sample of sixty radio producers from ten community radio stations, two communication collectives, and three community communication associations participated in the mnemonic mapping exercise. The group of sixty community radio producers was divided according to municipality.[5] Each group of five or six participants produced one mnemonic map showing all the relationships they remembered their community radio station as having with other organizations and entities at the municipal, regional, national and international levels. The data-collection process was developed as follows:

(a) Each participating community radio station (or communication collective) produced one mnemonic map, giving a total of fifteen mnemonic maps. The first element participants drew on their map was their radio station. Next, participants drew all the local, regional, national or international organizations with which they could remember their station having a relationship. After that, each relationship was characterized or classified (as an alliance, joint work, instrumental, commercial or political). The different stages of those relationships were taken into account; older and newer relationships were represented using different colours.
(b) Each group analysed its mnemonic map and identified common, contradictory and complementary patterns among the relationships represented, as well as links and networks among these relationships.
(c) Afterwards, the members of each group reflected on the mnemonic mapping exercise and identified issues that arose during the memory-reconstruction process, such as the lack of relationships their station had with grass-roots organizations, its strong connections with local schools, or its problematic relationships with local government authorities.

(d) In a plenary session, each group reported their conclusions concerning points (b) and (c). All maps were assembled into a single map of the Magdalena Medio community radio stations and their networks of relationships. The participants discussed what the general 'master' map expressed. All the group discussions and the plenary session were recorded and transcribed.

The entire methodological process was based on the assumption that each community radio station team operates as a 'collective I', or an 'us' existing as a collective subject. The mnemonic mapping exercise allowed participants to materially represent all the other 'collective subjects' with which their radio stations maintain relationships. The maps, tables, comments and discussions during the plenary session served as data for the following analysis.

AREDMAG's community radio stations and their networks

The following analysis articulates a series of tensions that emerged from the discussions and fifteen mnemonic maps described above. We use the term 'tensions' to refer to complex, push-and-pull forces experienced by each community radio station. During the plenary session in which the mnemonic maps were discussed, the participants described these tensions in a variety of ways: as accomplishments, challenges or unmet goals for their community radio station.

First tension: level of integration with local and regional organizations

The community radio producers recognized a tension in the following questions. To what extent are AREDMAG and its radio stations political subjects with a significant impact on local and regional decision-making processes? Do these community radio stations act as a space where local citizens can have a say in decisions?

The concerns of the community radio broadcasters around this tension emerged in several ways:

(a) the capacity of each community radio station to include programming produced by various local organizations;
(b) the ability of radio stations to call upon the various participants and points of view co-existing in the region and make them accessible to the public;
(c) the participation of representatives from radio stations and AREDMAG in the decisions made at municipal and regional levels (for instance, decisions concerning local government policies, public forums organized by local civil society groups and collectives, and the design and allocation of municipal budgets).

Concerning (a), the production of radio programmes by local organizations, the results show a wide variety. While some radio stations, such as Puerto

Wilches Estéreo (19 programmes produced weekly by local organizations), Santa Rosa Estéreo (14 programmes) and Campo Serrano Radio (13 programmes), have numerous programmes produced by different organizations, others have only a few. For example, Emisora Comunitaria 89.2 La FM de Gamarra (two programmes produced by local organizations) and La Inmaculada de Río Negro (just one programme) have very little locally produced programming.

It should be made clear that municipalities like Río Viejo, San Alberto and San Pablo do not yet have legal radio stations; they are now just collectives in the process of trying to secure a broadcasting licence and, therefore, have not developed their own programmes.

The preceding analysis shows that, as far as radio stations are concerned, there are different levels of inclusion of local and regional actors in the production of meaning. A community radio station's capacity to act as a citizens' medium for community members in their own environment is determined by the strength of the radio station's relationships with local and regional organizations. It would be impossible to determine the 'ideal' ratio of local programming that a community radio station should have for it to 'count' as a citizens' medium. It can be assumed, however, that radio stations with a greater number of programmes produced by local and regional organizations are more legitimate, address a larger number of issues and, therefore, can act as citizens' radio stations in the sense suggested by Mouffe – that is, as political subjects.

With respect to (b), the stations' ability to give visibility to and express local and regional subjects, voices and points of view, the mnemonic maps demonstrate that radio stations involve social, cultural and political subjects in a variety of ways beyond programming produced by local and regional organizations. Our evaluation study showed that AREDMAG's stations maintain a number of diverse relationships with a wide variety of local, regional, national and even international entities.

The data demonstrate that relationships with political community organizations are the most frequently reported by the radio stations. These include labour unions, peasants, fishermen, palm and cacao growers' associations, women's groups and youth collectives (these types of organizations appeared 56 times in the mnemonic maps of 15 municipalities). These results are significant because they reveal an intention on the part of the radio stations to establish relationships with social change agents in the form of grass-roots organizations and social movements. The second most frequently mentioned type of organization comprises religious groups and churches (appearing 29 times in all the mnemonic maps). Although the Catholic Church is most often represented, there are several cases of other religious groups (mainly Christian, including Protestants, Jehovah's Witnesses and Adventists, among others) having programmes broadcast by AREDMAG's community radio stations. Universities are the third most frequently mentioned type of organization (23 times). Next in rank are some national ministries and government entities (mentioned 22 times), and the business and private sectors (mentioned 21 times) which are linked to the radio stations through advertising or sponsorships.

Even though the integration of community radio stations with their environments is recognized as a strength, it has also become a source of anxiety for community radio broadcasters. According to some of the mapping workshop participants, achieving full community involvement is still a challenge to be faced. In the words of one participant at the plenary session:

> I believe that we, as members of the radio station teams, need to be more involved with our communities. If we think about it – and it is in this type of meeting that we do – so it seems as though only two or three people work in the community radio stations, the rest of them are just barely meeting their responsibilities and working their set hours, without any real commitment. We seem to be more interested in music programmes than in the processes being carried out in the region. I have seen this in many radio stations and the situation is the same in ours. Although we have managed to overcome this situation to a great extent and now people are more involved, we have failed at being more closely involved with our communities in general.
>
> (Testimony of one of the participants in the Evaluation Workshop held in Bucaramanga, Colombia, 15–18 October 2004)

At the local level, nearly all radio stations report having a relationship with their town council. In most cases, this relationship is made explicit, and only in three of the fifteen mnemonic maps was such a relationship absent.

In reference to (c), the function of radio stations as participants in local decision-making processes, the mnemonic maps show that in some municipalities this function is complicated by the types of power relationships in place. We did find that the participation of AREDMAG's community radio stations in Territorial Planning Councils was mentioned four times, and most radio stations openly reported relationships with the Peace and Development Programme (PDPMM) – one of the most important decision-makers in MM.

During the plenary session in which the mnemonic maps of the fifteen municipalities were discussed, the radio programmers' commitment to the participation of radio stations in local and regional decision-making processes was evident. Radio programmers want AREDMAG's community radio stations to become strong political subjects in their municipalities and in the region as a whole.

The following three testimonies from plenary participants illustrate this:

> If community radio stations do not get into the political structures of the municipality, they will never manage to be sustainable; this means that they must participate in the budget planning and allocation groups.
>
> (Testimony of one of the participants in the Evaluation Workshop held in Bucaramanga, Colombia, 15–18 October 2004)

> The discussion should move from the number of municipalities we reach – is it ten or forty – or the size of our audience – is it big or small – to the number of organizations that are participating in the community radio station, and whether the station is a political actor involved in the political processes of those organizations, in the Territorial Planning Councils, or in the local planning systems, for it is there that the true legitimacy of the radio station can be observed.
> (Testimony of one of the participants in the Evaluation Workshop held in Bucaramanga, Colombia, 15–18 October 2004)

> We believe in communication as a way of social development; our communication project is clearly reflected in our programmes. Somehow, this situation has to do with us: most of us did not participate in the stages previous to the emergence of the radio stations; we just appeared on stage (before we were mere listeners who got involved in the community radio station). The context has forced us to become political actors, to do things we were not used to because we were ordinary people: watchmakers, mechanics, repairmen, or electronic technicians. But once we are part of the public sphere, we must start to think about the political options that we have as individuals.
> (Testimony of one of the participants in the Evaluation Workshop held in Bucaramanga, Colombia, 15–18 October 2004)

Finally, as a way to conclude the discussion of this first tension, we cite a dialogue in which workshop participants discussed the solidification of AREDMAG as a political protagonist in the MM. The statements of the participants are based on the mnemonic maps as well as on their past experiences interacting with external institutions:

> I believe that the political subject mentioned by Adolfo, and later on by Melba, already exists. But I have a question. You all seem to have a very clear idea of the issue. I say so because during the last three years I've had the chance to talk about AREDMAG in other contexts; I've talked about it before the European Union and the United Nations. For them, AREDMAG is a very strong network and an extremely important actor in the Magdalena Medio. They also see AREDMAG as a very strong group. But I wonder if we feel that strong when we sit down to negotiate with them.
> (Testimony of one of the participants in the Evaluation Workshop held in Bucaramanga, Colombia, 15–18 October 2004)

> I think we are political actors, but invisible ones. If we were strong, visible political actors, we would have the possibility of negotiating, on equal terms, budget and resource allocations for our projects. We haven't been

> able to do so because the only person in charge of negotiating with the European Union and the Peace Laboratory is Julio [reference is made to Julio Hoyos, chair of AREDMAG's Board of Directors]. He is there, all by himself, because he has not been supported by the rest of us. Think of the moment when a call is made to renew AREDMAG's board! It is always the same group of people trying to decide who will face the situation because no one is really willing to get involved. Until when should we wait?
> (Testimony of one of the participants in the Evaluation Workshop held in Bucaramanga, Colombia, 15–18 October 2004)

Second tension: quality vs. participation

The second tension emerges from the community broadcasters' concern for producing good quality programmes, while at the same time opening the stations up to community participation. In other words, the tension is felt as a push-and-pull between professionalizing the media through the improvement of production quality and keeping the station doors open, allowing for media that is participatory, inclusive and accessible to ordinary local citizens. In the words of participants:

> We should also think of quality when we talk about programming. This is very important because opening programming for many people to participate does not mean having good quality radio programmes. We tend to think that having many programmers equals good quality, but we are ignoring an important aspect here. It turns out that it is quality that makes the difference between us and commercial radio stations. Our programmes are boring, they are half-an-hour or one-hour-long tedious programmes and we don't care about their quality. Quality should be the objective of a radio station's network.
> (Testimony of one of the participants in the Evaluation Workshop held in Bucaramanga, Colombia, 15–18 October 2004)

> The most difficult task when opening the radio station to community groups and organizations is the sustainability and continuity of those programmes. The key question is: how are we going to achieve that? Very often, community organizations start participating in radio programming but they don't continue; they begin and one month later they do not come back, or three months later the programmes become boring. There is no planning at all. We should think of a strategy for community radio stations to prevent this situation.
> (Testimony of one of the participants in the Evaluation Workshop held in Bucaramanga, Colombia, 15–18 October 2004)

Members of AREDMAG revealed an important strategy informing this tension. They explained their belief that community radio stations should serve as community educators in matters concerning radio broadcasting. In their view, a community radio station should offer training in both technical and political aspects of media:

> How to achieve good quality programmes while opening radio stations' programming to the community? An option is that of radio stations functioning as schools of radio broadcasting; people must go through a training process before they start making programmes; meanwhile, they not only get involved in radio programming but also start thinking about the role of community radio stations and citizens' communication. After the training process, people are expected to have a clear communication project in mind and to have the abilities and competences necessary to make a radio programme.
>
> (Testimony of one of the participants in the Evaluation Workshop held in Bucaramanga, Colombia, 15–18 October 2004)

Third tension: audiences vs. local interaction

A third tension emerged in the discussion among the community radio producers in terms of the logic of their actions in the local context. The Magadalena Medio community radio broadcasters questioned whether they should focus on trying to improve radio production processes to reach larger audiences, or concentrate on strengthening their relationships with grass-roots organizations and local and regional social movements:

> We are the voice of this whole region; we are not a radio station for 15,000 people, but a network of 700,000 inhabitants capable of making our own decisions. We can talk to the Peace and Development Programme officers, to the government or to any other authority, and let them know that we do have a say in the region, and that they must listen to us.
>
> (Testimony of one of the participants in the Evaluation Workshop held in Bucaramanga, Colombia, 15–18 October 2004)

> What radio stations should do now is attract social movements and grass-roots organizations. This should be our main task from now on. Our main duty is not to know how big our audiences are but what kind of audiences we have, how community organizations are participating in our radio programmes, and how our radio stations are participating in the processes of those organizations as political actors.
>
> (Testimony of one of the participants in the Evaluation Workshop held in Bucaramanga, Colombia, 15–18 October 2004)

Fourth tension: economic sustainability vs. autonomy

The fourth tension that emerged has to do with the radio stations' sustainability measured against adherence to their stated goals. While commercialization grants a station economic sustainability, without commercialization the radio stations can function as autonomous institutions independent of any economic or political interests – the kind of institutions that communities can identify as their own. The discussion of this tension revolved around the identification of these media as citizens' media:

> I would like to mention here one key word that seemed controversial at the beginning of this plenary session: the word 'sustainability' … Community radio stations do need economic resources to survive and to improve their work, but they also must train people.
> (Testimony of one of the participants in the Evaluation Workshop held in Bucaramanga, Colombia, 15–18 October 2004)

> Just like AREDMAG, which is very weak in this respect, I think that nearly 80 per cent or 90 per cent of the community radio stations face this problem. The service they render is mainly social and, consequently, they have economic problems. I insist on the idea that if we are not economically strong, we can hardly promote social development.
> (Testimony of one of the participants in the Evaluation Workshop held in Bucaramanga, Colombia, 15–18 October 2004)

Fifth tension: institutional articulation vs. political control

Another tension was felt in the process of integrating AREDMAG's radio stations with municipal authorities. Community radio broadcasters believe that involving municipal authorities in their radio stations will provide them with economic support, but they are wary of how this involvement could influence the political control of their radio stations:

> What kind of relationship are municipal authorities establishing with community radio stations? Let me explain. In almost all cases, municipal authorities are important figures. What we should think here is who needs whom. Does the mayor need the radio station? Does the radio station need the mayor? Thus, we should question ourselves about this reality.
> (Testimony of one of the participants in the Evaluation Workshop held in Bucaramanga, Colombia, 15–18 October 2004)

> I would like to ask AREDMAG and the universities here represented to help us in the design of a strategy to approach town mayors and municipal

> councils in order to create a sustainability fund without any conditions being imposed on us. As members of the community radio station of San Vicente, we have tried to do so but conditions immediately arise. Municipal authorities or council members soon want the radio station to be under their control. I believe that if a town mayor has the possibility of running the radio station, he will certainly allocate economic resources to it. But to what extent should we allow this situation?
> (Testimony of one of the participants in the Evaluation Workshop held in Bucaramanga, Colombia, 15–18 October 2004)

Sixth tension: AREDMAG being just a node or the centre of the network

The last tension worth mentioning here emerged from the differing perceptions of AREDMAG as a community radio network. Magdalena Medio community radio broadcasters question the centrality of AREDMAG as a single entity in charge of integrating community radio stations and mediating between them. They suggest the possibility of a horizontal communication scheme among the radio stations; the goal to be met is to become a real network where communication flows from node to node without having to go through the centre (AREDMAG's board):

> I am very surprised by the fact that the maps do not reflect any relations among radio stations. For me, it is clear that a real network, which differs from an association or some other type of organization, is characterized by the possibility of any of its nodes to communicate with another one without having to pass through a central point. Therefore, I wonder if AREDMAG is really a network since, apparently, every interaction or communication with a radio station must always go through the center. I think that we should work hard on the possibility of one node communicating with another one without having to go all the way to Barrancabermeja.[6]
> (Testimony of one of the participants in the Evaluation Workshop held in Bucaramanga, Colombia, 15–18 October 2004)

> The internal relations that make up a real network are not evidenced here. The network of radio stations is not an institution, it is not AREDMAG … or any other leader. It is all of us. When I travel around the region, I see the links between the radio stations, of Rio Negro and Betulia, or those between Puerto Wilches and San Vicente. But for some reason these relationships did not appear on the maps. Why are the relations among radio stations not reflected? Why did we conceal such relationships if they are what makes us a strong network?
> (Testimony of one of the participants in the Evaluation Workshop held in Bucaramanga, Colombia, 15–18 October 2004)

Conclusion

The tensions pointed out above give rise to a series of challenges that can only be addressed through a recognition of the progress already made by these community radio stations. Facing and welcoming these challenges create the possibility for AREDMAG and its radio stations to ease the tensions and strengthen each station and the network as a whole.

The first challenge requires the coalescing of a type of radio programming based on appropriation of the production process by different social subjects. In facing this challenge, AREDMAG could establish a set of goals and policies, taking into account the characteristics of the region and identifying specific local needs for radio production training. Another challenge could be met by drawing a map of local and regional decision-making bodies, and designing a strategy that would allow AREDMAG to increase the participation of its community radio stations in those bodies. This strategy requires the training and preparation of AREDMAG's cadres.

To maintain relevance, AREDMAG should improve the ability of the network and the radio stations to negotiate, so that they can establish stronger relationships with different local, regional and national organizations. This means that those involved in the network and in the radio stations must develop the necessary competencies to negotiate with government authorities and participate in decision-making forums.

AREDMAG must design a plan in which community radio stations train community members in the area of communication so that all members of the community can participate in radio production without compromising programme quality. Radio stations should have a wide range of coverage and reach large audiences in order to be economically sustainable. It is also critical that they be part of the social fabric of their communities at the local level, through links with community organizations and social movements, in order to guarantee their social and political sustainability.

Horizontal communication processes need to be strengthened, and alliances among radio stations should be promoted in an effort to reinforce AREDMAG as a true network. Such alliances could result in collective radio production and programme exchange.

Finally, since there is a strong need for evaluation research, training and competency development, the involvement of universities and academics is vital in effectively responding to the challenges identified here. However, the research and training offered by the academic community should always be driven by the needs and challenges of citizens' media, not by academic needs.

The initial purpose of this study was to provide the members of AREDMAG with some themes for reflection, but the following considerations, generally applicable to citizens' media, can be derived from this study. As academics, we need to research the relative autonomy of citizens' media and their roles in local contexts. Autonomy should be seen as a dynamic process. Citizens' media oscillate, in ways that are context-specific, in response to the tensions and pressures exerted by different local, regional and national entities. This makes it impossible to establish ideal formulas, models or patterns to assess citizens' media autonomy. Instead, we need to design long-term studies and flexible, plastic methodologies to monitor and understand the continuous movement towards (or away from) 'connected autonomy' – meaning strong connections with local organizations while also maintaining the medium's autonomy.

In order to understand the political influence of community radio stations in their specific contexts, it is crucial to identify and map the links these media have with various institutions (grass-roots organizations, social movements, local government authorities, etc.). This process of identification and mapping can be the first step in strengthening the participation of community radio stations in the construction of a local and regional public sphere. Although mnemonic mapping does not provide exact information about the links and relationships of citizens' media, it is a significant tool for understanding the way these media perceive and represent themselves and the relationships they have with different organizations. In other words, the maps express to what extent community media broadcasters perceive their medium as a political subject.

Acknowledgements

Many thanks to Orley Durán, Melba Quijano, Amparo Cadavid, Oscar Moreno, Julio Oyos, Manfry Gómez Ditta, Omaira Arrieta and all the other people from the community radio stations in Magdalena Medio who believed in us and trusted us with their stories and their lives. It is thanks to their faith in the power of communication, their courage, and especially their love for Colombia that this text was possible.

Notes

1 Better known in Latin America as *Nuevo Orden Mundial de la Información y la Comunicación* NOMIC – or New World Information and Communication Order (NWICO).

2 In 1978 Pasquali was invited to join the UNESCO committee in charge of the New World Information and Communication Order project, which led to the MacBride Report *Many Voices: One World*, published by UNESCO in 1980 (UNESCO, 1980).

3 For further information on Liberation Theology, see Levine (1986) and Gutierrez (1988).

4 Colombia has one of the highest homicide rates in the world at 66 per 100,000 inhabitants. In the United States, it is 5.7 per 100,000 inhabitants.

5 In Colombia, community broadcasting legislation assigns one community radio licence per municipality. Thus, each mnemonic map was produced by community radio people from the same municipality/station.

6 Refers to the city where AREDMAG has its central office.

References

Freire, P. (1980) *Educación como práctica de la libertad*. Mexico: Siglo XXI.

—— (2005) *Pedagogía del oprimido*. Mexico: Siglo XXI.

Gumucio-Dagrón, A. (2005) Discussion on Community Media in Latin America, Personal communication, 10 July 2005.

Gutierrez, G. (1988) *A Theology of Liberation*. New York: Orbis Books.

Katz García, M. (n.d.) A Regional Peace Experience. The Magdalena Medio Peace and Development Programme. Available at www.c-r.org/accord/col/accord14/regionalpeaceinit.shtml (accessed 14 November 2006).

Kivisto, P. and Faist, T. (2007) *Citizenship: Discourse, Theory and Transnational Prospects*. Oxford: Blackwell.

Levine, D.H. (ed.) (1986) *Religion and Political Conflict in Latin America*. Chapel Hill, NC: University of North Carolina Press.

McClure, K. (1992) On the Subject of Rights: Pluralism, Plurality and Political Identity, in C. Mouffe (ed.) *Dimensions of Radical Democracy: Pluralism, Citizenship, Community*. London: Verso, pp. 108–25.

Mouffe, C. (1988) Hegemony and New Political Subjects: Towards a New Conception of Democracy, in L. Grossberg and C. Nelson (eds) *Marxism and the Interpretation of Culture*. Urbana: University of Illinois Press, pp. 89–102.

—— (ed.) (1992) *Dimensions of Radical Democracy: Pluralism, Citizenship, Community*. London: Verso.

Pasquali, A (1979) *Comprender la comunicación*. Caracas: Monte Avila Editores.

Riaño-Alcalá, P. (1998) Recuperar las memorias y elaborar los duelos [Recovering memory and processing pain], in I. Cepeda and C. Girón (eds) *Duelo, memoria, reparación* [Mourning, memory, reparation]. Bogotá: Fundación Manuel Cepeda, pp. 103–18.

—— (1999) La piel de la memoria [The skin of memory], *Nova y Vetera*, 36: 79–85.

—— (2000a) Recuerdos metodológicos: El taller y la investigación etnográfica [Methodological memories: workshops and ethnographic research], *Revista de Estudios Sociales*, 7: 48–60.

—— (2000b) La memoria viva de las muertes: Lugares e identidades juveniles en Medellín [Living memory of death. Place and youth identities in Medellín], *Análisis Político*, 41: 23–39.

—— (2006) *Dwellers of Memory: Youth and Violence in Medellín, Colombia*. New Brunswick, NJ: Transaction.

Rodríguez, C. (2001) *Fissures in the Mediascape: An International Study of Citizens' Media*. Cresskill, NJ: Hampton Press.

—— (2003) The Bishop and His Star: Citizens' Communication in Southern Chile, in N. Couldry and J. Curran (eds) *Contesting Media Power: Alternative Media in a Networked World*. Boulder, CO: Rowman and Littlefield, pp. 177–94.

Rodríguez, C. and Murphy, P. (1997) The Study of Communication and Culture in Latin America: From Laggards and the Oppressed to Resistance and Hybrid Cultures, *Journal of International Communication*, 4(2): 24–45.

UNESCO (1980) *Many Voices, One World: Report by the International Commission for the Study of Communication Problems*. Paris: UNESCO.

Part IV

Pedagogic parameters

Internationalizing media syllabi

Chapter 15

Internationalizing media ethics studies

Cees J. Hamelink

Around the world courses and textbooks on media ethics proliferate. A simple Google search yields over seven million hits. One can easily understand this growing interest in reflections on the moral issues that the ever-expanding use of media evokes. Among the factors are the industrialization and commercialization of media, the global proliferation of advertising, concerns about children's use of the media, the political doctoring of the news and reporting about armed conflict. Among the topics in media ethics studies we find: undercover journalism, professional conduct and its self-regulation, the relations between journalists and PR professionals, conflicts of interest, deceptive reporting, the protection of privacy, the presumption of innocence, dealing with violence, gender and race reporting, truth and fairness.

Raising the question of internationalizing media ethics studies poses three sub-questions.

Are studies in media ethics internationalizing?

This is the simple question as it asks whether media ethics studies – increasingly – give attention to such issues as global disparities, intercultural encounters, international protection of copyright or international reporting. Judging from media ethics studies curricula around the world, the answer is positive. Generally, media ethics studies engage with the increasingly global nature of the media in both entertainment and news, and in both the realm of conventional media and the domain of such new media as the internet.

Should media ethics studies internationalize?

This is a slightly more complex, normative question that can be answered by referring to the efforts to develop a global approach to ethics. One illustration is 'Towards a Global Ethic: An Initial Declaration', signed at the 1993 Parliament of the World Religions, which proposes as basic and global standards: non-violence, respect for life, solidarity, tolerance, truthfulness and equal rights (www.weltethos.org).

Similarly, the report *Our Global Neighbourhood* of the Commission on Global Governance (1995) proposes that 'the world is now ready to accept a global civic ethics based on a set of core values that can unite people of all cultural, political, religious, or philosophical backgrounds' (www.sovereignty.net/p/gov/gganalysis.htm).

Can media ethics studies internationalize?

This is the difficult question! It asks whether moral issues related to the media can be meaningfully studied in an international context. To deal with this question it would seem helpful to distinguish between ethics and morality. Ethics can be seen as the philosophical process of critical reflection on human morality. Morality can be seen to encompass the normative standards people apply in their behaviour with others. There is a good deal of evidence that morality – although there may be a limited set of globally shared normative assumptions (Renteln, 1990) – is largely bound to people's localities and sub-localities. The 1993 Vienna Final Declaration of the UN World Conference on Human Rights reconfirmed the universal validity of human rights principles. 'The universal nature of these rights and freedoms is beyond question.' At the same time, however, the Declaration proposed that the implementation of these standards should take place within local cultural interpretative frameworks. In dealing with moral choice situations, it seems likely that people are inclined to look for solutions that have a comfortable degree of 'cultural proximity' and thus make sense within a normative framework people are familiar with. The question whether media ethics studies can realistically be expected to internationalize poses the further question whether the prevailing (and almost globally applied) approaches to morality and moral choice lend themselves to internationalization.

By and large media ethics studies are characterized by a common and conventional structure. The prevailing theories on morality and moral choice are presented, such as deontological (duty-based) approaches or consequentialist (utilitarian) approaches, and these are discussed in the context of concrete case stories.

The deontological or duty-based approach to moral choice

This approach represents the position that rules based upon moral principles can provide guidance in moral choices. In essence the method searches in concrete situations of moral choice for the moral rule that applies. In professional practice such rules may be articulated in a so-called Code of Conduct. However, given the great variety of situations and the inevitable general nature of the rules embedded in codes, these moral rules are not likely to provide concrete moral guidance. Moral prescriptions in codes suggest an almost universal applicability, which is not realistic since actors, situations and interests differ greatly over time and from place to place. Across the world societies are likely to entertain very different and often conflicting value-based interpretations of what constitute 'good' versus 'bad' consequences of human decisions.

The rules of a code may prescribe that professionals should be truthful, but they usually do not explain how this general principle should be applied in concrete situations. The code will generally not tell its users when justifiable exceptions to its rules can and must be made. Also, the different rules in a code may conflict with each other, and the code does not explain how choices should be made when its basic moral principles clash.

The consequentialist (effects-based) approach to moral choice

An important attraction of this approach is that it takes the consequences of moral choices seriously. A complex problem, however, is that most of the time people cannot know the consequences of their acts. Moreover, consequentialist-type approaches imply the risk that beneficial ends justify immoral means. In professional practice the optimal consequences of moral decision-making are often identified as those effects that serve the 'common good'. This suggests a societal consensus about the notion of 'common good'. In reality, this is a highly evasive concept that has many different interpretations, and in all societies opinions about what constitutes the 'common good' are divided. Actually, its meaning is often defined by the most powerful groups in society and rarely coincides with the needs of the less powerful.

The discursive approach to moral choice

Conventional approaches are not well suited to the internationalization of studies in media ethics, due to their embeddedness in local interpretations. A more promising approach may be offered by discursive ethics. This approach proposes that moral choice can evolve in a legitimate fashion only through dialogue among all those concerned. German social philosopher Jürgen Habermas suggests that moral standards are valid only when those concerned would give their consent following their common deliberations (Habermas, 1993: 66). Herewith the basis is given of what has been termed a communicative or discursive ethics. In the dialogue it is explored upon which 'minima moralia' societies can find basic and common agreement. Since there are never ideal solutions for moral choices and since all moral choices are essentially contestable, the dialogue presupposes that there are always various plausible solutions to choice-situations. A discursive approach does not focus on the identification of the single, correct moral solution but proposes a reiterative and dynamic process that takes account of the reality that moral situations and moral standards change over time and space.

The core of ethics as a reflexive approach is the acceptance that since moral choices are always contestable, they should be accounted for. The professional who is willing to accept the challenge of ethical dialogue takes seriously his/her ability to account for professional choices. Herewith, he or she lives up to the ancient Socratic insight that since professionals know what they do and why they do it, they are also capable of public accountability for their practices.

The key question for media ethics studies thus becomes: how can responsible procedures be developed for media decision-making? Responsible procedures can be designed through systematic and regular professional ethical dialogues that do not depart from a consensus on fundamental moral values, but seek those solutions to moral dispute that optimally accommodate the parties' interests and principles. The leading assumption is that in choice-situations there are always different plausible solutions. Those involved in the decision-making process accept that all moral choices are essentially contestable. It is important to conduct such discursive processes regularly. The capacity to participate in these processes needs to be learned and demands considerable practice. This could be the essential mission of media ethics studies. In fact, this represents a universal challenge since moral reasoning is nowhere an inherent talent and needs to be learned everywhere!

The reflexive approach extends media ethics beyond issues of the media production practice. It asks that also the other actors in the media reflect critically on their choices and account for them. The usual question is: do the media have bad effects on their audiences? But we should equally ask: do audiences have bad effects on media? Do sources have bad effects? Do employers have bad effects? Most work in the field of media ethics focuses on media producers. From such early classics as Merrill and Barney (1975) to more recent studies by Christians *et al.* (1993), most books on media ethics deal with the resolution of the moral dilemmas that media producers face in the execution of their profession. The existing codes of professional ethics address the rights and wrongs of professional producers.

However laudable all the efforts in the field of professional ethics may be, they leave the issues of freedom, quality and responsibility as the sole concern of the professional. This is odd since professions necessarily imply relationships between professionals and clients. If one accepts the interactive character of the professional–client relationship, it follows that media ethics cannot be limited to the rights and wrongs of the producers only. It should also be an ethics for media users.

Mass media performance concerns not only media producers. It also involves client communities. The interactive relation between professionals and clients also implies that media users have moral choices to make and have to assume accountability for these choices. The design of a user ethics should be inspired by ethical enquiry and not limited to moralistic rules of conduct (Hamelink, 2000: 400).

The reflexive approach makes the 'glocalization' of media ethics studies possible. The 'locality' of moral preferences in moral choice-situations can be fused with the 'globality' of reflection on such preferences. The best way to 'glocalize' media ethics studies would seem to be to teach and discuss moral issues in settings where students from different cultural backgrounds participate. In such settings students may explore the need to be creative and to think 'out of the box'. Moral issues tend to be treated in a bi-polar fashion as dilemmas where choices have to be made between basic moral premises and other pressing interests, or where choices have to be made between basic moral principles that are equally valid but that demand different and possibly conflicting courses of action. The classical example is the moral choice between publishing private information and thus violating someone's privacy or not publishing such material and thus violating the free speech principle. Creative thinking – reflexivity – would imply that such dilemmas can be transformed into multidimensional exercises of brainstorming about what other options there might be.

Conclusion

Media ethics studies can be internationalized if respect for local moralities is fused with engagement in the global challenge of discursive reflexivity. Eventually, it could well be that through sharing the reflexive process students of media ethics across the globe will discover common moral ground!

References

Christians, C.G., Ferré, J.P. and Fackler, P.M. (1993) *Good News: Social Ethics and the Press*. New York: Oxford University Press.

Commission on Global Governance (1995) *Our Global Neighbourhood*. New York: Oxford University Press.

Habermas, J. (1993) *Moral Consciousness and Communicative Action*. Cambridge, MA: MIT Press.

Hamelink, C.J. (2000) Ethics for Media Users, in B. Pattyn (ed.) *Media Ethics Opening Social Dialogue*. Leuven: Peeters, pp. 393–401.

Merrill, J.C. and Barney, R.D. (eds) (1975) *Ethics and the Press: Readings in Mass Media Morality*. New York: Hastings House.

Renteln, A.D. (1990) *International Human Rights: Universalism versus Relativism*. London: Sage.

Chapter 16

Media studies as an academic discipline[1]

Kaarle Nordenstreng

The concept of 'media studies' or 'media and communication' is widely used in referring to an academic discipline established in universities as a major or minor subject, a department or institute and sometimes even a school or college. It is typically implied that this relatively young field is by now a discipline in its own right alongside such traditional disciplines as history, literature, sociology and political science. However, the nature of the discipline remains unclear, while it is determined by administrative convenience and market demand rather than analysis of its historical development and scholarly position within the system of arts and sciences. This chapter discusses the nature of the discipline, using examples from Finland and other Nordic countries.

The field expanded and diversified

Throughout the past fifty years, the field of media studies has expanded perhaps more than any other academic field, apart from computer science and biomedicine. This may be a wild generalization – not based on systematic data covering all disciplines around the world (hardly available anywhere) – but it is supported by other colleagues (notably Donsbach quoted below). In any case, the status of media studies has been consolidated, next to the old-established fields, but its expansion has also led to friction with the old 'ivy league' sciences, which often view this rising and popular field as 'Mickey Mouse studies' (see the British debate in the *Times Higher Education Supplement*). The conflicts are not just based on prestige and jealousy but literally on the vital prospects of each field – not least the old and established – in the midst of the so-called structural adjustment of universities.

In its expansion, the field has become more and more diversified. Different media (newspapers, magazines, radio, television, cinema, etc.) and different aspects of communication (journalism, visual communication, media culture, media economy, etc.) have emerged as more or less independent branches of the field. This multiplication process has not been halted by the convergence brought about by the digitization of media production and distribution.

Placed in the broader perspective of the history of science, such multiplication is quite problematic as the field runs the risk of both deserting its scholarly roots and embracing just the surface of reality. I have addressed this problem in my response to Brenda Dervin's question 'How do you account for the field's many approaches, foci, methodologies, methods? Is this diversity strength or weakness?'[2] Both. But today I mostly warn about diversity turning into surfing. The rapidly expanded field has become more and more differentiated and the recent development of convergence has not stopped this tide. Rather the contrary, new media, the internet, etc., have given further grounds for specialized approaches in media studies, these often gaining the status of other major subjects and disciplines in academic nomenclature. With such a trend the field is both losing its healthy roots in basic disciplines (sociology, political science, linguistics, literature, etc.) and also becoming more and more dependent on empirical and practical aspects of reality. This means, typically, applied research serving existing institutions, i.e. administrative instead of critical research. It is an unhealthy illusion to celebrate the popularity of media studies with the distinction of an independent discipline or several disciplines. I would call for serious soul searching and critical examination of the identity of the field. It is time again to return to the crossroads of Schramm, Berelson *et al.*

In this situation there are indeed good reasons to return to the crossroads question discussed by Bernard Berelson (1959) and Wilbur Schramm (1959) in the late 1950s: is mass communication research really a discipline or just a field? I made an early excursion into this topic already in the 1960s on the basis of my experiences in the US – including personal interviews with Berelson, Schramm and Harold Lasswell (Nordenstreng, 1968). Since then this soul searching has been fed by indispensable material from the 'ferment in the field' exercise which George Gerbner as editor of the *Journal of Communication* mobilized in the early 1980s among colleagues to review the field from the point of view of research paradigms and their challenges – not least the challenge posed by leftist-critical thinking. The resulting special issue (summer 1983, vol. 33, no. 3) did not reveal any final truth about the state of the art, but it did serve as a welcome reminder of the need to periodically take a meta look at what we are doing. A new look at the ferment in the field was taken by the same journal ten years later (summer and autumn 1993, vol. 43, nos. 3 and 4), but that turned out to be just another panorama of the field 'between fragmentation and cohesion' (the title of the issue).

More of that ferment is exposed by histories of the field, whether of the whole international landscape (e.g. Pietilä, 2005), particular national arenas (e.g. *European Journal of Communication* 1990 special issue, 5:2–3), a focused area of journalism and mass communication (e.g. Leung *et al.*, 2006) or anthologies of the classics (e.g. Katz *et al.*, 2003; Peters and Simonson, 2004). A useful overview of the present global landscape was provided by Wolfgang Donsbach in his presidential address to the ICA conference in New York in 2005 (Donsbach, 2006). His first thesis is that communication as a research field has seen the greatest growth of probably all academic fields over the last thirty years, but he has a counter-thesis to problematize the growth perspective: 'Communication still lacks, and even loses, identity' (based on a survey of ICA members, pp. 439–43). His second thesis is that we have accumulated a lot of good empirical evidence on the communication process, while his counter-thesis admits: 'The field increasingly suffers from epistemological erosion' (pp. 444–6). Donsbach's third thesis says: 'We have precise and sound knowledge in many areas – but (counter-thesis) we tend to lose normative orientation in empirical research' (pp. 446–7). I fully agree with these points, the last of them included already in my reading of the field in the late 1960s (Nordenstreng, 1968).

The big picture over the past fifty years is that the field has indeed undergone an impressive expansion and consolidation. Instead of withering away as suggested by Berelson (1959), the field has seen a phenomenal growth which has brought communication and media studies to the centre of contemporary paradigms of socio-economic development, including the Information Society (e.g. Webster, 2006). As Gerbner (1983: 358) put it in the editor's epilogue to the ferment issue: 'if Marx were alive today, his principal work would be entitled *Communications* rather than *Capital*'.

But I do have mixed feelings about this success story. I see that the field, with all the expansion and diversity, runs the risk of becoming professionally self-centred and scientifically shallow. Therefore one of the first points I nowadays make in the introductory course to the most popular subject at my home university is what I call 'the paradox of media studies': our task is to deconstruct the naive view that communication is the core of society and thus we specialize in undoing media hubris.

Accordingly, there are good grounds to search for the identity of the field. Moreover, in addition to these reasons for soul searching, which stem from the field itself, Europe has an additional challenge for reform of its whole higher education system.

The challenge of Bologna

The site of Europe's oldest university has become a byword for the latest reform of higher education in this part of the world as a result of a declaration in 1999 by 29 ministers of education from various European countries. The Bologna Declaration confirmed an initiative taken one year earlier at the Sorbonne by the ministers of education of France, Germany, Italy and the UK. Bologna was followed up by even broader meetings of education ministers in Prague in 2001 and in Berlin in 2003, where the Bologna process was extended to 40 countries, including Russia and the Vatican. The latest ministerial meetings were hosted by Bergen in 2005 and London in 2007, with the number of countries increased to 46. The next meeting will be hosted by Leuven in 2009 (Benelux Bologna Secretariat, 2007).

This reform seeks to replace the different systems of higher education in European countries by a common 'European Higher Education Area' (EHEA) with increased mobility of students, teachers, researchers and administrative staff, and with easily readable and comparable degrees (using the 'European Credit Transfer System' [ECTS] and a Diploma Supplement). The reform boils down to a uniform degree structure with two main degrees, Bachelor's in 3 years and Master's in 1–2 more years, followed by a doctoral degree in 3–4 more years. The two-cycle basic degrees are supposed to create a competitive and attractive market for academic studies in Europe compared to the US.

What is called for is both a rejuvenation of the often outdated academic systems – as typically happened in France and elsewhere after 1968 – and a push for academic institutions to serve more directly the needs of the European labour market. The Berlin Communiqué refers to the EU's commitments from Lisbon (2000) and Barcelona (2002) aimed at making Europe 'the most competitive and dynamic knowledge-based economy in the world, capable of sustainable economic growth with more and better jobs and greater social cohesion'. But the Communiqué also stresses research and doctoral studies with a more ecumenical approach:

> Ministers agree that efforts shall be undertaken in order to secure closer links overall between the higher education and research systems in their respective countries. The emerging European Higher Education Area will benefit from synergies with the European Research Area, thus strengthening the basis of the Europe of Knowledge. The aim is to preserve Europe's cultural richness and linguistic diversity, based on its heritage of diversified traditions, and to foster its potential of innovation and social and economic development through enhanced co-operation among European Higher Education Institutions.

Moreover, the Communiqué declares in its preamble:

> Ministers reaffirm the importance of the social dimension of the Bologna Process. The need to increase competitiveness must be balanced with the objective of improving the social characteristics of the European Higher Education Area, aiming at strengthening social cohesion and reducing social and gender inequalities both at national and at European level. In that context, Ministers reaffirm their position that higher education is a public good and public responsibility. They emphasize that in international academic cooperation and exchanges, academic values should prevail.

Accordingly, the Bologna process includes positive elements from the point of view of critical and progressive interests. Yet it would be naive not to admit the overwhelming economic and market interest behind Bologna – a paradox given the name symbolizing institutions of free academia. The current Bologna process is indeed full of contradictions.

This is particularly true of media studies and communication research. Throughout Europe the field is rapidly moving to the two-tier degree system, which brings further ferment. Bologna invites – in practice compels – each major subject to rewrite its curriculum in terms of the two-tier degree BA–MA system, and in this process one cannot help defining the disciplinary profile and core elements of each subject. This will naturally lead to soul searching not only within each department but also at higher faculty or college level. Especially challenging prospects are provided by interdisciplinary programmes, which seem to become popular at the MA level, opening the possibility of combining different BA backgrounds and focusing on cutting-edge topics such as ICT and new media.

A survey in Scandinavia

An illustrative case of the state of the art is provided by the Scandinavian countries of Denmark, Finland, Norway and Sweden (this time excluding the fifth Nordic country, Iceland). Some years ago I suggested in the context of the biannual Nordic conferences a systematic survey of the concepts and terms by which the field of (mass) communication is defined in our universities. The motivation was both theoretical-intellectual in terms of the philosophy of science and practical-bureaucratic in terms of the names given to disciplines, departments and positions. Both aspects have become more and more intriguing with the development of new media, convergence and globalization. The field in this connection refers broadly to all approaches to media and communication within the humanities, social sciences and arts, apart from purely technical approaches, and it covers both research and education.

Such an inventory based on lists of all the relevant departments and disciplines to be found in the Nordic universities proved to be too ambitious to be completed as first planned by 2003. I underestimated the difficulties of ascertaining the disciplinary profiles from published materials and websites. I therefore started from what Nordicom had already compiled: a country-by-country listing of university programmes in the field, indicating for each its institutional frame (university, faculty, department), name of subject or discipline, level and length of programme, as well as keyword-type characterization of the programme content.[3] My preliminary survey[4] was based on this Nordicom mapping of the situation in 2002, and the following national characteristics are summarized from the latest update in 2006.

Sweden has nearly 20 institutions which offer BA/MA-level studies, 15 of them also MA programmes and six of them doctoral studies. Practically all of these use the same name for the discipline: 'media and communication science' (*medie-och kommunikationsvetenskap*, MKV). In addition there are eight journalism programmes. Nordicom's inventory of Swedish programmes does not include the institutions of film studies, nor those of library studies. Of all 20 institutions in Sweden, 11 are called universities in Swedish, while 9 are colleges with the Swedish name 'högskolan' (literally 'high school'). Most of these colleges translate their name as 'university' – quite confusing as the status of these colleges is inferior to that of proper universities; for example, they do not have the right to grant doctoral degrees.

Finland has 10 universities which offer BA/MA + PhD programmes either in media or, beyond media, in speech communication, organizational communication or library and information studies – generally designated as 'communication sciences' (*viestintätieteet*). The number of different departments or institutes in these universities is 17 and the total number of programmes or disciplines is 22. Outside these are non-university-level polytechnics (misleadingly calling themselves 'universities of applied science'), which offer nearly 20 programmes in media and communication, not least related to new media. Finnish university programmes have no common name for the discipline; several labels are used, each with a specific meaning determined by the history of the academic subject and its professorship.

Norway used to have only 4 institutions in 2001, with 'media science' (*medievitenskap*) as the national discipline label, except for one with 'film science' (*filmvitenskap*). In addition, there were several institutions for professional journalism and library studies. But by 2006 9 regional institutions of higher education, called 'högskolen' and translated in English as 'university colleges', have entered the field so that the latest Norwegian count is 13 institutions with a variety of discipline labels such as 'media studies' (*mediefag*), 'digital media technology', 'film and TV production'.

Denmark has 5 institutions but no common label for the discipline. 'Media science' (*medievidenskap*) is used in Aarhus and South Denmark, 'film and media science' (*film og medievidenskap*) in Copenhagen, 'communication' (*kommunikation*) in Aalborg and Roskilde, while the labels 'multi-media' and 'humanistic informatics' are also used. Other pre-university institutions/programmes offer education for professional journalism and librarianship.

In general, the Nordic landscape of the academic discipline gives rise to the following observations.

The field in Sweden and Finland is institutionally quite abundant and diverse. In these countries the discipline is represented in the faculties of both the humanities and the social sciences, and those fairly evenly. Moreover, Finland also brings to the field the faculty of art and design (Helsinki, Rovaniemi), while Sweden's list includes a technical university. Sweden has a nationally used umbrella term for the discipline in contrast to Finland's anarchic terminology. However, this terminological difference may be more cosmetic than real.

Denmark and Norway have fewer institutions and programmes, although Norway has increased its supply. In these two countries the discipline is mostly administered by the faculty of humanities, but the actual study programmes and research activities display more or less a balance between humanities and social sciences. Actually, the difference between humanities and social sciences appears to be largely artificial and obsolete in this discipline.

The true nature of the discipline is revealed only through a careful examination of its historical evolution and its institutional position in each case. There is no shortcut to map out the disciplinary landscape; a proper survey requires thorough knowledge of the respective national territory. Such an in-depth survey is still waiting to be carried out.

The current challenge posed by new information technologies, on the one hand, and the Bologna process, on the other, has led most institutions and programmes in the field to critically assess the foundations of their discipline. Regardless of such reflection, institutional changes occur, notably mergers between classic humanistic media studies and (post)modern information sciences, as experienced in Denmark and Norway in the first years of the new millennium.

The last-mentioned changes are symptomatic of a more general trend, well known in the USA, where multimedia and digital media are no longer designators for a pilot speciality but part and parcel of mainstream media studies. Take the Department of Information and Media Studies at the University of Aarhus, Faculty of Humanities. This is how it describes its departmental profile (see http://www.imv.au.dk/eng/unit/presentation):

> The research and teaching at the Institute fall broadly within the scope of Information and Media Studies. The institutional research in Information Studies includes historical, sociological, communicative, and design-oriented approaches to the study of the development and application of information technology on the level of individuals, organizations and society. Institutional research in Media Studies includes projects concerning production aesthetics, textual analysis and reception within print media, radio, TV, film and the internet, as well as topics concerning the theory, policy, history, and institution of the media. Between these two fields, where information and media studies increasingly meet, research is carried out in areas such as IT and Learning, the Internet, and Multimedia.

This profile is clearly more technology-oriented than the earlier programme of Media Studies, which grew out of Nordic Literature. A reorientation was natural, given the fact that the department incorporated a branch of computer science.[5] A similar merger was recently carried out in Bergen, motivated by the new media society and prospects of convergence.[6] On the other hand, such a merger did not materialize at the University of Tampere in Finland, where a new Faculty of Information Sciences was established, with Computer Science and Information Studies brought under the same umbrella. Journalism and Mass Communication was invited to join the new faculty, but it preferred to remain in the Faculty of Social Sciences, alongside Sociology and Political Science, rather than move into what it considered too much of a 'bits and bytes faculty'.[7]

By and large, this survey of Scandinavia presents a fairly typical picture of contemporary media studies worldwide. It leads us to reflect on the nature of the discipline in greater detail – both regarding contemporary media studies and regarding the status of academic disciplines in general.

Nature of media studies

As suggested in my response to Brenda Dervin's survey above, lack of scientific depth follows all too easily from an eclectic and multidisciplinary approach. Both are important as such for the healthy evolution of a discipline, but in a rapid pace of development they may become too dominant and offset the foundations of the body of knowledge. Such a 'surfing syndrome' applies particularly to studies of fashionable topics such as information technology. As a matter of fact, information technology tends to lead not only to excessive eclecticism but also to the neglect of other phenomena. I have introduced the term 'Nokia syndrome' to refer to the risks of a fashionable dominance of technology.[8]

A particular problem in the field is its own scientific identity and its genealogical nature, not least regarding the concept of communication. Within the field, communication is typically understood as the constituting factor of related studies and disciplines, whereby various aspects of human communication – from speech and organizational communication to different media – have their specialities, which are based on this core concept and its foundational theory.[9] However, it is by no means self-evident that communication should be taken as the core of related disciplines. True, communication may be understood as the essence of social relations, and society may be understood not only as something held together by the 'glue' of communication but also as something that itself is made up of communication in the Luhmannian sense. On the other hand, communication can be seen merely as camouflage distracting attention from more fundamental levels such as economics or socio-political power structures. This latter perspective does not support the idea of communication studies as an independent discipline or a group of disciplines united by the foundational concept of communication; it rather takes communication as a complementary aspect of more fundamental factors and thus communication studies as a loosely constructed field.

The question about the nature of communication and the related problem of discipline vs. field is far from settled and therefore should be actively discussed instead of being brushed under the carpet, either by overlooking it or by addressing it with clichés. Pursuing this and other issues raised above leads us ultimately to the philosophy of science – asking how scientific knowledge is constructed and organized, and what are the principles which designate sciences and disciplines. This examination includes the well-known distinctions between basic and applied research: whereas basic sciences are supposed to describe, explain and help to understand, applied sciences are supposed first and foremost to predict; the basic sciences tell us what *is* and predictive applied sciences tell us what *will be*. In addition to these two main types, there is an often overlooked form of applied science which tells us what *ought to be* so that we can attain a given goal. These 'design sciences' are not supposed to produce true or false knowledge, or to predict correctly what will happen, but to enhance human skills and to generate instrumental knowledge for the manipulation of both natural and artificial systems – something that is highly relevant in communication studies.

The distinction between critical and administrative research cuts across both basic and applied sciences, including design sciences. These categories should not be vulgarized by identifying critical research only with basic theorizing and administrative research only with applied data gathering and processing. Both theoretical and empirical research can be critical as well as administrative, and critical scholars should be particularly wary of simplistic labelling of this or that orientation.

Consequently, I make a strong claim for the philosophy of science in order to deal with the concept of communication and its relation to the system of sciences. At the same time I call for continuous study of the history of ideas in the field. However young the field, and however burning the challenges of the day, it is vital to realize how it has evolved and how it relates to other fields of research. Being aware of one's own research tradition is a precondition for the organic growth of science – and a medicine against the 'surfing syndrome'.

Accordingly, all masters-level communication study programmes should have a module on the history of the field and on the nature of the discipline. Likewise, all established institutions of communication studies should maintain some research on research, not only by mapping out the development of their research agenda, both in terms of topics and underlining paradigms, but also by examining the nature of the field.[10]

Challenging academic disciplines

With all its expansion and diversity the field has given rise to a growing category of researchers and their associations (at the global level the IAMCR http://www.iamcr.org/, see Nordenstreng, 2008). President François Heinderyckx (2007) of the European Communication Research and Education Association (ECREA, http://www.ecrea.eu/) has fittingly characterized the field by dividing its scholars into two camps: 'communication natives', who were trained by communication departments and hold their degrees, and 'communication migrants', who were trained in other disciplines and brought to communication by their research interests and projects. Five decades after Berelson's 'obituary' of communication research and Schramm's defence of the field's vitality, the president of a rapidly growing European association reminds us that not only has the field survived and developed into a distinct area of scholarship but it also remains a crossroads for migrants from various other fields. As a whole the communication research community is 'an open club', and becoming a communication researcher is 'a self-affiliation process' (Heinderyckx, 2007: 360).

Heinderyckx (2007) points out that being a 'communication scientist' does not constitute a recognized category and that even the 'natives' are far from a coherent and homogenous group. 'In fact, communication may not be a discipline in the classic institutional sense of the word, not even in the making' (ibid.: 359). Instead, the field suffers from 'an academic identity crisis'. The crisis is both intellectual, given the internal divisions of a multidisciplinary field, and administrative, given an underdog position when competing for funding with the established disciplines. The identity crisis may be a permanent feature of the field and it can even be seen as 'the secret of our remarkable capacity to innovate, to renew research and to keep pace with the rapid evolution of our objects' (ibid.). On the other hand, such a field is particularly vulnerable to the current general trend towards applied research with short-term benefits, with researchers expected to behave 'more and more as experts and less and less as scholars' (ibid.: 362).

So we are back to the 'Nokia syndrome'. But we are also back to the conflict between 'ivy league' disciplines and 'Mickey Mouse' studies. And this conflict is not only about struggle over resources and students but also fundamentally about the intellectual power in determining what is and what is not a legitimate academic discipline. Cultural studies – a still younger candidate entering the family of arts and sciences – has experienced a lot of resistance from the established disciplines. A series of testimonies on cultural studies and the politics of disciplinarity (Nelson and Parameshwar Gaonkar, 1996) provides a telling story of how 'disciplines police their boundaries, by training their members to internalize them, neutralize them, and then fancy themselves free as birds' (ibid.: 3).

Media studies, like cultural studies, serves as an exemplary case of a more general question regarding the nature of academic cultures as 'tribes' defending their disciplinary territories (Becher and Trowler, 2001). Media studies invites us also to consider the fundamental issue of scientific enquiry and the system of sciences – including multidisciplinarity, interdisciplinarity and crossdisciplinarity (e.g. Gieryn, 1999; Moran, 2002). And a real challenge is provided by historical reviews of the social sciences from the eighteenth century to the twenty-first century (Wallerstein, 1999; Wallerstein, 1996). In such a crude reality the disciplinary landscape is shaped by 'academics as social animals' (Becher and Towler, 2001, 161):

> The tribes of academia, one might argue, define their own identities and defend their own patches of intellectual ground by employing a variety of devices geared to the exclusion of illegal immigrants. [...] To be admitted to membership of a particular sector of the academic profession involves not only a sufficient level of technical proficiency in one's intellectual trade but also a proper measure of loyalty to one's collegial group and of adherence to its norms.
>
> (ibid.: 47)

Nevertheless, disciplines are not completely determined by powers outside the scientific substance and method. Although shaped by power games with political and commercial factors, academic disciplines still retain a more or less pure intellectual rationale. Admittedly, this rationale is not based on a transcendental interest in universal truth but is historically constructed to generate knowledge for a particular stage of socio-economic-cultural development, notably modernization in the Western world from the eighteenth century to the present day. But all the same academic disciplines represent a degree of intellectual autonomy, which leaves some ground for academic idealism and reforms instead of succumbing to defeatism and reductionism.

Media studies as an academic discipline has a fairly advantageous position in the middle of this conflicting landscape. Despite pressures from the 'ivy league' disciplines, media studies has enough scientific substance to defend its existence in the intellectual realm; it is undeniably a mixed bag with a rich multidisciplinary legacy, but its centrality in social sciences and humanities is indisputable. It also has a lot of administrative bonuses on its side in the contemporary world given its popularity, especially among the younger generation, and its resonance within the media industry.

Like media as an institution, media studies as an academic discipline or field is also largely international by its very nature. Therefore there is no need for a separate excursion on the international level; all the foregoing applies to both national and international perspectives. In the context of the present chapter we may even say that internationalizing is an imperative inherent in media studies. And it is particularly the intellectual realm of scientific enquiry that is immanently international, while the administrative power game is a typically local and national phenomenon. Consequently, the greater the internationalism, the higher the scientific level.

Notes

1 This chapter is based on the author's two earlier articles: 'Ferment in the Field: Notes on the Evolution of Communication Studies and Their Disciplinary Nature', published in 2004 in the journal *Javnost – The Public* 10(3): 5–18 (special issue 'New Perspectives on Critical Communication Studies'), available at http://www.uta.fi/jour/laitos/nordenstrenge.html; 'Field or Discipline? Soul-Searching in Communication Research', published in *Nordicom Review*, Jubilee Issue 2007: 211–22, available at http://www.nordicom.gu.se/common/publ_pdf/248_248_nordenstreng1.pdf.

2 Brenda Dervin provided an insightful addition to historical reflections about the field in a survey for the 2004 ICA conference in New Orleans on 'Navigating Methodological Divides in the Communication Field'; see Dervin and Song (2004).

3 'Utbildningar i medie-och kommunikationsämnen vid universitet och högskolor in Norden' (2001), published in a slightly abridged form in 2002 by *Nordicom Information*, 24(4): 105–11. (For Nordicom publications, see http://www.nordicom.gu.se/eng.php?portal = publ.) A second useful source was 'Utvärdering av medie-och kommunikationsvetenskapliga utbildningar vid svenska universitet och högskolor', the evaluation report of Sweden's media and communication study programmes, produced in 2001 by the Swedish Högskoleverket with an appendix overview of media and communication education in other Nordic countries, based on the same Nordicom survey. An updated list of institutions and programmes of media and communication studies in the Nordic countries is published by *Nordicom Information* each year in issue number 3.

4 First presented as the paper 'Disciplines of Media and Communication – A Survey of the Field' at the 16th Nordic Conference of Media and Communication Research (Kristiansand, Norway, August 2003) in Working Group 25: Media Theories – Media Studies – Media Research.

5 An interesting – even ironic – aspect of this case is the fact that the department has been headed by Professor Frands Mortensen, who was Denmark's leading leftist scholar of communication in the late 1960s and the early 1970s. He and other young scholars were instrumental in importing Habermas, Negt and Kluge to Scandinavia, and Finns, for instance, got to know continental radicalism largely via Denmark. Mortensen has since continued to pursue media studies with a critical approach – no longer something that is dubbed 'radical', however. In any case, neither he nor anybody else would have imagined even in their wildest dreams in the 1960s that one day he would be the most senior professor at a department focusing on information technology in a fairly affirmative way.

6 The new Department of Information Science and Media Studies (Institutt for informasjons- og medievitenskap) is located, like the earlier Department of Media Studies, in both the Faculty of Arts and the Faculty of Social Sciences. The first head of the merged department is Professor Jostein Gripsrud, one of Scandinavia's leading critical media scholars.

7 A status quo solution regarding the faculty reform in 2001 did not mean that Journalism and Mass Communication wanted to avoid new media, digitization, convergence, etc. On the contrary, the department (http://www.uta.fi/laitokset/tiedotus/index1.html) was the first in Finland to introduce Master's programmes in this area and its Journalism Research and Development Centre (http://www.uta.fi/jourtutkimus/english.html) has focused largely on projects around new media. Regarding Information Studies, earlier named 'Library Science and Informatics', it also used to belong to the Faculty of Social Sciences, but unlike Journalism and Mass Communication, it decided to move to the new Faculty of Information Sciences.

8 Nokia is a perfect label to be used by someone coming from Tampere; the Finnish company started in the late nineteenth century in Nokia, a little township next to Tampere. The company, which adopted the name of its place of origin, began in wood processing, moving soon to rubber boots and later to car tyres and electric cables, followed by mobile phones as late as the 1980s. Now none of Nokia Corporation's business is located in the town of Nokia, whereas a good share of its R&D activity has landed in Tampere, next to the academic community.

9 This is manifested in colleges or schools of communication, which typically include departments of speech, journalism, radio/TV, PR and advertising. In Finland the idea of communication as a unifying concept in higher education and research is concretely suggested by the fact that there are several and different kinds of university departments concerned with communication and media at the graduate and postgraduate level – nearly 20 units in 10 universities – and that these departments have established a network for cooperation, University Network for Communication Sciences; see http://viesverk.uta.fi//index.php?option=com_contentandtask=sectionandid= 88888899andItemid = 88888967.

10 An exemplary project in this respect has been carried out at the University of Aarhus, Department of Information and Media Studies: 'Theories of Media and Communication – Histories and Relevance' sought to highlight the theory of the field – meta-theory – as a special area of study; see Brügger (2003) and http://www.medieteori.dk/english/.

References

Becher, Tony and Trowler, Paul (2001) *Academic Tribes and Territories: Intellectual Enquiry and the Culture of Disciplines*. Buckingham: Open University Press, second edn.

Benelux Bologna Secretariat (2007) Bologna Process Website, http://www.ond.vlaanderen.be/hogeronderwijs/bologna/.

Berelson, Bernard (1959) The State of Communication Research, *Public Opinion Quarterly*, 23(1): 1–6.

Brügger, Niels (2003) *Theories of Media and Communication: Histories and Relevance*. Aarhus: University of Aarhus, Department of Information and Media Studies. Online at http://www.medieteori.dk/publikationer/001_bruegger.pdf.

Dervin, Brenda and Song, M. (eds) (2004) Communication as a Field – Historical Origins, Diversity as Strength/Weakness, Orientation toward Research in the Public Interest. Background paper for the 'Strength of Our Methodological Divides: Five Navigators, Their Struggles and Successes plenary and post-plenary dialogue, International Communication Association annual meeting, 27–31 May, New Orleans, LA. Online at http://communication.sbs.ohio-state.edu/sense-making/artdirect/artdervinsong04ica.html.

Donsbach, Wolfgang (2006) The Identity of Communication Research, *Journal of Communication*, 56(3): 437–48.

Gerbner, George (1983) The Importance of Being Critical – In One's Own Fashion, *Journal of Communication*, 33(3): 355–62.

Gieryn, Thomas (1999) *Cultural Boundaries of Science: Credibility on the Line*. Chicago: University of Chicago Press.

Heinderyckx, François (2007) The Academic Identity Crisis of the European Communication Researcher, in Nico Carpentier, Pille Pruulmann-Vengerfeldt, Kaarle Nordenstreng, Maren Hartmann, Peeter Vihalemm, Bart Cammaerts and Hannu Nieminen (eds) *Media Technologies and Democracy in an Enlarged Europe*. Tartu: Tartu University Press, pp. 357–62.

Katz, Elihu, Peters, John Durham, Liebes, Tamar and Orloff, Avril (eds) (2003) *Canonic Texts in Media Research: Are There Any? Should There Be? How About These?*. Cambridge: Polity.

Leung, Kenneth, Kenny, James and Lee, Paul S.N. (eds) (2006) *Global Trends in Communication Education and Research*. Cresskill, NJ: Hampton Press.

Moran, Joe (2002) *Interdisciplinarity*. London: Routledge.

Nelson, Cary and Parameshwar Gaonkar, Dilip (eds) (1996) Cultural Studies and the Politics of Disciplinarity: An Introduction, in Cary Nelson and Dilip Parameshwar Gaonkar (eds) *Disciplinarity and Dissent in Cultural Studies*. New York: Routledge, pp. 1–19.

Nordenstreng, Kaarle (1968) Communication Research in the United States: A Critical Perspective, *Gazette*, 14(3): 207–16. Online at http://www.uta.fi/laitokset/tiedotus/laitos/Gazette1968.pdf, accompanied by original interviews as MP3 files – interview with Bernard Berelson, interview with Harold Lasswell.

—— (2008) Institutional Networking: The Story of the International Association for Media and Communication Research (IAMCR), in David Park and Jefferson Pooley (eds) *The History of Media and Communication Research: Contested Memories*. New York: Peter Lang, pp. 225–48. Online at http://www.uta.fi/laitokset/tiedotus/laitos/Nordenstreng.pdf.

Peters, John Durham and Simonson, Peter (eds) (2004) *Mass Communication and Social Thought: Key Texts 1919–1968*. Lanham, MD: Rowman and Littlefield.

Pietilä, Veikko (2005) *On the Highway of Mass Communication Studies*. Cresskill, NJ: Hampton Press.

Schramm, Wilbur (1959) Comments on Berelson's Article, *Public Opinion Quarterly*, 23(1): 6–9.

Wallerstein, Immanuel (1996) *Open the Social Sciences: Report of the Gulbenkian Commission on the Restructuring of the Social Sciences*. Stanford, CA: Stanford University Press.

—— (1999) *The End of the World as We Know It: Social Science for the Twenty-First Century*. Minneapolis: University of Minnesota Press.

Webster, Frank (2006) *Theories of the Information Society*. London: Routledge, third edition.

Chapter 17

International media studies in the US academy

A sampling of programmes and textbooks[1]

John D.H. Downing

I am presenting here a preliminary analysis of the coverage of international and global communication in (1) the teaching programmes of a number of US universities, and (2) some of the most widely used introductory media studies textbooks for undergraduates. The significance of these findings lies in the considerable hegemony that US university communication programmes wield across the planet, given the number of departments globally which have been founded and staffed by doctoral graduates of those programmes. Equally, these introductory foundation textbooks and degree courses will shape US undergraduates' framing of this field, as they either graduate in the field or retain a memory of those priorities and issues while pursuing other academic pathways. In their subsequent professional careers, too, in or out of the communication industries or the academy, these formative influences will in many cases continue to exert a pull.

In this study I have focused on the extent to which global media issues are or are not taught, or how far they are engaged with in introductory textbooks, within the United States. I have not, however, engaged with a critique of the detailed content of courses and textbooks covering these issues, which would be a worthwhile but mammoth task.

Methodology

The procedures I adopted, and some of the complications I encountered in following them, were as follows. For university programmes, I chose eight private universities[2] generally recognized as among the top campuses in the US, and eight public universities[3] with a similarly high reputation, either across the board or in one or more branches of communication scholarship and teaching. My reasoning was that leading universities, or university programmes, typically exert a considerable influence over the formation of academic programmes nationally. My decision was also based on a subsidiary research question, namely the extent to which the 'top-of-the-tree' campuses have engaged with this field or have shunned it, at least in their teaching programmes.

The complications included the following. (1) Not all webpages are born equal, at least as regards their layout and level of detail. (2) Some programmes may be currently under development and renewal, such as my own at Southern Illinois, and this process may not have gelled sufficiently to be put on the website. (3) In some cases, where the university bureaucracy grinds exceedingly slowly in the endorsement of new course topics, a standard response is to create one or more 'Special Topics' courses that only have to be approved by the department, but which may run for years without being specifically named in the catalogue (such is the case at the University of Texas, Austin). (4) Some webpages provide the curriculum semester by semester, others the curriculum as a whole, with the result that in the former case the course listings may be under-represented, while in the latter there may be courses on the books that are rarely if ever taught. (5) In many communication programmes, there are a substantial number of practicum and 'learning-by-doing' courses, whose descriptions focus on the 'hands-on' content, but which may or may not incorporate attention to global communication issues of one kind or another. It is to be hoped that they would, and that these issues are not simply the preserve of media analysis courses, but in the nature of things such decisions are usually left to the individual instructor, so it is impossible to ascertain how far international issues surface. (6) There is, predictably, a categorization problem in this area: does a course with 25 per cent or more international content get classified as international, and even if the answer is yes, how can one tell this from the routine three-line course summaries that are to be found on university webpages? And finally (7), as noted, this initial mapping cannot provide information for a detailed critique and mapping of typical course content, which only a study of specific syllabi could enable.

As regards introductory textbooks, there is a convenient web source, Faculty Online,[4] which lists the US campuses using each book, as well as the number of editions each one has gone through and the date of its most recent edition. Both these last indices are very helpful in filling out the picture of both the longevity and the currency of the textbooks in question. Faculty Online is a free service provided by Monument Information Resource, which in turn is a project of R.R. Bowker, a long-established US firm that amongst other activities establishes the ISBN numbers for all books published in the US. Faculty Online surveys over twelve hundred US university and college campuses. The webpage also frequently provides short summaries of chapter content, if provided by the publisher.

As regards complications in using this source, occasionally Faculty Online's data may be slightly out of date, and sometimes books are listed as basic textbooks introducing media studies which are really monographs, such as Herman and Chomsky's *Manufacturing Consent*. Furthermore, quite a proportion of the textbooks listed are on topics such as media ethics, public relations, advertising, and media law. Although their international content would be interesting to study, insofar as it exists, a cursory examination suggested to me that this category of textbook rarely if ever ventures outside the US. I have therefore excluded them from this study. The data here were initially researched and compiled in early autumn 2006.

The private universities

Of the private universities surveyed, four – New York University, Northwestern University, Stanford, and the University of Southern California – boasted Communication Departments. In Columbia there was just a graduate Journalism School, and Yale had just a Film Studies programme – though the Columbia Journalism teaching faculty had substantial international experience, and the Yale film programme was quite heavily oriented towards world cinema. Harvard and Princeton had nothing by way of a department (as no doubt befits aged and sclerotic institutions whose existing professoriate ferociously guards its turf). NYU, Northwestern, Stanford and USC are of course relative latecomers compared to the Ivy League schools. Of those four, Stanford had the smallest programme, one department of nine permanent faculty; Northwestern had a School of Communication and a School of Journalism; NYU had no less than five departments or programmes across three schools,[5] and USC had a huge School of Cinema and Television, mostly professionally oriented, plus the very sizeable Annenberg School for Communication with over 40 permanent faculty, as well as the Annenberg School of Journalism.

It is sometimes possible to find communication courses, and more specifically, in terms of our focus here, courses on international communication, in other programmes. Harvard, for example, has some 27 communication courses scattered across a number of different programmes, including one on global media, and some others on health and development communication which have a degree of international content.[6] Columbia's School of International and Public Affairs listed a couple on global media, out of 189 registered courses all told on a great range of global topics. However, Yale's International Studies programme listed no courses at all on this topic out of the 45 taught, and nor did its long-running MA in International and Development Economics. The Woodrow Wilson School of Public and International Affairs at Princeton had a single undergraduate course on media and public policy, and while 18 out of 52 listed courses were international in scope, none touched upon communication issues. The Princeton University French Department averaged one course each in five foreign language departments (French ½ a course, German 1, Russian 1, Italian 1½, Spanish 1½), all on film. The Programme on Visual Arts had two, while East Asian Studies, Japanese, African Studies, and even Media and Modernity, all had zero. The tiny Journalism programme, however, had five courses in total, out of which one was on comparative objectivity/accuracy issues, and a second on reporting on repressive regimes.

To turn to the private universities that do sport communication departments, Stanford had around 45 courses per quarter, of which one in the autumn 2006 quarter was on comparative journalism. Its Janet M. Peck Chair in International Communication, James Fishkin, is a specialist on deliberative democracy and has conducted research on that topic in seven or more countries, but in terms of the curriculum – disputed though the specific merits of their contributions may be – the research focus of Wilbur Schramm and Everett Rogers on global communication has virtually evaporated.

Northwestern University, a major private university near Chicago, has a substantial School of Communication and the renowned Medill School of Journalism. In the former, the Radio-Television-Film department offered two globally focused undergraduate courses out of 19 in total, and the Communication Studies department two out of 63. Out of the seven required courses in their joint PhD programme, one global course was stipulated. The Medill School offered zero international journalism courses at the undergraduate level, though required one course in International Studies. Its Master's degree provided for ten-week residencies in foreign newsrooms, but offered no international courses as such.

The two privates that take this focus seriously were New York University and the University of Southern California. NYU's Cinema Studies Department offered two out of 22 courses on global media topics (data for spring 2007). However, nearly half of its 14 faculty had an international focus to their own research, so we might be safe in assuming their courses would often reflect this expertise. The enormous and very famous Maurice Kanbar Institute of Film and Television, whose emphasis is overwhelmingly on 'how-to' courses, was offering two undergraduate courses, out of 41, on global media issues, and none in its graduate programme. Out of 39 'how-to' courses in the Interactive Telecommunications Programme, there were precisely zero focused on any global issue.

In the Culture and Communication Department, founded by the late Neil Postman, things perked up, with seven of 55 undergraduate courses on global themes, plus two of 21 graduate courses, and a further two six-credit international summer schools. The NYU Journalism School offered three composite Master's programmes with other units, in Latin American and Caribbean Studies, Near Eastern Studies and French Studies. However, its specialist graduate programme in Science, Health and Environmental Reporting made no mention of international issues; nor did its Cultural Reporting and Criticism specialization, or its Business and Economic Reporting specialization. At the undergraduate level, none of the Journalism School's required courses focused on international topics.

The globalist gorilla among the private campuses, however, is the University of Southern California. The Annenberg School for Communication had no fewer than 20 out of 65 courses at three levels on international issues, including Global Organizational Communication, Global Culture, National Development,

Global Edutainment, International Entertainment Industries, and Globalization and Culture. Sometimes standard Communication Policy, Law or Economics courses noted global issues as an element, and sometimes they were focused, for instance a course on Communication Policy in the Global Marketplace or on the Political Economy of Global Telecommunications and Information.

In the School of Cinema and Television's Critical Studies Department, two courses on international cinema were required at both undergraduate and graduate levels, out of a total programme of 58 undergraduate and grad courses. Three other 'generic rubric' international or comparative courses were also listed. The Journalism School was rather more fixated on domestic dimensions, with only seven out of 106 courses focused on some aspect of international issues.

Summarizing these eight leading private US universities, we could say the following. (1) The more encrusted the campus, the less likely it was to have Communication Studies anywhere, let alone as a department, and therefore the less likely to address global media issues. (2) The campuses running international studies programmes very rarely featured courses on international communication topics. (3) Courses in world cinema were more likely to be found than on any other topic. (4) Journalism programmes tended to be overwhelmingly domestic in focus.

The public universities

Historically in the public universities of the US, journalism programmes and public speaking/rhetoric programmes[7] have been nurtured 'officially' as educational supports for a functioning, participative democracy that absorbs talent from those not born with silver spoons in their mouths. Not surprisingly, then, such programmes are much more visible and normal in public universities than on the older private campuses. (I say 'officially' – I am not making claims here concerning the actual democratic role of US universities, which is a much more contested issue.)

The three largest state flagship campuses are Texas (Austin), Minnesota (Minneapolis) and Ohio State (Columbus), in descending order. Texas has a very large College of Communication, with over 120 faculty, 4,000 students, and five departments. International Communication was mostly taught in the Radio-Television-Film Department, and was offered as a specialized course at the introductory undergraduate level and on up through higher undergraduate and graduate levels. Six out of 29 faculty, including two teaching film production, had substantial international interests, and a few others shared these interests in part. Because of the rather inflexible procedures for approving new courses, as noted earlier, the official course schedule did not fully reflect this heavy international dimension. The Journalism School at Texas offered two international courses at undergraduate level (out of 37 total), and two at graduate level (out of 14 total).

Distressingly, however, the other two huge campuses offered virtually nothing in the international field. The Communication Studies Department at Minnesota offered 36 undergraduate courses but not one on global communication, and the Journalism and Mass Communication Department offered just one out of 43 listed overall. At Ohio State University, 54 courses were listed at undergraduate and graduate levels, with not a single one on global media issues.

The Institute of Communication Research at the University of Illinois at Urbana-Champaign (also founded by Wilbur Schramm) offered three undergraduate international courses out of a total of 29, and one at graduate level out of a total of 11, in autumn 2006. The University of Wisconsin at Madison offered seven out of 74 in total in the Communication Arts Department, mostly on world cinema; and five out of 55 in the Journalism and Mass Communication Department. My own College of Mass Communication and Media Arts at Southern Illinois University, Carbondale, with a 40-year-old doctoral programme, was in the process of expanding its international focus substantially. It officially ran five international courses out of 105 in the three undergraduate departmental programmes, and two such courses out of 39 at the College's MA, MS, MFA and PhD levels. Its profile neatly illustrates some of the methodological issues raised earlier,[8] especially as regards 'general rubric' Special Topics courses.

The highly respected Journalism schools at the University of California, Berkeley and the University of Missouri differed somewhat from each other in this respect. Berkeley ran two courses out of a total of 32 on international topics, whereas Missouri ran two out of 64. Missouri also has a small Communication Department, offering 42 undergraduate courses, yet none focused on international issues.

Summarizing the picture in these eight public universities with large Communication and Journalism programmes, we may say (1) that 'Communication Studies' programmes (in the restricted sense) seemed the least likely to show curricular interest in the world outside the United States. The only format in which they did so on a routine basis was in the study of what is called Intercultural Communication, which in practice veers between (a) the study, through highly empiricist methods, of interpersonal and organizational communication in culturally diverse settings, and (b) 'cookbook courses' for future executives to advise them how not to sour a foreign business deal by such ill-conceived actions as burping at business lunches (or, perhaps, failing to).

We may say (2) that, while acknowledging the difficulty of judging precisely what students are exposed to on a routine basis from the website versions of academic programmes, the percentage of internationally focused Communication, Media Studies and Journalism courses on these eight campuses appeared to vary for the most part between 5 and 10 per cent. Some, such as Texas, had a higher percentage, though two standout failures or near-failures in this regard were the very large Minnesota and Ohio State campuses, and the two Missouri programmes.

Questions left unanswered to date concern further key issues such as (1) the proportion of required international courses to optional ones; and (2) the relevance of overseas placements/internships, either as stand-alone opportunities or as linked to analytical coursework.

Introductory media studies textbooks

Just as we could not provide a critical evaluation of detailed course content from the data surveyed, so too this initial mapping exercise can only establish *whether* global media issues are addressed in some of the most widely selling textbooks, but not how. However, this is one way of ascertaining across many campuses the extent to which international communication topics were put on undergraduate students' agendas – and in turn, obviously, the degree to which their instructors thought this important, or not. I restricted myself to textbooks published in fresh editions since 1999.

The introductory textbooks used in 408 colleges and universities did not, from their publicity chapter summaries, engage with international issues. The 408 figure was dominated by one textbook, which accounted for 106 of these sites. There were a further five textbooks, used in 104 colleges or universities, which addressed global issues in a single chapter, normally the last, 'tack-on' chapter, or in one case as significant parts of a couple of chapters. It is important to realize that many of these textbooks have gone through multiple editions, some as many as eight (the case of the 106-campus textbook mentioned, for instance), and the practice of tacking on chapters about currently faddish topics – gender, 'race', war, international communication, video games – is popular among textbook publishers. They can then exploit students whom their instructors tell to buy the latest edition, not the previous one, available second-hand. It is also the case that instructors do not necessarily use all chapters, especially if their number exceeds the number of weeks in the semester, so in some courses that token gesture towards the global may never be taken up at all.

There were three introductory textbooks used on at least 64 campuses which did engage consistently with global issues,[9] and a further seven which focused specifically on global media issues (though in one or two cases on a generous interpretation). These latter were used currently on 168 campuses, which is the most encouraging news out of this otherwise rather dispiriting survey. It is almost certain, however, that they are mostly used in specialist elective courses, not as part of a standard introduction to the field.[10]

Conclusions

There is likely to be a considerable parallel between communication courses and texts and those in sociology, political science, history, education, psychology, and perhaps other areas. I doubt that communication teaching is unique in the US in its overwhelming focus on domestic issues. This most likely being the case, the findings here are part of a broader tapestry which contains considerable implications for the outlook on the rest of the world among *university-educated* citizens of the US. There were certainly important exceptions in the Communication field, which have been noted and for which we need to be grateful, but it is evident that the trend is strongly in the direction of insularity rather than internationalism.[11]

Some of the most prestigious and/or largest universities are central actors in the continuing construction of this unnerving deficit. It is a deficit which plausibly has immense implications for the readiness of many university-educated US citizens – in other words, cultural leaders in their communities – to endorse or at least tolerate the long succession of foreign wars in which US administrations have engaged, directly or by proxy, since the Second World War (e.g. Korea, Vietnam, Lebanon, Angola, Afghanistan, Nicaragua, El Salvador, Kosovo, Iraq).[12] To be sure, American students were very energetically active in opposition to the Vietnam war, once conscription was expanded to their ranks. But, in general, insularity reigns.

The exceptions, as I have suggested elsewhere (Downing, 1990), are to be found in two circles within the US: (a) the foreign policy establishment, whose official mission it is to study the rest of the world, for whom the journals *Foreign Affairs* and *Foreign Policy* are standard reading; and (b) the establishment's penumbra, meaning principally readers of *Time*, *Newsweek*, the *New York Times*, the *Los Angeles Times*.

It is at this point that the simple dichotomy between knowledge of and interest in the rest of the world and insular, university-formed ignorance of the rest of the world, has to be qualified. Where detailed international information *is* available in the US to those citizens eager to hunt it out, it is largely framed within the priorities and dictates of successive US administrations' foreign policy. As Herman and Chomsky (1988) have argued, policy rifts do appear within the US corporate and government establishment that in turn often open up rival interpretations and competing information sources on foreign affairs within mainstream news media. Yet the core presumption of the contending parties is typically the same, namely how what *they* define as US global interests may best prevail? Within this US-centred framework, attention to the legitimate interests of the rest of the planet is a tactical matter, in no way a matter of real significance. Thus 'mere knowledge' of the rest of the planet through university courses and textbooks, though crucial, is still liable to be framed through the various vectors of US corporate interests. In professional foreign policy schools (e.g. at Harvard, Tufts, Yale, Princeton, Georgetown) this is particularly likely to be the case, but these elite schools' influence radiates way beyond their campuses.

There is therefore a significant challenge to be taken up, or neglected, by communication researchers, and not just by those for whom international communication issues may be their hobby.

Notes

1 Earlier versions of this chapter were presented to the Internationalizing Media Studies conference, University of Westminster, London, September 2006; the International Communication Association conference, San Francisco, May 2007; and the International Association for Media and Communication Research conference, Paris, July 2007.

2 Columbia, Harvard, New York University (NYU), Northwestern, Princeton, Stanford, University of Southern California (USC), Yale.

3 University of California at Berkeley, Illinois at Urbana-Champaign, Minnesota, Missouri, Ohio State, Southern Illinois at Carbondale, Texas, Wisconsin at Madison. Texas at Austin, Ohio State and Minnesota are also the three most populous campuses in the US, though NYU is not far behind.

4 http://www.facultyonline.com/browse_form.asp?client = 70752.

5 Cinema Studies; Culture and Communication; Film and Television; Interactive Telecommunications Programme; Journalism. The first, third and fourth are in the School of the Arts; the second in Education; and Journalism in Graduate Arts and Sciences.

6 My thanks to Dr Vish Viswanath of the Dana Farber Institute in Harvard Medical School for the information on Harvard's courses.

7 Currently, 'Communication Studies' is the preferred self-designation for programmes whose genesis was in public speaking and rhetoric, but which have also embraced Interpersonal and Organizational Communication over the past few decades.

8 Over three years I alone taught the two international focus graduate courses officially on the books, and two others, quite different, listed under the Special Topics rubric.

9 One is published by a small press, and no figures are given for its campus use, probably because the press's marketing operation is attenuated.

10 The '408' figure is composed of Biagi, *Media and Impact*, 2004; Bryant, *Fundamentals of Media Effects*, 2001; Bucy, *Living in the Electronic Age*, 2004; Creech, *Electronic Media Law and Regulation*, 2003; DeFleur and Dennis, *Understanding Mass Communication*, 2001, 7th edn; Dominick, *Dynamics of Mass Communication in the Digital Age*, 2004, 8th edn; Leighley, *Mass Media and Politics*, 2001; Sloan, *Media in America*, 2002; Wimmer and Dominick, *Mass Media Research*, 2005, 8th edn. The '104' group consists of Baran, *Introduction to Mass Communication*, 2004; Pavlik, *Journalism and Mass Communication in the Digital Age*, 2003; Vivian, *The Media of Mass Communication*, 2005; Folkerts, *Voices of a Nation*, 2001, 4th edn; Gross, *Telecommunications*, 2005, 8th edn. The '64' group consists of Straubhaar and Rose, *Media Now*, 2003, 4th edn; Turow, *Media Today*, 2003, 3rd edn; Croteau and Hynes, *Media/Society*, 2002, 3rd edn. The '168' group consists of Crowley, *Communication in History*, 2002, 4th edn; Kamalipour, *Global Communication*, 2006, 2nd edn; Mody, *International and Development Communication*, 2003; Thussu, *International Communication*, 2006, 2nd edn; de Beer, *Global Journalism*, 2003, 4th edn; Hachten and Scott, *The World News Prism*, 2002, 6th edn.

11 Among counter-currents to the general trend, I would note the efforts of the US International Communication Association over the past few years to expand its non-US membership, and the existence of International Communication divisions/sections not only in its ranks but also in the Association for Education in Journalism and Mass Communication, and in the National Communication Association. However, these efforts need to be read in the light of the argument in the final paragraphs to this chapter. See Marques de Melo (2007) for a withering critique of US Communication conference organizations' repeatedly dismissive posture toward Latin American research in the field. Marques has been a prime agent over 30+ years in developing communication research in Latin America and scholarly connections with the US academy.

12 There are other factors in the cauldron, including the long cultural history of defining the US nation as under imminent threat from malevolent forces, visible not only in US history but also in British history before 1776 (Downing, 2007).

References

Downing, J. (1990) US Media Discourse on South Africa: The Development of a Situation Model, *Discourse and Society*, 1(1): 39–60.

—— (2007) The Imperiled 'American': Visual Culture, Nationality and US Foreign Policy, *International Journal of Communication*, 1: 318–41 [http://ijoc.org/ojs/index.php/ijoc/article/view/111/74].

Herman, E. and Chomsky, N. (1988) *Manufacturing Consent: The Political Economy of the Mass Media*. New York: Pantheon.

Marques de Melo, J. (2007) La Comunicación Latinoamericana frente al desafío de la globalización: sueños y pesadillas de la comunidad académica, *Revista Latinoamericana de las Ciencias de la Comunicación* 7: 38–52.

Chapter 18

Re-conceptualizing media studies in Africa

Winston Mano

Academic fields in Africa, including the relatively new communication and media studies, are undergoing major changes, in parallel with global trends. However, the study of media, as of other academic fields, has been undermined by the colonial legacy as well as economic difficulties and political instability (Chimutengwende, 1988; Ronning, 1991; Bourgault, 1995). This chapter explores ways in which the teaching and study of media in Africa, as seen by those teaching and researching it, could be re-conceptualized to make it more responsive to local and international demands.

While the notion of 'African' is not unproblematic, it is fair to suggest that beyond differences in the histories of the continent's 54 countries there is a shared concern about former colonial powers continuing to dominate the education sector. As recently as the 1990s, this consensus was manifest in what was seen as a new awakening in Africa, born out of disillusionment and resentment of Western domination in intellectual, political and economic terms (Mafeje, 1992). African scholarship has engaged critically with Eurocentric approaches, and in the area of media this has meant rejecting the universalizing pretensions of Western theorizing and evidence, and paying more attention to neglected 'indigenous' forms of communication and languages (Salawu, 2006). The growing body of literature on endogenous forms of communication and how they can be used for human development can be seen as a specific response to continued Eurocentricism in African education[1] (Ugboajah, 1985; Ansu-Kyeremeh, 2005; Banda *et al.*, 2007).

Africans have long been misrepresented, both in history and in the academy (Mudimbe, 1988). Colonial domination in education matters because it makes Africa more 'amenable to control by Western social and cultural influences' (Mukasa and Becker, 1992: 36). Debates among African scholars have focused on the meaning and relevance of existing media education in Africa (Chimutengwende, 1988; M'Bayo and Nwanko, 1989). A review of mass communication research in west Africa by Edeani (1988), covering the period from the 1930s to 1980s, noted that much of the excitement that attended the emergence of communication and media research activities in the 1960s appeared, as early as the 1970s, to have given way to sober reflection on what African research was offering social science and Africa:

> A number of searching questions began to be asked: Was that research advancing scientific knowledge as it was supposed to be doing? Was the research capable of serving the social, economic, political, cultural, and other developmental needs of Africa? And were foreign Africanists really genuinely committed to the study of Africa as an intellectual pursuit or were they involved for certain ulterior motives?
>
> (Edeani, 1988: 157)

Although these questions were not adequately answered, continued 'soul-searching' helped uncover further epistemological issues, mainly about the crude importation to Africa of theories and measuring instruments developed in and for Western societies. To illustrate the magnitude of this problem, out of a survey of 20 randomly selected papers read at a 1987 communications conference in Nigeria, 87 per cent of citations were from Western sources, suggesting strong evidence of Western dominance in African media education (Mukasa and Becker, 1992: 36). Such evidence clearly showed that Western 'liberal-democratic' perspectives dominated existing scholarship on the media's role in post-colonial African societies (Wasserman, 2006). The solution to the domination of Western knowledge systems in media studies requires more than 'decolonization' (Ngugi, 1986) or 'de-Westernization'[2] (Curran and Park, 2000). There is a need to incorporate history in a dual sense: specific African cultural histories, accompanied by an honest discussion of the academic history of existing concepts and approaches.[3] African media studies, as suggested by McMillin (2007: 194), must go beyond the present and 'draw in the residual function of colonial pasts or religious and traditional structures, in informing how viewers interpret and make use of media technologies and texts'.

The problem in media education is that it was firmly entrenched in the European colonial system in Africa. Journalism and mass communication were based on 'teaching materials, trainers and curricula from the respective colonizing powers whose policies were to ensure the dominance of their [European] culture in their colonial enclaves' (Mukasa and Becker, 1992: 41). Early African media education, therefore, saw syllabi transplanted into training institutions, for example with the Jackson College of Journalism (now the Department of Mass Communication) superimposing its entire curricula on the University of Nsukka, Nigeria. American universities, funded by substantial American aid, supplied the structure, staff and much of the university curricula, including an entire journalism programme and, in some cases, the journalists themselves, who were mostly Western-trained (Mukasa and Becker, 1992). Western media theories and concepts based on 'liberalism, rationalism, realism and pragmatism' are not always applicable to Africa, yet Africa has continued to rely on the West for communication syllabi and theories (Ndlela, 2007). UNESCO has raised concerns about the implications of Westernized forms of training in Africa:

> The source of inspiration of teachers, curricula and textbooks is Western. Teachers are mostly Western educated, curricula are drawn from Western models and most textbooks are authored and published in the West and North America. Under these circumstances, communication training in Africa can hardly be said to be culturally relevant, although cultural inculcation was usually the main justification for its introduction and sustainability.
>
> (UNESCO, 2002: 1)

The dominance of Western models in African media education has far-reaching consequences. Even in fairly advanced African nations such as South Africa, journalism and media were accused of being 'firmly grounded in a Western epistemology influenced by the Enlightenment and thus with an emphasis on observable and measurable facts, and on individualism' (Fourie, 2005: 15). The very codes of ethics and professional values used by journalists in Africa today are heavily inspired by Western or Western-derived international codes; though some apply to Africa, most imported codes tend to dwell in the main on issues of relevance to the West (Nyamnjoh, 2005: 87).[4] However, it remains crucial that those who make inputs in African mass media are guided by socio-historical and cultural values that condition the production of knowledge (M'Bayo and Nwanko, 1989; Ronning and Kupe, 2000). Some have suggested rethinking communication, journalism and media studies in terms of 'African-based epistemology' (Fourie, 2005: 15). South Africa, to its credit, has initiated broad and deeper debates on the meaning and relevance of its media education (Tomaselli and Teer-Tomaselli, 2007).[5] However, it is important briefly to map out other problems facing media studies in Africa.

Major problems impeding the academic study of media in Africa mainly result from the lack of a coherent policy on the nature and distribution of media education centres. More than two decades ago, Zimbabwean scholar Chimutengwende (1988) pointed out how countries such as Nigeria, Kenya, Ghana and Egypt had more than two media training institutions covering mid-career training for graduates who want to enter the communication field. He suggested that 'ideally there should be at least one national communication training centre in each country for mid-career training under a ministry of information apart from the in-service training programmes of individual media organizations' (Chimutengwende, 1988: 39). He observed that existing communication institutions were too few and not well distributed geographically: 'The few which exist lack adequate facilities, funds and are under-staffed. They are, therefore, not well prepared for the tasks for which they were established. They cannot as yet train enough media educators, practitioners, researchers, administrators, planners, technicians and other categories of media workers' (ibid.: 40).

Such problems have multiplied or evolved into new ones, as will be shown below. Apart from a Western-dominated theoretical base there is little agreement in terms of what and how media should be taught, resulting in different emphases among the existing journalism and communication training programmes. For example:

> In east and southern Africa, except South Africa, the emphasis is mainly on skills training with print and broadcast journalism, advertising and public relations dominating the curricula. In west and central Africa, as well as in South Africa, the curricula generally combine theoretical and practical courses. Programmes offered range from certificate and diploma courses and the Bachelor of Arts/Science in east, central, west and southern Africa to the Doctor of Philosophy in Nigeria and South Africa.
>
> (UNESCO, 2002: 2)

It is possible to understand the above variations in training in terms of historical, political and regional factors. There are historical differences dating back to the carving up of Africa by European powers at the Berlin conference in 1884, which created rigid vertical lines of command with little lateral interaction between African institutions, countries and regions:

> Thus the French colonies became an extension of the French colonial culture and social system. The communication education curriculum in Francophone Africa was modelled after schools of journalism in Paris, Lille and Strasbourg (Domatob, 1989). Students from journalism schools in Senegal and Cameroon did their third year in France, Britain, or North America, especially Quebec in Canada. The same applied to colonial empires of the British, the Belgians and the Portuguese. It is not surprising that communication and transport structures in colonial Africa linked the colonies directly with their colonial overlords with little or no lateral links or networks … In this respect communication education and journalism practice produced practitioners who had a tunnel vision about the world around them – not only in neighbouring countries but also in rural areas. They were essentially urban elites with strong organic ties to their colonial metropoles where they often went for internship or further training.
>
> (Mukasa and Becker, 1992: 40–1)

This elitist tendency in media education has not gone away in post-colonial Africa, partly because of staff shortages and inadequate media training facilities. Well-trained, competent and experienced educators are subjected to extremely poor working conditions and low salaries. As a result staff turnover is high, as many opt to join the private sector. The media studies programme at the University of Zimbabwe, formed in 1994, has lost all but one of its founding staff members to jobs elsewhere. Young staff members left because they were unable to provide for their families on monthly salaries that averaged less than $100. Those who stayed behind have had to 'moonlight' in the non-governmental sector. There was even a joke suggesting that such academics worked from, rather than for, the University of Zimbabwe.

The recurrent shortage of relevant basic teaching resources for media courses is another issue that has made research and teaching exceedingly difficult. The few available textbooks are not sufficient for the huge classes, and in any case they are published and written principally for 'Western' communication studies. For African media students and teachers the harsh reality is that:

> The content of these publications is, thus, often irrelevant to the social, political, economic and cultural reality in African countries. Besides, the textbooks are insufficient in quantity and variety, partly because of prohibitive costs. Apart from the textbooks, other teaching and training materials including libraries, radio and television studios, photographic laboratories, computers, printing machines and other equipment are rare in many African communication training institutions. It is evident then that communication training in African countries faces a catalogue of problems of which curriculum improvement is only a part.
>
> (UNESCO, 2002: 2)

Researching media studies in Africa

Doing research on media studies in Africa is made difficult by poor communication facilities, as most training institutions in Africa do not have (functioning) web presences (Berger and Matras, 2007). What follows is based on information gathered in 2007 from research visits to the University of Lagos, the University of Ibadan in Nigeria, Uganda's Makerere University, the University of Zimbabwe, the National University of Science and Technology (Bulawayo, Zimbabwe) and Witwatersrand University, Johannesburg. At the time of writing the author was acting as an external examiner at two of the universities under study. Some of the evidence is from the author's experiences as a graduate media student in 1994 and later as a lecturer in the English and Media Studies Department, University of Zimbabwe. For research on South Africa, particularly useful were documented resources on journalism studies, especially papers presented at the 2004/5 colloquium on 'Teaching of South African Journalists: 1994–2014' held at the University of Rhodes. The chapter also benefited from ongoing debates about media studies, both in and outside of Africa.[6]

Survey of issues in media studies in sub-Saharan Africa

The study of communication and media has been in existence in Africa for many decades (Bourgault, 1995; Akinfeleye and Okoye, 2003; Tomaselli and Teer-Tomaselli, 2007). In sub-Saharan Africa, the Ghana Institute of

Journalism, established in 1959, was the first journalism institution in the region. African independence in the 1960s and 1970s witnessed the growth and development of journalism training schools (Mukasa and Becker, 1992: 42). Among the oldest is the mass communication programme at the University of Lagos (UNILAG), the 'home of mass communication', established in 1964. This arose from a regional meeting of African broadcasters organized by UNESCO, which recommended the establishment of a regional African radio and television training centre in Nigeria (interview with staff at UNILAG, June 2007). Subsequently, the UNDP, UNESCO and the government of Nigeria started the programme at the University of Lagos in 1966. Throughout Africa, similar university-level courses were introduced under different names: Communication and Language Arts (at the University of Ibadan, Nigeria); Media Studies (University of Botswana); Journalism and Media Studies (National University of Science and Technology, Zimbabwe, and Rhodes University in South Africa); Mass Communication (University of Lagos in Nigeria and Makerere University in Uganda). At the University of Zimbabwe, the Media Studies Programme in the English Department offers specific media degree and diploma courses to graduate students. Other African universities offer separate courses in both media and journalism, as is the case at the University of Witwatersrand, Johannesburg. The programmes were first established in 2001, under the leadership of Zimbabwean Tawana Kupe (formerly of the University of Zimbabwe and Rhodes University). The media studies option in 2002, its second year, attracted 100 students. The University of Witwatersrand's Postgraduate Journalism and Media Studies programme was reshaped in 2002, with honours and master's degree programmes being offered, following the appointment of Anton Harber, co-founder of the *Weekly Mail* (now *Mail and Guardian*) newspaper and now professor in journalism (interview, Johannesburg, 23 August 2007).

The Mass Communication degree programme at Makerere University, introduced in 1988, is an example of foreign involvement in the establishment of media training in post-colonial Africa. This came about through support from the United States Information Agency (now United States Information Service) through its Fulbright programme, which was influential in the establishment of the course, originally hosted by the Literature Department at Makerere University. American-trained lecturers in the Mass Communication department, together with practitioners, drew up the first curriculum and helped with the recruitment of staff. For the first few years, the American Embassy offered scholarships for staff to be trained in the United States, donated books and materials and sent staff on the Fulbright exchange programme. Its name and course content had a clear American bias.

The Department of Communication and Media Studies at Nigeria's Ajayi Crowther University started degree-level training in media in 2007 under the title 'Mass Communication'. According to its head: 'We decided to retain the name Mass Communication for the programme so that we can remain within the ambit of the National Universities Commission which regulates University programmes in Nigeria' (interview, July 2007). It can be argued that such new departments, although headed by locally trained staff, are good evidence of the reproduction of foreign-inspired programmes in Africa, especially when they uncritically adopt materials and syllabi produced by early programmes set up by foreign agencies.

The purpose of media studies in Africa

The primary objective of media studies in Africa, according to my respondents, was both 'professional and academic'. It was pointed out that research and teaching should engage and critique existing theory, 'with the option to accept it, debunk it or improve on/contextualize it. Its role should also be to prepare scholars and practitioners so that they become relevant to both African and global theoretical and practical realities' (interview with teaching staff, Makerere University, 20 August 2007). Staff at the University of Lagos, whose four-year degree programme catered for media, public relations, advertising and marketing, believed that media studies should focus on using the media for development, a sentiment echoed by the head of department at Ajayi Crowther University, who suggested that media must dwell on 'issues that are of relevance to African needs, society and culture' (interview, 23 May 2007).

At Makerere University, media studies helped teach the 'political and media history of their respective country, region' and the continent as a whole, 'issues/challenges of professional' practice, and the area of communication for development. The medium of radio (the emphasis in Uganda is on the print media), it was argued, should receive more focus in the curricula. It was also suggested that it had become necessary to be more responsive to the needs of employers, as one staff member noted: 'We mostly target the mainstream media industry in Uganda as well as the public relations sector. Recently, we have been more deliberate about training communication practitioners to work for NGOs and other development agencies' (interview, 20 August 2007). Others posited that media studies syllabi should pay more attention to 'the role of the local languages in making the media meaningful for a participatory democracy' (interview with teaching staff, 20 August 2007). One lecturer wanted to see more research by African scholars on Africa's indigenous knowledge, which has not been properly harnessed: 'We should not look down on African traditional knowledge as primitive or useless!' (interview, 20 August 2007). The same point was made more forcefully by the head of department at the University of Ibadan, when he stated that the 'African traditional knowledge system should provide the bedrock of communication studies in Africa. It should explore the possibilities of exogenous and endogenous communication systems' (interview, 23 May 2007). The above views demonstrate the need to re-conceptualize the purpose and goal of existing media studies on the continent, making them draw more meaningfully from the local and global, so that they can engage with the changing needs of Africa.

The composition and role of staff in media studies departments

In the institutions surveyed, not all staff were adequately trained to cover key aspects of media studies. This was particularly so at Makerere University:

> At the theoretical level, depending on where they did their postgraduate studies, some may have a [theoretical] grounding in the behavioural paradigm, while only a smaller number had a background in the 'critical' or 'postmodernist' paradigms. The majority of staff's training leans towards mainstream media practice, and particularly the print media. At Ajayi Crowther staff had not been sufficiently trained to cover all aspects of the course, with a relatively smaller number focusing 'on communication as opposed to journalism'.
>
> (interview, July 2007)

As for the role of media studies teachers, one member of staff said: 'I believe one important role media teachers have in African intellectual development is to generate theory that takes cognizance of African political, social, economic and cultural realities and popularize it through research and dissemination of this research through their teaching, conferences and publication' (interview, Makerere University, 20 August 2007). At the University of Ibadan, it was felt that media studies teachers in Africa should advance the cause of African intellectual development by paying more attention to democracy and development, through communication. The role of African media departments should be to help produce 'indigenous' media texts. The theoretical and evidential basis of media studies was meant to be worked out from a synthesis of the 'past and present', 'African and non-African' scholarly traditions and from taking cognizance of African realities: 'It should certainly not be an unquestioning adaptation of theory handed to us via available textbooks' (interview, Makerere University, July 2007). Media studies had a role in helping 'improve the level of discourse about the media, and explore the dialectics involved in media offerings' from local and global perspectives (interview, University of Lagos, 23 May 2007). The main challenge and impediment to achieving these goals was the limited resource base at most institutions.

Resources for media studies in Africa

The study was also keen to discover the rationale for choosing reading lists at the departments visited. Staff at Makerere University revealed that most of their existing 'course content is developed by staff who teach that [particular] course'. Staff who take over courses are not always keen to amend/update the courses developed by their predecessors. The prevailing tendency is to 'follow' the existing syllabus (interview, July 2007). Access to up-to-date books was a general problem. There was limited access to publications from other regions in the South. In some cases, existing texts were outdated. At Ajayi Crowther University, students were using 'mostly foreign (American) books' but, because of the local publishing industry, the students would sometimes access work by Nigerian authors. At the University of Lagos funds to buy foreign books were not adequate and as a result students had to use locally produced books. At Makerere University, too, staff were worried about the lack of access to texts: 'The basic [undergraduate] textbooks would be similar to the standard textbooks used in an American undergraduate class. However, our graduate classes are more open to journals from all parts of the world and have access to recent African scholars' work. It is helpful that some members of staff have studied in South Africa and that we have had external examiners hailing from east, central and southern Africa. These normally infuse some "Africanness" in our repertoire of teaching/reference materials' (interview, August 2007). It should be added that at Makerere staff had access to foreign media journals and were provided with local and international publishing opportunities. Some were using their own publications in their teaching.

Internationalizing media studies in Africa

The above discussion shows that media studies in Africa is perhaps too internationalized: most syllabi were conceived abroad, most students and staff are still trained abroad, and the major books and theories used are mainly written by Westerners for Western students in the first instance. The study sought to investigate this issue further by asking questions about the role played by African media scholars located in the West. In Nigeria it was felt that ongoing internationalization of the discipline would lead to a healthy 'cross-pollination of key ideas', and lecturers are as a result getting increased opportunities to train abroad, attend conferences and publish in leading journals.

Internationalization also benefited Zimbabwe's National Science University, where in 2007 four staff were awarded grants for PhD-training in Britain, the US and South Africa, and a Fulbright professor was seconded to teach in the department of journalism and media studies. Witwatersrand media studies programme employed Zimbabwean academics trained in Norway, with one assuming the position of executive dean of the faculty. A Kenyan professor was also teaching in the department. Similarly, the media studies programme at the University of Zimbabwe has involved teaching staff, external examiners and students from other countries, especially from Nigeria, Norway, Britain, Kenya and the Netherlands.

Increased internationalization and networking were seen as positive at Makerere University:

> African scholars based in the West could play a linking role between African and Western universities, in terms of staff exchanges, with the idea

> that African staff can share some African insights/experiences with their Western colleagues and their Western colleagues can share experiences with African universities and because they understand the conditions and needs in Africa. African scholars living in the West could also help identify relevant teaching/learning resources. They could also be key partners in collaborative research that gives a more balanced picture of the realities in the area of media studies.
>
> (Interview, Makerere University, August 2007)

Ugandans also wanted to establish partnerships with Asian scholars. It was felt that African media teachers could go for further studies in India and China. One respondent suggested that China should put some of its profits from increased trading with Africa into 'communication and cultural research'. The above problems should not be used to generalize about media education in Africa, as challenges and prospects are different from one country to another and to some extent between regions.

Media studies in South Africa: a model case

South Africa could be considered a model case for the rest of the continent in that it has a big 'community of media trainers' in constant dialogue about trends, prospects and future directions of media training in the country and in Africa as a whole. For years, communication and media issues have been debated in such journals as *Rhodes Journalism Review*; *Critical Arts: A Journal of Media and Cultural Studies* (KwaZulu Natal University) and *Ecquid Novi* (Stellenbosch University), which in 2007 relaunched as *Ecquid Novi: African Journalism Studies* (Tomaselli and Teer-Tomaselli, 2007). Two major colloquia about the teaching of journalism were organized in October 2004 and June 2005 at Rhodes University to 'foster timely dialogue among teachers, and between them and industry, at a significant moment in South African history; Renew and deepen the community of journalism educators at tertiary level' (Berger, 2005: 2).

The colloquia showed that, although advanced, South African media education had its share of problems, including the poor quality of students in media education. Media training departments have to enrol underprepared students because of 'enormous market pressure from students and their families looking for qualifications that will give them immediate employment opportunities' (Gibbon, 2005). This has parallels with Makerere University, where dwindling government support in 2007 prompted the department to offer more donor-driven courses so that it could attract regional students and donor funding. Withdrawal of donor funding at the University of Zimbabwe has meant that the media studies programme selects students according to their ability to pay rather than on academic merit. Another major challenge for South African universities is how to make media educational institutions 'fit for purpose' in a democratic society. This means having to (re-)define their missions so that they become relevant to post-apartheid reconstruction (Berger, 2005: 17).

The post-1994 democratic context has compelled South African academics to rethink journalism studies and media education and emphasize the need for media education with a progressive agenda to effect social intervention and change (Wasserman, 2005). Emerging out of debates is the question about indigenization/Africanization of media education, inviting increased focus on the 'history, symbolic forms, culture(s), achievements and needs of Africa' as well as involving 'decolonizing the mind ... a break with and questioning of Western epistemology(ies) as the foundation of thinking reality' (Fourie, 2005: 15). In such arguments there is an implied rejection of excessive Westernization at the expense of the local. African concepts such as *ubuntu*[7] should be debated, with intellectual skills preceding but not replacing professional training.

One major problem in South Africa, as well as in other African countries, 'is the lack of debate and self-reflection about paradigms, and about the field itself. Little discussion occurs on the relationship between journalism education, or media studies, to broader social issues ... Adopting canons, rather than debating their relevance, seems to be an overriding imperative' (Tomaselli and Shepperson,1999: 238). Nyamnjoh expresses disappointment with how 'scholars of and in Africa have, in the main, championed Western intellectual hegemony, instead of restructuring, modifying, enriching and remodelling existing concepts and theories in order to accommodate the broader experiences and contextual variations that the continent offers' (1999: 16). The theoretical 'poverty' discussed above could be a result of many factors that include poor training and a lack of attention to conditions in the African context. UNESCO has attempted to redress such problems in its model curricula discussed below.

The 'model' curricula for media studies in Africa

UNESCO has developed 'model curricula' for degree and non-degree-level communication training in Africa, necessitated because 'a number of issues seem to place Africa more at a disadvantage than other regions of the world with regard to the capacity to properly manage the transition from largely poor, non-industrial social formations to post-industrial information societies that the realities of the twenty-first century demand' (UNESCO, 2002: 9). It was felt that Africa's economic backwardness and poverty increased its need for information and communication technologies, if it was to progress. Communication and information are necessary to engender the idea of community and improve social life and have significant functions to help fulfil Africa's political and governance goals. The contextual issues taken into account by UNESCO recognized the important role played by communication in the realm of kinship – family, values and interactions among social groups.

The initial stage of building 'model curricula' in communication training in Africa came in 1996, when UNESCO decided to survey the curricula used in existing institutions in Cameroon, Côte d'Ivoire, Ghana, Kenya, Nigeria, Senegal, South Africa, Tanzania, Uganda, Zambia and Zimbabwe. It made three key findings. First, the main areas of communication training were traditional print and broadcast journalism, advertising, public relations and mass communication subjects. Lacking were policy-related courses and subjects such as new media, media management, community media, and communication for social change, democracy and human rights. Second, the communication training institutions surveyed faced shortages of qualified staff, and motivation among the existing educators was found to be low. Third, some of the communication training centres surveyed periodically revised their curricula in response to the media market or industry.

A meeting on curricula for communication training was organized by UNESCO and the African Council for Communication Education (ACCE) in Cape Town in 1996, which made a number of recommendations on communication education in general and communication training in particular, including the suggestion that curricula developers must take into account the social, economic, political and cultural contexts in Africa. It was also emphasized that such communication training must be both inter- and multi-disciplinary (UNESCO, 2002: 4). In 1998 a follow-up workshop was held in Nairobi, and, based on its recommendations, UNESCO organized regional workshops of communication trainers in Zambia in November 2000 for trainers from east and southern Africa; in Accra in December 2000 for trainers in English-speaking west African countries; and in Yaounde in June 2001 for trainers in Francophone Africa.

UNESCO's concern in media curriculum development went beyond the mere selection and organization of subjects into core/options or theory/practice. It involved establishing a consistent relationship between general goals and specific objectives to guide media teaching, carefully ensuring a sound sequence or continuity and balance in the curriculum (UNESCO, 2002: 2). Questions were asked about the purpose, aim and content of the curriculum, including its assessment criteria. More importantly, UNESCO emphasized that various professional areas, such as print journalism, broadcasting, public relations, marketing, advertising, publishing and development communication, needed both technical skills and philosophical knowledge.

The proposed curricula included courses such as African media history; media economics; research methods; African languages; journalism; publishing; film; public relations and advertising. One key missing course was on audience studies – African researchers need to put people at the centre of what they do. Work on audience would help engage Eurocentrism in media studies and contribute to generating new perspectives more relevant to the African context.

Re-conceptualizing media studies in Africa

The level of agreement among African media educators and scholars on the need to rethink the role and quality of media education in Africa offers a sound basis to re-conceptualize media studies in Africa. In many ways, this study has shown that the process has already started. In 2007 a team of African media researchers led by Arnold de Beer submitted a report to the World Conference on Journalism Education (WCJE) on what needs to be done to improve communication and media studies in Africa.[8] The report included a critique of the continued dominance of American and European approaches in media studies in Africa (de Beer *et al.*, 2007: 10). It noted that 'in order to enter the international and increasingly the national higher echelons of academe, individuals, just as institutions such as universities, will need to play the game according to the hegemonic rules of the North. This process is already quite clear, for instance, in South Africa, where, apart from a journal list kept by the Department of Education, journalism and media authors only get full research credit if they publish in one of the few journalism/media/communication journals indexed in the North by ISI and/or IBSS' (ibid.: 5).

To redress this imbalance, the report suggests a progressive two-way scholarly system, a model in which 'American publishers and journalism authors take cognizance of African scholarship and publishing possibilities. African journalism authors then ought to make their voices pro-actively heard in the field of journalism scholarship publishing for and in Africa.' Approached that way, the publishing hegemony of the North could then become a 'valuable stepping-stone for the development of a viable and vibrant journalism publishing in Africa and other continents in the South' (ibid.: 9).

Another attempt to re-conceptualize the field of media studies is contained in a report which examined the capacity and potential for excellence of almost one hundred journalism schools across Africa, using a set of indicators and criteria for measuring potential for institutional excellence. 'The criteria and indicators for defining potential excellence offer each institution with an interest in self-improvement a tool for honest self-assessment' (Berger and Matras, 2007: 27). Such a project forced media training schools to scrutinize themselves, according to 'standardized' criteria, and gave them an opportunity to compare their provision with that of other centres. There is no doubt that a momentum for change in African media education is in evidence, indicated also by initiatives by associations for academics, collaborative publishing projects, conferences and staff exchanges.

Concluding reflections

It is clear from the above that media education in Africa is being re-conceptualized to make it more relevant to the needs of the continent. Interdisciplinary approaches could help deepen the theoretical element in African media education. However, I would qualify the view that Africa has a 'different tradition, philosophy, values and history' (Mukasa and Becker, 1992: 45). By focusing on radio, theatre, audiences and aspects of endogenous communication in rural Africa, where the majority lives, media scholarship might be able to meaningfully engage with local issues. It is equally important for scholars to explore beyond traditional areas to encompass issues of global media industries, culture, ethics and other worldwide processes of media production and consumption (*Global Media and Communication*, 2007). Themes of power and domination need to be central to media studies in Africa for the simple reason that the continent is affected by the rapid political and technological reordering led by US-dominated global media industries.

Ultimately, media education in Africa ought to be freed from what Zeleza, in relation to African history, has called 'the epistemological traps of Eurocentricism, the tropes of the "colonial library"'. Such a struggle requires a double intellectual manoeuvre, involving 'provincializing' Europe, which has monopolized universality, and globalizing Africa beyond its Eurocentric 'provincialization':

> The answer to Eurocentricism does not lie, I believe, in ever more refined auto-critiques within the 'Western' tradition itself, as seen in the fulminations of postmodernism, or endless critiques from its physical or paradigmatic peripheries, the province of post-colonialism, but in stripping this tradition of its universalistic pretensions and universalizing propensities, in producing new or alternative histories based on a fundamental reconstitution of world history, or what I would call human history, and the reconstruction of the provincial histories of the world's major regions including Africa and Europe in that history.
>
> (Zeleza, 2006: 3)

This radical model suggests that having deconstructed West-centric disciplines in Africa, academics need to participate more actively in the deconstruction of West-centric subjects and disciplines in the West itself. It is posited that the discipline of history offers a powerful entry point because colonialism conjoined African and European histories and, over the last 50 years, the discipline of African history has 'developed the critical tools to undress the emperor' (ibid.: 4). Media studies could learn from history and other disciplines. There is a need for it to firmly (re-)embrace living local cultures, languages, African philosophies, values and concepts. African media scholars abroad need to participate in the ongoing deconstruction of West-centric media studies. This would help establish a new generation of media scholarship and curricula in Africa that engage with issues in ways that meaningfully respond not only to individual but also to local, national, regional and international imperatives. It would allow the nascent academic field of media studies the space to evolve indigenized and internationalized theories, in tandem with other regional initiatives.

Notes

1 Africans particularly resented 'the most often mistaken impression that the Western text and Western ways of making meaning are universal, and therefore to be copied by academics the world over' (Nyamnjoh, 1999: 17–18).
2 The solution is not to de-link African media studies from international media studies but to focus on critical local academic work while making links with other regional media studies networks. In saying this, I am inspired by such academic journals as *Inter-Asia Cultural Studies*, which, among other things, sees its role as responding 'to the re-centering of cultural studies outside the Anglo-American axis and participating in cultural politics at a local level, but with an international agenda'.
3 Downing has observed how certain concepts have enjoyed the privilege of academic scrutiny over the decades: '[I]deology and the state were big in the 1970s, hegemony and discourse in the 1980s, and information society and public sphere in the 1990s, identity and globalization and civil society in the 2000s' (cited in McMillin, 2007: 194).
4 Couldry has suggested that one should not argue for de-nationalization or de-Westernization but rather for 'global media ethics' whose aim is to generate an entirely new discourse whose reference points are, from the outset, global: 'Global media ethics asks: what things should media professionals – in fact anyone who makes inputs to the media process – aim for, if media are to contribute to us living a good life, both individually and collectively?' This view is premised on the fact that 'everyone is affected by the way the media represent the world and its divisions' (Couldry, 2007: 249).
5 For example, the two major meetings of South African journalism educators organized by Rhodes University in 2004 and 2005. For a discussion of the history of communication debates in South Africa see Tomaselli and Teer-Tomaselli (2007).
6 The Internationalizing Media Studies conference, organized by Daya Thussu and his colleagues at the University of Westminster in September 2006, is a good example of these initiatives.
7 An African philosophy which emphasizes collectivism, sharing, community and participation in a collective life.
8 Presenters of the report to the WCJE in Singapore, and representing the Trans-African Council on Communication Education, were Fackson Banda (Rhodes University, South Africa), John Mukela (Southern African Media Training Trust, Mozambique) and Arnold de Beer (Stellenbosch University, South Africa).

References

Akinfeleye, R.A. and Okoye, I.E. (eds) (2003) *Issues in Nigerian Media History: 1900–2000 AD*. Lagos: Malthouse Press.

Ansu-Kyeremeh, Kwasi (ed.) (2005) *Indigenous Communication in Africa: Concept, Application and Prospects*. Accra: Ghana University Press.

Banda, F., Beukes-Amiss, C.M., Bosch, T., Mano, W., McLean, P. and Steenveld, L. (2007) Contextualising Journalism Education and Training in Southern Africa, *Ecquid Novi: African Journalism Studies*, 28(1–2): 156–75.

Berger, G. (2005) Fit for Purpose – Towards Tracking the Quality of University Education of Entry-Level Journalists, *Colloquium 2: Teaching South African Journalists, 1994–2014*, School of Journalism and Media Studies, Rhodes University, Grahamstown.

Berger, G. and Matras, C. (2007) *Criteria and Indicators for Quality Journalism Training Institutions and Identifying Potential Centres of Excellence in Journalism Training in Africa*. Paris: United Nations Educational, Scientific and Cultural Organization (UNESCO).

Bourgault, L.M. (1995) *Mass Media in Sub-Saharan Africa*. Bloomington: Indiana University Press.

Chimutengwende, C. (1988) The Role of Communication Education in the Development and Democratization of African Society, *Africa Media Review*, 2(2): 29–45.
Couldry, N. (2007) Comparative Media Research as If We Really Meant It, *Global Media and Communication*, 3(3): 247–50.
Curran, J. and Park, M.J. (eds) (2000) *De-Westernizing Media Studies*. London: Routledge.
de Beer, A., Banda, F. and Mukela, J. (2007) Looking for Journalism Education Scholarship in Some Unusual Places: The Case of Africa. Paper presented at the16th AMIC Annual Conference/1st World Journalism Education Congress, 25–8 June, Singapore.
Domatob, J.K. (1989) Liberating Strategies for Communication Training for Tropical Africa: Challenges and Options, in *Communication and Democratization in Africa: 6th Biennial Conference Report*. Nairobi: ACCE.
Edeani, D.O. (1988) West African Mass Communication Research at Major Turning Point, *Gazette*, 41(3): 151–83.
Fourie, P. (2005) Thinking about Journalists' Thinking, *Colloquium 2: Teaching South African Journalists, 1994–2014*, School of Journalism and Media Studies, Rhodes University, Grahamstown.
Gibbon, T. (2005) The Flaw in the Ceiling: Antinomies of Higher Education Transformation and Implications for the Curriculum, *Colloquium 2: Teaching South African Journalists, 1994–2014*, School of Journalism and Media Studies, Rhodes University, Grahamstown.
Global Media and Communication (2007) Editorial, special themed issue on Internationalizing Media Studies, *Global Media and Communication*, 3(3): 243–5.
McMillin, D. (2007) *International Media Studies*. Oxford: Blackwell.
Mafeje, A. (ed.) (1992) *In Search of an Alternative: A Collection of Essays on Revolutionary Theory*. Harare: Sapes.
M'Bayo, R. and Nwanko, R.N. (1989) The Political Culture of Mass Communication Research and the Role of African Communication Scholars, *Africa Media Review*, 3(2): 1–15.
Mudimbe, V.Y. (1988) *The Invention of Africa: Gnosis, Philosophy, and the Order of Knowledge*. Bloomington: Indiana University Press.
Mukasa, S.G. and Becker, L.B. (1992) Toward an Indigenised Philosophy of Communication: An Analysis of African Communication Educational Resources and Needs, *Africa Media Review*, 6(3): 31–50.
Ndlela, N. (2007) Reflections on the Global Public Sphere: Challenges to Internationalising Media Studies, *Global Media and Communication*, 3(3): 324–9.
Ngugi, W. (1986) *Decolonising the Mind: The Politics of Language in African Literature*. London: James Currey.
Nyamnjoh, F.B. (1999) African Cultural Studies, Cultural Studies in Africa: How to Make a Useful Difference, *Critical Arts: A Journal of Cultural Studies in Africa*, 13(1): 15–39.
—— (2005) *Africa's Media: Democracy and the Politics of Belonging*. London: Zed Books.
Rønning, H. (1991) *Media and Democracy: Theories and Principles with Reference to an African Context*. Harare: Sapes Books.
Rønning, H. and Kupe, T. (2000) The Dual Legacy of Democracy and Authoritarianism: The Media and the State in Zimbabwe, in J. Curran and M.J. Park (eds) *De-Westernizing Media Studies*. London: Routledge, pp. 157–177.
Salawu, A. (ed.) (2006) *Indigenous Language Media in Africa*. Lagos: Centre for Black and African Arts and Civilization.
Tomaselli, K.G. and Shepperson, A. (1999) The Poverty of Journalism: Media Studies and 'Science', *Continuum: Journal of Media and Cultural Studies*, 13(2): 237–53.

Tomaselli, K.G. and Teer-Tomaselli, R.E. (2007) Internationalizing Media Studies: The Southern African Communication Association, *The International Communication Gazette*, 69(2): 179–91.

Ugboajah, F.O. (1985) Oramedia, in F.O. Ugboajah (ed.) *Mass Communication, Culture and Society in West Africa*. Oxford: Hans Zell Publishers.

UNESCO (2002) *Communication Training in Africa: Model Curricula*. Paris: United Nations, Educational, Scientific and Cultural Organization (UNESCO).

Wasserman, H. (2005) Journalism Education as Transformative Praxis, *Ecquid Novi*, 26(2): 159–74.

—— (2006) Globalized Values and Postcolonial Responses: South African Perspectives on Normative Media Ethics, *International Communication Gazette*, 68(1): 71–91.

Zeleza, P.T. (2006) Banishing the Silences: Towards the Globalization of African History, available at: www.codesria.org/Links/conferences/general_assembly11/papers/zeleza.pdf (accessed 30 July 2006).

Interviews

Staff interviews, Mass Communication Department, University of Lagos, Nigeria, 21–2 May 2007.

Staff interviews, Communication Arts and Languages Department, University of Ibadan, Nigeria, 23 May 2007.

Interview with Head of Department of Mass Communication, Ajayi Crowther University, Ibadan, Nigeria, 23 May 2007.

Staff interviews, Mass Communication Department, Makerere University, Kampala, Uganda, 18–20 August 2007.

Staff interviews, Media Studies Department, Witwatersrand University, Johannesburg, South Africa, 23 August 2007.

Staff interviews, Journalism and Media Studies Department, National University of Science and Technology, Bulawayo, Zimbabwe, 22 August 2007.

Chapter 19

The internationalization of the internet and its implications for media studies

Gerard Goggin and Mark McLelland

As new media gain in cultural and economic significance, various academic disciplines have searched for new concepts, methods, frameworks and insights to understand the nature of the internet and associated developments such as the convergence of media applications, the rise of the mobile phone, as well as mobile and wireless media in general.

New interdisciplinary undertakings have emerged, dedicated to aspects of new media. We now have, for instance, a fairly well-established field of internet studies, represented by the Association of Internet Researchers (AOIR, aoir.org; see Goggin, 2004; Nissenbaum and Price, 2004; Wellman and Haythornwaite, 2002), as well as the prior formation of critical internet culture (Lovink, 2002 and 2007). There is also an overlapping but distinct group of researchers centring on the mobile phone embodied in the Society for the Social Study of Mobile Communication (www.sociomobile.org; see also Katz, 2007; Nyíri, 2007).

Established disciplines such as media studies now need not only to grapple with the internet as another object of consideration, but also to rethink their approach to traditional media in today's era of rapid technological and cultural globalization and convergence. In the context of the imperative to internationalize media studies, the case of the internet offers a number of useful considerations.

First, the nature of the internet as an international medium underlines the way that contemporary media need to be grasped by genuinely international approaches. Indeed we often see within media studies that the internet is presented as a pre-eminent case of media globalization. However, this is only a starting point, and often the internet is misconstrued in such framing.

So the second consideration is that discussions of the internet within media studies – or indeed within the specialized field of internet studies – are not actually informed by a recognition of the implications of acknowledging the internet as international. In our minds, the problem here is that dominant notions of the internet, like those of media or culture generally, are still modelled on a limited range of experiences, deployments and conceptions of the internet.

The shorthand version of our argument is that the dominant ways of seeing the internet in Western scholarship are still largely based on the perspectives of Anglophone users, especially North Americans, who featured prominently among early pioneers (as well as some European nations). The cultural, linguistic and social values of such Anglophone users have had a strong influence, even in the inscription of such values at the level of technical protocols (as in the centrality of English to domain names, for instance). At the present time, however, English is fast on its way to becoming a minority language on the internet, and certainly English-language users are being overtaken by Chinese, Japanese, Korean, Spanish, Russian and other language communities in the appearance and domestication of various internet technologies, applications and cultures.

If this critique is correct, then the third thing we would suggest is that research and theory are now needed to reconstruct the basic, shared understandings of the internet to reflect this extraordinary variety of use, and its social, cultural, political and even technical underpinnings. Within internet studies, we have contributed a collection that gathers together leading work in this area, calling for an internationalizing of internet studies (Goggin and McLelland, 2009). Such a project stands to offer a timely contribution to the project of internationalizing media studies, the subject of this volume. In our chapter we wish to focus on the pedagogical implications for media studies of the internet as an international phenomenon.

International pedagogies for the internet

At the level of pedagogy, a range of subjects in cultural studies, media and communication studies, and journalism studies, as well as in other disciplines such as sociology, anthropology, commerce and marketing, law, economics and design, are being rewritten to acknowledge the recent shift to a convergent digital media environment. While much has occurred in this area since the inception of the mass internet in the mid-1990s, we suspect syllabi still do not adequately register the international nature of this medium – which may not be surprising, given the state of research and the paucity of suitable work available.

Such a reworking of curricula is not only important in its own right in order to adequately and critically teach about the internet, it is doubly important given the salience of internet technologies in the actual habitus and practice of teaching, student learning and the environments in which this takes place. Universities, institutes of advanced, further and technical education, and schools around the world, especially in the wealthier countries, have become highly media-saturated environments, with digital, networked technologies now providing the infrastructure and also circuits and routines of pedagogy.

A further pressure for the internationalizing of the curriculum comes from the changing nature of universities competing globally. Many universities in

Anglophone societies such as Australia and the US have high numbers of overseas students (primarily from East Asia) taking these subjects and some of these universities now run offshore programmes in Asia, thus necessitating that the curriculum be broadened beyond a local or regional focus. As Australia-based researchers into Asian media, who also have taught and conducted research in offshore communication studies programmes in Hong Kong, it is apparent to us that students in these different locales have very different experiences of the online environment, and it is the Australian students who have a less rich and less sophisticated engagement with a range of new media, especially mobile and convergent applications of the internet.

Until recently, it used to be difficult for us to find useful research dealing with the cultural aspects of new media use in Asian societies that could be set for classroom discussion, but things now seem to be changing for the better, with a range of new publications looking at the different histories and cultural uptakes of new media technologies across the globe (Cunliffe and Herring, 2005; Danet and Herring, 2007; Ess, 2001; Luo *et al.*, 2006; Pertierra and Koskinen, 2007; Thorseth and Ess, 2005).

In this chapter, we propose to look at some of this work, particularly that focusing upon the societies of East Asia, in order to emphasize the importance of drawing upon a wide range of cultures of use in the media studies classroom.

Korean internet use – at home and abroad

Of particular interest from an Australian perspective is the work of Larissa Hjorth (2007), who has surveyed Korean students studying in Melbourne to uncover the kind of online lives they enjoyed in Korea and to find out what happens when these students arrive in a less well-connected internet environment. Like its neighbour Japan, South Korea is a techno-savvy society that displays extremely high rates of broadband connectivity. While the development of a high-speed optical cable internet service has been stalled in Australia due to disputes between government and industry providers, South Korea is reported as having the best e-government in the world. Proactive government initiatives, alongside convenient demographics (three-quarters of the population live in seven major cities in high-rise developments equipped with high-speed internet), have resulted in South Korea becoming a world leader in high-speed internet accessibility, ahead of the US, Canada and Japan (Yoo, 2009).

Hjorth's survey of Korean students reveals a dense and sophisticated engagement with online communication that both reinforces and augments offline connections. She focuses her analysis upon one site in particular, Cyworld, a provider of mini-homepages (known as minihompy) to one-third of the South Korean population. Hjorth notes how users' minihompy are constantly updated with blogs, photos and messages (including those posted by friends), so that the pages give a snapshot of what the user is up to that day or even that hour or moment. It is not a fantasy space for identity play or subversion, as Hjorth notes: 'Cyworld does not aim to substitute the virtual for the actual but rather to use technological space to further connect individuals with the real world.' It is a kind of 'third space' between home and work, and the way in which users interact in this space mirrors offline relations. As Hjorth points out, the Korean notion of *chon* or degrees of kinship is reflected in how far another user can get into your profile, many 'rooms' in your minihompy being restricted to those who are friends (*ilchon*, literally 'one remove'). Thus, to be granted *ilchon* status and to be allowed to move freely around a friend's or relative's minihompy is a sign of 'co-presence' and 'establishes a correspondence between online and offline identities'. It is a way of maintaining intimacy and a sense of connectedness despite geographical separation.

Given the above, the minihompy would seem to be an ideal means for Korean students studying in Australia to maintain contact with their friends and family at home. However, as Hjorth indicates, it does not work out that way since 'almost 90 per cent of respondents [expressed frustration with] the lack of speedy and efficient broadband and lack of wireless services taken for granted in their homeland'. Hjorth's investigation reveals that the lower quality of Australia's internet service has made it difficult to update the minihompys, and as a result Korean students tend to revert to previous technologies such as email and voice calling to keep in touch with folks at home. As Hjorth points out, '[o]ne of the marked features of the internet is that, as a "global" technology, its adaptation at the level of the local is far from homogenous', and, as her case study shows, it is not the case that local internet cultures can simply be reproduced anywhere in the world, even among developed nations.

The English language and the architecture of the internet

Many native English-speaking students are unaware of the extent to which their online experience has been facilitated by the fact that the computer and the internet were largely US inventions and that English (or the roman script more generally) has become embedded in the very architecture of computer programming languages and key aspects of the internet protocol. Likewise, the QWERTY keyboard, which has remained unchanged since the invention of the typewriter, is still the main human–computer interface.

The historical dominance of English has resulted in numerous problems for non-English users. Technical computer language, for instance, because of the primacy of US companies such as IBM and Apple, has been developed in English. This leads to problems when computer interfaces are translated into other languages. Nokia, for instance, found it difficult to come up with a Hindi interface when marketing its mobile phones to India, noting that 'the terms call divert, data, fax, call register, prepaid credit, incoming call alert, and infrared, don't have good Hindi analogs' (Konkka, 2003). Also, research by Moukdad and Cui (2005) shows how general search engines such as Google and AltaVista, which were developed using algorithms based on roman script, are less able to comprehend queries in non-roman scripts, particularly Chinese, since they cannot identify word segments (Chinese is written with no spaces between the characters).

Language issues are one reason why societies in the East-Asian cultural sphere have developed internet cultures that differ markedly from the more PC-based interfaces characteristic of the US, Europe and Australia. Japan, Korea and China never went through the same kind of office automation phase characteristic of Western countries in the post-war period because it was very difficult to create simple machines such as typewriters to reproduce their scripts – Japanese uses about 2,000 characters in daily life, Chinese over 5,000 (Gottlieb, 2000). The advent of personal computers in the mid-1980s helped to solve this problem, but there were considerable technical hurdles to overcome in developing a programming language that could handle the transmission of so much data. Japanese, for instance, uses three different scripts (four if you include roman). The total number of distinct Chinese characters is over 10,000, and there are two very different ways of writing the characters, traditional (Taiwan, Hong Kong) and simplified (mainland and Singapore).

The different orthographies of the languages in the region necessarily impacted upon the take-up of computerization in general and the internet in particular, and led to different developmental trajectories and patterns of use that diverge in many important ways from those characteristic of Western nations. Although in the Western context the movement from manual typewriter to electric typewriter to personal computer was fairly seamless – given that the QWERTY keyboard has remained the main human–machine interface on all these devices – this kind of office automation and computerization presented a challenge to users of non-alphabet-based Asian languages. It is no surprise, then, that in Japan and elsewhere in East Asia the PC did not emerge as the main interface through which consumers access the internet, but rather a range of hand-held and mobile devices that rely on a ten-digit keypad have proven more popular (Gottlieb and McLelland, 2003; Ito *et al.*, 2005).

Computer codes have struggled with the difficult task of being able to represent the symbols, letters and characters not just in the orthography of one language, such as English, but also in the rich range of world languages that started to be used for computers and data networking:

> Fundamentally, computers just deal with numbers. They store letters and other characters by assigning a number for each one … there were hundreds of different encoding systems for assigning these numbers. No single encoding could contain enough characters: for example, the European Union alone requires several different encodings to cover all its languages. Even for a single language like English no single encoding was adequate for all the letters, punctuation, and technical symbols in common use.
>
> (Unicode, 2007)

The advent of Unicode, a standard that assigns a unique number for every character, regardless of language or platform, has provided a boost to the computer representation of languages and the incorporation of a much wider range of languages into computer programming, protocols, applications and hardware. Currently around the world there is a great deal of activity under way in language communities, and among those with an interest in them (such as local and transnational businesses), to indigenize existing internet technologies and ensure new and future technologies work for desired languages. This is necessary because of the different layers and complex interoperability issues of the myriad technologies that constitute today's multimedia, interactive internet.

Language and internet technology, for instance, has been a key issue in internet governance. It was an overarching concern raised with great passion by countries and civil society groups, particularly at the World Summit on the Information Society through 2002 to 2005 (Goggin, 2008). Language has been an important issue in the debates around domain-name regulation and standards, given the difficulty of putting web addresses into non-roman scripts (Mueller, 2005). The implications of language in the constitution of polities, and their claims to sovereignty, have also been an important issue raised as the internet has internationalized. For some language communities, whose claims to territory or nationhood are not well recognized by global norms and conventions, the internet has assumed a vital role in linguistic maintenance and cultural survival.

A fascinating example of this is the case of Catalan, discussed by Josep Lluís Micó and Pere Masip. The Catalan romance language is native to Catalonia, a territory designated as autonomous by the Spanish constitution, but Catalan speakers are dispersed across three other European countries (not to mention diasporic communities across the world). Catalan speakers are also contending with the immigration of other language speakers (from South America, Asia and the Magreb) into Catalonia (Micó and Masip, 2009). Thus, as Micó and Masip chronicle: 'Catalan has found in the internet a suitable platform for consolidating and promoting the language, overcoming the economic and political problems of the "real world"' (Micó and Masip, 2009). One fascinating consequence of this investment of the Catalan community in the internet was their successful bid to obtain a domain name. When first devised, the taxonomy of domain names was based on the international standard of country codes (names). As Catalonia was not recognized as a country in this standard, and other international conventions, at first its citizens were refused their own domain name. Eventually, in September 2005, ICANN (the regulator of domain names) relented and Catalan was given the top-level domain '.cat' (Gerrand, 2006; Micó and Masip, 2009).

In the Asia-Pacific, there has been important work around raising regional issues of language and culture, seeking to have these reflected in the governance arrangements of the internet, but also the actual technical standards and technology implementations themselves (Banerjee, 2007). Here we would point to the account offered by Danny Butt and Norbert Klein, who suggest that it 'is not possible for the Domain Name System (DNS) as it stands to incorporate full Unicode script encoding to be used in top-level domains' (Butt and Klein, 2006: 78). Butt and Klein emphasize that 'the internationalization of domain names is a cultural issue. There remain serious problems with both the ability of the DNS system to handle non-roman domain names, as well as inadequate procedures to facilitate this occurring' (Butt and Klein, 2006: 82).

Another key locus of activity around the shaping of internet technology in accordance with the needs and values of language users and their cultures is localization of software. Broadly speaking, proprietary software development is driven by the imperative of targeting profitable markets, and so software design is likely to incorporate the characteristics of major language communities. Microsoft's Windows Operating System and its word-processing program Word now incorporate many language groups, but in their earlier instances, for commercial reasons and as a result of the history of internet and computer development we have outlined, this would not have been the case. Many language groups, then, find that they are hamstrung in using important software, and are forced to lobby for or to initiate projects to 'localize' software, making it 'native' for their own languages. As well as working with, and exerting pressure on, software companies such as Microsoft, those engaged in localization also turn to the resources of the free and open source software movements (FOSS, for short). For example, discussing the internet in Wales, Daniel Cunliffe notes that:

> There is a strong tradition of software localization into Welsh, often volunteer-based and focused on open source software, in some cases with financial support from the Welsh Language Board … Agored based on OpenOffice; Gwe-lywiwr Mozilla … as well as a variety of other software, such as spelling and grammar checkers. There is also a Welsh version of Unix called Cymrux. Commercial software developers in Wales are also providing bilingual and Welsh language software. In December 2004 the Welsh Language Board and Microsoft launched Welsh language interface packs for Office 2003 and Windows XP.
>
> (Cunliffe, 2009)

In their primer on software localization in the Asia-Pacific, Souphavanh and Karoonboonyanan (2005: 1) observe that: 'It is almost impossible to use a computer if you cannot read the instructions, buttons and menus. Thus it is not surprising that many countries in Asia lag behind Europe and America in the adoption and use of modern computer technologies at work, in schools, and in the home.'

They strongly advocate that countries adopt the non-proprietary software approach:

> It is an acknowledged fact that the near-monopoly of English language software, controlled by English-speaking companies, does not serve the long-term needs of any country. Microsoft and a few other large US corporations dominate the international software market, earning large profits and wielding enormous power ... If a corporation decides to no longer support software in another language, only those who are fluent in English would be able to operate computers effectively.
>
> (ibid.: 1)

Souphavanh and Karoonboonyanan (2005: 5–16) offer a number of case studies of software localization in the Asia-Pacific, including:

- the well-funded and promoted joint 'CJK' programmes of China, Japan and Korea;
- 'multiple localized Indic language versions of GNU/Linux, Mozilla and OpenOffice.org', enabled by the 'depth of technical experience of Indian programmers in localization';
- fledgling voluntary efforts to localize software for the Vietnamese language;
- the ambitious but underfunded Khmer Software Initiative;
- the success of localization of the complex Thai language, underpinned by a sustained push for incorporation of Thai in international standardization efforts.

The mobile internet in East Asia

Once the 'black box' of the internet is opened up, and the intertwined social, linguistic, cultural, political and economic forces shaping even fundamental aspects of the technology are traced, the pedagogical scene is set for challenging basic assumptions about what the internet is understood to be – and instead focusing classroom discussion and enquiry on the realities, and figuring what the processes and politics of internationalization entail.

So, for instance, the history of internet take-up in Japan is useful in shaking many Western students' assumption that their societies are always at the forefront of innovation. Regarding the uptake of mobile communications, Castells *et al.* note that the 'United States lags behind Europe and Japan and Japan is ahead of Europe in the uses of the wireless Internet' (2006: 2). Indeed, a 'broad consensus has been formed that the usage of *keitai* [mobile phones], including especially the myriad wireless internet applications, is central to the transformation of the Japanese information society', and that this usage represents 'a process significantly distinct from the development of the computer-based Internet in other countries' (2006: 103).

The importance of understanding the particular developmental trajectories of the mobile internet is highlighted by the popularity in the mid-1990s of paging devices among high-school girls (a mobile communications phase absent in the youth cultures of Australia, Europe and the US). Okada (2005) notes how in the mid-1990s schoolgirls in Japan appropriated paging devices originally developed for the (male) business market, using the keypad on telephones to send simple text messages to the LCD displays of friends' pagers. This led to a distinct *poke-kotoba* (pager-lingo) among the sub-culture and assisted young people in organizing their private lives outside of parental supervision and control. The prior popularity of pagers among youth groups impacted upon the functions of early models of mobile phones, which included SMS services and from 1999, via a service known as i-mode, internet-enabled e-mail, which enabled subscribers to write longer messages and also include graphics, audio, video and web links (Matsuda, 2005: 35). In Japan these were innovations driven by and for the youth market. Indeed, mobile uptake among young people is evident across East Asia and has resulted in a 'juvenation' of the technology (that is, a movement away from a business model of mobile telecommunications towards a model that focuses on young people's recreational patterns of use – SMS, gaming, ring tones, downloads, and so on).

While not 'unique' to Japan (since Japanese patterns of usage are similar in some respects to those in South Korea), it is clear that pre-existing Japanese cultural norms and practices have exerted a strong influence on the development of *keitai* technology and its deployments. In Japan (and to an extent in other East-Asian societies), mobile telephony, unlike the internet, was not 'conceived by an elite and noncommercial technological priesthood and disseminated to the masses' (Ito *et al.*, 2005: 9) but emerged out of young Japanese consumers' love of 'gadget fetishism and technofashion'.

The astonishing uptake of the mobile internet in Japan, from only one million i-mode subscribers in 1999 to over 46 million in 2006, is also related to a host of other specific factors, not least the problematic blurring of public and private space occasioned by the advent of the mobile phone. In Japan spoken communication via mobiles that takes place 'in public' on buses and trains is frowned upon and needs to be handled with particular decorum. As Matsuda (2005: 24) points out, the 'physical noise is not the problem. Rather, *keitai* conversations disrupt the order of urban space' by confusing the boundaries of private and public. Okabe and Ito (2005) point out how from 1996, when young people became the main demographic to take up the mobile phone, there developed a voluble media discourse about their use in public settings. (Indeed, in Japanese switching one's phone to vibrate/silent is referred to as 'manner mode'.) Public transport in Japan is 'characterized by precise technical and social regulation and very low rates of disorder' (2005: 208), supported by commuters' willing acquiescence to a system of 'mutual surveillance, regulation and sanctioning' (2005: 208). Consequently, on the whole, answering the phone or making a call while on public transport is to be avoided.

One way around this impasse is of course the use of SMS and e-mail, which can be actioned with limited disturbance to those around. However, internet-enabled mobile phones are deployed in many other ways by commuters on their long trips to and from their places of work. As in South Korea, the almost ubiquitous provision of wireless access to fast broadband networks makes the receipt and transmission of information quick and efficient. Innovative payment systems, where the user pays per packet downloaded to the phone and receives each month an itemized bill for this service, also encourage commuters to surf the internet via their *keitai* screens – downloading mp3 files, updating their websites, engaging in chat, looking up news and sport, TV and show schedules, or even finding a specific kind of restaurant via the phone's satellite navigation function. It is no surprise, then, that Apple's recently released i-phone seems 'so yesterday' in the East-Asian context (Manabe, 2009).

The case of Japan (and that of Korea discussed earlier) helps Australian students, and we suspect their counterparts in North America and elsewhere, to imagine the online experience outside of the PC interface that characterizes the bulk of their experience. It comes as a surprise to students that i-mode, which was only recently introduced to Australia (and which has had only limited take-up), was a relatively inexpensive and popular service in Japan as early as 1999. Moreover, students are impressed to learn that Japanese phone carriers introduced 3G, which offers broadband internet access over mobile phones, in 2001 – three years before Verizon rolled out its 3G platform in the United States. As of March 2006, 3G accounted for 53 per cent of all mobile subscribers in Japan. Polyphonic ringtones, or *chaku-mero* as they are called in Japan, were released only three years ago in the United States, but had already been developed by Japanese karaoke companies by 1996 and were commonplace in Japan by 1999. Camera phones were also common throughout Japan by 2001, two years before they began to be marketed in the United States (Manabe, 2009; Ito *et al.*, 2005).

Hence, despite a slow start due to orthographic difficulties, Asian societies such as Japan, Korea and China have become leaders in mobile internet access and have much more sophisticated hardware (and software) available than is the case in Australia or even the US. Also, it is important to introduce the idea that the use of character-based scripts is not necessarily a handicap – although characters take longer to input, they take up less display space. Thus it is possible to display more complex messages on a small screen in Chinese characters than it is in roman script – making for a richer and more sophisticated short-messaging culture. In Chinese, for instance, popular fiction can be downloaded and read on the small screen. The diverse experience of East-Asian societies is important, then, when leading classroom discussions about 'the internet'. It is important to stress that we are dealing with a range of different histories and experiences and that we cannot generalize from 'our' use of the internet to that of other people, even other people in our own communities.

Conclusions

It is not really possible to talk about 'the internet' as if it were a single phenomenon or has a simple history. Accessing the internet via a small mobile device is going to be very different from accessing it via a PC – different hardware both enables and disables certain kinds of use and creates particular kinds of internet experiences. Similarly, the wider telecommunications environment of different societies (such as Korea and Australia), which is determined as much by population densities and natural topography as by government policies and strategies, has an enormous impact on the kinds of electronic cultures that develop around the internet.

In addition, different kinds of internet applications and cultures have quite different functions and significances in different societies. How does the massive Persian blogosphere (Alavi, 2005; Khiabany and Sreberny, 2009) contribute to our understanding of the uses of blogs, which is still largely predicated on the Western, and in particular North American, origins of blogs? Does blogging differ in, say, Indonesia or Iran? How does it constitute various kinds of transnational communities, based on music, faith and culture, for instance (Lim, 2009)? At the time of writing there is much excitement around notions of 'Web 2.0', 'social media' and 'social networking', but to what extent are such ideas informed by the Korean Cyworld or Japanese mobile internet cultures rather than, say, MySpace, Facebook or YouTube?

Also, language is not a 'neutral' vehicle for the communication of information but is deeply embedded with cultural ideologies. Likewise, the power of English (despite the gradual decline in its percentage of internet content) is still apparent in the architecture of the internet – the predicament of domain names (and hence web addresses) being based on roman scripts – and the interface problems that remain for the transfer and display of other scripts via the internet, as well as mobile and wireless devices. A disproportionate amount of the world's information is also stored in English, and existing search engines work better for English-language queries. Then there is the issue of the linguistic and cultural assumptions reflecting the politics of globalization that shape software.

Clearly, while the internet experiences of individuals living in Japan, Korea and China are very different from those of individuals in Australia, the US or the UK, it is not sensible to contrast 'our' use with a singular 'Asian' online environment. What is emerging in recent work by internet researchers studying Asian societies is not so much a sense of common issues, but rather a common understanding that 'the internet', which is so often positioned as a 'global' and 'deterritorialized' technology, should, in fact, be understood in relation to different cultures of use which are still very much influenced by geographical location. As Ito *et al.* (2005: 7) point out, technologies are not universal; rather, it is necessary to attend to 'the heterogeneous co-constitution of technology across a transnational stage'.

To capture this sense of heterogeneity is the current challenge for media studies researchers and teachers, who now need to engage with the contemporary internet and international frameworks for understanding it. Related to this is the task of focusing learning and teaching on the realities of describing, analysing, understanding and debating how the internet is actually being constituted through processes of internationalization as well as regional and local indigenization.

The good news is that there is now a growing body of scholarly work, as well as other literatures from governmental, corporate and civil society bodies interested in the internet in different settings. In addition, students' own experience of digital technologies can be an excellent starting point for reflection, placing their own social settings and cultural and linguistic practices in critical, comparative contexts. This is not a case of essentializing students as 'digital natives' (all too common in pedagogical discourses on e-learning); rather it requires focusing sustained attention on how the internet is constituted in different ways in particular societies, something that leaves its mark on the culturally diverse, globally dispersed space of educational institutions.

References

Alavi, Nasrin (2005) *We Are Iran: The Persian Blogs*. Brooklyn, NY: Softskull Press.

Banerjee, Indrajit (ed.) (2007) *The Internet and Governance in Asia: A Critical Reader*. Singapore: Asian Media Information and Communication Centre.

Butt, Danny and Klein, Norbert (2006) Internet Governance and Socio-cultural Inclusion, in Danny Butt (ed.) *Internet Governance: Asia-Pacific Perspectives*. Bangkok: UNDP Asia-Pacific Development Information Programme; New Delhi: Elsevier; http://www.apdip.net/publications/ict4d/igovperspectives.pdf.

Castells, Manuel, Fernandez-Ardevol, Mireia, Qiu, Jack Linchuan and Sey, Araba (2006) *Mobile Communication and Society: A Global Perspective*. Cambridge, MA: MIT Press.

Cunliffe, Daniel (2009) The Welsh Language on the Internet: Linguistic Resistance in the Age of the Network Society, in Gerard Goggin and Mark McLelland (eds) *Internationalizing Internet Studies: Beyond Anglophone Paradigms*. New York: Routledge, pp. 96–111.

Cunliffe, Daniel and Herring, Susan C. (eds) (2005) Minority Languages, Multimedia and the Web, *New Review of Multimedia and Hypermedia*, 11(2), special issue.

Danet, Brenda and Herring, Susan (eds) (2007) *The Multilingual Internet: Language, Culture, and Communication Online*. New York: Oxford University Press.

Ess, Charles (ed.) (2001) *Culture, Technology, Communication: Towards an Intercultural Global Village*. Albany, NY: State University of New York Press.

Gerrand, Peter (2006) Cultural Diversity in Cyberspace: The Catalan Campaign to Win the New.cat Top Level Domain, *First Monday*, 11(1), http://firstmonday.org/issues/issue11_1/gerrand/index.html.

Goggin, Gerard (ed.) (2004) *Virtual Nation: The Internet in Australia*. Sydney: University of New South Wales Press.

—— (2009) The International Turn in Internet Governance: A World of Difference?, in Gerard Goggin and Mark McLelland (eds) *Internationalizing Internet Studies: Beyond Anglophone Paradigms*. New York: Routledge. pp. 48–62.

Goggin, Gerard and McLelland, Mark (eds) (2009) *Internationalizing Internet Studies: Beyond Anglophone Paradigms*. New York: Routledge.

Gottlieb, Nanette (2000) *Word-Processing Technology in Japan: Kanji and the Keyboard*. Oxford: RoutledgeCurzon.

Gottlieb, Nanette and McLelland, Mark (2003) The Internet in Japan, in Nanette Gottlieb and Mark McLelland (eds) *Japanese Cybercultures*. London: Routledge, pp. 1–16.

Hjorth, Larissa (2007) Home and Away: A Case Study of Cyworld Minihompy by Korean Students Studying Abroad, *Asian Studies Review*, 31(4): 397–407.

Ito, Mizuko, Okabe, Daisuke and Matsuda, Misa (eds) (2005) *Personal, Portable, Pedestrian: Mobile Phones in Japanese Life*. Cambridge, MA: MIT Press.

Katz, James (ed.) (2007) *Handbook of Mobile Communication Studies*. Cambridge, MA: MIT Press.

Khiabany, Gholam and Sreberny, Annabelle (2008) The Internet in Iran: The Battle over an Emerging Public Sphere, in Gerard Goggin and Mark McLelland (eds) *Internationalizing Internet Studies: Beyond Anglophone Paradigms*. New York: Routledge.

Konkka, Katja (2003) Indian Needs – Cultural End-User Research in Mumbai, in Christian Lindholm, Turkka Keinonen and Harri Kiljander (eds) *Mobile Usability: How Nokia Changed the Face of the Mobile Phone*. New York: McGraw-Hill.

Lim, Merlyna (2009) Muslim Voices in the Blogosphere: Mosaics of Local–Global Discourses, in Gerard Goggin and Mark McLelland (eds) *Internationalizing Internet Studies: Beyond Anglophone Paradigms*. New York: Routledge, pp. 178–195.

Lovink, Geert (2002) *Dark Fiber: Tracking Critical Internet Culture*. Cambridge, MA: MIT Press.

—— (2007) *Zero Comments: Blogging and Critical Internet Culture*. New York: Routledge.

Luo, Peilin, Fortunati, Leopoldina and Yang, Shanhua (eds) (2006) *New Technologies in Global Societies*. Singapore: World Scientific.

Manabe, Noriko (2009) Ring My Bell: The Impact of Cell Phone Downloads on the Japanese Music Markets, in Gerard Goggin and Mark McLelland (eds) *Internationalizing Internet Studies: Beyond Anglophone Paradigms*. New York: Routledge, pp. 316–332.

Matsuda, Misa (2005) Discourses of Keitai in Japan, in Mizuko Ito, Daisuke Okabe and Misa Matsuda (eds) *Personal, Portable, Pedestrian: Mobile Phones in Japanese Life*. Cambridge, MA: MIT Press, pp. 19–40.

Micó, Josep Lluís and Masip, Pere (2009) The Fight of a Minority Language against the Force of Globalization: The Case of Catalan on the Internet, in Gerard Goggin and Mark McLelland (eds) *Internationalizing Internet Studies: Beyond Anglophone Paradigms*. New York: Routledge, pp. 112–127.

Moukdad, Haidar and Cui, Hong (2005) How Do Search Engines Handle Chinese Queries?, *Webology*, 2(3), www.webology.ir/2005/v2n3/a17.html.

Mueller, Milton (2005) *Ruling the Root: Internet Governance and the Taming of Cyberspace*. Cambridge, MA: MIT Press.

Nissenbaum, Helen and Price, Monroe (eds) (2004) *Academy and the Internet*. New York: Peter Lang.

Nyíri, Kristóf (ed.) (2007) *Mobile Studies: Paradigms and Perspectives*. Vienna: Passagen Verlag.

Okabe, Daisuke and Ito, Mizuko (2005) Keitai in Public Transportation, in Mizuko Ito, Daisuke Okabe and Misa Matsuda (eds) *Personal, Portable, Pedestrian: Mobile Phones in Japanese Life*. Cambridge, MA: MIT Press, pp. 205–18.

Okada, Tomoyuki (2005) Youth Culture and the Shaping of Japanese Mobile Media: Personalization and the Keitai Internet as Multimedia, in Mizuko Ito, Daisuke Okabe and Misa Matsuda (eds) *Personal, Portable, Pedestrian: Mobile Phones in Japanese Life*. Cambridge, MA: MIT Press, pp. 41–60.

Pertierra, Raul and Koskinen, Ilpo (eds) (2007) *The Social Construction and Usage of Communication Technologies: European and Asian Experiences*. Singapore: Singapore University Press.

Souphavanh, Anousak and Karoonboonyanan, Theppitak (2005) *Free/Open Source Software: Localization*. United Nations Development Programme, Asia Pacific Development; New Delhi: Elsevier; http://www.iosn.net/l10n/foss-localization-primer/foss-localization-primer.pdf.

Thorseth, May and Ess, Charles (eds) (2005) *Technology in a Multicultural and Global Society*. Trondheim: Norwegian University of Science and Technology.

Unicode (2007) What Is Unicode?, www.unicode.org/standard/WhatIsUnicode.html.

Wellman, Barry and Haythornwaite, Caroline (eds) (2002) *The Internet in Everyday Life*. Oxford: Blackwell.

Yoo, Seunghyun (2009) Characteristics and Capacity of a Korean Online Community: What Keeps Them Going?, in Gerard Goggin and Mark McLelland (eds) *Internationalizing Internet Studies: Beyond Anglophone Paradigms*. New York: Routledge, pp. 217–236.

Index

Page numbers in *italics* denote a figure/table